"Michael Shermer is our most fearless explorer of alternative, crackpot, and dangerous ideas, and at the same time one of our most powerful voices for science, sanity, and humane values. In this engrossing collection, Shermer shows why these missions are consistent: it's the searchlight of reason that best exposes errors and evil."

STEVEN PINKER, Johnstone Professor of Psychology, Harvard University, and author of *Enlightenment Now: The Case for Reason, Science, Humanism, and Progress*

"This is a rather difficult book for me to blurb, given that an entire chapter is devoted to criticizing my claims about pragmatic truth vis-à-vis scientific truth. However, Dr. Michael Shermer is a very clear thinker, and the kind of skeptic that is always necessary to ensure that public thought, scientific and otherwise, maintains a certain clarity. He's a passionate advocate of free speech, for this and many other reasons – to the point of entitling his new book *Giving the Devil His Due*, which is devoted to many worthwhile topics, but to free speech above all. Despite our disagreements, this is a necessary book for our times. Read it. And thank God and the powers that be that you have the right to do so."

JORDAN B. PETERSON, Professor of Psychology, University of Toronto, and author of *12 Rules for Life: An Antidote to Chaos*

"Michael Shermer is a fearless defender of free speech, open inquiry, and freedom of thought and conscience, including – and especially – for those with whom he disagrees. *Giving the Devil His Due* is one of the strongest bulwarks against the tyranny of censorship that I have read."

NADINE STROSSEN, Professor, New York Law School, former President of the ACLU, and author of *Hate: Why We Should Resist it with Free Speech, Not Censorship*

". . . a detailed roadmap for thinking well and clearly about interesting and challenging ideas. This vivid, erudite, broad, and deep collection of essays is marvelously written – so much so that, as you finish one essay, you cannot resist starting the next. And the range – from ancient civilizations to the colonization of Mars, from free speech on campus to gun control in cities – is as astonishing as it is engaging."

NICHOLAS A. CHRISTAKIS, MD, PhD, author of *Blueprint: The Evolutionary Origins of a Good Society*

"As always, Michael Shermer is hard-hitting, thought-provoking, and brilliant. The fascinating essays in this wide-ranging book will make you think – and then rethink."

AMY CHUA, Yale Law Professor, and author of *Battle Hymn of the Tiger Mother and Political Tribes: Group Instinct and the Fate of Nations*

"Michael Shermer is the voice of reason, and this is a book of his best essays – the ones we most need to read to understand the madness of our time and to imagine a more reasonable future. The range of questions Shermer addresses and the breadth of his knowledge make this book a delight to read."

JONATHAN HAIDT, New York University, author of *The Righteous Mind*, and co-author of *The Coddling of the American Mind*

Reviews for the Hardback Edition

"...Shermer skims over the usual constitutional analysis to instead cast free speech as the cornerstone of democracy and knowledge."

MICHAEL BOBELIAN, *The Washington Post*

"A powerful case is made here for why free speech is the best way to drive out bad ideas and fake news."

DAVID AARONOVITCH, *The Times*

"*Giving the Devil His Due* is a joy to read for its penetrating insights on a wide range of subjects."

RALPH LEWIS, MD, *Psychology Today*

"*Giving the Devil His Due* is a treasure trove for lovers of the humanities and society at large as viewed through the perspective of scholarly minds, treatises, and essays. It's marvelously ripened and full of wonderful tales..."

ROBERT HUNZIKER, *Counterpunch*

"A collection of skilful elucidations of academic ideas."

CHRISTOPHER SILVESTER, *The Critic*

"Each essay is well crafted to provoke thoughtful reflection and amply referenced for those who wish to dig deeper into each topic ... However, for any reader new to scepticism, *Giving the Devil his Due* would be an auspicious place to start."

DON CARPENETTI, *Chemistry World*

GIVING THE DEVIL HIS DUE

Who is the "Devil"? And what is he due? The devil is anyone who disagrees with *you*. And what he is due is the right to speak his mind. He must have this for your own safety's sake because his freedom is inextricably tied to your own. If he can be censored, why shouldn't you be censored? If we put barriers up to silence "unpleasant" ideas, what's to stop the silencing of any discussion? This book is a full-throated defense of free speech and open inquiry in politics, science, and culture by the *New York Times* bestselling author and skeptic Michael Shermer. The new collection of essays and articles takes the devil by the horns by tackling five key themes: free thought and free speech, politics and society, scientific humanism, religion, and the ideas of controversial intellectuals. For our own sake, we *must* give the devil his due.

Michael Shermer is Presidential Fellow at Chapman University, USA, the Publisher of *Skeptic* magazine, the host of the Science Salon podcast, and for eighteen years he was a monthly columnist for *Scientific American*. He is the author of a number of *New York Times* bestselling books including: *Heavens on Earth*, *The Moral Arc*, *The Believing Brain*, and *Why People Believe Weird Things*. His two TED talks, viewed over nine million times, were voted into the top 100 out of more than 2,000 TED talks.

GIVING THE DEVIL HIS DUE

Reflections of a Scientific Humanist

Michael Shermer

Chapman University

CAMBRIDGE
UNIVERSITY PRESS

CAMBRIDGE
UNIVERSITY PRESS

University Printing House, Cambridge CB2 8BS, United Kingdom

One Liberty Plaza, 20th Floor, New York, NY 10006, USA

477 Williamstown Road, Port Melbourne, VIC 3207, Australia

314–321, 3rd Floor, Plot 3, Splendor Forum, Jasola District Centre,
New Delhi – 110025, India

103 Penang Road, #05–06/07, Visioncrest Commercial, Singapore 238467

Cambridge University Press is part of the University of Cambridge.

It furthers the University's mission by disseminating knowledge in the pursuit of
education, learning, and research at the highest international levels of excellence.

www.cambridge.org
Information on this title: www.cambridge.org/9781108489782
DOI: 10.1017/9781108779395

© Michael Shermer 2020

Graphs and charts courtesy of Pat Linse

First published 2020
Reprinted 2020
Paperback edition first published 2021

Printed in the United Kingdom by TJ Books Limited, Padstow Cornwall

A catalogue record for this publication is available from the British Library.

ISBN 978-1-108-48978-2 Hardback
ISBN 978-1-108-74758-5 Paperback

This book is dedicated to my friends Christopher Hitchens and Steven Pinker, peerless champions of liberty who have always given the devil his due . . . for our own safety's sake.

Contents

Acknowledgments

Thank you to Janka Romero, Bethany Johnson, Kilmeny MacBride, Chloe Bradley, Phyllis van Reenen, Emily Watton, Diana Rissetto, David Repetto, Diane Kraut, and the staff at Cambridge University Press.

Thank you to Pat Linse for producing the graphs and charts for the book.

Thank you to the following publications and publishers for originally publishing the articles and essays in this volume: the *New York Times*, the *Los Angeles Times*, *Scientific American*, the *Journal of Bioeconomics*, *Quillette*, *Skeptic*, the *Journal of Criminal Justice*, the journal *Theology and Science*, *The Palgrave Handbook of Philosophy and Public Policy*, Palgrave, Oxford University Press, Prometheus Books, and Bloomsbury/Continuum.

Thank you to my wife Jennifer . . . for loving me . . . forever.

Who Is the Devil and What Is He Due?

"**F**IRE. FIRE. FIRE! NOW YOU'VE HEARD IT,**"** Christopher Hitchens declared in an auditorium that bore some resemblance to a theater, the type specimen on offer by the United States Supreme Court Justice Oliver Wendell Holmes of where and when speech should be restricted.[1] To wit, Justice Holmes' unanimous opinion in the 1919 case of *Schenck v. United States* included these now famous and oft-quoted lines:

> The most stringent protection of free speech would not protect a man in falsely shouting fire in a theatre and causing a panic ... The question in every case is whether the words used are used in such circumstances and are of such a nature as to create a clear and present danger that they will bring about the substantive evils that Congress has a right to prevent. It is a question of proximity and degree.[2]

What were the falsely shouted utterances that Justice Holmes feared constituted *a clear and present danger*? They were 15,000 fliers distributed to draft-age men during the First World War that encouraged them to "Assert your rights," "Do not submit to intimidation," and "If you do not assert and support your rights, you are helping to deny or disparage rights which it is the solemn duty of all citizens and residents of the United States to retain." The right to what? Freedom. Freedom from what? Slavery.

Slavery? Yes. According to the distributors of the fliers – Charles Schenck and Elizabeth Baer, members of the Executive Committee of the Socialist Party in Philadelphia – military conscription constituted involuntary servitude, which is strictly prohibited by the Thirteenth

Amendment of the US Constitution. "When you conscript a man and compel him to go abroad to fight against his will, you violate the most sacred right of personal liberty, and substitute for it what Daniel Webster called 'despotism in its worst form,'" they wrote in their broadside, elaborating:

> A conscript is little better than a convict. He is deprived of his liberty and of his right to think and act as a free man. A conscripted citizen is forced to surrender his right as a citizen and become a subject. He is forced into involuntary servitude. He is deprived of the protection given him by the Constitution of the United States. He is deprived of all freedom of conscience in being forced to kill against his will.[3]

For this treasonous act of voicing their opposition to the draft (and US involvement in a largely European war), Schenck and Baer were convicted of violating Section 3 of the Espionage Act of 1917, passed shortly after US entry into the Great War in order to prohibit interference with government recruitment into the armed services, and to prevent insubordination in the military and/or support for enemies of the United States during wartime.[4] It sounds like an antiquated law applicable to a darker time in American history, employed as it was to silence such socialists as the newspaper editor Victor Berger, the labor leader and Socialist Party of America Presidential candidate Eugene V. Debs, anarchists Emma Goldman and Alexander Berkman, communists Julius and Ethel Rosenberg, and Pentagon Papers revealer Daniel Ellsberg. But, in fact, the Act is still used today as a cudgel against such whistleblowers as diplomatic cable leaker Chelsea Manning and National Security Agency contractor Edward Snowden, still on the lam in Moscow for his Wikileaks revelations about spying (and other questionable activities) on both American citizens and foreign actors (including German Chancellor Angela Merkel) by the United States government.

Tellingly, as mission creep set in and "clear and present danger" expanded to include speech unrelated to military operations or combating foreign enemies, Holmes dissented in other cases, reverting to a position of absolute protection for nearly all speech short of that intended to cause criminal harm, concluding that the "marketplace of ideas" of open discussion, debate, and disputation was the best test of their verisimilitude. Interestingly, in an earlier and similar case that came before the court involving anti-draft protesters convicted for obstructing recruitment and enlistment services that the Supreme Court of the United States (SCOTUS) voted to affirm, Holmes dissented thusly:

> Real obstructions of the law, giving real aid and comfort to the enemy, I should have been glad to see punished more summarily and severely than they sometimes were. But I think that our intention to put out all our powers in aid of success in war should not hurry us into intolerance of opinions and speech that could not be imagined to do harm, although opposed to our own. It is better for those who have unquestioned and almost unlimited power in their hands to err on the side of freedom.[5]

Err on the side of freedom. Call it Holmes' Axiom. Erring on the side of freedom is not just for champions of free speech but, instead, is intended to counter those who would censor speech in the name of some alleged threat.

After admonishing Holmes' errant decision involving fires and theaters, Hitchens identified what he considers to be the three founding documents of free speech: John Milton's 1644 *Areopagitica*, Thomas Paine's introduction to his 1794 *The Age of Reason*, and John Stuart Mill's 1859 *On Liberty*.[6] Daring to "summarize all three of these great gentlemen of the great tradition of especially English liberty in one go," Hitch affirmed:

> It is not just the right of the person who speaks to be heard, it is the right of everyone in the audience to listen and to hear, and every time you silence somebody you make yourself a prisoner of your own action because you deny yourself the right to hear something. In other words, your own right to hear and be exposed is as much involved in all these cases as is the right of the other to voice his or her view.

These are such monumental works of freedom of thought and expression that select quotes are warranted. From John Milton's *Areopagitica* (in seventeenth-century English not altogether familiar to twenty-first-century eyes):

> Give me the liberty to know, to utter, and to argue freely according to conscience, above all liberties.
>
> I cannot praise a fugitive and cloister'd vertue, unexercis'd & unbreath'd, that never sallies out and sees her adversary, but slinks out

of the race, where that immortall garland is to be run for, not without dust and heat. Assuredly we bring not innocence into the world, we bring impurity much rather: that which purifies us is triall, and triall is by what is contrary.

And though all the windes of doctrin were let loose to play upon the earth, so Truth be in the field, we do injuriously, by licencing and prohibiting to misdoubt her strength. Let her and Falshood grapple; who ever knew Truth put to the wors, in a free and open encounter.

Let Truth and Falsehood grapple in a free and open encounter. Wise words.

From Thomas Paine's *The Age of Reason,* in his opening remarks addressed "to my fellow-citizens of the United States of America":

You will do me the justice to remember, that I have always strenuously supported the Right of every Man to his own opinion, however different that opinion might be to mine. He who denies to another this right, makes a slave of himself to his present opinion, because he precludes himself the right of changing it. The most formidable weapon against errors of every kind is Reason. I have never used any other, and I trust I never shall.

The most formidable weapon against errors of every kind is Reason. And to reason with others we must be free to speak.

From John Stuart Mill's 1859 essay *On Liberty,* arguably the most poignant and powerful articulation of why, precisely, we should protect thought and speech:

If all mankind minus one, were of one opinion, and only one person were of the contrary opinion, mankind would be no more justified in silencing that one person, than he, if he had the power, would be justified in silencing mankind ... But the peculiar evil of silencing the expression of an opinion is, that it is robbing the human race; posterity as well as the existing generation; those who dissent from the opinion, still more than those who hold it. If the opinion is right, they are deprived of the opportunity of exchanging error for truth: if wrong, they lose, what is almost as great a benefit, the clearer perception and livelier impression of truth, produced by its collision with error.

Truth produced by its collision with error. Call it Mill's Maxim.

In his always learned but never too pedantic rhetorical style, Hitch offered his preferred representatives of the genre (paraphrasing their positions). From his "personal heroine" Rosa Luxemburg:

The freedom of speech is meaningless unless it means the freedom of the person who thinks differently.

From Hitch's former *National Review* editor John O'Sullivan:

If you hear the Pope saying he believes in God you think, "well the Pope's doing his job again today." If you hear the Pope saying he's really begun to doubt the existence of God, you begin to think "he might be on to something."

Apropos to my own work, Hitch asserted that someone who denies the Holocaust

doesn't just have a right to speak, that person's right to speak must be given *extra* protection because what he has to say must have taken him some effort to come up with.

And

What would you do if you met a flat Earth society member? Come to think of it, how can I prove the Earth is round? Am I sure about the theory of evolution? I know it's supposed to be true. Here's someone who says no such thing, it's all intelligent design. How sure am I in my own views?

Indeed, most people cannot articulate why the Earth is round and the theory of evolution true, so in responding to the claims of the flat-Earthers and creationists we are vouchsafed the opportunity to outline exactly how we know these things are true. As much as I am reticent to admit it, I have been forced by creationists and Holocaust deniers to improve my knowledge of and explanations for evolution and the Holocaust, and by so doing my confidence in their authenticity was elevated.

In summing together these observations, Hitch affirmed, in such poignant language we should give it the honorific of *Hitchens' Theorem*:

Don't take refuge in the false security of consensus.

Hitchens' Theorem should not be confused with what I called (in my *Scientific American* column of November, 2010) *Hitchens' Dictum*: "What can be asserted without evidence can also be dismissed without evidence."[7] This is an important proviso in any discussion of freedom of speech: While we may grant others the right to speak their views – however unfounded or unjustified we may think them – we are not obliged to respond (much less help them publish or otherwise disperse their ideas). It is axiomatic in skeptical and scientific reasoning that the *burden of proof* is on the speaker, not the listener. You think Big Foot is real? Show me the body, otherwise I can dismiss your claim as presently unsupported (even while being open to the possibility new evidence will present itself). You believe aliens from other worlds have landed on Earth? Show me the spaceship (or alien bodies), otherwise there is nothing for me to explain (and blurry photographs, grainy videos, and blacked-out paragraphs in government documents do not count as proof, even though we should keep an open mind that more solid evidence might be forthcoming). You contend that God exists and that there is an afterlife to which we go after death? Show me the evidence for either or both that goes beyond faith and cultural conventions, otherwise I shall remain skeptical (even while willing to be pleasantly surprised if it turns out my current atheism was mistaken – although in this case I might query the divine One why He didn't make His existence more obvious).

A qualification: In these claims, and many others I have investigated over the decades, I am not against their possible authenticity. Indeed, finding another bipedal primate that didn't go extinct – like Neanderthals and other hominids did over the past several hundred thousand years – and is still living in the hinterlands of Canada or the Himalayas would be the most spectacular find in biology since the discovery of the mountain gorilla in 1902 by Captain Robert von Beringe in German East Africa (present-day Burundi, Rwanda, and part of Tanzania). The discovery of or contact with an extraterrestrial intelligence and/or the finding of their interstellar vehicle, would be the greatest scientific story since ... the New World? The Atom? Gravity? Evolution? Ever?

An encounter with the deity who created our universe and (presumably) the heavenly cloud where our connectome souls are uploaded after death would very probably top all of these encounters, given its implications for our future existence, not to mention the opportunity to answer science's deepest questions from the ontological source itself: What is dark energy and dark matter? What was there before the Big Bang? Did you create our universe out of a singularity, and if so how did you do that . . . and why?

We only have our thoughts and the tools of communicating those thoughts through speech and writing. Thus, free thought and free speech are the epistemological primitive, the ground of all other rights. Human and moral progress can only come about when people are free to think and speak their minds and their conscience. Why? The aforementioned classics in liberty cited by Hitch make the case more elegantly than I, but over the years in speeches and writings, I have assembled lists of succinct arguments that audiences unfamiliar with the longer and more literary sources can digest in bullet-point (and PowerPoint) form. To that end, here are my *Ten Commandments of Free Speech and Thought* against censorship:

1. Who decides which speech and thought is acceptable and which is unacceptable? You? Me? The majority? A thought committee? The language police? The control of speech is how dictatorships and autocracies rule. We must resist the urge to control what other people say and think.

2. What criteria are used to censor certain speech? Ideas that I disagree with? Thoughts that differ from your thoughts? Anything that the majority determines is unacceptable? This is another form of tyranny, a tyranny of the majority.

3. It is not just the right of the speaker to speak but for listeners to listen. When colleges deplatform speakers or students succeed in silencing a speaker through the heckler's veto, the right of the audience to hear the speaker's ideas is violated.

4. We might be completely right but still learn something new in hearing what someone else has to say.

5. We might be partially right and partially wrong, and by listening to other viewpoints we might stand corrected and refine and improve our beliefs.

6. We might be completely wrong, so hearing criticism or counterpoint gives us the opportunity to change our minds and improve our thinking. No one is infallible. The only way to find out if you've gone off the rails is to get feedback on your beliefs, opinions, and

even your facts. Alternative facts are corrected by confirmed facts, but the confirmation bias means we are all subject to seeking only confirming evidence for our beliefs. To overcome it we must listen to our critics.

7. Whether right or wrong, by listening to the opinions of others, we have the opportunity to develop stronger arguments and build better facts for our positions. If you know only your own position, you do not know it as well as you would if you knew your opponent's position.

8. Arguments made in favor of censorship and against free speech are automatically gainsaid the moment the speaker speaks – otherwise we would be unaware of their arguments if they were censored.

9. Freedom of inquiry – a form of free thought and speech – is the basis for all human progress because of human fallibility. We are all wrong some of the time (and many of us, most of the time) so the only way to know if you've gone off the rails is to tell others about your beliefs so that they may be tested in the marketplace of ideas. In science this is called *conjecture and refutation,* or hypothesis testing.

10. My freedom to speak and dissent is inextricably tied to your freedom to speak and dissent. If I censor you, why shouldn't you censor me? If you silence me, why shouldn't I silence you? Once customs and laws are in place to silence someone on one topic, what's to stop people from silencing anyone on any topic that deviates from the accepted canon?

This final argument against censorship – and the source for the title of this book – was well articulated in Robert Bolt's 1960 play, *A Man for All Seasons,* based on the true story of the sixteenth century Chancellor of England, Sir Thomas More, and his collision with King Henry VIII over the monarch's divorce from Catherine of Aragon. In the play, a dialogue unfolds between More and his future son-in-law, Roper, over the changing of the law. Roper urges him to arrest a man whose testimony could condemn More to death, even though no laws were broken.

MORE: And go he should, if he were the Devil himself, until he broke the law!

ROPER: So now you'd give the Devil benefit of law!

MORE: Yes. What would you do? Cut a great road through the law to get after the Devil?

ROPER: I'd cut down every law in England to do that.

MORE: Oh? And when the law was down, and the Devil turned round on you – where would you hide, Roper, the laws all being flat? This country is planted thick with laws from coast to coast . . . and if you cut them down . . . do you really think you could stand upright in the winds that would blow then? Yes, I'd give the Devil benefit of law, for my own safety's sake.[8]

* * *

For our own safety's sake, we must give the Devil his due.

But who is the devil, and what is he due? In short, the devil is anyone who disagrees with you or someone else, and what he is due is the right to speak his mind. In my case, my devils include creationists who reject the theory of evolution, Holocaust deniers who reject the theory that the Nazi regime intended to exterminate European Jewry, scientists who risk their reputations and careers to study such radioactive topics as racial group differences in IQ and gender differences in cognitive abilities or career preferences, and conservatives and centrists who challenge the far-left dogma on college campuses and find themselves deplatformed before speaking or vetoed by hecklers while speaking.

These are the devils of Part I of this book, *The Advocatus Diaboli: Reflections on Free Thought and Free Speech,* and I try to give them their due through a fair hearing of their opinions, even when I reject them. Even the Catholic Church employed an *Advocatus Diaboli* – a Devil's Advocate – tasked with arguing "against the canonization (sainthood) of a candidate in order to uncover any character flaws or misrepresentation of the evidence favoring canonization."[9] The position was established in 1587 by Pope Sixtus V when it became apparent to the church that many claims of miracles – offered to elevate favored candidates to sainthood – were bogus, such as pieces of the true cross, saints' relics, weeping statues, bleeding paintings, and especially miraculous healings that might have happened by chance or through the natural healing capacities of the body.

In acting as a modern-day *Advocatus Diaboli,* I have approached my would-be saints not just through books and articles, but through direct contact and interaction with adherents and skeptics of each such claim. It has been my good fortune, as the Editor-in-Chief of *Skeptic* magazine for a quarter-century and a monthly columnist for *Scientific American* for nearly eighteen years, to have met and dialogued with a great many renowned and respected scientists and scholars, along with many famous – and, in some cases, infamous – claimants of pseudoscience, pseudohistory, and all manner of what most mainstream scientists and scholars consider to be bunkum. This collection of articles and essays from the past fifteen years takes its title from the first essay, "Giving the Devil His Due," in which I make the case for why freedom of thought, conscience, inquiry, and speech is inviolable for science and politics and sacrosanct to civilization.

But this book is far more than just reflections on free speech. *Giving the Devil His Due* is much broader, being (as noted in the subtitle) *Reflections of a Scientific Humanist*. It is a collection of articles and essays classified by subject into five parts: Free Thought and Free Speech, God and Religion, Politics and Society, Scientific Humanism, and Controversial Intellectuals. At the beginning of each chapter, I explain why I wrote it, where it was originally published, any updates where appropriate, and why they're included in the book. Thus each chapter reads as it did in its original form, with the exception of a few factual corrections and errata. Note on referencing: Some chapters in this volume are heavily referenced, others lightly referenced, and some contain no references at all. This reflects the varying type of publications in which they were originally published: some in scholarly or scientific journals, which require formal referencing, others in magazines or newspapers that require no references at all.

In Part II, *Reflections on God and Religion*, I explore the true meaning of the Latin phrase *E Pluribus Unum* for a modern pluralistic society like ours and why it must include not just all faiths but no faiths; why political freedom for people of all faiths somewhat ironically leads to religious skepticism and is, in part, the reason for the rise of the Nones – those who have no religious affiliation; why I believe Scientology is a cult, yet why I also defend their right to hold their beliefs but how the wide distribution via the Internet of their "secret" theological doctrines and the transparency of their practices will very likely result in either the end of the cult or the transformation of it into a mainstream religion, along the lines of what happened to the Mormon religion in the 1890s when they banned the practice of polygamy (under pressure from the federal government when Utah lobbied to become a state in the union); finally, in this section, I consider from a scientific perspective the two biggest questions of all: Does the universe have a purpose? and Why is there something rather than nothing? Constructing a worldview of scientific humanism means we must provide answers to these most meaning-laden questions, even if our answers are provisional.

In Part III, *Deferred Dreams: Reflections on Politics and Society*, I take on identity politics, intersectionality theory, and tribalism in modern politics and why this has corrupted Martin Luther King, Jr.'s dream that we should judge people by the content of their character instead of the color of their skin; I propose classical liberalism as a mediating political position between Left and Right as a means of healing the bonds of affection so torn asunder since the 2016 election; I also consider the matter of how we're going to govern Mars when colonists set up a new society there – that is, what lessons in governance from the Blue Planet we can take with us to the Red Planet; I include three articles and essays I wrote on guns and gun control, another contentious current issue, reviewing what scientific research shows we can and cannot do about gun violence, and giving the devils on both sides of this debate their due through debates I have done (and the fact that I've been on both sides); finally, I include a long review essay on economics related to evolutionary theory because, as with most social and political issues, I contend that approaching such issues from a scientific perspective with the best tools of science that we have is the only hope for solving problems, and this is what I mean by the blended label of scientific humanism.

Part IV, *Scientia Humanitatis: Reflections on Scientific Humanism* is, as it were, a manifesto of my life's work inasmuch as I see myself as a child of the Enlightenment, that age of reason following the Scientific Revolution that applied the tools of science to any and all human problems; to that extent I plead with my fellow scientists and philosophers to tear down the wall separating science and morality – David Hume's Is-Ought barrier, or the naturalistic fallacy – because if we are not going to base our values and morals on reality as best described by science, what are we going to base them on? In the final two essays in this section, I look at the bigger picture of how we can achieve Civilization 1.0 (on the Kardashev scale of civilizational types) and what we can and cannot control in our lives, as I consider another big subject of how lives turn out.

In the final section of the book, Part V, *Transcendent Thinkers: Reflections on Controversial Intellectuals,* I return to the devils in my own camp – scientists, philosophers, and scholars – who challenged the false security of consensus in science and society. These include Paul Kurtz, the philosopher who took on all manner of superstition and supernatural beliefs when it was unsafe to do so, and as a result became one of the founding fathers of the modern skeptical and humanist movements – the foundation of scientific humanism; Christopher Hitchens and what he really believed, in the context of those who – as is customary after a famous intellect dies – attributed the equivalent of a deathbed confession to Hitch (I also offer some reflections on Hitch's personality and intellectual style, as I knew him personally); Richard Dawkins, whom I call "the Skeptic's Chaplain," given his formidable influence in the furtherance of scientific humanism in his fearless application of the methods of science to all of human beliefs, most famously religion. In the penultimate chapter of the book, I take on Jordan Peterson, the man who is arguably the most controversial intellect of the twenty-first century, whom I have gotten to know so that I can better understand his ideas and the phenomenon surrounding him. Peterson is the perfect embodiment of my trope about devils and what they are due, as he has emerged as one of the most polarizing figures in intellectual life since, perhaps, Noam Chomsky. Peterson is not the devil, but a surprising number of highly intelligent and highly regarded scientists and scholars seem to think he is, so I consider why that is and – fitting the underlying theme of this book – why he must be given his due so that we may accept or reject his ideas according to their evidentiary standing instead of their emotional evocation. I then end the book with my analysis of Graham Hancock, an alternative archaeologist and audacious autodidact who is challenging what mainstream science says about our past in a way I consider to be the embodiment of why we must listen to outsiders – devils who should be given their due – because although they are often wrong, they turn out to be right just often enough that we must not dismiss them out of hand.

* * *

What about *hate speech?* Surely there are reasonable arguments to be made for censoring words that offend others or are generally agreed upon to be deeply offensive, the N-word being the most obvious? No. Hate speech is best countered with free speech, better speech, or no speech at all (just ignore them). As I have posted on social media many times (often in real time during their events), if you really want to hurt provocateurs like Milo Yiannopoulos, Ann Coulter, Richard Spencer, or Jared Taylor, just ignore them when they come to your town or campus to speak. As a professional public speaker myself, I can affirm that there is nothing public speakers hate more than an empty auditorium. By contrast, what such agitators really want is exactly what their opponents have been giving them: protests that erupt in violence that draw huge crowds and generate extensive media coverage. This turns hate-speech bigots into free-speech martyrs, recognition that they most assuredly do not deserve. So don't give it to them. If a rebuttal is in order then calmly explain why they are wrong by countering their claims with facts, evidence, and reason. This can be done directly in the question-and-answer period of the person's talk, or in an opinion editorial in the campus or city newspaper, in a book or magazine article, in a blog or podcast, on Facebook or Instagram, or any of a number of other venues now readily available online at virtually no cost and with no barrier to entry.

The reasons to counter hate speech with free speech are covered in my Ten Commandments of Free Speech and Thought above (especially numbers 1, 2, and 3), but to punctuate the point I offer this poignant observation of Christopher Hitchens, who cautioned:

> To whom do you award the right to decide which speech is harmful, or who is the harmful speaker? Or to determine in advance what are the harmful consequences going to be, that we know enough about in advance to prevent? To whom would you give this job? To whom are you going to award the job of being the censor?[10]

In her monumental 2018 treatise on *Hate: Why We Should Resist it with Free Speech, not Censorship,* former American Civil Liberties Union (ACLU) president Nadine Strossen points out that one man's hate speech is another man's free speech. To wit, during the 1830s many southern states enacted laws to "protect" their citizens from hearing abolitionist speech, arguing that it could lead to slave rebellions and violence, and that abolitionists "libeled the South and inflicted emotional injury," in the words of South Carolina senator John C. Calhoun. In the twentieth century civil rights activists opposed viewpoint-based censorship, knowing that their call for black Americans to be granted the same rights as white Americans would be considered "hate speech" by a great many southern citizens. And there are countless examples of autocrats, theocrats, and dictators of various political stripes silencing their critics by enacting hate speech laws. As the ACLU noted in their defense of neo-Nazis to demonstrate in Skokie, Illinois, in 1977, such laws "could have been used to stop Martin Luther King, Jr.'s confrontational march into Cicero, Illinois, in 1968." As Strossen concludes: "Notably, the asserted harms that abolitionist speech was feared to cause – libel, emotional injury, and violence – are the very same harms that are now cited in support of 'hate speech' laws." Hate speech laws, Strossen concludes "undermine universal principles of liberty, equality, and democracy."[11]

To be sure, I will confess that when I see racist assholes like Richard Spencer and Jared Taylor spouting their ignorant beliefs about blacks and Jews in half-empty hotel conference rooms or to a rag-tag mob of tiki-torch-carrying thugs in a public park, the urge to "punch a Nazi" wells up inside, as it did for the man who sucker punched Spencer during a television interview near President Trump's inauguration in January 2017. But we must resist the primal urge that bubbles up in our primate brains to fight hate with hate, and instead follow the sage advice of Martin Luther King, Jr. when he reproved in 1958:[12]

> Hate begets hate; violence begets violence; toughness begets a greater toughness. We must meet the forces of hate with the power of love.

And again in 1963:

> Darkness cannot drive out darkness; only light can do that. Hate cannot drive out hate; only love can do that. Hate multiplies hate, violence multiplies violence, and toughness multiplies toughness in a descending spiral of destruction ... The chain reaction of evil – hate begetting hate, wars producing more wars – must be broken, or we shall be plunged into the dark abyss of annihilation.

Not even "fighting words" should be censored, as the SCOTUS ruled in a 1949 case (*Terminiello v. Chicago*) in which a Catholic priest named Arthur Terminiello was convicted of "breach of the peace" after he gave an inflammatory speech to over 800 people in a packed Chicago auditorium with a thousand protesters outside. Such speech, the law read, "may constitute a breach of the peace if it stirs the public to anger, invites dispute, brings about a condition of unrest, or creates a disturbance, or if it molests the inhabitants in the enjoyment of peace and quiet by arousing alarm." Did it? According to Supreme Court Justice Douglas, writing for the majority opinion that overturned Terminiello's conviction, Terminiello "condemned the conduct of the crowd outside and vigorously, if not viciously, criticized various political and racial groups whose activities he denounced as inimical to the nation's welfare." Why shouldn't this form of speech be censored, indeed punished? Because, Justice Douglas continued:

> [The] function of free speech under our system of government is to invite dispute. It may indeed best serve its high purpose when it induces a condition of unrest, creates dissatisfaction with conditions as they are, or even stirs people to anger. Speech is often provocative and challenging. It may strike at prejudices and preconceptions and have profound unsettling effects as it presses for acceptance of an idea. That is why freedom of speech, though not absolute, is nevertheless protected against censorship or punishment.

When I argue that free speech is inviolable and sacrosanct, I mean this in the broadest sense, even while acknowledging that some restrictions are both legally and morally necessary, such as leaking the nuclear codes to an enemy nation, libeling someone in a way that damages their reputation and income, extorting others to give up money or freedom, and fraudulently stealing from others what isn't rightfully yours through persuasion. But as the Harvard psychologist Steven Pinker explained,

> these exceptions must be strictly delineated and individually justified; they are not an excuse to treat speech as one fungible good among many. Despots in so-called "democratic republics" routinely jail their opponents on charges of treason, libel, and inciting lawlessness. Britain's

lax libel laws have been used to silence critics of political figures, business oligarchs, Holocaust deniers, and medical quacks. Even Oliver Wendell Holmes's famous exception to free speech – falsely shouting "Fire!" in a crowded theater – is easily abused, not least by Holmes himself. He coined the meme in a 1919 Supreme Court case that upheld the conviction of a man who distributed leaflets encouraging men to resist the draft during World War I, a clear expression of opinion in a democracy.

And if you object to these arguments – if you want to expose a flaw in my logic or a lapse in my accuracy – it's the right of free speech that allows you to do so.[13]

It is for these reasons – and many others – that this book is dedicated to my friends Christopher Hitchens and Steven Pinker, peerless champions of liberty who have always given the devil his due ... for our own safety's sake.

PART I

THE ADVOCATUS DIABOLI: REFLECTIONS ON FREE THOUGHT AND FREE SPEECH

CHAPTER 1

Giving the Devil His Due

*Why Freedom of Inquiry and Speech in Science
and Politics Is Inviolable*

PREAMBLE

This article was originally published in the November/December 2018
issue of the *Journal of Criminal Justice* as a "Special Issue on the Study of
Ethnicity and Race in Criminology and Criminal Justice," addressing
a target article by the psychologist James Flynn on "Academic Freedom
and Race," dealing with the always-controversial topic of racial group
differences in IQ scores. The subject of this issue is not the IQ test and
whether or not group differences are real (and if they are what the cause
of those differences might be). Instead, we were tasked with thinking
about to what extent scientists and scholars (and anyone else) should be
free to inquire into the matter and, especially, whether they should be
free to report their findings and opinions, regardless of the political or
cultural implications.

This topic was radioactive even before I started college in 1972 when
I took my first psychology course in which the professor introduced us to
the controversy. I recall at the time deciding then and there that were I to
major in psychology (which I ultimately did, earning a BA in psychology
from Pepperdine University and an MA in experimental psychology from
California State University, Fullerton), I would not study intelligence,
especially racial group differences in IQ scores. I could see even back
then that such ventures could torpedo one's career and, since there were
so many other interesting subjects to explore and problems to solve,
I didn't see any reason to unduly burden my life.

Nevertheless, I feel quite strongly that anyone who does explore the
topic absolutely should be free to do so unencumbered by political or
cultural restraints. To do otherwise – to censor knowledge we don't

like – is the antithesis of free speech and inquiry, for knowledge is what will ultimately set us free.

* * *

I N THE 1990s I UNDERTOOK AN EXTENSIVE ANALYSIS OF THE Holocaust and those who deny it that culminated in *Denying History*, a book I coauthored with Alex Grobman.[1] Alex and I are both civil libertarians who believe strongly that the right to speak one's mind is fundamental to a free society, so we were surprised to discover that Holocaust denial is primarily an American phenomenon for the simple reason that America is one of the few countries where it is legal to doubt the Holocaust. Legal? Where (and why) on earth would it be illegal? In Canada, for starters, where there are "anti-hate" statutes and laws against spreading "false news" that have been applied to Holocaust deniers. In Austria it is a crime if a person "denies, grossly trivializes, approves or seeks to justify the national socialist genocide or other national socialist crimes against humanity." In France it is illegal to challenge the existence of "crimes against humanity" as they were defined by the Military Tribunal at Nuremberg "or in connection with any crime within the jurisdiction of the Tribunal, whether or not in violation of the domestic law of the country where perpetrated." The "Race Relations Act" in Great Britain forbids racially charged speech, "not only when it is likely to lead to violence, but generally, on the grounds that members of minority races should be protected from racial insults." Switzerland, Belgium, Israel, Italy, New Zealand, and Sweden have all passed similar laws.[2] In 1989 the New South Wales parliament in Australia passed the "Anti-Discrimination Act" that includes these chilling passages, Orwellian in their implications:

> The law invests in the Anti-Discrimination Board the power to determine whether a report is "fair," and whether a discussion is "reasonable," "in good faith," and "in the public interest." The Board will pronounce upon the acceptability of artistic expression, research papers, academic controversy, and scientific questions. An unfair (i.e., inaccurate) report of a public act may expose the reporter and the publisher to damages of up to $40,000.[3]

Even at the University of California, Berkeley, home of the Free Speech Movement of the 1960s, they apparently have abandoned teaching this most basic principle. On Friday, February 3, 1995, for example, the controversial historian David Irving was invited to speak on campus, leading 300 protesters to show up and block the 113 ticket holders from entering the building and prevent Irving from speaking about his alternative views of the Holocaust and the Second World War. Campus police were roused to action to control the unruly crowd, and Irving had to seek protection behind his book table until order was restored.[4] Frank Miele, one of my editors for *Skeptic* magazine, attended the event and reported the mayhem:

> The people outside the door were screaming at Irving and the rest of us inside the room. They tried to force their way in, but the Berkeley police prevented this. At one point an older-looking man with a gray stubbly beard came from the back of the crowd and made his way through the demonstrators and into the room. Irving grabbed his cash box from the display table of books and retreated peacefully to the wall. The old man pushed the books off the table and then physically pushed and shoved Irving. The Berkeley police finally restored order, moving the crowd out of the building and into the street, where they continued to chant, shout, and demonstrate. When the old man physically assaulted Irving, a muscular young man in a black T-shirt came forward and decked him with one right cross. The young man made no attempt to attack or injure him further, and the Berkeley police took the old man out of the room.[5]

Since Irving's invitation to speak came from the Berkeley Coalition for Free Speech, they apparently also no longer teach irony at that institution.

* * *

Given the fact that the Shoah took place in Europe, it is perhaps understandable that some countries there would be hypersensitive to the denial of it. And given the horrific history of race relations in America, such hate speech laws could be rationalized as relevant to the claim that there are genetically determined differences between blacks and whites in intelligence, because such information (whether true or false) might lead white supremacists and other bigots to commit violence against blacks. Or, considering the long struggle women have had to gain parity to men, one could argue that research on gender differences in cognitive abilities could turn back the clock on women's rights should a disparity be found in favor of the gender still dominant in positions of power. Since people act on their beliefs, and beliefs are expressed in the form of speech, isn't it reasonable to argue that certain scientific findings be categorized as a form of hate speech that should be censored?

No.

The justification of such laws in the consequentialist argument that people might be incited to discrimination, hate, or violence if exposed to such ideas fails the moment you turn the argument around and ask: What happens when it is *you and your* ideas that are determined to be dangerous? This argument against censorship was well articulated in Robert Bolt's 1960 play, *A Man for All Seasons*, based on the true story of the sixteenth-century Chancellor of England, Sir Thomas More, and his collision with King Henry VIII over his divorce from Catherine of Aragon. In the play, a dialogue unfolds over the changing of the law, between More and his future son-in-law, Roper, who urges him to arrest a man whose testimony could condemn More to death, even though no laws were broken. "And go he should, if he were the Devil himself, until he broke the law!" More entices.

ROPER: *So now you'd give the Devil benefit of law!*

MORE: *Yes. What would you do? Cut a great road through the law to get after the Devil?*

ROPER: *I'd cut down every law in England to do that.*

MORE: *Oh? And when the law was down, and the Devil turned round on you – where would you hide, Roper, the laws all being flat? This country is planted thick with laws from coast to coast ... and if you cut them down ... do you really think you could stand upright in the winds that would blow then? Yes, I'd give the Devil benefit of law, for my own safety's sake.*[6]

Pretend for a moment that the majority of people deny the Holocaust (or believe that racial and gender differences are real and innate) and that they are in the positions of power. If a mechanism for censorship of unwanted speech exists, then the believer in the reality of the Holocaust (or the skeptic of racial and gender differences) may now be censored. Would we tolerate this? Of course not.

In America, the First Amendment protects the right of citizens to express their opinions on anything they like, no matter how extreme, evil, conniving, or crazy. Here you are free to doubt the Apollo moon landing, the JFK assassination single-bullet theory, the existence of God, the divinity of Jesus, the verisimilitude of the Quran, the prophetic nature of Moses or Muhammad, al Qaeda's role in 9/11, and even the president's birthplace. No matter how much one may dislike someone else's opinion – even if it is something as disturbing or potentially disruptive as denying that the Holocaust happened or that some people may not be as successful because of innate racial or gender differences – that opinion is protected by the First Amendment. More than a legal right, I also believe we have a moral duty to speak our minds.

I am therefore in unwavering agreement with James Flynn in his target article on "Academic Freedom and Race" in the *Journal of Criminal Justice*, that "There should be no academic sanctions against those who believe that were environments equalized, genetic differences between black and white Americans would mean that blacks have an IQ deficit." Flynn's courage and integrity go even further when he argues, "Moreover, research into this question should not be forbidden. This is so, no matter what the outcome of the race and IQ debate, that is, no matter whether the evidence eventually dictates a genetically caused deficit of nil or 5 or 10 or 20 IQ points." That principle – the freedom to participate in the dialogue that the philosopher Karl Popper called "conjecture and refutation" – is at the heart of both the scientific method and the political process.[7]

The reason we need critical feedback from others is that our brains come equipped with a set of cognitive heuristics – or rules of thumb, or shortcuts – that help us navigate through the buzzing blurring confusion of information coming in through our senses. These heuristics are also known as *cognitive biases* because they often distort our percepts to fit preconceived concepts, and they are part of a larger process called "motivated reasoning," in which no matter what belief system is in place – religious, political, economic, or social – they shape how we interpret information that comes through our senses and motivate us to reason our way to finding the world to be precisely the way we wish it were. As I argue in *The Believing Brain*, our beliefs are formed for a variety of subjective, emotional, psychological, and social reasons and then are reinforced through these belief-confirmation heuristics and justified and explained with rational reasons.[8] The confirmation bias, the hindsight bias, the self-justification bias, the status quo bias, the sunk-cost bias, the availability bias, the representative bias, the believability bias, the authority bias, and the consistency bias are just a few of the ways cognitive psychologists have discovered that we distort the world.

It is not so much that scientists are trained to avoid these cognitive biases – as I argued in *Why People Believe Weird Things*, smart people can be even better at rationalizing beliefs they arrived at for nonsmart reasons – as it is that science itself is designed to force you to ferret out your errors and prejudices because if you don't someone else will, often with great glee in a public forum, from peer-review commentary to social media (where all pretentions to civil discourse are stripped away). Science is a competitive enterprise that is not for the thin-skinned or faint of heart. Most ideas that people come up with are wrong. That is why science is so cautious about tossing aside old ideas that have already survived the competitive marketplace, and why scientists tend to dismiss out of hand new ideas that threaten a tried-and-true research paradigm, especially before the revolutionary theory has been properly vetted by professionals in the field. That process of generating new ideas and introducing them to your peers and the public where they can be skeptically scrutinized in the bright light of other minds is the only way to find out if you've come up with something true and important or if you've been immersed in self-deception.

James Flynn hits the mark on this point when he writes, "I know of no alternative to the scientific method to maximize accumulation of truth about the physical world and the causes of human behavior. If scholars are to debate this issue, do we not want the best evidence possible – and this can only come from science." What if it turns out that the primary cause of racial differences in IQ is the environment but, due to academic censorship of sensitive topics, the only people doing research in this area are those who believe that all such differences are to be found in our genes? Where is the environmental refutation to the genetic conjecture? "There will be bad science on both sides of the debate," Flynn admits. But "The only antidote I know for that is to use the scientific method as scrupulously as possible." By way of example, Flynn says he discovered his eponymous effect – the "Flynn Effect" that IQ points have been increasing on average about three points every ten years for almost a century[9] – by reading Arthur Jensen's research on IQ and "g" (the general intelligence factor), which no one else noticed because of their reluctance to give any credence to Jensen's work as a result of his association with the genetic position on racial differences in IQ. Flynn asks rhetorically, "Does academia really want to ally itself with those who reserve free discussion to Philosopher Kings, and create dogmas to deaden the minds of all others?" The answer for many academics, I'm sorry to say, is a resounding yes. They see themselves as Philosopher Kings who know what is best for the masses, whom they believe are incapable of thinking as deeply as themselves.

This elitist arrogance goes a long way to explaining the recent and disturbing trend on college campuses to censor unwanted speech and thought (yes, thought crimes!), well documented by Greg Lukianoff, President of the Foundation for Individual Rights in Education (FIRE), in his 2014 booklet *Freedom from Speech*.[10] Readers may recall the wave of "disinvitations" at universities who invited controversial (or simply interesting but politically diverse) speakers to enlighten their students, only to disinvite them after waves of protest from some students and faculty that the speakers' words might offend. FIRE has documented 257 such incidents since 2000, 111 of which were successful in preventing the invited speakers from delivering their speeches (75 disinvitations, 20 speaker withdrawals, and 16 "heckler's vetoes" in which student hecklers shouted down or chased off stage the speakers).[11] Potentially offensive words are the basis of "trigger warnings" professors are supposed to supply to their students in classroom lectures that might cause them discomfort (these include sex, addiction, bullying, suicide, sizeism, ableism, homophobia, transphobia, slut-shaming, and victim-blaming),[12] as if a university classroom were designed to infantilize students and treat them like children instead of preparing them for adulthood and the real world where they most certainly will not be so shielded.

This is why the principle of free speech and the arguments in its favor apply to the political world as well as the scientific one, and why no Philosopher King or Benevolent Dictator can ever be allowed to rule. As I explained in my 2015 book *The Moral Arc*:

Democracies developed in response to the monarchic autocracies of the eighteenth and nineteenth centuries and to the dictatorship regimes of the 20th century because democracies empower individuals with a methodology instead of an ideology, and it is to this extent that we can see that the scientific values of reason, empiricism and antiauthoritarianism are not the *product* of liberal democracy but the *producers* of it. Democratic elections are analogous to scientific experiments: every couple of years you carefully alter the variables with an election and observe the results. If you want different results, change the variables. The political system in the United States is often called the "American experiment," and the founding patriarchs referred to it as such, and thought of this experiment in democracy as a means to an end, not an end in itself.

Many of the founding fathers were, in fact, scientists who deliberately adapted the method of data gathering, hypothesis testing, and theory formation to their nation building. Their understanding of the provisional nature of findings led them to develop a social system in which doubt and dispute were the centerpieces of a functional polity. Jefferson, Franklin, Paine, and the others thought of social governance as a *problem to be solved* rather than as power to be grabbed. They thought of democracy in the same way that they thought of science – as a method, not an ideology. They argued, in essence, that no one knows how to govern a nation so we have to set up a system that allows for experimentation. Try this. Try that. Check the results. Repeat. That is the very heart of science.[13]

The freedom of speech has been one of the driving forces behind moral progress through science and reason because it enables the search for truth. "There must be no barriers to freedom of inquiry," J. Robert Oppenheimer wrote in 1949. "The scientist is free, and must be free to ask any question, to doubt any assertion, to seek for any evidence, to correct any errors." Reflecting on the history of science and extrapolating to wider spheres, he noted: "Our political life is also predicated on openness. We know that the only way to avoid error is to detect it and that the only way to detect it is to be free to inquire. And we know that as long as men are free to ask what they must, free to say what they think, free to think what they will, freedom can never be lost, and science can never regress."

It is my belief that truth will win out when the evidence is made available for all to see. "It is error alone which needs the support of government," Thomas Jefferson wrote in his *Notes on Virginia*. "Truth can stand by itself."[14] And as Jefferson articulated the principle in his original draft of the Declaration of Independence, arguably the greatest free-speech statement ever penned, "And, finally, that truth is great and will prevail if left to herself; that she is the proper and sufficient antagonist to error, and has nothing to fear from the conflict unless by human interposition disarmed of her natural weapons, free argument and debate; errors ceasing to be dangerous when it is permitted freely to contradict them."[15]

Thus it is that the human mind, no matter what ideas it may generate, must never be quashed.

CHAPTER 2

Banning Evil

In the Shadow of the Christchurch Massacre, Myths about Evil and Hate Speech Are Misleading

PREAMBLE

As we were putting together this volume of essays, the tragedy in Christchurch, New Zealand, took place when a deranged white supremacist shot up two mosques, killing fifty people, wounding another fifty, and leading to a mass call for action, from outlawing assault rifles to banning hate speech. As I discuss below, it is possible that a ban on such firearms in a small and relatively homogeneous country like New Zealand might work to prevent another such occurrence, as it did with a similar ban in Australia in the 1990s. But banning hate speech is another thing entirely and something that we know will not work, especially in the age of Internet access to virtually all of human knowledge, in which almost anyone anywhere can set up a web page and publish their ideas, no matter how hateful. But when I saw that a New Zealand bookstore chain decided to discontinue carrying the books of the Canadian psychologist Jordan Peterson – about whom I write in the penultimate essay of this volume – while they continued stocking copies of Adolf Hitler's *Mein Kampf,* I had to respond with this essay on the idea of banning evil in all forms, originally published in *Quillette* on March 26, 2019. In short, it can't be done. You can combat evil, as when police forces catch criminals and military services counter terrorists and challenge insurgents and threats. But the idea – and it is an idea that can only be heard in an environment of free speech – that one can simply ban bad, dangerous, or hateful ideas has a historical track record of failure to do so, while snagging it its net good, useful, and productive ideas and their human generators. As I conclude, following the old saying that the answer to the problems of democracy is more democracy, the solution to hate speech is more speech.

* * *

O N MARCH 15, A TWENTY-EIGHT-YEAR OLD AUSTRALIAN GUNMAN named Brenton Tarrant allegedly opened fire in two Christchurch, New Zealand mosques, killing fifty and wounding fifty more. It was the worst mass shooting in the history of that country. Prime Minister Jacinda Ardern, who was rightly praised for her response to the murders, declared, "While the nation grapples with a form of grief and anger that we have not experienced before, we are seeking answers."

One answer took form a week later, when Ms. Ardern announced legislation that would ban all military-style semiautomatic weapons, assault rifles and high-capacity magazines. Will such gun-control measures work to reduce gun crime? Maybe. They did in Australia following a 1996 mass shooting in Tasmania in which thirty-five people were murdered. A 2006 follow-up study showed that in the eighteen years prior to the ban, there had been thirteen mass shootings.[1] But in the decade following, there had been none. Gun culture is different in every country. But there is at least an arguable case to be made that the newly announced controls will make New Zealand a safer country.

The problem with banning the weapons of evil is that Australia and New Zealand are not comparable to America and other large and diverse nations. Their populations are much smaller and more homogeneous, the number of guns in circulation is orders of magnitude smaller, and the "gun culture" there is nothing like it is in America. Any attempt by the federal government to confiscate or even "buy back" such firearms would likely result in a Ruby Ridge or Waco-like incident ... every week. With over 300 million guns in circulation and, apparently, easy to obtain if one so desires, I do not think there are any gun-control measures that would greatly reduce mass public shootings, much less bring them down to zero. Even the comparatively small and homogeneous Norway with very restrictive gun-control laws failed to stop Anders Breivik, the Norwegian terrorist who murdered seventy-seven people there in 2011. The reason is that such events are far too random. They are Black Swan events, or as I called them *Sandy Hook Events*, namely: *high-profile, improbable, rare, and unpredictable mass murders*.[2] We cannot and never will be able to predict such events, much less prevent them.

But banning certain tools that may be used to commit murder is one thing. Tarrant's rampage also has led to calls to block *ideas* that allegedly fuel murderous extremism. In the immediate aftermath of tragedy, it is understandable that every conceivable means should be employed to prevent a recurrence. But censorship is almost invariably the wrong response to evil actions. You cannot ban evil.

Before the killings, Tarrant authored a rambling seventy-four-page manifesto titled *The Great Replacement*. The document is difficult to find online, as most platforms took to blocking it as soon as its appearance was flagged. I was quick to grab a copy early on, however, because such documents inform my longstanding research into extremist groups and ideologies (e.g., Holocaust denial).[3]

The Great Replacement was inspired by a 2012 book of the same title by the French author Renaud Camus – a right-wing conspiracy theorist who claims that white French Catholics in particular, and white Christian Europeans in general, are being systematically replaced by people of non-European descent, especially from Africa and the Middle East, through immigration and higher birth rates. The manifesto is filled with white-supremacist fearmongering. "If there is one thing I want you to remember from these writings, it's that the birthrates must change," the author tells his audience (whom he presumes to be white). "Even if we were to deport all Non-Europeans from our lands tomorrow, the European people would still be spiraling into decay and eventual death." The result, he concludes apocalyptically, is "white genocide."

Like many cranks and haters of this type, Tarrant has a weakness for codes and slogans. He references the number 14 to indicate the fourteen-word slogan originally coined by white supremacist David Lane while imprisoned for his role in the 1984 murder of Jewish radio talk-show host Alan Berg: "We must secure the existence of our people and a future for white children." Lane, for his part, explicitly extolled the writings of white supremacist William Pierce, who in turn inspired Timothy McVeigh to blow up the Oklahoma City federal building in 1995, killing 168 people.

Accusations of racism and white supremacism are thrown around so casually these days that the meaning of these terms has become diluted and ambiguous. So, for clarity, I will state the obvious by emphasizing that the writings of Tarrant, Lane, and Pierce all reflect attitudes that are completely racist and hateful, as such terms are properly used.

And yes, there is a connection with Nazism. The number 14 is sometimes rendered as 14/88, with the 8s representing the eighth letter of the alphabet – H – and 88 or HH standing for *Heil Hitler*. Lane, who died in 2007, was inspired by *Mein Kampf*, in which the Nazi Party leader declared: "What we must fight for is to safeguard the existence and reproduction of our race and our people, the sustenance of our children and the purity of our blood, the freedom and independence of the fatherland, so that our people may mature for the fulfillment of the mission allotted it by the creator of the universe."

But even here, the bibliographical trail of hatred doesn't end – because Hitler copied much of his anti-Semitic conspiracism from *The Protocols of the Learned Elders of Zion*, a tragically popular hoaxed document purporting to record the proceedings of a secret meeting of Jews plotting global domination, which a number of prominent people at the time believed, including the American industrialist Henry Ford, who published his own conspiratorial tract titled *The International Jew: The World's Foremost Problem*. He later recanted and withdrew the book from circulation when he found out the conspiracy theory was a fake.

Nor was the *Protocols* itself conceived out of thin air: It was plagiarized from *Biarritz*, a luridly anti-Semitic nineteenth-century novel; and a propaganda tract called *Dialogues in Hell between Machiavelli and Montesquieu*, which had been written by a French lawyer as an act of protest against Louis-Napoléon Bonaparte; both of which, in turn, drew on anti-Semitic tropes going back to Roman times. So, if you're looking to root out and ban the political ideology that produced Tarrant, you're going to have to purge whole library shelves. The same goes for Islamophobia, anti-black racism, and virtually every other kind of bigotry you could name.

And yet, there are those who argue that mass censorship is justified in the name of heading off hateful indoctrination. That group apparently would include leaders of the Whitcoulls bookstore chain in New Zealand. Late last week, the company announced it was banning one popular book, "in light of some extremely disturbing material being circulated prior, during and after the Christchurch attacks." Yet the book wasn't *Mein Kampf*, which you can still buy on the company's site for $44.95 – or

Michael Shermer ✓
@michaelshermer

If you think @jordanbpeterson / 12 Rules for Life explains the New Zealand massacre you've lost your mind. If you think Cambridge U students would be harmed hearing Jordan's ideas, you shouldn't be in the education business. This is getting insane & has to stop.

Figure 2.1 Tweet from Michael Shermer (@michaelshermer), March 21, 2019. The thread is available at: https://bit.ly/2JHCR2n

anything of its ilk. Rather, the chain is boycotting Jordan Peterson's *12 Rules for Life*, a self-help book that has no connection at all with the mosque attacks or their perpetrator. The announcement from their customer service department reads:

> Thank you for contacting us. Unfortunately 12 Rules for Life is currently unavailable, which is a decision that Whitcoulls has made in light of some extremely disturbing material being circulated prior, during and after the Christchurch attacks.
>
> As a business which takes our responsibilities to our communities very seriously, we believe it would be wrong to support the author at this time.
>
> Apologies that we're not able to sell it to you but we appreciate your understanding.

What is the "extremely disturbing material" in Peterson's book? Whitcoulls doesn't say. I've read the entire book, along with much of the University of Toronto professor's 1999 massive first book, *Maps of Meaning*. And I've watched many of his YouTube videos and media interviews. I have yet to find anything remotely reminiscent of white supremacy, racism, anti-Semitism, or Islamophobia. On Twitter, I suggested that those who think Peterson is the ideological culprit behind the New Zealand massacre have lost their minds (see Figure 2.1).

I added that I'm no toady for Jordan Peterson, inasmuch as I disagree with him on many subjects – including his theory of truth and his largely uncritical endorsement of religious myths as an organizing principle for human cultures.[4] But the banning of Peterson on any theory related to preventing mass murder doesn't even rise to the level of wrong: It's demonstrably absurd – akin to banning spoons and skateboards as a strategy to stave off prospective arsonists.

When I asked my social-media followers for examples of anything Peterson had said or done that could be construed as inviting mass murder, the only remotely relevant responses I got pointed to photos that random fans had taken with Peterson, one of which featured a guy sporting a T-shirt proclaiming himself to be an "Islamaphobe,"[5] and another (more ambiguous)[6] example of someone holding a Pepe the Frog banner.[7] But this proves nothing. Peterson has taken photos with tens of thousands of people at public events in recent years. In a typical fan-photo cattle call, fans are cycled into frame with a celebrity roughly every five or six seconds – typically by handlers, not the celebrity acting in his or her personal capacity. I've done a number of these during book tours and can attest to the fact that it's completely unrealistic to think that Peterson could screen the clothes worn by all these legions of photo seekers for ideological purity – even if this were something he aspired to do.

On March 23, I received an email from Change.org, the left-leaning political action group whose stated mission is to "empower people everywhere to create the change they want to see." In this case, the change users wanted to see in response to the New Zealand massacre was the banning of PewDiePie from YouTube. "One of the largest platforms for white supremacist content is PewDiePie's YouTube channel," the petition informs us. "PewDiePie has on many occasions proven once and again to promote and affiliate himself with white supremacist and Nazi ideologies." The petitioners then list the YouTuber's alleged sins, including using the N-word, playing videos of Adolf Hitler's speeches, and giving the Nazi heil in a video.

For those unaware, PewDiePie is a Swedish comedian and video game player named Felix Arvid Ulf Kjellberg, whose YouTube channel has a massive following and whom Tarrant referenced in his manifesto (along with Candace Owens, Donald Trump, and others). It is true that PewDiePie once used the N-word during a video game competition (and then apologized profusely for doing so).[8] He also has used brief audio and video snippets of Nazi imagery as part of satirical responses to attacks against him that he lampooned as melodramatic.[9] The idea that any of this betrays PewDiePie as a closet white supremicist is absurd. Even without Change.org's urging, YouTube already has demonetized the videos of such avowedly anti-racist and anti-supremacist moderates as Dave Rubin and Gad Saad, as well as anti-anti-Semite conservatives such as Dennis Prager. YouTube is acting on an ideological hair trigger: If there were any evidence whatsoever that PewDiePie had expressed real Nazi sympathies, he would have been axed from the platform long ago.

Responding to evil by banning random controversial authors or YouTubers is completely irrational. But that doesn't make it *inexplicable.* Manifestations of great evil provoke a desire to do something – anything – to reestablish moral order. Remember when millions of people tweeted #BringBackOurGirls after the terrorist organization Boko Haram kidnapped dozens of Nigerian students in 2014? Murderous rapists don't give a fig about being mobbed on Twitter. But it made people feel useful for an instant – as if they had *done* something. We all entertain some version of this instinct in times of tragedy – a reflex satirized by *The Onion* in the days after 9/11 with the headline *Not Knowing What Else To Do, Woman Bakes American-Flag Cake.*

Intertwined with this instinct is the idea that there is some abstract force called *evil* that exists in the cosmos, a force that we are all called upon to confront and defeat. As I argued in my 2003 book, *The Science of Good and Evil,* this belief – that pure evil exists separately from individuals – is a myth. Evil is an adjective, not a noun, inasmuch as the latter implies an existence all its own, as in an "evil force" or an "evil person." It is in this sense that *there is no such thing as evil.* There is no mysterious force operating outside the realm of the known laws of nature and human behavior that we can call evil.

Thus concluded social psychologist Roy Baumeister, as reported in his 1997 book about serial killers and other career criminals, *Evil: Inside Human Violence and Cruelty.* The problem, he discovered, is that nearly everyone who has ever committed what most of us would consider evil think that they did it for perfectly good reasons. "The essential shock of banality is the disproportion between the person and the crime," Baumeister writes, referencing Hannah Arendt's famous description of Adolf Eichmann, chief orchestrator of the Final Solution, as the *banality of evil.* "The mind reels with the enormity of what this person has done, and so the mind expects to reel with the force of the perpetrator's presence and personality. When it does not, it is surprised." Ironically,

Baumeister found that the myth of evil existing as a standalone force may, itself, lead societies to become more violent:

> The myth encourages people to believe that they are good and will remain good no matter what, even if they perpetrate severe harm on their opponents. Thus, the myth of pure evil confers a kind of moral immunity on people who believe in it ... belief in the myth is itself one recipe for evil, because it allows people to justify violent and oppressive actions. It allows evil to masquerade as good.

The explanation for the surprise can be found by contrasting the victim's perspective with that of the perpetrator. In his 2011 book *The Better Angels of Our Nature*, Steven Pinker called this the "moralization gap," and it can be instructive – even shocking – to stand on both sides of the gap and look into the dark abyss between them. To a man (and they're almost exclusively men), these violent criminals justified their evil acts. This helps explain the grimly bizarre means by which violent criminals and terrorists find ways to justify even the most horrifying and nihilistic acts. Consider this 1994 police record of Frederick Treesh, a spree killer from the Midwest who explained, "Other than the two we killed, the two we wounded, the woman we pistol-whipped, and the light bulbs we stuck in people's mouths, [my accomplice and I] didn't really hurt anybody." After killing thirty-three boys, the serial killer John Wayne Gacy explained, "I see myself more as a victim than as a perpetrator. I was cheated out of my childhood."

Modern campaigns aimed at shutting down this or that speaker implicitly present evil as something that may be communicated from one person to another, like bacteria. By this model, censorship is akin to quarantine. But Baumeister tells us "you do not have to give people reasons to be violent, because they already have plenty of reasons. All you have to do is take away their reasons to restrain themselves." It is absolutely true that some extremist ideologies can encourage adherents to abandon the sense of restraint that Baumeister describes. But the campaign to ban the likes of Jordan Peterson and PewDiePie – individuals whose work bears no relationship at all to the extreme forms of hatred we should be most concerned about – suggests that censors aren't actually thinking through such propositions. Instead, they seem to be operating on the idea of evil as a quasi-mystical force akin to Satan. In this conception, Peterson and PewDiePie are seen as *carriers* of evil, much like witches channeling demons from below, no matter that they never actually say or do anything evil in nature.

As Baumeister argued, this mythical idealization of evil as being an actual force in our universe, rather than a descriptor of human motivations, isn't merely harmless ersatz spiritualism: It causes people to act more immorally, sometimes murderously so, by allowing them to imagine the locus of evil as lying completely outside their own intentions and actions. This was the observation made by Aleksandr Solzhenitsyn, who knew a few things about evil from his experiences in the Soviet gulag system. As he noted in his classic work *The Gulag Archipelago*:

> If only there were evil people somewhere insidiously committing evil deeds, and it were necessary only to separate them from the rest of us and destroy them. But the line dividing good and evil cuts through the heart of every human being. And who is willing to destroy a piece of his own heart?[10]

To obtain a scientific understanding of evil, it is necessary to take both perspectives into account – that of the victim and that of the perpetrator – even though our natural propensity is to side with the victim and moralize against the perpetrator. If evil is explicable – and I believe that it is – then remaining detached is imperative, as the scientist Lewis Fry Richardson put it in his statistical study of war:

> For indignation is so easy and satisfying a mood that it is apt to prevent one from attending to any facts that oppose it. If the reader should object that I have abandoned ethics for the false doctrine that "to understand all is to forgive all", I can reply that it is only a temporary suspense of ethical judgment, made because "to condemn much is to understand little".[11]

Which gets to the (necessarily political) question of who should be identified, stigmatized, and even punished for being a "carrier" of evil? Who gets to define that class of people? Me? You? The majority? An evil-thought committee? The government? Social-media companies? We already have law enforcement and the military to deal with evil *deeds*. Controlling evil thoughts is far more problematic.

Campaigns aimed at banning evil in its own (mythical) right almost always include efforts to ban evil speech – or even, as in the aftermath of the New Zealand mass murder, speech from someone who has not said anything remotely evil, but is seen, in some vague sense, to be contaminated by evil. When Western societies were religious, evil speech was tantamount to anti-Christian speech. In a secular age, we call it "hate speech," a reformulation that does nothing to solve the always contentious issue of distinguishing between evil speech and free speech, and the problem of who gets to decide where one ends and the other begins.

It is my contention that we must protect speech no matter how hateful it may seem. The solution to hate speech is more speech. The counter to bad ideas is good ideas. The rebuttal to pseudoscience is better science. The answer to fake news is real news. The best way to refute alternative facts is with actual facts. This is just as true now as it was in the moment before fifty innocent Muslim lives were taken in New Zealand – even if our emotionally felt need to put a name and form to evil now makes this truth harder to see.

CHAPTER 3

Free Speech Even If It Hurts

Defending Holocaust Denier David Irving

PREAMBLE

This essay was originally published as an opinion editorial in the *Los Angeles Times* as "Free Speech, Even If It Hurts" on February 22, 2006. It was in response to the news that Holocaust denier David Irving, whom I wrote about in my coauthored 2000 book (with Alex Grobman) *Denying History* (2nd Edition 2009), had been sentenced to three years' imprisonment in Austria for violating one of their "hate crime" laws, a misguided, impractical, and, in my opinion, immoral attempt to combat hate speech with censorship (and punishment) rather than with free speech. Unbidden and unbeknownst to him, before Irving's sentencing I wrote a letter to the judge along the lines of what I argue here, asking not just for leniency in his sentencing but for Irving's freedom. I have no idea if the judge ever read my letter, and, unfortunately, I no longer seem to have a copy of it in my archives. That Irving was arrested at the airport in Austria well before he was scheduled to deliver his speech means that this was worse than an assault on free speech; it was an assault on free thought – literally a thought crime. How Orwellian.

∗ ∗ ∗

> More women died in the back seat of Edward Kennedy's car at Chappaquiddick than ever died in a gas chamber at Auschwitz.

IS THIS LINE MORE OFFENSIVE TO JEWS THAN AN EDITORIAL cartoon depicting the prophet Muhammad with a turban bomb is to Muslims?

Apparently it is, because the editorial cartoonists are still free, whereas the man who made this statement – British author David Irving – was sentenced on February 20, 2006 to three years in an Austrian jail for violating an Austrian law that says it is a crime if a person "denies, grossly trivializes, approves or seeks to justify the National Socialist genocide or other national socialist crimes against humanity."

Irving had traveled to Austria in November 2005 to deliver a lecture to a far-right student fraternity but was arrested on a warrant dating back to 1989, when he gave a speech and interview denying the existence of gas chambers at Auschwitz. After pleading guilty to the charge, Irving told the court, "I made a mistake when I said there were no gas chambers at Auschwitz," and "The Nazis did murder millions of Jews."

That David Irving has been, and probably still is, a Holocaust denier is indisputable. In 1994 I interviewed him for a book on Holocaust denial, and he told me then that no more than half a million Jews died during the Second World War and that most of those deaths were due to disease and starvation. Irving also added that Hitler was the Jews' best friend: "Without Hitler, the State of Israel probably would not exist today so to that extent he was probably the Jews' greatest friend." In 2000, the judge in his libel trial in England called him "an active Holocaust denier ... anti-Semitic and racist." And, in April 2005, I attended a lecture Irving gave in Costa Mesa at an event sponsored by the Institute for Historical Review, the leading voice of Holocaust denial in America, where he employed the Chappaquiddick line and, holding his right arm up, boasted, "This hand has shaken more hands that shook Hitler's hand than anyone else in the world."

The important question here is not whether Irving is a Holocaust denier (he is), or whether he offends people with what he says (he does), but why anyone, anywhere should be imprisoned for expressing dissenting views or saying offensive things. Today, you may be imprisoned or fined for dissenting from the accepted Holocaust history in the following countries: Australia, Austria, Belgium, Canada, Czech Republic, France, Germany, Israel, Lithuania, New Zealand, Poland, Romania, Slovakia, and Switzerland.

Given their disastrous history of being too lenient with fringe political ideologues, it is perhaps understandable that countries like Germany and Austria have sought to crack down on rabble-rousers whose "hate speech" can and has led to violence and pogroms. In some cases, the slippery slope has only a few paces between calling the Holocaust a "Zionist lie" to the neo-Nazi desecration of Jewish property.

And as we have witnessed repeatedly, Europeans have a different history and culture of free speech than we do in this country. In Germany, for example, the "Auschwitz-Lie" law makes it a crime to "defame the memory of the dead." In May of 1992, Irving told a German audience that the reconstructed gas chamber at Auschwitz I was "a fake built after the war." (It is, in fact, a postwar reconstruction made by the Soviets running the camp museum, but it was never intended to deceive tourists into believing it was the original structure.) The following month when he landed in Rome, he was surrounded by police and put on the next plane to Munich where he was fined 3,000DM. Irving appealed the conviction, but it was upheld and the fine increased to 30,000DM (about $20,000) after he publicly called the judge a "senile, alcoholic cretin."

In England, libel law requires the defendant to prove that he or she did not libel the plaintiff, unlike US law that puts the onus on the plaintiff to prove damage, and they recently debated the merits of banning religious hate speech. In France, it is illegal to challenge the existence of "crimes against humanity" as they were defined by the Military Tribunal at Nuremberg, and another law, on the books until January 2006, required that France's colonial history (which was not always "humane") has to be taught in a "positive" light.

Even in the traditionally liberal Canada, there are "anti-hate" statutes and laws against spreading "false news." In late 1992, Irving went to Canada to receive the George Orwell Award from a conservative free-speech organization, whereupon he was arrested by the Royal Canadian Mounted Police, led away in handcuffs, and deported on the grounds that his German conviction made him a likely candidate for future hate speech violations. Again, another thought crime.

Even in the land of Thomas Jefferson and the First Amendment, freedom of speech does not always ring. On Friday, February 3, 1995, Irving was invited by the Berkeley Coalition for Free Speech to lecture at the University of California, Berkeley. More than 300 protesters surrounded the hall and prevented Irving and the 113 ticket holders from entering. (That, however, is quite different from passing a law to bar him from speaking.)

Austria's treatment of Irving as a political dissident should offend the same people who defend the rights of political cartoonists to express their opinion of Islamic terrorists, and of the civil libertarians who leapt to the defense of the University of Colorado Professor Ward Churchill when he exercised his right to call the victims of 9/11 "little Eichmanns." Why doesn't it? Why aren't liberty lovers everywhere offended by Irving's conviction?

Freedom is a principle that must be applied indiscriminately. We have to defend David Irving in order to defend ourselves. My freedoms are inextricably tied to Irving's freedoms. Once the laws are in place to jail dissidents of Holocaust history, what's to stop those same laws from spreading to dissenters of religious or political histories, or to skepticism of any sort that deviates from the accepted canon?

David Irving's three-year prison sentence for denying the Holocaust may please his detractors, but it is an assault on the civil liberties of us all. No one should be required to facilitate the expression of Holocaust denial, but neither should there be what the US Supreme Court Justice Louis Brandeis called "silence coerced by law – the argument of force in its worst form." Call David Irving the devil if you like – the principle of free speech gives you the right to do so. [Here I quoted the dialogue from Robert Bolt's 1960 play, *A Man for All Seasons*, included in the previous essay, so it is redundant to repeat it.] But we must give the devil his due.

Let David Irving go, for our own safety's sake.

[*Note*: Irving ended up serving thirteen months of his three-year sentence after an appeals process was heard by the court. On December 20, 2006, Irving was released from prison, and the next day he was banned from ever returning to Austria. To her credit, the Holocaust historian whom Irving sued for libel years before – Deborah Lipstadt – flew her free-speech colors when she told the media, "I am not happy when censorship wins, and I don't believe in winning battles via censorship. The way of fighting Holocaust deniers is with history and with truth." Bravo.]

POSTSCRIPT ON DAVID IRVING AND THE EICHMANN PAPERS

In the Austrian trial, Irving admitted that he denied the Holocaust in 1989, telling the court: "I said that then, based on my knowledge at the time, but by 1991 when I came across the Eichmann papers, I wasn't saying that anymore and I wouldn't say that now. The Nazis did murder millions of Jews."

Not quite. Here Irving is engaged in some personal historical revisionism. While researching my book, *Denying History*, Irving told me the story about the Eichmann papers. Here is what actually happened.

Adolf Eichmann was one of the prime architects of the Final Solution. In 1991 David Irving was on a lecture tour in Argentina. Immediately following a lecture, Irving explained,

> a guy came out to me with a brown-paper package. And he said, "You're obviously the correct repository for these papers that we've been looking after since 1960 for the Eichmann family." See, the Eichmann family panicked when he was kidnapped in the streets. And they took all his private papers which they could find, that had any kind of bearing, put them into brown paper and gave them to a friend. Then he gave them to this man who gave them to me, who gave them to the German government.

In the manuscript, Irving explains, Eichmann "refers on many occasions to a discussion he had with Heydrich at the end of September or October 1941, in which Heydrich says, in quotation marks, these two lines: 'I come from the Reichführer [Himmler]. He has received orders from the Führer for the physical destruction of the Jews.'"

It could not be any clearer than that, right? Wrong. A master rhetorician like Irving can spin-doctor any potentially damaging document. While admitting that "it rocked me back on my heels frankly because I thought 'Oops!,'" he recovered in time to "tell myself, 'Don't be knocked off your feet by this one.'" The easy solution was to announce that the Eichmann memoir was a fake (along the lines of Hitler's diaries, which Irving helped expose as fake), but this would appear to contradict the verdict of the German Federal Archives at Koblenz, who determined that the memoir is authentic.

In 1992, Irving confessed that "Quite clearly this has given me a certain amount of food for thought and I will spend much of this year thinking about it. They show that Eichmann believed there was a Führer order (*Führerbefehl*)." So, Irving's initial conclusion hints at intellectual honesty: "It makes me glad I have not adopted the narrow-minded approach that there was no Holocaust."

As time passed, however, Irving found a way out of his predicament. The memoirs are real, but Eichmann lied about the *Führerbefehl*. Why? As he told the journalist Ron Rosenbaum in an elaborate rationalization, during the Suez crisis in 1956 Eichmann worried that if Israel conquered Cairo they might intercept intelligence files on fugitive Nazis in South America, possibly leading to his capture and arrest. Irving picks up the story (from his imagination, of course):

> Eichmann must have had sleepless nights, wondering what he's going to do, what he's going to say to get off the hook. And though he's not consciously doing it, I think his brain is probably rationalizing in the background, trying to find alibis. The alibi that would have been useful to him in his own fevered mind would be if he could say that Hitler – all he did was carry out [Hitler's] orders.

Eichmann, Irving speculates, inserted into his memoirs the phrase "*Der Führer hat richt der Ausrottung der Juden befohlen*" – "The Führer has ordered the extermination of the Jews" – so that if he were ever captured his defense would be that he was merely following orders. Eichmann was, of course, captured and tried, and his defense included this argument, along with a moral equivalency one where all sides in the war were equally guilty of atrocities. The defense worked about as well as it did at Nuremberg – Eichmann was executed.

CHAPTER 4

Free to Inquire

The Evolution–Creationism Controversy as a Test Case in Equal Time and Free Speech

PREAMBLE

This article first appeared as a book chapter in the *Handbook of Philosophy and Public Policy*, edited by David Boonin and published by Palgrave in 2018. I was tasked with finding a test case of freedom of speech and inquiry from the sciences, in the larger context of free-speech issues as related to public policy and the law. I have already written extensively about evolution and creationism, most notably in my 1997 book *Why People Believe Weird Things* and my 2006 book *Why Darwin Matters*, so here I engage the creationist movement as a free-speech issue inasmuch as its proponents hold a minority viewpoint as far as the scientific community is concerned. Nevertheless, I contend that they should be free to believe, teach (and preach) whatever they like about the origins and diversity of life and that, in the well-trodden principle, sunlight is the best disinfectant (to which Supreme Court Justice Louis Brandeis added "electric light the most efficient policeman").

* * *

D URING THE SECOND WEEK OF MARCH 1837, BARELY A YEAR and a half after circumnavigating the globe in the HMS Beagle, Charles Darwin met with the eminent ornithologist John Gould, who had been studying Darwin's Galápagos bird specimens. With access to museum ornithological collections from areas of South America that Darwin had not visited, Gould corrected a number of taxonomic errors Darwin had made, such as labeling two finch species a "Wren" and an "Icterus," and pointed out to him that although the land birds in the Galápagos were endemic to the islands, they were notably South American in character.

According to the historian of science Frank J. Sulloway, who carefully reconstructed Darwin's intellectual voyage to the discovery of the theory of evolution by means of natural selection, Darwin left the meeting with Gould convinced "beyond a doubt that transmutation must be responsible for the presence of similar but distinct species on the different islands of the Galápagos group. The supposedly immutable 'species barrier' had finally been broken, at least in Darwin's own mind."[1] That July, Darwin opened his first notebook on *Transmutation of Species*. By 1844 he was confident enough to write in a letter to his botanist friend and colleague Joseph Hooker, "I was so struck with distribution of Galapagos organisms &c &c, & with the character of the American fossil mammifers &c &c, that I determined to collect blindly every sort of fact which cd bear any way on what are species." Five years at sea and nine years at home pouring through "heaps" of books led Darwin to admit, "At last gleams of light have come, & I am almost convinced, (quite contrary to opinion I started with) that species are not (it is like confessing a murder) immutable."[2]

Like confessing a murder. How could a solution to a technical problem in biology, namely the immutability of species, generate such angst in its discoverer? The answer is obvious: if new species are created naturally instead of supernaturally, there's no place for a creator God. No wonder Darwin waited twenty years before publishing his theory, and he would have waited even longer had he not rushed into print for priority's sake because the naturalist Alfred Russel Wallace had sent Darwin his own theory of evolution in 1858, the year before Darwin published *On the Origin of Species*.[3] And no wonder it took some time for Darwin to convince others of the theory's veracity. The geologist Charles Lyell, a close friend and colleague of Darwin who groomed him into the world of British science and whose geological works Darwin read on the *Beagle*, withheld his support for a full nine years and even then pulled back from fully embracing naturalism, leaving room for providential design underlying the entire natural system. The astronomer John Herschel sniffed at natural selection, calling it the "law of higgledy-piggledy." In a review in the popular *Macmillan's Magazine*, the statesman and economist Henry Fawcett spoke of a great divide created by Darwin's book: "No scientific work that has been published within this century has excited so much general curiosity as the treatise of Mr. Darwin. It has for a time divided the scientific world with two great contending sections. A Darwinite and an anti-Darwinite are now the badges of opposed scientific parties."[4]

Darwinites and anti-Darwinites. After a century and a half, there is now overwhelming consensus within the scientific community that evolution happened and that natural selection is the driving force behind it. Among scientists, there are only Darwinites. Publicly, however, the picture is disturbingly divided, especially along political and religious lines, where the anti-Darwinites have captured a sizable portion of the populace. A 2005 Pew Research Center poll, for example, found 42 percent of Americans holding strict creationist views that "living things have existed in their present form since the beginning of time." The survey also found that 64 percent said they were open to the idea of teaching creationism in addition to evolution in public schools, while 38 percent said they think evolution should be completely *replaced* by creationism in biology classrooms. Most alarmingly, a sizable 41 percent believe that parents, rather than scientists (28 percent) or school boards (21 percent) should be responsible for teaching children about the origin and evolution of life.[5] More recent polling data found similar percentages of belief in creationism and skepticism about evolution. In a 2014 Gallup poll, 42 percent of Americans said that "God created humans in [their] present form" while 31 percent said "Humans evolved, with God guiding." There was a slight uptick to 19 percent of Americans who agreed that "Humans evolved, but God had no part in the process," but that was at least a significant gain from the paltry 9 percent in 1982.

None of this polling data should matter. Truth in science is not determined by vox populi. It shouldn't matter how many people support one or another position. As Einstein said in response to a 1931 book skeptical of relativity theory titled *Hundert Autoren gegen Einstein (A Hundred Authors Against Einstein)*, "Why one hundred? If I were wrong, one would have been enough."[6] A theory stands or falls on evidence, and there are few theories in science that are more robust than the theory of evolution. Arguably the most culturally jarring theory in the history of science, the Darwinian revolution changed both science and culture in at least five ways:

1. The static creationist model of species as fixed types was replaced with a fluid evolutionary model of species as ever-changing entities.

2. The theory of top-down Intelligent Design through a supernatural force was replaced with the theory of bottom-up natural design through natural forces.

3. The anthropocentric view of humans as special creations above all others was replaced with the view of humans as just another animal species.

4. The view of life and the cosmos as having design, direction, and purpose from above was replaced with the view of the world as the product of bottom-up design through necessitating laws of nature and contingent events of history.

5. The view that human nature is infinitely malleable and primarily good, or born in original sin and inherently evil, was replaced with the view of a constraining human nature in which we are both good and evil.[7]

When he first heard Darwin's theory, the man who would earn the moniker "Darwin's Bulldog" for his fierce defense of evolution, Thomas Henry Huxley, called Darwin's *On the Origin of Species* "the most potent instrument for the extension of the realm of knowledge which has come into man's hands since Newton's *Principia*."[8] A century later, the Harvard evolutionary biologist Ernst Mayr opined, "it would be difficult to refute the claim that the Darwinian revolution was the greatest of all intellectual revolutions in the history of mankind."[9] And in the memorable and oft-quoted observation by the evolutionary theorist Theodosius Dobzhansky, "Nothing in biology makes sense except in the light of evolution."[10]

WHY PEOPLE DO NOT ACCEPT EVOLUTION

If the theory of evolution is so proven and profound, why doesn't everyone accept it as true? It is evident that there are a number of extrascientific variables that factor into the beliefs people hold about scientific theories, and in this case additional polling data show who is more or less likely to accept evolution based on their religious and political attitudes. In the 2014 Gallup poll mentioned above, 69 percent of Americans who attend religious services weekly embrace creationism over evolution, compared to only 23 percent of those who seldom or never attend religious services.[11] A 2013 Pew Research Center survey found that white evangelical Protestants are more likely to believe that humans have existed in their present form since the beginning of time, at 64 percent, compared to half of black Protestants and only 15 percent of white mainline Protestants.[12] A 2017 Gallup poll found that 57 percent of those with no religious preferences agreed with the statement "Humans evolved, God had no part in process" compared to only 6 percent of Protestants and 11 percent of Catholics, and only 1 percent of those who attend church weekly agreed with this statement, compared to 35 percent who rarely attend church.[13]

The underlying foundation behind this religious-based skepticism of evolution may be traced back to the early twentieth century when anti-evolution legislation was sweeping southern states, most famously Tennessee. At the climax of the 1925 Scopes "monkey" Trial in Dayton, William Jennings Bryan, testifying on behalf of the prosecution against a young biology teacher named John T. Scopes, prepared a final statement, summarizing what he understood to be what was really at stake in the trial. The judge determined that Bryan's speech was irrelevant to the case – the same ruling he made against the defense when they called on evolutionary biologists as expert witnesses – so it was published posthumously (Bryan died two days after the trial ended) as *Bryan's Last Speech: The Most Powerful Argument Against Evolution Ever Made*.[14] The most telling summation of the anti-evolution position in Bryan's view was as follows:

> The real attack of evolution, it will be seen, is not upon orthodox Christianity or even upon Christianity, but upon religion – the most basic fact in man's existence and the most practical thing in life. If taken seriously and made the basis of a philosophy of life, it would eliminate love and carry man back to a struggle of tooth and claw.

This is what troubles people about evolutionary theory and leads them to doubt its verisimilitude, not the technical details of the science. The syllogistic reasoning goes like this:

> The theory of evolution implies that there is no God.
> Without a belief in God there can be no morality or meaning.

Without morality and meaning there is no basis for a civil society. Without a civil society we will be reduced to living like brute animals.

This sentiment was expressed by the Intelligent Design theory supporter Nancy Pearcey in a briefing before a House Judiciary Committee of the United States Congress, when she quoted from a popular song urging "you and me, baby, ain't nothing but mammals so let's do it like they do on the Discovery Channel." She went on to claim that since the US legal system is based on moral principles, the only way to generate ultimate moral grounding is for the law to have an "unjudged judge," an "uncreated creator."[15] The neoconservative social commentator Irving Kristol was even more bleak in a 1991 statement: "If there is one indisputable fact about the human condition it is that no community can survive if it is persuaded – or even if it suspects – that its members are leading meaningless lives in a meaningless universe."[16]

In an attempt to distance themselves from "scientific creationists," Intelligent Design theorists have emphasized that they are only interested in doing science. According to the prominent ID proponent William Dembski, for example, "scientific creationism has prior religious commitments whereas intelligent design does not."[17] This is disingenuous. On February 6, 2000, Dembski told the National Religious Broadcasters at their annual conference in Anaheim, California:

Intelligent Design opens the whole possibility of us being created in the image of a benevolent God ... The job of apologetics is to clear the ground, to clear obstacles that prevent people from coming to the knowledge of Christ ... And if there's anything that I think has blocked the growth of Christ as the free rein of the Spirit and people accepting the Scripture and Jesus Christ, it is the Darwinian naturalistic view.[18]

In a feature article in the Christian magazine *Touchstone*, Dembski was even more succinct: "Intelligent design is just the Logos theology of John's Gospel restated in the idiom of information theory."[19]

The sentiment was echoed by one of the fountainheads of the modern Intelligent Design movement, Phillip Johnson, at the same National Religious Broadcasters meeting at which Dembski spoke:

Christians in the twentieth century have been playing defense. They've been fighting a defensive war to defend what they have, to defend as much of it as they can. It never turns the tide. What we're trying to do is something entirely different. We're trying to go into enemy territory, their very center, and blow up the ammunition dump. What is their ammunition dump in this metaphor? It is their version of creation.[20]

Johnson was even blunter in 1996: "This isn't really, and never has been, a debate about science ... It's about religion and philosophy."[21] In his book *The Wedge of Truth*, Johnson explained: "The Wedge of my title is an informal movement of like-minded thinkers in which I have taken a leading role. Our strategy is to drive the thin end of our Wedge into the cracks in the log of naturalism by bringing long-neglected questions to the surface and introducing them to public debate." This is not just an attack on naturalism – it is a religious war against all of science.

It is time to set out more fully how the Wedge program fits into the specific Christian gospel (as distinguished from generic theism), and how and where questions of biblical authority enter the picture. As Christians develop a more thorough understanding of these questions, they will begin to see more clearly how ordinary people – specifically people who are not scientists or professional scholars – can more effectively engage the secular world on behalf of the gospel.[22]

The new creationism may differ in the details from the old creationism, but their ultimate goals run parallel. The veneer of science in the guise of Intelligent Design theory is there to cover up the deeper religious agenda.

EQUAL TIME AND FREE SPEECH

Engrained in the American public psyche is the sense of fair play for all ideas and free speech for everyone. What's wrong with giving equal time to evolution and creationism and letting the people decide for themselves? This is, in fact, what has become known as the "equal time" argument proffered by proponents of "Creation Science" in the 1980s and "Intelligent Design" in the 1990s. It's an argument that appeals to fair-minded people but that cannot be put into practice in public schools, which is where the evolution–creation battles have been fought. The problem is that there are so many creation stories and so little classroom time, already filled with science curricula. Here, for example, are at least ten different positions one might take on the creationism continuum:

Flat-Earthers, who believe that the shape of the earth is flat and round like a coin, which some believers contend has a biblical basis.

Geocentrists, who believe that the earth is spherical but that the planets and sun revolve around it; this belief is grounded in Genesis scriptures.

Young-Earth Creationists, who believe that the earth and all life on it was created within the last ten thousand years.

Old-Earth Creationists, who believe that the earth is ancient and micro-evolution may alter organisms into different varieties of species but that all life was created by God and that species cannot evolve into new species.

Gap Creationists, who believe that there was a large temporal gap between Genesis 1:1 and 1:2, in which a pre-Adam creation was destroyed, after which God recreated the world in six days; the time gap between the two separate creations allows for an accommodation of an old earth with the special creation.

Day-Age Creationists, who believe that each of the six days of creation represents a geological epoch and that the Genesis sequence of creation roughly parallels the sequence of evolution.

Progressive Creationists, who accept most scientific findings about the age of the universe and that God created "kinds" of animals sequentially; the fossil record is an accurate representation of history because different animals and plants appeared at different times rather than having been created all at once.

Intelligent Design Creationists, who believe that the order, purpose, and design found in the world is proof of an intelligent designer.

Evolutionary Creationists, who believe that God used evolution to bring about life according to his foreordained plan from the beginning.

Theistic Evolutionists, who believe that God used evolution to bring about life but intervenes at critical intervals during the history of life.[23]

If equal time were granted to all of these positions, along with the many other creation myths from diverse cultures around the world, when would students have time to learn science? Given limited time and resources, and the ever-expanding body of scientific knowledge that students in a twenty-first-century society simply must learn for our nation to stay relevant technologically and economically, such ideas have no place in science classrooms where curricula are determined by the consensus science of the field, not polls on what the public believe. The place for introducing these ideas is in courses on history, cultural studies, comparative mythology, and world religions.

In any case, as far as public policy is concerned, creationists have lost all major court cases of the past half-century – most notably *Epperson v. Arkansas* in 1968, *McLean v. Arkansas Board of Education* in 1982, *Edwards v. Aguillard* in 1987, and *Kitzmiller et al. v. Dover* in 2005 – so legal precedent means that the chances of creationists or Intelligent Design proponents gaining access to public school science classrooms through legislation is nil.[24] Consensus science cannot be legislated by fiat from the top down. In the 1920s when evolutionary theory was not widely accepted and politically connected religious groups were successful in passing anti-evolution legislation making it a crime to teach Darwin's theory in public schools, the noted attorney and civil liberties defender Clarence Darrow made this case against the censorship of knowledge in the Scopes case:

> If today you can take a thing like evolution and make it a crime to teach it in the public school, tomorrow you can make it a crime to teach it in the private schools, and the next year you can make it a crime to teach it in the hustings or in the church. At the next session you may ban books and the newspapers. Soon you may set Catholic against Protestant and Protestant against Protestant, and try to foist your own religion upon the minds of men. If you can do one you can do the other. Ignorance and fanaticism is ever busy and needs feeding. Always it is feeding and gloating for more. Today it is the public school teachers, tomorrow the private. The next day the preachers and the lecturers, the magazines, the books, the newspapers. After a while, your honor, it is the setting of man against man and creed against creed until with flying banners and beating drums we

are marching backward to the glorious ages of the sixteenth century when bigots lighted fagots to burn the men who dared to bring any intelligence and enlightenment and culture to the human mind.[25]

In America, the First Amendment protects the right of citizens to express their opinions on anything they like, no matter how unconventional, crazy, conniving, or evil. You are free to doubt not just evolution, for example, but the Big Bang theory, vaccines, the germ theory of disease, and global warming. You can believe that JFK was assassinated by the KGB, Castro, the Mafia, Lyndon Johnson, and the Military Industrial Complex. You can contend that Princess Diana faked her death, along with Hitler and Elvis. You can even challenge the existence of God, Jesus, and the universe itself. No matter how much one may dislike someone else's opinion – even if it is something as disturbing or potentially disruptive as denying that the Holocaust happened or that some people may not be as successful because of innate racial or gender differences – that opinion is protected by the First Amendment. Not everyone thinks such freedom is good for a safe civil society. In particular, and paradoxically given the fact that the Free Speech Movement began at UC Berkeley in the 1960s, the past several years have seen campuses around the country erupt in flames over these charged issues, issuing lists of microaggressions that might offend people, trigger warnings about books that might upset readers, safe spaces to go to for protection from dangerous ideas, and the disinvitation of speakers who might espouse ideas different from the majority of people in the audience.[26] Shouldn't we protect people from speech that might be hateful and thus harmful? No. Here are eight reasons why.

1. Who decides which speech is acceptable and which is unacceptable? You? Me? The majority? The control of speech is how dictatorships and autocracies rule. We must resist the urge to control what other people say and think.
2. What criteria are used to censor certain speech? Ideas that I disagree with? Thoughts that differ from your thoughts? Anything that the majority determines is unacceptable? That's another form of tyranny, a tyranny of the majority.
3. It is not just the right of the speaker to speak but for the listeners to listen.

4. We might be completely right but still learn something new.

5. We might be partially right and partially wrong, and by listening to other viewpoints we might stand corrected and refine and improve our beliefs.

6. We might be completely wrong, so hearing criticism or counterpoint gives us the opportunity to change our minds and improve our thinking. No one is infallible. The only way to find out if you've gone off the rails is to get feedback on your beliefs, opinions, and even your facts.

7. Whether right or wrong, by listening to the opinions of others we have the opportunity to develop stronger arguments and build better facts for our positions.

8. My freedom to speak and dissent is inextricably tied to your freedom to speak and dissent. If I censor you, why shouldn't you censor me? If you silence me, why shouldn't I silence you? Once customs and laws are in place to silence someone on one topic, what's to stop people from silencing anyone on any topic that deviates from the accepted canon?

There are exceptions to the purely civil libertarian case for free speech, of course, most notably that you are not free to spread lies about someone that damage their reputation, safety, or income, nor are you free to distribute national secrets like the nuclear codes to known enemies. But never in history have a people been so free to speak their mind, and from that freedom emerges the truth, for the only way to know if your idea is wrong is to allow others to critique it.

CHAPTER 5

Ben Stein's Blunder

Why Intelligent Design Advocates Are Not Free Speech Martyrs

PREAMBLE

I penned this essay in 2008 shortly after the release of a documentary film titled *Expelled: No Intelligence Allowed*. Directed by Nathan Frankowski and starring the popular conservative financial commentator Ben Stein, it featured many of the major proponents of creationism and Intelligent Design theory that I have debated or engaged with publicly in the past, including William Dembski, Stephen Meyer, Jonathan Wells, and Paul Nelson. The film also includes interviews with such noted scientists and scholars as Richard Dawkins, William B. Provine, Eugenie Scott, Michael Ruse, and Christopher Hitchens. Since I was also interviewed for the film and made an appearance therein, I was surprised to see how it turned out, given that it was pitched to me with an entirely different premise.

I include the essay in this section on freedom of speech as the central premise of *Expelled* is that there is an academic conspiracy afoot among scientists and scholars to censor the speech of creationists and Intelligent Design advocates. As the film appeared in over a thousand movie theaters and grossed $7.7 million (on a budget of $3.5 million) and was widely discussed in popular culture and the media, evidently we aren't very adept at censorship. More importantly, I felt I needed to set the record straight about what the film is really about and why the speech of those who hold a different view of the origins and evolution of life on earth is not being suppressed. The government never moved to censor the film, theater owners gladly screened it, and a nontrivial portion of the public viewed it. What Stein and his on-camera voices object to is that their theory (that's too lofty a word – call it conjecture) of a top-down intelligent designer of life is rejected by scientists for lack of empirical evidence and internal coherency. As I wrote an entire book explaining this failure – *Why Darwin Matters* – I do not address that issue in this piece.

* * *

I N 1974 I MATRICULATED AT PEPPERDINE UNIVERSITY AS A BORN-again Christian who rejected Darwinism and evolutionary theory, not because I knew anything about it (I didn't) but because I thought that in order to believe in God and accept the Bible as true you had to be a creationist. What I knew about evolution came primarily from creationist literature, so when I finally took a course in evolutionary theory in graduate school I realized that I had been hoodwinked. What I discovered is a massive amount of evidence from multiple sciences – geology, paleontology, biogeography, zoology, botany, comparative anatomy, molecular biology, genetics, and embryology – demonstrating that evolution happened.

It was with some irony for me, then, that I saw Ben Stein's anti-evolution documentary film, *Expelled: No Intelligence Allowed*, opens with the actor, game-show host, and speech writer for Richard Nixon addressing a packed audience of adoring students at Pepperdine University, apparently falling for the same trap I did.

Actually, they didn't. The biology professors at Pepperdine assure me that their mostly Christian students fully accept the theory of evolution. So who were these people embracing Stein's screed against science? Extras. According to Lee Kats, Associate Provost for Research and Chair of Natural Science at Pepperdine, "the production company paid for the use of the facility just as all other companies do that film on our campus" but that "the company was nervous that they would not have enough people in the audience so they brought in extras. Members of the audience had to sign in and the staff member reports that no more than two to three Pepperdine students were in attendance. Mr. Stein's lecture on that topic was not an event sponsored by the university." And this is one of the least dishonest parts of the film.

AT THE CROSSROADS OF CONSPIRACY

Ben Stein came to my office to interview me about what I was told was a film about "the intersection of science and religion" called *Crossroads* (yet another deception). I knew something was afoot when his first question to me was on whether or not I think someone should be fired for expressing dissenting views. I pressed Stein for specifics: Who is being fired for what, when and where? In my experience, people are usually fired for reasons having to do with budgetary constraints, incompetence, or not fulfilling the terms of a contract. Stein finally asked my opinion on people being fired for endorsing Intelligent Design. I replied that I know of no instance where such a firing has happened.

This seemingly innocent observation was turned into a filmic confession of ignorance when my on-camera interview abruptly ends there, because when I saw *Expelled* at a preview screening at the National Religious Broadcasters' convention (tellingly, the film is being targeted primarily to religious and conservative groups), I discovered that the central thesis of the film is a conspiracy theory about the systematic attempt to keep Intelligent Design creationism out of American classrooms and culture.

Stein's case for conspiracy centers on a journal article written by Stephen Meyer, a senior fellow at the Intelligent Design think tank, the Discovery Institute, and professor at the theologically conservative Christian Palm Beach Atlantic University. Meyer's article, "The Origin of Biological Information and the Higher Taxonomic Categories," was published in the June 2004 *Proceedings of the Biological Society of Washington*, the voice of the Biological Society, with a circulation of less than 300 people. In other words, from the get-go this was much ado about nothing.

Nevertheless, some members of the organization voiced their displeasure, so the society's governing council released a statement explaining, "Contrary to typical editorial practices, the paper was published without review by any associate editor; Sternberg handled the entire review process. The Council, which includes officers, elected councilors, and past presidents, and the associate editors would have deemed the paper inappropriate for the pages of the *Proceedings*." So how did it get published? In the words of the journal's managing editor at the time, Richard

Sternberg, "it was my prerogative to choose the editor who would work directly on the paper, and as I was best qualified among the editors I chose myself." And what qualified Sternberg to choose himself? Perhaps it was his position as a fellow of the International Society for Complexity, Information, and Design, which promotes Intelligent Design, along with being on the editorial board of the Occasional Papers of the Baraminology Study Group, a creationism organization committed to the literal interpretation of Genesis. (Baraminology is the classification of organisms based on the biblical doctrine of "special creation" and has nothing to do with the classification systems used by evolutionary biologists.) Or perhaps it was the fact that he is a signatory of the Discovery Institute's "100 Scientists Who Doubt Darwinism" statement.

Meyer's article is the first Intelligent Design paper ever published in a peer-reviewed journal, but it deals less with systematics (or taxonomy, Sternberg's specialty) than it does paleontology, for which many members of the society would have been better qualified than he to peer-review the paper (in fact, at least three members were experts on the Cambrian invertebrates discussed in Meyer's paper). Meyer claims that the "Cambrian explosion" of complex hard-bodied life forms over 500 million years ago could not have come about through Darwinian gradualism. The fact that geologists call it an "explosion" leads creationists to glom onto the word as a synonym for "sudden creation." After four billion years of an empty earth, God reached down from the heavens and willed trilobites into existence *ex nihilo*. In reality, according to paleontologist Donald Prothero in his 2007 magisterial book *Evolution: What the Fossils Say and Why It Matters* (Columbia University Press):

> The major groups of invertebrate fossils do not all appear suddenly at the base of the Cambrian but are spaced out over strata spanning 80 million years – hardly an instantaneous "explosion"! Some groups appear tens of millions of years earlier than others. And preceding the "Cambrian explosion" was a long slow buildup to the first appearance of typical Cambrian shelled invertebrates.

If an intelligent designer did create the Cambrian life forms, it took eighty million years of gradual evolution to do it.

Stein, however, is uninterested in paleontology, or any other science for that matter. His focus is on what happened to Sternberg, who is portrayed in the film as a martyr to the cause of free speech. "As a result of publishing the Meyer article," Stein intones in his inimitably droll voice, "Dr. Sternberg found himself the object of a massive campaign that smeared his reputation and came close to destroying his career." According to Sternberg, "after the publication of the Meyer article the climate changed from being chilly to being outright hostile. Shunned, yes, and discredited." As a result, Sternberg filed a claim against the Smithsonian for being "targeted for retaliation and harassment" for his religious beliefs. "I was viewed as an intellectual terrorist," he tells Stein. In August 2005 his claim was rejected. According to Jonathan Coddington, his supervisor at the Smithsonian Institution, Sternberg was not discriminated against, nor was he ever dismissed because, in fact, he was not even a paid employee but just an unpaid research associate who had completed his three-year term!

WHO SPEAKS FOR SCIENCE?

The rest of the martyrdom stories in *Expelled* have similar less menacing explanations, detailed at https://bit.ly/2kdL1Xl, where physical anthropologist Eugenie Scott and her tireless crew at the National Center for Science Education have tracked down the specifics of each case. Astronomer Guillermo Gonzales, for example, did not get tenure at Iowa State University and is portrayed in the film as sacrificed on the altar of tenure denial because of his authorship of a pro-Intelligent Design book entitled *Privileged Planet* (Regnery Publishing, 2004). As Scott told me, "Tenure is based on the evaluation of academic performance at one's current institution for the previous seven years." Although Gonzales was apparently a productive scientist before he moved to Iowa State, Scott says that "while there, his publication record tanked, he brought in only a couple of grants, one of which was from the Templeton Foundation to write the *Privileged Planet* [a creationism-based documentary film], didn't have very many graduate students and those he had never completed their degrees. Lots of people don't get tenure, for the same legitimate reasons that Gonzales didn't get tenure."

Tenure in any department is serious business because it means, essentially, employment for life. Tenure decisions for astronomers are based on the number and quality of scientific papers published, the prestige of the journal in which they are published, the number of grants obtained (universities are ranked, in part, by the grant-productivity of their faculties), the number of graduate students who completed their program, the amount of telescope time allocated – and the trends (up or down) in each of these categories – indicating whether or not the candidate shows potential for continued productivity. In point of fact, according to Gregory Geoffroy, president of Iowa State University, "Over the past ten years, four of the 12 candidates who came up for review in the physics and astronomy department were not granted tenure." Gonzales was one of them, and for good reasons, despite Stein's claim of his "stellar academic record."

For her part, Scott is presented in the film as the cultural filter for determining what is and is not science, begging the rhetorical question: Just who does she think she is anyway? Her response to me was as poignant as it was instructive: "Who is Ben Stein to say what is science and not science? None of us speak for science. Scientists vary all over the map in their religious and philosophical views, for example, Francis Collins [the evangelical Christian and Human Genome Project director], so no one *can* speak for science."

FROM HAECKEL TO HITLER

Even more disturbing than these distortions is the film's other thesis that Darwinism inexorably leads to atheism, Communism, Fascism, and the Holocaust. Despite the fact that hundreds of millions of religious believers fully accept the theory of evolution, Stein claims that we are in an ideological war between a scientific natural worldview that leads to the gulag archipelago and Nazi gas chambers, and a religious supernatural worldview that leads to freedom, justice, and the American way. The film's visual motifs leave no doubt in the viewer's emotional brain that Darwinism is leading America into an immoral quagmire; we're going to hell in a Darwinian handbasket. Cleverly edited interview excerpts from scientists are interspersed with various black-and-white clips for guilt by association, including bullies beating up on a 98-pound weakling, Charlton Heston's character in *Planet of the Apes* being blasted by a water hose, Nikita Khrushchev pounding his fist on a United Nations desk, East Germans captured while scaling the Berlin Wall in search of freedom in the West, and Nazi crematoria remains and Holocaust victims being bulldozed into mass graves. This propaganda production would make Joseph Goebbels proud.

It is true that the Nazis did occasionally adapt a warped version of social Darwinism proffered by the nineteenth-century German biologist Ernst Haeckel in a "survival of the fittest races" mode. But this rationale was only in the service of justifying the anti-Semitism that had been inculcated into European culture centuries before. Because Stein is Jewish, he surely knows that the pogroms against his people began ages before Darwin and that the German people were, in Harvard University political scientist Daniel Goldhagen's apt phrase (and book title), "Hitler's willing executioners."

When Stein interviewed me and asked my opinion on the impact of Darwinism on culture, he seemed astonishingly ignorant of the many other ways that Darwinism has been used and abused by political and economic ideologues of all stripes. Because Stein is a well-known economic conservative (and because I had just finished writing my book *The Mind of the Market*, a chapter of which compares Adam Smith's "invisible hand" with Charles Darwin's "natural selection"), I pointed out how the captains of industry in the late nineteenth and early twentieth centuries justified their beliefs in laissez-faire capitalism through the social Darwinism of "survival of the fittest corporations." And, more recently, I noted that Enron's CEO, Jeffrey Skilling, said his favorite book in Harvard Business School was Richard Dawkins' *The Selfish Gene* (first published in 1976), a form of Darwinism that Skilling badly misinterpreted ("read by title only" in Dawkins' apt phrase to describe those who misread the book). Scientific theorists cannot be held responsible for how their ideas are employed in the service of nonscientific agendas.

QUESTIONING DARWINISM

A final leitmotif running through *Expelled* is inscribed in chalk by Stein in repetitive lines on a classroom blackboard: "Do not question Darwinism."

Anyone who thinks that scientists do not question Darwinism has never been to an evolutionary conference. At the World Summit on Evolution held in the Galápagos Islands in June 2005, for example, I witnessed a scientific theory rich in controversy and disputation. UCLA paleontologist William Schopf, for instance, explained that "We know the overall sequence of life's origin, that the origin of life was early, microbial and unicellular, and that an RNA world preceded today's DNA-protein world." He openly admitted, however, "We do not know the precise environments of the early earth in which these events occurred; we do not know the exact chemistry of some of the important chemical reactions that led to life; and we do not have any knowledge of life in a pre-RNA world."

Stanford University biologist Joan Roughgarden declared that Darwin's theory of sexual selection (a specific type of natural selection) is wrong in its claim that females choose mates who are more attractive and well-armed. Calling neo-Darwinians "bullies," the University of Massachusetts biologist Lynn Margulis pronounced that "neo-Darwinism is dead" and, echoing Darwin, she said, "It was like confessing a murder when I discovered I was not a neo-Darwinist." Why? Because, Margulis explained, "Random changes in DNA alone do not lead to speciation. Symbiogenesis – the appearance of new behaviors, tissues, organs, organ systems, physiologies, or species as a result of symbiont interaction – is the major source of evolutionary novelty in eukaryotes: animals, plants, and fungi." Finally, Cornell University evolutionary theorist William Provine (featured in *Expelled*) presented eleven problems with evolutionary theory, including "Natural selection does not shape an adaptation or cause a gene to spread over a population or really do anything at all. It is instead the result of specific causes: hereditary changes, developmental causes, ecological causes, and demography. Natural Selection is the result of these causes, not a cause that is by itself. It is not a mechanism."

Despite this public questioning of Darwinism (and neo-Darwinism), which I reported on in *Scientific American* ("Rumsfeld's Wisdom," September 2005), Schopf, Roughgarden, Margulis, and Provine have not been persecuted, shunned, fired, or even expelled. Why? Because they are doing science, not religion. It is perfectly okay to question

Darwinism (or any other *ism* in science), as long as there is a way to test your challenge. Intelligent Design creationists, by contrast, have no interest in doing science. In the words of mathematician and philosopher William Dembski of Southwestern Baptist Theological Seminary and a key witness in Stein's prosecution of evolution, from a 2000 speech at the National Religious Broadcasters convention in Anaheim, California, "Intelligent Design opens the whole possibility of us being created in the image of a benevolent God . . . And if there's anything that I think has blocked the growth of Christ as the free reign of the Spirit and people accepting the Scripture and Jesus Christ, it is the Darwinian naturalistic view."

When will people learn that Darwinian naturalism has nothing whatsoever to do with religious supernaturalism? By the very definitions of the words, it is not possible for supernatural processes to be understood by a method designed to analyze natural causes. Unless a deity reaches into our world through natural and detectable means, God remains wholly outside the realm of science.

So, yes Mr. Stein, sometimes walls are bad (Berlin), but other times good walls make good neighbors. Let's build up that wall separating church and state, along with science and religion, and let freedom ring for all people to believe or disbelieve what they will.

CHAPTER 6

What Went Wrong?

Campus Unrest, Viewpoint Diversity, and Freedom of Speech

PREAMBLE

The impetus for this article, originally published in *Skeptic* in 2016, began with a question I was tasked to answer:

"Is Freedom of Speech Harmful for College Students?"

The query came (via my lecture agency) from my alma mater California State University, Fullerton (MA 1978, Experimental Psychology), for a 2015 symposium they were hosting on the title question, partly in response to a controversy the year before captured in this headline in the *Orange County Register*.

Cal State Fullerton Sorority Sanctioned for "Taco Tuesday" Party

What was the sorority's sin? "Cultural appropriation." That is, appropriating someone else's culture as your own, for which members of the originating group are allegedly offended (there's no evidence that this is the case generally, much less for Hispanics experiencing nonHispanics consuming Mexican food).

My initial response was "Seriously?" How could free speech possibly be harmful to anyone, much less college students whose introduction to the invigorating world of ideas begins with the premise that any and all topics are open for debate and disputation? Since I matriculated as an undergraduate in the early 1970s on the wave crest of the Free Speech Movement of the late 1960s, I was taken aback that the anyone would doubt this central tenet of liberty. I shouldn't have been, given that signs had appeared the previous few years – starting around 2013 – with the deplatforming (disinvitation) of controversial speakers; the emphasis on protecting students' feelings from ideas that might challenge their beliefs; the call for trigger warnings about sensitive subjects in books, films, and lectures; the opening of safe spaces for students to retreat to when encountering ideas they find offensive; and the dispersal of lists of microaggressions – words, phrases, statements, and questions that might offend people.

We now know that 2013 was a pivotal year as this is when the iGen (or Gen Z) generation of students born in 1995 or after began to enter college, and as Greg Lukianoff and Jonathan Haidt demonstrate in their 2018 book *The Coddling of the American Mind*, this generation differs significantly from Millennials (born after 1981), Gen Xers (born mid 1960s), and Baby Boomers (born after the Second World War), most notably in how they were raised (helicopter parenting) and what that means for how a "coddled" generation handles challenges. But there is much more to the story as I see it, and this article is my hypothesis of what went wrong.

* * *

THE FRENCH POLITICAL JOURNALIST AND SUPPORTER OF THE Royalist cause in the French Revolution, Jacques Mallet du Pan, famously summarized what often happens to extremists: "the Revolution devours its children."[1] I was thinking about this idiom – and it's doppleganger "what goes around comes around" – while writing a lecture for a talk I was invited to give at my alma mater, California State University, Fullerton, on the topic: "Is freedom of speech harmful for college students?" The short answer is an unflinching and unequivocal "No."

Why is this question even being asked? When I was in college, free speech was the *sine qua non* of the academy. It is what tenure was designed to protect! The answer may be found in the recent eruptions of student protests at numerous American colleges and universities, including Amherst, Brandeis, Brown, Claremont McKenna, Oberlin, Occidental, Princeton, Rutgers, University of California, University of Missouri, Williams, Yale, and others.[2] Most of these paroxysms were under the guise of protecting students from allegedly offensive speech and disagreeable ideas – defined differently by different interest groups – with demands for everything from trigger warnings and safe spaces to microaggressions and speaker disinvitations.

TRIGGER WARNINGS

Before readings, classroom lectures, film screenings, or public speeches, professors and administrators are now supposed to warn students that they will be exposed to certain possibly sensitive ("triggering") topics such as sex, addiction, bullying, suicide, eating disorders, and the like, involving such supposed prejudices as ableism, homophobia, sizeism, slut-shaming, transphobia, victim-blaming, and who-knows-what-else, thereby infantilizing students instead of preparing them for the real world where they most assuredly will not be so shielded.[3] At Oberlin College, for example, students leveled accusations against the administration of imperialism, white supremacy, capitalism, and the *ne plus ultra* in gender politics, cissexist heteropatriarchy, the enforcement of "gender binary and gender essentialism" against those who are "gender variant (non-binary) and trans identities."[4] The number of such categories has expanded into an alphabet soup of labels, LGBTQIA, or lesbian, gay, bisexual, trans, queer/questioning, intersex, asexual, and any other underrepresented sexual, gender, and/or romantic identities.[5] This is not your parents' protest against Victorian sexual mores, and the list of demands by Oberlin students would be unrecognizable to even the most radical 1960s hippies:

- The creation of a school busing system for Oberlin, Ohio's K-12 schools, paid for by the college.
- The establishment of special, segregated black-only "safe spaces" across campus.
- A more inclusive audition process in the Conservatory that does not privilege Western European theoretical knowledge over playing ability.
- The creation of a bridge program that will recruit recently released prisoners to enroll at Oberlin for undergraduate courses.

The most audacious demand was "an $8.20/hour stipend for black student leaders who are organizing protest efforts." These students wanted to be paid for protesting!

As often happens in moral movements, a reasonable idea with some evidentiary backing gets carried to extremes by engaged moralists eager for attention, sympathy, and the social standing that being a victim or perpetrator-shamer brings. Soldiers suffering from PTSD, for example, may be "triggered" by the backfire of a nearby automobile, but no one has proposed that automobile manufacturers put "trigger warnings" on cars to accommodate soldiers. As well, the Harvard psychologist Richard McNally points out that trigger warnings may have the opposite effect for which they are intended, because "systematic exposure to triggers and the memories they provoke is the most effective means of overcoming the disorder." McNally sites an analysis by the Institute of Medicine, which found that "exposure therapy is the most efficacious treatment for PTSD, especially in civilians who have suffered trauma such as sexual assault."[6] In other words, face your problems head-on and deal with them. An additional problem with trigger warnings is that the number of triggers has expanded to the point where nearly every speech and lecture could contain triggering words, turning communication into a moral hazard. Finally, who determines what is "triggering" anyway? The very concept is a recipe for censorship.

SAFE SPACES

According to the organization Advocates for Youth, a safe space is "A place where anyone can relax and be fully self-expressed, without fear of being made to feel uncomfortable, unwelcome or challenged on account of biological sex, race/ethnicity, sexual orientation, gender identity or expression, cultural background, age, or physical or mental ability; a place where the rules guard each person's self-respect, dignity and feelings and strongly encourage everyone to respect others."[7] Some such places even contain pillows, soothing music, milk and cookies, and videos of puppies.

No doubt there is a wide range of practices for safe spaces. While writing this article, for example, I attended a safe-space workshop at Chapman University and found it to be completely innocuous. Attended mostly by members of the LGBTQ community and supporters, people swapped stories about their own and others' experiences of bias and persecution on campus or in the local community (Orange/Anaheim), and how best to respond. When I inquired as to the frequency of such incidents, I was informed that no reliable data exists, so there is no way to know if rates of discrimination and bias are going up, down, or are about the same. Still, as a social primate species, we need our communities of like-minded people to gripe about the slings and arrows of life, so I don't see anything wrong with this type of safe space. I have my own in the form of weekly cycling training rides with my buddies in which we swap stories about irksome things that are troubling us that week.

By contrast, the safe space at Duke University – announced in a school newspaper headline that read "Duke offers men a 'safe space' to contemplate their 'toxic masculinity'" – is especially instructive as it has a reversed valance: punishment instead of protection. This is evidenced in the excerpted comment from the student newspaper that the new program was "not a reeducation camp," the term historically used to describe what dictatorships did with dissenters.

The deeper problem with safe spaces, however, is that in addition to infantilizing adults, they often end up protecting students from opinions that they don't happen to agree with or shielding them from ideas that challenge their beliefs, which has always been one of the most valuable benefits of a college education. In any case, college campuses, along with the cities and states they're in, are already designed to be safe from violence and discrimination based on the rule of law enforced by the police and courts. In point of fact, most of these colleges nestled in American cities are among the *safest* places on earth. If you want to build a safe space for people who really need it, go to Syria or Somalia. And if this opinion triggers you or makes you feel unsafe, then you haven't been paying attention to what's going on in the world.

MICROAGGRESSIONS

Comments or questions that slight, snub, or insult someone, intentionally or unintentionally, in anything from casual conversation to formal discourse, are now labeled as microaggressions.[8] According to the University of California publication *Recognizing Microaggressions*, examples include (see Figure 6.1 for a full list):

- Asking, "Where are you from or where were you born?" or "What are you?" This implies someone is not a true American.

Tool: Recognizing Microaggressions and the Messages They Send

Microaggressions are the everyday verbal, nonverbal, and environmental slights, snubs or insults, whether intentional or unintentional, that communicate hostile, derogatory, or negative messages to target persons based solely upon their marginalized group membership *(from Diversity in Classroom, UCLA Diversity & Faculty Development, 2014).* **The first step in addressing microaggressions is to recognize when a microaggression has occured and what message it may be sending. The context of the relationship and situation is critical.** Below are common themes to which microaggressions attach.

THEMES	MICROAGGRESSION EXAMPLES	MESSAGE
Alien in One's Own Land When Asian Americans, Latino Americans and others who look different or are named differently from the dominant culture are assumed to be foreign-born	• *"Where are you from or where were you born?"* • *"You speak English very well."* • *"What are you? You're so interesting looking!"* • A person asking an Asian American or Latino American to teach them words in theirnative language. • Continuing to mispronounce the names of students after students have corrected the person time and time again. Not willing to listen closely and learn the pronounciation of a non-English based name.	You are not a true American. You are a perpetual foreigner in your own country. Your ethnic/racial identity makes you exotic.
Ascription of Intelligence Assigning intelligence to a person of color or a woman based on his/her race/gender	• *"You are a credit to your race."* • *"Wow! How did you become so good in math?"* • To an Asian person, *"You must be good in math, can you help me with this problem?"* • To a woman of color: *"I would have never guessed that you were a scientist."*	People of color are generally not as intelligent as Whites. All Asians are intelligent and good in math/science. It is unusual for a woman to have strong mathematical skills.
Color Blindness Statements that indicates that a White person does not want to or need to acknowledge race.	• *"When I look at you, I don't see color."* • *"There is only one race, the human race."* • *"America is a melting pot."* • *"I don't believe in race."* • Denying the experiences of students by questioning the credibility /validity of their stories.	Assimilate to the dominant culture. Denying the significance of a person of color's racial/ethnic experience and history. Denying the individual as a racial/culture being.
Criminality/Assumption of Criminal Status A Person of color is presumed to be dangerous, criminal, or deviant based on his/her race.	• A White man or woman clutches his/her purse or checks wallet as a Black or Latino person approaches. • A store owner following a customer of color around the store. • Someone crosses to the other side of the street to avoid a person of color. • While walking through the halls of Chemistry building, a professor approaches a post-doctoral student of color to ask if she/he is lost, making the assumption that the person is trying to break into one of the labs.	You are a criminal. You are going to steal/you are poor, you do not belong. You are dangerous.

Figure 6.1 Tool: Recognizing microaggressions and the messages they send. Reproduced in part, with permission from Sue, D. W., *Microaggressions in Everyday Life: Race, Gender and Sexual Orientation,* Wiley & Sons, 2010.

- Inquiring, "How did you become so good in math?" (to people of color) or suggesting "You must be good in math" (to an Asian), which is stereotyping.

- Proclaiming, "There is only one race, the human race" or "I don't believe in race." This denies the significance of a person of color's racial/ethnic experience and history.

- Opining, "I believe the most qualified person should get the job" or "America is the land of opportunity." This suggests that the playing field is level, so if women or people of color do not fill all jobs and careers in precise proportion to their population percentages, it must mean that the problem is with them, or that they are lazy or incompetent and just need to work harder.[9]

Yes, language matters, and some comments that people make are cringeworthy (e.g., saying "you people" to a group of African Americans, or "you're a girl, you don't have to be good at math"). But do we really need a list of dos and don'ts handed out to students and reviewed as though they were five-year-olds being taught how to play nice with the other kids in the sandbox? Can't adults work out these issues themselves without administrators stepping in as surrogate parents? And who determines what constitutes "hate," "racist," or "sexist" speech? Who it happens to bother or offend? Students? Faculty? Administration? And as with the problem of trigger words, the list of microaggressions grows, turning normal conversation into a cauldron of potential violations that further restricts speech, encourages divisiveness rather than inclusiveness, and forces people to censor themselves, dissemble, withhold opinion, or outright lie about what they believe.

An incident at Brandeis University in 2015 is instructive: When Asian American students installed an exhibition on microaggressions, other Asian American students claimed that the exhibit was itself a microaggression that triggered negative feelings, leading the president to issue an apology to anyone "triggered or hurt by the content of the microaggressions."[10] I agree, blurting out "Why do you Asians always hang out together?" is lame, but at this point in history it just makes the communicant sound more like a bore than a bigot and more deserving of eye rolls than public humiliation.

SPEAKER DISINVITATIONS

Cancellations of invited speakers have been accelerating over the past decade.[11] According to the Foundation for Individual Rights in Education (FIRE), 257 such incidents have occurred since 2000, 111 of which were successful in preventing the invited guests from giving their talks.[12] In 2014, for example, Ayaan Hirsi Ali was invited to give the commencement speech at Brandeis University, where she was to also receive an honorary doctorate.[13] After students protested, citing her criticism of Islam for its mistreatment of women, the administration caved in to their demands and Ali was no-platformed (as it is called in England). Worse, in this theater of

the absurd, students from UC Berkeley attempted to no-platform the comedian and social commentator Bill Maher for his alleged "Islamophobia,"
code for anyone who criticizes Islam for any reason. Maher delivered his
commencement oration nonetheless, telling the very liberal student body
that "Liberals should own the First Amendment the way conservatives own
the Second Amendment," pointing out that apparently irony is no longer
taught at this birthplace of the 1960s Free Speech Movement.[14] This was
topped by students at Williams College who, in October 2015, succeeded in
disinviting Suzanne Venker, author of *The Flipside of Feminism*. Venker was
invited to participate in the college's "Uncomfortable Learning" lecture
series but, well, she made some students feel too uncomfortable. "When you
bring a misogynistic, white supremacist men's rights activist to campus in
the name of 'dialogue' and 'the other side,'" whined one student on
Facebook, it causes "actual mental, social, psychological, and physical
harm to students."[15] Physical harm?

The effects of such protests are often the opposite of what the protesters sought. Ayaan Hirsi Ali's speech, for example, was printed in the
Wall Street Journal where it was seen by that paper's 2.37 million readers
(under the title "Here's What I Would Have Said at Brandeis"), many
orders of magnitude more than would have heard it on campus.[16] Bill
Maher turned his Berkeley brouhaha into a bit for his HBO television
show *Real Time*, which carries over four million viewers. More irony.

What may have started out as well-intentioned actions at curbing prejudices and attenuating bigotry, with the goal of making people more tolerant,
has now metamorphosed into thought police attempting to impose totalitarian measures that result in silencing dissent of any kind. The result is the
very opposite of what free speech and a college education is all about.

Why such unrest in the academy – among the most liberal institutions
in the country – surrounded as these students are by so many liberal
professors and administrators? Here I will offer five proximate (immediate) causes, one ultimate (deeper) cause, and some solutions.

PROXIMATE CAUSES

(1) Moral Progress. As I document in *The Moral Arc*,[17] we have made so much
moral progress since the Enlightenment – particularly since the civil rights

and women's rights movements that launched the modern campus protest movement in the first place – that our standards of what is tolerable have been ratcheted ever upward to the point where students are hypersensitive to things that, by comparison, didn't even appear on the cultural radar half a century ago. This progress has happened gradually enough on the news cycle measure of days and weeks to be beneath the awareness of most observers, but fast enough that it can be tracked on timescales ranging from years to decades. For example, remember when interracial marriage was a divisive debate? Me neither. But recall the now-jarring words of the trial judge Leon M. Bazile, who convicted Richard and Mildred Loving in the case (*Loving v. Virginia*) that ultimately made its way to the Supreme Court in 1967 and overturned laws banning interracial marriage: "Almighty God created the races white, black, yellow, malay and red, and he placed them on separate continents. The fact that he separated the races shows that he did not intend for the races to mix."[18] Same-sex marriage went through a similar evolution as interracial marriage, culminating in the 5–4 decision by the Supreme Court of the United States in 2015 to make same-sex marriage the law of the land, another data point in the long-term trend toward granting more rights to more people.

Interracial marriage and same-sex marriage are themselves the legacy of the rights revolutions that first took off in the late 1700s when the idea of rights was invented and then demanded, first in the American Revolution (starting with the Declaration of Independence in 1776), then in the French Revolution (with the *Declaration of the Rights of Man and of the Citizen* in 1789), inspiring subsequent rights revolutions and documents (for example, *Declaration of the Rights of Woman and of the Citizen* in 1791). The result, two and a half centuries later, has been the abolition of slavery, the eradication of torture, the elimination of the death penalty in all modern democracies save America, the franchise for all adult citizens, children's rights, women's rights, gay rights, animal rights, and even the rights of future generations to inhabit a liveable planet. Who knows, perhaps one day soon we'll even grant rights to Artificially Intelligent robots. In other words, most of the big moral movements have been fought and won, leaving today's students with comparatively smaller causes to promote and evils to protest, but with moral emotions just as powerful as those of previous generations, so their outrage seems disproportionate.

(2) Transition from a Culture of Honor to a Culture of Victimhood. In a *culture of honor*, one settles minor disputes oneself and leaves the big crimes to the criminal justice system. Over the past two decades this has been eroded and is being replaced by a *culture of victimhood* in which one turns to parent-like authorities (faculty and college administrators, but not the law) to settle minor disputes over insults and slights.[19] The *culture of honor* leads to autonomy, independence, self-reliance, and self-esteem, whereas the *culture of victimhood* leads to dependence and puerile reliance on parental figures to solve one's problems. In this victimhood culture, the primary way to gain status is to either be a victim or to condemn alleged perpetrators against victims, leading to an accelerating search for both.[20] A student at the University of Oxford named Eleanor Sharman explained how it happened to her after she joined a campus feminist group named *Cuntry Living* and started reading their literature on misogyny and patriarchy:

> Along with all of this, my view of women changed. I stopped thinking about empowerment and started to see women as vulnerable, mistreated victims. I came to see women as physically fragile, delicate, butterfly-like creatures struggling in the cruel net of patriarchy. I began to see male entitlement everywhere.

As a result she became fearful and timid, afraid even to go out to socialize:

> Feminism had not empowered me to take on the world – it had not made me stronger, fiercer or tougher. Even leaving the house became a minefield. What if a man whistled at me? What if someone looked me up and down? How was I supposed to deal with that? This fearmongering had turned me into a timid, stay-at-home, emotionally fragile bore.[21]

It is not that there are no longer real victims of actual crimes, but it is a disservice to them to equate the trivial peccadillos of micro-aggressions or triggering words with brutal rapes and murders. A feminist blogger named Melody Hensley, for example, claims that years of online stalking and social-media trolls gave her PTSD on par with that of combat soldiers, disabling her from being able to work. Not surprisingly, war vets were not sympathetic.[22]

(3) From Anti-Fragile to Fragile Children. One response to the 1970s and 1980s crime wave was a shift toward "helicopter parenting" in which children were no longer allowed to be, well, children. The social psychologist Jonathan Haidt explains why through the concept of anti-fragility:

> Bone is anti-fragile. If you treat it gently, it will get brittle and break. Bone actually needs to get banged around to toughen up. And so do children. I'm not saying they need to be spanked or beaten, but they need to have a lot of unsupervised time, to get in over their heads and get themselves out. And that greatly decreased in the 1980s. Anxiety, fragility and psychological weakness have skyrocketed in the last 15–20 years.[23]

Those kids are today's college students, and as a consequence they have brittle bones and thin skins. An example of an anti-fragile person with strong bones and thick skin is the model Isabelle Boemeke, who tweeted what she does when verbally harassed on the streets by ogling men (see Figure 6.2).

If your Spanish is rusty, a biblical metonymy may be found in the command to "go forth and multiply" (with your mother).

(4) Puritanical Purging. Social movements tend to turn on themselves in puritanical purging of anyone who falls short of moral perfection, leading to preemptive denunciations of others before one is so denounced. The witch crazes of the seventeenth century degenerated into such anticipatory condemnations, resulting in a veritable plethora of nonexistent sorceresses being strapped to faggots and torched. The twentieth century witnessed Marxist and feminist groups undergoing similar purges as members competed for who was the purist and defenestrated those who fell below the unrealizable standard. On the other side of the political spectrum, Ayn Rand's objectivist movement took off in a frenzied buildup after the publication of *Atlas Shrugged* in 1959, but, by the time the philosopher-novelist died in 1982, most of the insider "collective" had been expunged for various sins against the philosophy,

Isabelle Boemeke
@isaboemeke

Here's what I do when catcalled: roll my eyes, if he's Hispanic say "chinga tú madre!", put earphones on, continue with life.

Figure 6.2 Tweet from Isabelle Boemeke (@isaboemeke), February 10, 2016.

from listening to the wrong music to challenging the founder on any point of substance or minutia.[24] Such purification purges are among the worst things that can happen to a social movement.

(5) Virtue Signaling. Related to puritanical purging is virtue signaling, in which members of a movement compete to signal who is the most righteous by (a) recounting all the moral acts one has performed and (b) identifying all the immoral acts others have committed. This leads to an arms race to signal moral outrage over increasingly diminishing transgressions, such as unapproved Halloween costumes at Yale University, which led to a student paroxysm against a faculty member, a cell-phone video of which went viral and nearly brought the campus to a standstill.[25] This is an example of what Maajid Nawaz means by "Regressive Liberalism" (sometimes called the "Regressive Left"), where freedom of speech and expression are sacrificed in the name of tolerance, which is actually intolerance.[26] One of the first acts of totalitarian regimes is to restrict dissent and free speech, so perhaps it should be called *Totalitarian Liberalism,* or the *Totalitarian Left.*

AN ULTIMATE CAUSE

A deeper reason behind the campus problem is a lack of diversity. Not ethnic, race, or gender diversity, but *viewpoint diversity,* specifically, *political* viewpoint. The asymmetry is startling. A 2014 study conducted by UCLA's Higher Education Research Institute found that 59.8 percent of all undergraduate faculty nationwide identify as far left or liberal, compared with only 12.8 percent as far right or conservative.[27] In a 2015 study published in *Behavioral and Brain Sciences* Arizona State University psychologist José Duarte and his colleagues reported that 58–66 percent of social science professors identify as liberals, compared to only 5–8 percent as conservatives.[28] Figure 6.3 captures the political bias in the social sciences – those fields most equipped to understand the problem of bias – from a study conducted by Daniel B. Klein and Charlotte Stern and published in the journal *Critical Review* as "Professors and Their Politics: The Policy Views of Social Scientists."

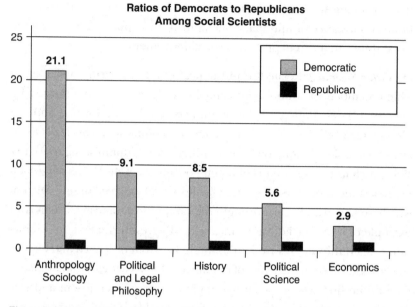

Figure 6.3 Ratios of Democrats to Republicans among social scientists.

Given the power of beliefs to drive actions, college students today stand next to no chance of receiving a balanced education on the most important topics of our time and which social science is best equipped to study.

What goes around comes around. Today's liberal college professors were radical college students in the 1960s and 1970s, protesting "the man" and bucking authority. One reason faculty and administrators are failing to stand up to student demands today is that they once wore those shoes. Raising children and students to be dismissive of law and order and mores and manners leads to a crisis in consciousness and the rejection of the very freedoms so hard-won by their parents and teachers. A generation in rebellion gave birth to a generation in crisis. Thus it is that the revolution devours its children.

SOLUTIONS

There is no magic-bullet solution to the problems the academy faces today, but, as liberals have known for some time, it takes decades – even generations – to right the wrongs of the past, so solutions are likely to be incremental and gradual, which is almost always a good thing when it comes to social change, as it leads to less violent and more peaceful actions on the part of both activists and their opponents. Contra Barry Goldwater, *extremism in the defense of liberty is no virtue; moderation in the pursuit of justice is no vice.*[29]

Hiring practices fall under this rubric. If the academy is already comfortable with and active in seeking to diversify its faculty by ethnicity, race, and gender, why not viewpoint as well? Given the entrenchment of tenure this will take time, but as that scribe of moral progress Victor Hugo observed, "Nothing is more powerful than an idea whose time has come."[30]

In the meantime, viewpoint diversity can be increased almost overnight by inviting speakers from a wide range of perspectives – political, economic, and ideological – even if (or especially) if they are offensive to faculty and students. *And no more disinvitations!* If you invite someone to speak, honor your word, own your decision, and stand up to the *cry bullies* (as they're called in this neologism). The assignment of books and papers for students to read – especially for courses in history, English literature, the humanities, and the social sciences – can and should include authors whose positions are at odds with those of most academicians and student bodies. And professors: in addition to assigning students articles and opinion editorials from the *New York Times*, give them a few from the *Wall Street Journal.* Balance the *Nation* magazine with *Reason* magazine, the *American Prospect* with the *American Spectator*, National Public Radio with Conservative Talk Radio, PBS with Fox News.

Viewpoint diversity, however, is subservient to the deeper principle of free speech, which should be applied indiscriminately across the academy, as it should across society and, ideally, the world. What does free speech mean? First, it does not mean that you can lie about someone. Libel laws are in place to protect people from defamation that causes reputational and financial harm. Second, free speech does not mean that the government, public institutions, or private persons, businesses, or publications are *required* to promote or publish the opinions of others. As the publisher of *Skeptic* magazine, for example, it is not incumbent on me to publish articles or accept advertisements just because we're in the business of publishing. Institutions should have the freedom to restrict the speech of anyone who utilizes resources within the jurisdiction of its own institution, such as a school newspaper. The government, however, cannot restrict citizens' speech just because it finds their opinions distasteful, offensive, or critical of its policies. (Exceptions have been made for treason and the passing on of national secrets to enemies, but crying "fire" in a crowded theater was most likely an exception that proves the rule.)

Holocaust deniers, creationists, and 9/11 truthers, for example, should have the right to publish their own journals and books, and to attempt to have their views aired in other publications and media venues, as in college newspapers and websites, but no one is obligated to publish them. Alex Grobman and I wrestled with the free-speech issue in our 2004 book *Denying History: Who Says the Holocaust Never Happened and Why Do They Say It?* As we opined: "Being in favor of someone's right to freedom of speech is quite different from enabling that speech." But we chose to write a book about their movement and arguments, quoting them extensively because, we believe, "In the bright light of open discussion the truth will emerge."[31] And although I declined to publish an ad submitted by a Holocaust denier in *Skeptic* (running an advertisement in our magazines carries the imprimatur of endorsement), I did debate Mark Weber, the director of the Institute for Historical Review (the leading Holocaust denier organization) in a public forum they hosted.[32]

The broader principle at work here is the Principle of Interchangeable Perspectives that I introduced in *The Moral Arc* (first articulated by Steven Pinker in *The Better Angels of Our Nature* in a larger context of moral principles): For me to expect you to listen to me, I must be willing to hear you. If I censor you, why shouldn't you censor me? If you silence me, why shouldn't I silence you? I want to protect the speech of people whose views I disagree with so that my speech is equally shielded from censorship by those who find my views disagreeable or offensive.

PART II

HOMO RELIGIOSUS: REFLECTIONS ON GOD AND RELIGION

CHAPTER 7

E Pluribus Unum for All Faiths and for None

The Case for Belief Pluralism

PREAMBLE

This essay was originally published in *eSkeptic* on December 20, 2011, as the run for the 2012 presidential election was ramping up and Republican candidates were scrambling to declare themselves more religious than thee (all Christian, of course). I found their rhetoric most off-putting, although not from my usual stance as a religious skeptic. Instead, I was offended as a US citizen who expects my elected officials – especially senators, representatives, and especially the president – to represent *all* Americans, not just Christian Americans, and to uphold their oath to protect and defend the *Constitution* of the United States, not the Bible. The figures I included in the essay for the "Nones" – those who affiliate with no religion – are from 2011 and have grown in number and percentage since: at the end of 2018, around 25 percent of all Americans and 33 percent of Millennials. I haven't seen data on iGens/Gen Zs, but I predict the percentage will be around half. I end this essay with what I would say if I were running for president and were asked my religious views, although rest assured I have no interest in going into politics.

* * *

FOREIGNERS COULD BE FORGIVEN FOR THINKING THAT America is fast becoming a theocracy. No fewer than three of the remaining Republican candidates (Rick Perry, Rick Santorum, and Michele Bachmann) have declared that they were called by God to run for the country's highest office. Congress recently voted to renew the country's motto of "In God We Trust" on nothing less than the coin of the realm. And this year's Thanksgiving Forum in Iowa (co-sponsored by the

National Organization for Marriage) featured most of the major presidential candidates competing for the title of God's quarterback.

Rick Santorum, for example, in the course of denouncing Islamic Sharia law, inadvertently endorsed the same as long as it is a Christian on the judge's bench: "Unlike Islam, where the higher law and the civil law are the same, in our case, we have civil laws. But our civil laws have to comport with the higher law." Not content to speak in such circular generalities, Santorum targeted his faith: "As long as abortion is legal – at least according to the Supreme Court – legal in this country, we will never have rest, because that law does not comport with God's law."

God's law? That is *precisely* the argument made by Islamic imams. But Santorum was only getting started. "Gay marriage is wrong. The idea that the only things that the states are prevented from doing are only things specifically established in the Constitution is wrong. ... As a president, I will get involved, because the states do not have the right to undermine the basic, fundamental values that hold this country together." Christian values only, of course.

The historically challenged Michele Bachmann minced no words when she declared: "I have a biblical worldview. And I think, going back to the Declaration of Independence, the fact that it's God who created us – if He created us, He created government. And the government is on His shoulders, as the book of Isaiah says." A Bachmann administration would apparently consult the Old Testament for moral guidance because, she pronounced with her usual hubris born of dunce-cap history, "American exceptionalism is grounded on the Judeo-Christian ethic, which is really based upon the Ten Commandments. The Ten Commandments were the foundation for our law." Really? Where in our laws does it prohibit belief in gods other than Yahweh, ban the manufacturing of graven images, forbid taking the Lord's name in vain, bar us from working on the Sabbath, require us to honor our parents, and interdict the coveting of our neighbor's house, wife, slave, servant, ox, and ass (or, in Christopher Hitchens' memorable rendering, coveting our neighbor's wife's ass)? Even the notoriously difficult to follow seventh commandment is not illegal, much to the relief of candidate Newt Gingrich, who was notoriously engaged in an extramarital affair while he was simultaneously prosecuting President Clinton for doing the same.

Surely the pluralism of America's religious diversity is what makes us great. Not so, said Texas Governor Rick Perry: "In every person's heart, in every person's soul, there is a hole that can only be filled by the Lord Jesus Christ." But don't politicians owe allegiance to the Constitution? Alas, pace Perry, no. "Somebody's values are going to decide what the Congress votes on or what the President of the United States is going to deal with. And the question is: Whose values? And let me tell you, it needs to be *our* values – values and virtues that this country was based upon in Judeo-Christian founding fathers." You mean the values and virtues of the atheist Thomas Paine and the deist Thomas Jefferson, the latter of whom rejected Jesus, the Resurrection, and all miracles as nonsense on stilts, and yet who nonetheless insisted on building an impregnable wall protecting religion from the encroachment of state abuse?

Finally, the erudite Newt Gingrich was more specific in his plan to bring about a Christian nation through legal means, starting by redacting the Fourteenth Amendment:

> I am intrigued with something which Robby George at Princeton has come up with, which is an interpretation of the 14th Amendment, in which it says that Congress shall define personhood. That's very clearly in the 14th Amendment. And part of what I would like to explore is whether or not you could get the Congress to pass a law which simply says: Personhood begins at conception. And therefore – and you could, in the same law, block the court and just say, "This will not be subject to review," which we have precedent for. You would therefore not have to have a Constitutional amendment, because the Congress would have exercised its authority under the 14th Amendment to define life, and to therefore undo all of *Roe vs. Wade*, for the entire country, in one legislative action.

If the Fourteenth Amendment can be averted on a technicality such as this, would the erstwhile Congressman from Georgia propose to do the same to the Thirteenth Amendment and thereby deprive African Americans of their freedom?

If you are a Christian, of course, all of this rhetoric is the mother's milk of nursing privilege. Power to the (Christian) people. It's the oldest trope in history – religious tribalism – and it's being played out in the land of liberty. So it is prudent for us to educe that other national motto found on the Seal of the United States that was first proffered by the founding patriarchs, John Adams, Benjamin Franklin, and Thomas Jefferson, and adopted by an Act of Congress in 1782:

E Pluribus Unum – Out of many, one.

How many make up our one? There are over 300 million Americans. Gallup, Pew, and other pollsters consistently find that about 10 percent of Americans do not believe in God. That's more than 30 million American religious skeptics. That's not all. A 2008 study by the American Religious Identification Survey (ARIS) revealed that between 1990 and 2008 the fastest growing religious group in America were the "Nones," or people who responded "None, No religion, Humanistic, Ethical Culture, Agnostic, Atheist, or Secular" in the survey. Remarkably, this group gained more new members (19,838,000) than either Catholics (11,195,000) or Protestants (10,980,000), and totals 15 percent, or 45 million Americans. (By 2018 the percentage of Nones had grown to 25 percent of 225 million Americans, or 56.25 million nonreligious Americans.)

Read that number again, candidates! If you are elected president of these United States, are you really going to dismiss and openly refuse to represent 45 million people living under the same Constitution as you? And that's just the Nones. Tens of millions more Jews, Mormons, Muslims, Buddhists, Hindus, Baha'i, Jains, Taoists, Wiccans, New Agers, and other law-abiding loyal Americans – many serving in the armed services protecting our liberty – are non-Christians who hold the same dreams and aspirations as Christians do for what this country has to offer. In fact, at most, Christians comprise 60–76 percent of all Americans, which means that somewhere between 72 million and 120 million US citizens are non-Christians no less deserving of representation in this democracy.

It's time for candidates and politicians to stop the God talk and start acting like true representatives of the people – *all of the people.* It's time for the 45 million Nones to demand both respect and representation no less than any other American, and for presidential candidates, when asked about their religion, to reply something along these lines:

> I understand why you are curious about my religious beliefs, but I am not running to represent only Americans who believe what I believe about God and religion. I am running to represent Americans of *all faiths*, and even the tens of millions of Americans who have *no religion*. If elected, *my allegiance is to the Constitution* and my duty is to uphold the laws of this great land, which are to be applied equally and without prejudice to all Americans no matter their color or creed.
>
> I realize that some candidates and politicians pander to their religious voting block in hopes of gaining support by tapping ancient tribal prejudices, but that is not my way.
>
> I get why other candidates are tempted to appeal to those deep emotions that are stirred by religious unity against those who believe differently, but I am trying to do something different.
>
> If elected, I fully intend to represent *all* Americans under my jurisdiction, not just those Americans whose beliefs I happen to share. I am trying to build a better America for *all* Americans, not just some Americans.
>
> The original motto of this country is *E Pluribus Unum*. It means "Out of many, one." It means that we are stronger together than separate, united by our common belief in liberty and the freedom to believe whatever you want as long as it doesn't harm others.
>
> As a candidate for the highest office of this noble nation, my faith is in its people – *all* of the people – and what we are able to do together to make the world a better place to live.

CHAPTER 8

Atheism and Liberty

Raising Consciousness for Religious Skepticism through Political Freedom

PREAMBLE

This essay was originally published in a 2008 book titled *The Edge of Reason? Science and Religion in Modern Society* (edited by Alex Bentley), published by Bloomsbury's book publishing company Continuum at a sticker-shock price (https://bit.ly/2SeBmLx) but is also available on Amazon at their usual deep discount (https://amzn.to/2AruUJX). The book asks:

> Should scientists challenge religious beliefs? Is religion inevitable in human society? Is religion harmful to society? Can science itself inspire spiritual wonder? Confrontation between science and religion has defined much public debate about religion in recent years ... This collection of essays gives voice to social scientists, natural scientists and theologians whose experience holds direct relevance on these major issues, and clarifies the position of science in the modern debate.

I took the opportunity to come at the problem from a different angle from that of the New Atheists' anti-theism strategy of attacking religion directly and argue instead for raising consciousness for religious skepticism through political freedom, namely protecting the rights of believers so that the rights of nonbelievers are equally protected.

* * *

OVER THE PAST SEVERAL YEARS, THE TRADITIONALLY STAID and academic field of science-and-religion studies has erupted in a paroxysm of public debate and disputation, landing theists and atheists on magazine covers and bestseller lists. Much has been made in the popular press about the "angry" attacks on religion by atheists and scientists, most notably Richard Dawkins (*The God Delusion*), Daniel Dennett (*Breaking the Spell*), Sam Harris (*The End of Faith* and *Letter to a Christian Nation*) and Christopher Hitchens (*God is Not Great*). I know all of these gentlemen quite well, consider them good friends, and agree with their arguments and conclusions on the God question. Indeed, I've made most of these arguments in my belief trilogy (*Why People Believe Weird Things, How We Believe,* and *The Science of Good and Evil*), yet I am often cast as a moderate for my more conciliatory approach towards religion. What is the right tactic to take? The answer depends on what one wants to accomplish.

Since the turn of the millennium, a new militancy has arisen among religious skeptics in response to three threats to science and freedom: (1) evolution education and stem cell research, (2) breaks in the barrier separating church and state, leading to political preferences for some faiths over others, and (3) fundamentalist terrorism here and abroad. In addition, they loudly and proudly proclaim that it is okay to be an atheist, and they free themselves of the burden of having to respect others' beliefs when they don't respect ours. Dawkins' program of "consciousness raising" is laudable and liberating. He wants to "raise consciousness to the fact that to be an atheist is a realistic aspiration, and a brave and splendid one. You can be an atheist who is happy, balanced, moral, and intellectually fulfilled." Dawkins wants atheists to quit apologizing for their religious skepticism. "On the contrary, it is something to be proud of, standing tall to face the far horizon, for atheism nearly always indicates a healthy independence of mind and, indeed, a healthy mind." Amen, brother.

Without question, whenever religious beliefs conflict with scientific facts or violate principles of political liberty, we must respond with appropriate aplomb. I understand and often share atheists' anger in the teeth of so much religious intolerance in today's society, especially the breathtakingly asinine notion that atheists are inherently incapable of being moral and dignified people and citizens. As a 1999 Gallup poll found, a gay black woman could be elected president before an atheist could, an appalling fact for a modern liberal democracy.

In point of fact, studies show that atheists are just as (if not more) moral than theists, even in studies conducted by the Christian pollster George Barna. In his 1996 *Index of Leading Spiritual Indicators*, Barna noted, "Born again Christians continue to have a higher likelihood of getting divorced [27 percent] than do non-Christians [24 percent]." In a 2001 survey, Barna found "33 percent of all born again individuals who have been married have gone through a divorce, which is statistically identical to the 34 percent incidence among non-born again adults." A tie.

More broadly, in a 2005 study published in the *Journal of Religion and Society* – "Cross-National Correlations of Quantifiable Societal Health with Popular Religiosity and Secularism in the Prosperous Democracies" – independent scholar Gregory S. Paul found an inverse correlation between religiosity (measured by belief in God, biblical literalism, and frequency of prayer and service attendance) and societal health (measured by rates of homicide, suicide, childhood mortality, life expectancy, sexually transmitted diseases, abortion, and teen pregnancy) in eighteen developed democracies. "In general, higher rates of belief in and worship of a creator correlate with higher rates of homicide, juvenile and early adult mortality, STD infection rates, teen pregnancy, and abortion in the prosperous democracies," Paul found. "The United States is almost always the most dysfunctional of the developed democracies, sometimes spectacularly so." Indeed, the USA scores the highest in religiosity and the highest (by far) in homicides, STDs, abortions, and teen pregnancies. Despite being the most religious nation of the sample (not to mention the most economically prosperous), the USA is at or near the bottom of every societal health measure.

The prejudices against us persist anyway. In America, atheists are associated with tree-hugging, whale-saving, hybrid-driving, bottled water-drinking, American Civil Liberties Union-supporting, pinko commie fags hell-bent on conning our youth into believing all that baloney about equal rights and evolution. When we hear such sentiments, we should not hesitate to respond, like Howard Beale in the 1976 film *Network*, by sticking our collective heads out of our windows and shouting, "I'm mad as hell and I'm not going to take this anymore."

Nevertheless, we must be cautious not to let this atheist reward center-stroking turn into the same form of intolerance and superiority to which we are often subjected. I wince when I hear religious people referred to as "faith-heads" and "clowns," as being less intelligent or poorly reasoned, or worse, deluded. I cringe when I hear their religious beliefs compared to cancer or to smoking cigarettes. And I grimace when religious moderates are called enablers of terrorism, their doctrines identified as Bronze Age relics, and prayer equated to talking to a hairdryer.

I cringe a little because I have religious friends and colleagues who do not in the least fit these descriptions; they are thoughtful, intelligent, educated people who abhor terrorism, who engage in prayer mainly for contemplative (not petitionary) purposes, and whose religions may have Bronze Age origins but are thoroughly modern in structure. I empathize at the pain such pejorative appellations cause them.

We need to raise our consciousness a little higher. Dawkins asks us, pace John Lennon, to "imagine no religion": "no suicide bombers, no 9/11, no 7/7, no Crusades, no witch-hunts, no Gunpowder Plot, no Indian partition, no Israeli/Palestinian wars, no Serb/Croat/Muslim massacres, no persecution of Jews as 'Christ-killers', no Northern Ireland 'troubles', no 'honor killings', no shiny-suited bouffant-haired televangelists fleecing gullible people of their money."

Indeed, all these, and more, we plainly could do without. But in my opinion, many of these events – and others often attributed solely to religion by atheists – were less religiously motivated than politically driven, or at the very least involved religion in the service of political hegemony. History, like life, is usually multivariate in its causes and consequences. And, I wonder, without religion, who would take care of the poor, the needy, the starving, the diseased, and the destitute? My atheist friends respond: "The government!" The government? You mean like they did for the victims of Katrina? As they have for inner-city slums and single-parent families?

According to Syracuse University professor Arthur C. Brooks in his 2006 book *Who Really Cares*, when it comes to charitable giving and volunteering, numerous quantitative measures debunk the myth of "bleeding heart liberals" and "heartless conservatives." Religious conservatives donate 30 percent more money than liberals (even when controlled for income), give more blood, and log more volunteer hours. In general, religious people are four times more generous than secularists to all charities, 10 percent more munificent to nonreligious charities, and 57 percent more likely than a secularist to help a homeless person. Those raised in intact and religious families are more charitable than those who are not. In terms of societal health, charitable givers are 43 percent more likely to say they are "very happy" than nongivers and 25 percent more likely than nongivers to say their health is "excellent" or "very good." Before we imagine a world without religion (or possessions?), we need to consider what social institutions will be substituted for all the good that religion does.

Instead of focusing our energy on eradicating religion, consider the following three observations and one principle.

1. **The Power of Positive Assertions.** Atheists champion science, reason, and rationality, which are best promoted through positive assertions. Here I take advice from Charles Darwin who, in 1880, clarified his reasoning on the question of science and religion to Edward Aveling, the noted British socialist. Aveling had solicited Darwin's endorsement of a group of radical atheists by asking his permission to dedicate a book Aveling edited entitled *The Student's Darwin*, a collection of articles discussing the implications of evolutionary theory for religious thought. The book had a militant anti-religious flavor that Darwin disdained. He declined the offer, elaborating his reason with his usual flair for quotable maxims:

   It appears to me (whether rightly or wrongly) that direct arguments against christianity & theism produce hardly any effect on the public; & freedom of thought is best promoted by the gradual illumination of men's minds which follow[s] from the advance of science. It has, therefore, been always my object to avoid writing on religion, & I have confined myself to science.

2. **Anti-Something Movements Are Doomed to Failure.** We cannot simply define ourselves by what do not believe, a principle I learned from the great Austrian economist and classical liberal Ludwig von Mises, who in 1956 warned his anti-Communist colleagues:

   An anti-something movement displays a purely negative attitude. It has no chance whatever to succeed. Its passionate diatribes virtually advertise the program they attack. People must fight for something that they want to achieve, not simply reject an evil, however bad it may be.

3. **Rational Consciousness Raising.** If it is our goal to raise the consciousness of as many people as possible to the wonders of science, the power of reason, and the virtues of rationality, we must apply science, reason, and rationality to our actions, not just our ideas. It is irrational to take an angry, hostile, demeaning, belittling, or condescending attitude towards religion. By so doing, we virtually guarantee that religious people will, in response, adopt an angry, hostile, demeaning, belittling, or condescending attitude towards science, reason, and rationality. In other words, our negative actions will have the exact opposite effect that we wish them to have, which is what makes them irrational.

Here I am not hypocritically pointing fingers, for I have been as guilty as anyone of biting and sardonic rejoinders to religious claims and people; instead, I simply call attention to a misdirection that our movement has taken. As Carl Sagan cautioned us in *The Demon-Haunted World*: "You can get into a habit of thought in which you enjoy making fun of all those other people who don't see things as clearly as you do. We have to guard carefully against it." We must direct our outrage at specific targets and heed the words of the greatest consciousness raiser of the twentieth century, Dr. Martin Luther King, Jr, in his now canonized "I Have a Dream" speech:

In the process of gaining our rightful place, we must not be guilty of wrongful deeds. Let us not seek to satisfy our thirst for freedom by drinking from the cup of bitterness and hatred. We must forever conduct our struggle on the high plane of dignity and discipline.

By the virtue of the golden rule, if we do not want theists to prejudge atheists in a negative light, then atheists must not do unto theists the same.

To this end I would like to propose that we raise our consciousness towards a higher goal that encompasses both science and religion, that allows for the free expression of both belief and disbelief, and in which science, reason, and rationality are subsumed within a broader principle, the *Principle of Freedom*: All people are free to think, believe, and act as they choose, as long as they do not infringe on the equal freedom of others.

This was the Enlightenment program as put into practice by Messrs Paine, Jefferson, and Mill, and carried on ever since by freedom fighters everywhere. With a higher goal of spreading liberty and freedom to more people in more places, science, reason, and rationality become the means towards an end, not ends in themselves.

With the *Principle of Freedom* in hand, we can see why we should be tolerant of religion: not because we want to "make nice" (which is patronizing); not because it is the polite thing to do in a polite society (true enough, but not good enough); and not because science fosters open discussion and dissent (it does, but we can reach higher still). We should conduct our struggle on the high plane of dignity and discipline because it is the rational thing to do: if we want the freedom to disbelieve, then we must grant others the freedom to believe. If it is our higher goal to attenuate intolerance, to expand the sphere of freedom to encompass all peoples, and to accentuate the free expression of both belief and disbelief, then the freedom of atheists not to worship God is inextricably bound to the freedom of theists to worship God. As Dr. King noted:

> The marvelous new militancy which has engulfed the Negro community must not lead us to a distrust of all white people, for many of our white brothers, as evidenced by their presence here today, have come to realize that their destiny is tied up with our destiny. And they have come to realize that their freedom is inextricably bound to our freedom. We cannot walk alone.

Read atheists for Negro and theists for white people. Then let freedom ring.

CHAPTER 9

The Curious Case of Scientology

Is It a Religion or a Cult?

PREAMBLE

The first section of this article served as an introduction to a special issue of *Skeptic* on Scientology,[1] inspired as it was by the publication of two new books on the church: Janet Reitman's *Inside Scientology: The Story of America's Most Secretive Religion* and Hugh Urban's *The Church of Scientology: A History of a New Religion*, both reviewed in a deep-dive essay by long-time Scientology scholar Jim Lippard.

After the publication of these works, the floodgates were opened, with Tony Ortega's *The Unbreakable Miss Lovely: How the Church of Scientology Tried to Destroy Paulette Cooper*, Lawrence Wright's *Going Clear: Scientology, Hollywood, and the Prison of Belief* and the accompanying 2015 HBO documentary film special based on the book, all exposing the abuses of the church in graphic detail. These were followed by insider tell-alls by Jenna Miscavige Hill, *Beyond Belief: My Secret Life Inside Scientology and My Harrowing Escape*, and by Ron Miscavige, *Ruthless: Scientology, My Son David Miscavige, and Me* – the niece and father of the current head of Scientology, David Miscavige. Most revealing (and damaging) was the 2016 memoir by ex-Scientologist and Hollywood star Leah Remini, *Troublemaker: Surviving Hollywood and Scientology*, followed by her A&E series, *Scientology and the Aftermath*, that featured a parade of ex-members recounting the horrors they experienced in the church.

The second section of this article was originally published as an opinion editorial in the *Los Angeles Times* in February of 2008, when Scientology was under public attack by a group calling itself Anonymous, which I found to be problematic, imagining what would have happened if a similar such anonymous group attacked Jews, and why most of us would find that offensive. Why don't we feel the same way about Scientologists?

The third section of this article is my brief response to the critics of the *LA Times* op-ed, primarily a historian of religion who upbraided me for using the pejorative term "cult" instead of the scholarly descriptor "New Religious Movement." I think the shorter lemma fits.

* * *

THE JET PROPULSION LABORATORY IN SOUTHERN CALIFORNIA is the home of many of the world's leading scientists and engineers, who shoot spacecraft deep into the solar system to find out what's out there. Apparently, they could save taxpayers a lot of money if they simply employed a different kind of science practiced by Scientologists, as described to me by one such rocket scientist who was once employed there:

> I was working at JPL, and my immediate supervisor was a dedicated Scientologist. This supervisor had just advanced from Clear to OT I. Some people at a meeting asked him what this meant, and he explained that he now had the ability to detach his Thetan from his body and cause it to perform useful out-of-body functions. For example, if he needed to purchase a certain item and he drove past a store that might or might not have that item, he could send his Thetan into the store to look for the item. If the Thetan reported the item was in stock, my boss would then park the car and go in and buy it. Unfortunately for JPL there was a senior NASA official in the audience. The official noted that NASA was about to spend hundreds of millions of dollars to send another robotic spacecraft to Mars. He asked if my supervisor would be willing to send his Thetan to Mars to gather the needed data, presumably at lower cost. The supervisor replied that this could in fact be done, and that other OTs from the Hollywood church would probably offer their services too. JPL was severely criticized by NASA, and warned of serious consequences if this got into the newspapers.

The Thetan reference stems from Scientology's genesis story that is only revealed after parishioners (aka customers) pay tens of thousands of dollars to reach Operating Thetan Level III. This science fiction UFO fantasy story is now so widely known that it was even featured in a 2005 episode of the animated sitcom television series *South Park*. Around seventy-five million years ago, Xenu, the story begins, the ruler of a Galactic Confederation of seventy-six planets, transported billions of his charges in spaceships similar to DC-8 jets to a planet called Teegeeack (Earth). He then vaporized them with hydrogen bombs, scattering to the winds their souls, called Thetans, which were then rounded up in electronic traps and implanted with false ideas. These corrupted Thetans attach themselves to people today, leading to drug and alcohol abuse, addiction, depression, and other psychological and social ailments that only Scientology "auditing" employing electropsychometers (E-meters) and numerous classes can cure.

As a student of religion curious about the genesis of such genesis stories, I tracked down the origin of the Xenu tale through the acclaimed science fiction author Harlan Ellison, who told me he was there at the birth of Scientology. At a late 1940s meeting in New York of a science fiction writers' group called the Hydra Club, Hubbard was complaining to L. Sprague de Camp and the others about writing for a penny a word.

> Lester Del Ray then said half jokingly, "What you really ought to do is create a religion because it will be tax free," and at that point everyone in the room started chiming in with ideas for this new religion. So the idea was a Gestalt that Ron caught on to and assimilated the details. He then wrote it up as "Dianetics: A New Science of the Mind" and sold it to John W. Campbell, Jr., who published it in *Astounding Science Fiction* in 1950.

Astounding indeed that anyone would accept such science fiction as fact, but such is the power of belief when coupled to a handful of powerful psychological principles. Consider *cognitive dissonance*, discovered by the psychologist Leon Festinger in 1954 when he joined a UFO end-of-the-world cult at the mountain top to record what would happen when the mothership failed to arrive at the designated midnight hour on December 21. Festinger saw this as an opportunity to study the phenomenon of mental tension created when someone holds two conflicting thoughts simultaneously:

Suppose an individual believes something with his whole heart; suppose further that he has a commitment to this belief, that he has taken irrevocable actions because of it; finally, suppose that he is presented with evidence, unequivocal and undeniable evidence, that his belief is wrong: what will happen? The individual will frequently emerge, not only unshaken, but even more convinced of the truth of his beliefs than ever before. Indeed, he may even show a new fervor about convincing and converting other people to his view.

That is exactly what happened with the UFO cult, whose members reduced the dissonance triggered by the failed prophecy by going out into the community to recruit new members. The greater the cost, the higher the gain on the dissonance dial that can only be assuaged by further reinforcing the veracity of the belief, no matter how preposterous it may seem to outsiders who do not share the dissonance that comes with their skepticism. So it is with Scientology, whose members pay a high price indeed in every sense of that word.

Is Scientology a cult? First, although it is recognized by the IRS as a tax-exempt religion, no other religion that I know of considers their theological doctrines and core religious tenets to be intellectual property accessible only for a fee. Envision converting to Judaism but having to pay for courses in order to hear the story of Abraham and Isaac, Noah and the flood, or Moses and the Ten Commandments. Or imagine joining the Catholic Church but not being told about the Crucifixion and the Resurrection until you have reached Operating Theological Level III, which can only be attained after many years and tens of thousands of dollars in church-run courses. That is, in essence, how the Church of Scientology dispenses its theology.

Second, a sociological definition of a cult is that it is a group with novel religious beliefs and a high degree of tension with the surrounding society (as contrasted with a sect, or a group with traditional religious beliefs and a low degree of tension with the surrounding society). The great sociologist of religion Rodney Stark has noted that most religions start out as cults, then either die out or become sects, which in turn either die out or transition into a mainstream religion.

Third, consider these characteristics of a cult:

- *Veneration of the Leader:* Excessive glorification of the leader to the point of virtual sainthood or divinity.
- *Inerrancy of the Leader:* Belief that the leader cannot be wrong in pronouncements on virtually all subjects, from existential to trivial.
- *Dissent Is Discouraged:* Questioning and doubt among members is punished.
- *Absolute Truth:* Belief that the leader and/or group has a method of discovering final knowledge on any and all subjects.
- *Absolute Morality:* Belief that the leader and/or the group have developed a system of right and wrong thought and action applicable to members and nonmembers alike.
- *In-Group/Out-Group Mentality:* Polarization of members and nonmembers into "us v. them."
- *Ends Justify the Means:* Leads to members doing things they would have considered reprehensible or unethical before joining the group.
- *Deceit and Hidden Agendas:* Potential recruits and the public are not given a full disclosure of the true nature of the group's beliefs and plans, and flaws of the leader or potentially embarrassing events in the group's history are covered up.
- *Financial and/or Sexual Exploitation:* Recruits and followers are persuaded to invest in the group, and the leader may develop sexual relations with one or more of the followers.
- *Mind-Altering Practices:* Meditation, chanting, speaking in tongues, denunciation sessions, and debilitating work routines are used to reinforce group think.
- *Lack of Accountability:* The group and leader are not accountable to any authorities.
- *Isolation from Friends and Family:* Normal reality checks are blocked for members.
- *Aggressive Recruitment Practices:* Members are strongly encouraged to bring in new members and raise money for the group.
- *Persuasive Techniques:* Special psychological methods are employed to recruit new followers and reinforce beliefs.

Fourth, compare this list with these noteworthy facts about Scientology as documented and described by the investigative journalist

Janet Reitman in her 2006 *Rolling Stone* magazine article and subsequently her 2011 book, *Inside Scientology*:

- Scientology's founder L. Ron Hubbard defined it as "the study of truth."
- Scientology calls itself "the world's fastest-growing religion" with 10 million members in 159 countries and more than 6,000 Scientology churches, missions, and outreach groups across the globe. In fact, a 2001 survey conducted by the City University of New York found only 55,000 people in the United States who claimed to be Scientologists. Worldwide, some observers believe a reasonable estimate of Scientology's core practicing membership ranges between 100,000 and 200,000.
- Scientology's holdings, which include real estate on several continents, are widely assumed to value in the billions of dollars.
- Scientology's practices and processes are highly controlled, and, at the advanced levels, highly secretive.
- Unique among religions, Scientology withholds key aspects of its central theology from all but its most exalted followers. This would be akin to the Catholic Church refusing to tell all but a select number of the faithful that Jesus Christ died for their sins.
- Members are isolated and live in a parallel world with the secular world.
- Scientology has its own nomenclature, guidelines for living, and ethical code that it enforces.
- The Bridge to Total Freedom is the goal, and it is expensive: Auditing is purchased in 12.5-hour blocks, known as "intensives." Each intensive can cost anywhere from $750 for introductory sessions to between $8,000 and $9,000 for advanced sessions. People spend tens to hundreds of thousands of dollars in auditing.

Is Scientology a cult? You be the judge. There is no scientifically determined set number of characteristics according to which the diagnostic label is determined, but as you read the *Skeptic* cover story on Scientology and as you read and hear about Scientology in the news, you might recall some of these salient points. In my opinion, if Scientology is not a cult, then nothing is a cult and the term has no meaning.

SCIENTOLOGY, ANONYMOUS

Imagine reading the following press release:

> Hello, Jews. We are anonymous. Over the years, we have been watching
> you. Your campaigns of misinformation; suppression of dissent; your
> litigious nature, all of these things have caught our eye ... Anonymous
> has therefore decided that your organization should be destroyed. For
> the good of your followers, for the good of mankind – for the laughs –
> we shall expel you ... and systematically dismantle Judaism in its
> present form. Your methods, hypocrisy, and the artlessness of your
> organization have sounded its death knell. You cannot hide; we are
> everywhere.

Are these the rantings of crazed neo-Nazis? No. Substitute "Jews" and
"Judaism" with "Scientologists" and "Church of Scientology" and you are
reading from a statement issued by a group of anti-Scientologists calling
themselves "Anonymous." This statement was released January 21, 2008
(read in a YouTube video in a Stephen Hawking-like computer voice). It
was followed by another on February 10, which coincided with demon-
strations at Scientology centers around the world at which protesters
donned masks (the Guy Fawkes variety from the movie *V for Vendetta*)
and waved posters that read, among other things, "Honk if you hate
Scientology."

Again, imagine if that sign read "Honk if you hate Jews." How innocuous would such a protest be in that case? And yet this latest turn against
the organization founded in 1954 by the former science fiction writer
L. Ron Hubbard has an air of farcical comedy to it. Why? Why aren't civil
rights organizations and anti-hate-speech activists pouncing on these
protesters? The reason, I suspect, is that most of us do not consider
Scientology a religion, at least not a religion that resembles in the
slightest the world's major faiths.

One clue to this interpretation can be seen in other protesters' signs:
"Religion is Free, Scientology is Not" and "Trade Secrets are for Business,
Not Religion." I'm a scientist who studies belief systems for a living, so
take it from me: Scientology is unlike any other religion in history. For
example, no other religion that I know of considers their theological

doctrines and core religious tenets to be intellectual property accessible only for a fee.

That is, in essence, how the Church of Scientology dispenses its theology, leading ex-members, critics, and journalists to divulge Scientology's sacred myth all over the Internet, in such national publications as the *New York Times* and *Rolling Stone* magazine, and even on the animated series *South Park*. As recounted earlier in this chapter (and bears repeating for proper context here), the story centers on Xenu the Galatic warlord, who seventy-five million years ago was in charge of seventy-six planets undergoing severe population pressures. Employing spaceships that resembled DC 9 planes, Xenu brought trillions of these alien beings to Earth (called Teegeeack) and placed them in select volcanoes. He then vaporized them with hydrogen bombs, scattering to the winds their souls, called Thetans, which were then rounded up in electronic traps and implanted with false ideas. These corrupted Thetans attach themselves to people today, leading to drug and alcohol abuse, addiction, depression, and other psychological and social ailments that only Scientology classes and "auditing" employing "e-meters" and numerous classes can cure. Paying customers, by the way, do not get to hear this story until they reach Operating Thetan Level III.

This peculiar story helps explain, in part, the often inexplicable Tom Cruise, whom we've all seen renouncing the evils of psychiatry and the drug industry on the *Today Show* and more recently in a viral YouTube video. There's nothing wrong with being skeptical of psychiatry – I publish *Skeptic* magazine that recently included an article by a psychiatrist who took his colleagues to task for overmedication and over-labeling as diseases what may just be unusual behavior. As well, self-help gurus such as Anthony Robbins have developed psychological techniques that may very well surpass psychiatry in helping people. But psychiatrists, drug companies, and motivation speakers pay taxes on their products and services and do not masquerade as religious leaders. This is yet another aspect of Scientology that provokes the type of animosity we are seeing in these recent attacks.

Humans are by nature tribal and xenophobic. We evolved a natural tendency to look askance at those who are different from us and, especially, to be suspicious of activities beyond our purview. Transparency and fairness are the key to trust, and trust is the social glue that binds a diverse society such as ours. This is why we insist on so many checks and balances in government, so many rules and regulations in markets, and equal treatment under the law. The reason people are suspicious of Scientology is because of its cult-like secrecy, its overly aggressive response to and legal attacks against critics, and especially the hypocrisy of comporting itself as a faux religion in a society willing to reward corporate success but not religious greed.

ORIGIN MYTHS OF RELIGIONS AND CULTS

In my November, 2011 column in *Scientific American*, titled "The Real Science Behind Scientology," I recounted the origin story of Xenu the Galatic warrior, concluding (with reference to the original 1950 publication of "Dianetics: A New Science of the Mind" by L. Ron Hubbard in the popular magazine *Astounding Science Fiction*):

> To be fair, Scientology's Xenu story is no more scientifically untenable than other faith's origin myths, and so if there is no testable means of determining which creation cosmogony is correct, then one might reasonably conclude that all religions are astounding science fictions.

It is with much interest, then, that my *Los Angeles Times* op-ed on Scientology (the second section of this chapter, "Scientology, Anonymous") generated a number of interesting responses published in that newspaper, including one by the UCLA historian of religions Jean E. Rosenfeld, who reproached me for concluding that Scientology is a cult and not a religion.[2] Her reasonable point is that all religions start out as cults, as the term is popularly employed today, but in fact they are better described as "new religious movements" (NRMs), and that the term "cult" is more appropriately used to describe "subgroups that express worship of a deity in a particular ritual, such as the cult of Mary that prays the rosary, or a cult of temple sacrifice that features a banquet." She asserts – in contradistinction of my own wording – that "a cult is not a 'faux religion.'"

Fine. I recognize the difference between scholarly and popular usages of language, and the difference between scholars who want to understand and activists who want to bring about change. (I vacillate between the two, at times, wanting to understand why people believe weird things and, at other times, wanting to talk them out of it, especially if the beliefs are harmful and dangerous.) But she then makes my point in my *Scientific American* column when she compares Scientology's origin myth with that of Christianity:

> All religions have origin myths, and all religions keep secrets from the uninitiated. If a nonbeliever were to tell the origin myth of Christianity, it would sound no less fantastic than the Thetan myth of L. Ron Hubbard: A spirit present as God before the creation of the universe splits off from Godhead after billions of years of Earth time and is born again as a flesh-and-blood person to a Jewish woman. The son gathers adherents, casts out demons from afflicted people, works miracles and finally confronts the evil king in the Jewish capital city. The evil empire's soldiers try, convict and kill him in a public execution. He then is resurrected before his disciples and tells them to spread his kingdom throughout the world. He promises to appear again and save those who believe in his message and condemn to eternal punishment those who do not. All of his followers will be resurrected after our Earth is destroyed by seven years of heaven-sent catastrophes that kill off most of the human race.

Rosenfeld then asks rhetorically: "Does this tale sound more convincing than Scientology's beliefs?" To which I reply, "No!"

But the point in distinguishing between religions and cults is not their ideas so much as what people *do* with those ideas – how they *act* on their beliefs – and after binge watching ex-Scientologist Leah Remini's A&E series *Scientology and the Aftermath*,[3] with its nonstop parade of victims of the organization's horrific treatment of them, including child labor, forced abortions, physical beatings, psychological torture, financial exploitation, and disconnection from families and loved ones – all of which the church denies in the teeth of overwhelming documentation in support of the victims' claims – I conclude that anyone who would join a Fair Play for Scientology Committee is either delusional or an academic historian who willingly and knowingly turns a blind eye to reality.

CHAPTER 10

Does the Universe Have a Purpose?

Alvy's Error and the Meaning of Life

PREAMBLE

This essay was originally published for the Templeton Foundation's Big Questions Online (BQO) program, "bringing before a wide public audience informative and accessible discussions by leading scholars who are working to address the Big Questions." I have, in fact, come at the question from different angles elsewhere, most forcefully in my 2018 book *Heavens on Earth*. It comes up a lot because it truly is one of life's Big Questions, and for too long theologians have had a monopoly on an answer. Unfortunately, many philosophers and scientists have punted on the question, preferring something along the lines of "the universe has no purpose – we have to create our own purposes" – which is true as far as it goes, but doesn't go far enough. One reason for the reticence of philosophers and scientists to speak out on the matter beyond this now-clichéd reply is that they fear being accused of the "naturalistic fallacy," or of bumping up against David Hume's Is-Ought wall (which I address in Chapter 20 in this volume). This is a red herring. We need not concede any ground to theists on this (or any other) question related to meaning, morals, and values, and to that end I append to this essay my February 2018 *Scientific American* column titled "Alvy's Error and the Meaning of Life," in which I come at the question from yet another perspective, this time demonstrating why theists' answer to the purpose question is not just misguided; it is wrong.

* * *

OVER THE PAST DECADE I HAVE PARTICIPATED IN SEVERAL debates over the question, *Does the Universe Have a Purpose?*, most recently in Puebla, Mexico in November, 2010 at the Ciudad de las Ideas

(City of Ideas) Conference, when Richard Dawkins, Matt Ridley, and I squared off (literally – in a boxing ring) against Rabbi David Wolpe and the theologians William Lane Craig and Douglas Geivett. The theists argued that without God the universe has no purpose, and they invested most of their time making the case for God's existence through standard apologetics arguments: the Big Bang had to have a first-cause which is God, the fine-tuning of the universe for stars, planets, and life could only have come about by God, the Intelligent Design of living organisms is only accountable for by an intelligent designer, the existence of consciousness is a product of the conscious agent who created the universe, and the moral sense of right and wrong could only have come from a moral law giver.

None of these arguments is relevant to the question because, I contend, whether there is a God or not, the universe per se cannot have a purpose in any anthropomorphic sense for which that term is usually employed. The universe is simply the collection of galaxies, stars, planets, comets, meteorites, and other solar system detritus, plus whatever dark matter and dark energy turn out to be. The universe is governed by laws of nature that themselves have no purpose other than dictating what matter and energy do. Stars, for example, convert hydrogen into helium, and they have no choice in the matter once they reach a certain size and temperature. Stars are not sitting around thinking "my purpose in life is to convert hydrogen into helium, so I better get on with it." Ditto everything else in the universe, including all living organisms, from *C. elegans* to *H. sapiens*.

Life began with the most basic purpose of all: survival and reproduction. For 3.5 billion years organisms have survived and reproduced in a lineal descent from the pre-Cambrian to us, an unbroken continuity that has endured countless terrestrial and extraterrestrial assaults and six mass extinctions. This fact alone ennobles us with a sense of cosmic purpose, but add to it the innumerable evolutionary steps from bacteria to big brains, and the countless points along the journey in which our lineage could have easily been erased, and we arrive at the conclusion that we are a glorious contingency in the history of life. As Charles Darwin wrote in the penultimate paragraph of his 1859 masterpiece *On the Origin of Species*, "When I view all beings not as special creations, but as the lineal descendants of some few beings which lived long before the first bed of the Silurian system was deposited, they seem to me to become ennobled."

Humans have an evolved sense of purpose – a psychological desire to accomplish a goal – that developed out of behaviors that were selected for because they were good for the individual or for the group. Although cultures may differ on what behaviors are defined as purposeful, the desire to behave in purposeful ways is an evolved trait. Purpose is in our nature. With brains big enough to discover and define purpose in symbolic ways inconceivable to billions of preceding and co-existing species, humans stand apart as genuinely unique in our attention to purposeful behavior. Evolution gave us a purpose-driven life.

How we define our purpose-driven lives may be personal, but there is an inherent structure to the human condition that helps delimit our search. Humans have evolved as a social primate species with a hierarchy of needs – depicted in Figure 10.1 – in which individuals belong to families, families to extended families, extended families to communities, communities to

Figure 10.1 Humans' hierarchy of needs.

societies, and most perceiving societies as part of the species, and the species as part of the biosphere.

At the bottom of the pyramid the individual's purposeful needs for survival and reproduction – food, drink, safety, and sex – are met through the family, extended family, and community. Moving up the pyramid, psycho-social needs – security, bonding, socialization, affiliation, acceptance, and affection – have evolved to aid and reinforce cooperation and altruism, traits that benefit both individuals and the group.

Selfish genes drive kin altruism (the propensity to help those who are genetically related to us), and social relations fuel reciprocal altruism (if you'll scratch my back, I'll scratch yours); but to achieve species- and bio-altruism, we need to learn higher-order pro-social behavior. Achieving the upper levels of the pyramid requires social and political action. We evolved in a manner in which our concern for the environment and biodiversity was restricted to a few tens of square kilometers, a couple of hundred of species, and a handful of decades. Global ecology and deep time were beyond anyone's conception until the past half-millennium, which is too short a time for evolution to fundamentally expand the range of our purposeful concerns. Higher purposes are learned and volitionally practiced.

What type of purpose should we practice? Although there are countless activities people engage in to feel purposeful, social scientists have discovered that there are a handful of powerful means by which we can bootstrap ourselves toward higher goals that have proven to be especially beneficial to both individuals and society. These include

1. *Deep love and family commitment* – the bonding and attachment to others increases one's circle of sentiments, and corresponding sense of purpose to care about others as much as, if not more than, oneself.
2. *Meaningful work and career* – the sense of purpose derived from discovering one's passion for work drives people to achieve goals so far beyond the needs of themselves that they lift all of us to a higher plane, either directly through the derivatives of the work itself or indirectly through inspiration and role modeling.
3. *Social and political involvement* – as a social species we have an obligation to community and society to participate in the process of determining how best we should live together.

4. *Transcendency and spirituality* – a capacity unique to our species that includes aesthetic appreciation, spiritual reflection, and transcendent contemplation through a variety of expressions such as art, music, dance, exercise, meditation, prayer, quiet contemplation, and religious reverie, connecting us on the deepest level with that which is outside of ourselves.

Evolution created in us a basic drive of purpose, but higher moral purposes are learned. To reach the highest levels of moral purpose that concern society, the species, and the biosphere, and especially with people who are not related to us, are not in our social group, or belong to other groups on other continents whom we shall never meet, requires volitional action and a social conscience. As one of the great consciousness raisers of the twentieth century, Helen Keller, wrote in a 1933 *Home Magazine* article entitled "The Simplest Way to be Happy":

I know no study that will take you nearer the way to happiness than the study of nature – and I include in the study of nature not only things and their forces, but also mankind and their ways, and the moulding of the affections and the will into an earnest desire not only to be happy, but to create happiness. It all comes to this: the simplest way to be happy is to do good.

In our debate in Mexico, I ended my talk by asking both the theists on the other side of the ring and the audience as a whole to try being an atheist for just an hour or two to see how it feels, and to ask themselves what would change if they stopped believing. Would you lose all purpose in life? Would you quit work? Would you stop being nice to other people? Would you cease loving your spouse, supporting your family, interacting with your extended family, contributing to your community, or participating in your society? Would you abandon all activities that lead to a sense of transcendency and spirituality? Of course not! Shouldn't we love our families, be nice to other people, and support our communities because those things are good in and of themselves? Of course!

Whether there is a God or not, all of these purposeful activities – and many more – stand as ends in themselves in the here-and-now, not as means to some other end in the hereafter. Purpose is not some prop on a momentary stage before an eternal tomorrow where its ultimate meaning will be revealed to us. Purpose is created by us through the courage of our convictions and the honor of our actions.

ALVY'S ERROR AND THE MEANING OF LIFE

In a flashback scene in the 1977 film *Annie Hall*, Woody Allen's character Alvy Singer is a depressed young boy who won't do his homework because, he explains to his doctor, "The universe is expanding. Well, the universe is everything and if it's expanding some day it will break apart and that will be the end of everything." His exasperated mother upbraids the youth, "What has the universe got to do with it?! You're here in Brooklyn. Brooklyn is not expanding!"

Call it *Alvy's Error: assessing the purpose of something at the wrong level of analysis.* The level at which we should assess our actions is the human timescale of days, weeks, months, and years – our three-score years + 10 lifespan – not the billions of years of the cosmic calendar. It is a mistake made by theologians when arguing that without a source external to our world to vouchsafe morality and meaning nothing really matters. One of the most prominent theologians of our time, William Lane Craig, committed Alvy's Error in a 2009 debate at Columbia University with the Yale philosopher Shelly Kagan when he pronounced:

> On a naturalistic worldview everything is ultimately destined to destruction in the heat-death of the universe. As the universe expands it grows colder and colder as its energy is used up. Eventually all the stars will burn out, all matter will collapse into dead stars and black holes, there will be no life, no heat, no light, only the corpses of dead stars and galaxies expanding into endless darkness. In light of that end it's hard for me to understand how our moral choices have any sort of significance. There's no moral accountability. The universe is neither better nor worse for what we do. Our moral lives become vacuous because they don't have that kind of cosmic significance.

Kagan properly nailed Craig, referencing the latter's example of godless Nazi torturers:

> This strikes me as an outrageous thing to suggest. *It doesn't really matter?* Surely it matters to the torture victims whether they're being tortured. It

doesn't require that this make some cosmic difference to the eternal significance of the universe for it to matter whether a human being is tortured. It matters to *them*, it matters to their *family*, and it matters to *us*.

Craig committed a related mistake when he argued that, "Without God there are no objective moral values, moral duties, or moral accountability." And "If life ends at the grave then ultimately it makes no difference whether you live as a Stalin or a Mother Teresa." Call this *Craig's Categorical Error: assessing the value of something by the wrong category of criteria.* In my 2018 book *Heavens on Earth: The Scientific Search for the Afterlife, Immortality, and Utopia,* I debunk this common belief that without God and the promise of an afterlife, this life has no morality or meaning. We live in the here-and-now, not the hereafter, so our actions must be judged according to the criteria of this category, whether or not the category of a God-granted hereafter exists. Whether you behave like a Russian dictator who murdered tens of millions of people, or a Roman Catholic missionary who tended to the poor, matters very much to the victims of totalitarianism and poverty.

Why does it matter? Because we are sentient beings designed by evolution to survive and flourish in the teeth of entropy and death. The Second Law of Thermodynamics (entropy) is the First Law of Life. If you do nothing, entropy will take its course and you will move toward a higher state of disorder that ends in death. So our most basic purpose in life is to combat entropy by doing something extropic – expending energy to survive and flourish. Being kind and helping others was one successful strategy and punishing Paleolithic Stalins was another, and from this we evolved morality. In this sense, evolution bestowed upon us a moral and purpose-driven life by dint of the laws of nature. We do not need any source higher than that to find meaning or morality.

In the long run entropy will spell the end of everything in the universe and the universe itself, but we don't live in the long run. We live now. We live in Brooklyn, so doing our homework matters. And so too does doing our duty to ourselves, our loved ones, our community, our species, and our planet.

CHAPTER 11

Why Is There Something Rather Than Nothing?

Answering the Biggest Question of Them All

PREAMBLE

This article grew out of my February 2017 *Scientific American* column titled "Imagine No Universe," eventually expanding into a feature-length cover story for *Skeptic*, necessarily an order of magnitude longer to nuance the many possible answers to the question. As readers will discover, far from a famine of scientific and philosophic answers to the question, we have a veritable feast to dine on. Which will turn out to be more or less supported by empirical research in both particle physics and cosmology remains to be seen – and it could be many decades to a century before we have a solid grasp of the problem – but do not succumb to the theists' transcendental temptation to evoke God as an answer in the teeth of so many elegant explanations already on our plate.

* * *

IN MY MANY DEBATES WITH THEISTS OVER THE DECADES, a handful of arguments for God's existence are routinely articulated as "proofs" of divine providence. These include the cosmological argument (that all natural things are contingent on something else for their existence so there necessarily exists a being independent of nature), the ontological argument (that we can conceive of an absolutely perfect being means it must exist because existence is a necessary feature of perfection), the design argument (the universe is fine-tuned for life, and life contains design features, therefore God is the fine-tuner and intelligent designer of life), the moral argument (without God anything goes, with God there is objective morality), the consciousness argument (the qualitative experience – qualia – of consciousness cannot be explained by the activity of neurons, and abstract concepts like logic and mathematics exist separate from brains, therefore God must be the source), and others.

All of these arguments (they are certainly not *proofs* in the mathematical sense) have counterarguments generated by philosophers over the centuries, but there is one that seems to trouble a great many thinkers of all persuasions, and that is why there should be anything at all. That is, all of the other arguments for God's existence presume that something exists that needs explaining. The argument that asks why there is something rather than nothing underlies all the other arguments and is cognitively challenging because it is simply not possible for existing beings to imagine not existing – not just themselves existing (which forms the cognitive foundation of afterlife beliefs), but to imagine nothing existing at all. Go ahead and try it. Picture nothing. When I ask myself this question, I start by visualizing dark empty space bereft of galaxies, stars, and planets, along with molecules and atoms. But this picture is incorrect because, if there were no universe, there would not only be no matter but there would be no space or time (or spacetime) either. There would be absolutely nothing, including no conscious being to observe the nothingness. Just ... nothing. Whatever that is.

This presents us with what is arguably the deepest of deep problems, the grandest of grand questions: *Why is there something rather than nothing?* In his 1988 blockbuster book *A Brief History of Time*, the late Cambridge theoretical physicist Stephen Hawking articulated the issue in his characteristically memorable manner:

> What is it that breathes fire into the equations and makes a universe for them to describe? The usual approach of science of constructing a mathematical model cannot answer the questions of why there should be a universe for the model to describe. Why does the universe go to all the bother of existing?[1]

Even if it could be established that something must exist, this does not necessarily mean that the something must be our universe with our particular laws of nature that give rise to atoms, stars, planets, and people. There could be universes whose laws of nature permit time and space but no matter or light; such universes could not be perceived because there would be no one to perceive the darkness.

Our universe has particular properties suited to planets and people. According to England's Astronomer Royal Sir Martin Rees, there are at least six constituents that are necessary for "our emergence from a simple Big Bang," including (1) Ω (omega), the amount of matter in the universe = 1: if Ω were greater than 1, it would have collapsed long ago, and, if Ω were less than 1, no galaxies would have formed. (2) ε (epsilon), how firmly atomic nuclei bind together = 0.007: if ε were even fractionally different, matter could not exist. (3) D, the number of dimensions in which we live = 3. (4) N, the ratio of the strength of electromagnetism to that of gravity = 10^{39}: if N were smaller, the universe would be either too young or too small for life to form. (5) Q, the fabric of the universe = $1/100,000$: if Q were smaller, the universe would be featureless, and, if Q were larger, the universe would be dominated by giant black holes. (6) λ (lambda), the cosmological constant, or "antigravity" force that is causing the universe to expand at an accelerating rate = 0.7: if λ were larger, it would have prevented stars and galaxies from forming.[2]

The most common reason invoked for our universe's "fine-tuning" is the "anthropic principle," most forcefully argued by the physicists John Barrow and Frank Tipler in their 1986 book *The Anthropic Cosmological Principle*:

> It is not only man that is adapted to the universe. The universe is adapted to man. Imagine a universe in which one or another of the fundamental dimensionless constants of physics is altered by a few percent one way or the other? Man could never come into being in such a universe. That is the central point of the anthropic principle. According to the principle, a life-giving factor lies at the center of the whole machinery and design of the world.[3]

So in addition to the grand question *Why is there something rather than nothing?*, we have a second question to answer: *Why this universe?* What follows is a number of responses, ranging from philosophical to scientific, that I have compiled from several sources, including a comprehensive taxonomic work by John Leslie and Robert Lawrence Kuhn titled *The*

Mystery of Existence: Why Is There Anything at All? that catalogues all extant explanations without religious, scientific, or philosophical prejudice.[4] It is a masterful compilation that anyone serious about the question should read.

EXPLANATIONS FOR NOTHING

NOTHING IS INCONCEIVABLE. First, as suggested above, it is impossible to conceptualize nothing – no space, time, matter, light, darkness, or even any conscious beings to perceive the nothingness. As Robert Kuhn conceives it: "Not just emptiness, not just blankness, and not just emptiness and blankness forever, but not even the existence of emptiness, not even the meaning of blankness, and no forever."[5] Inconceivable.

NOTHING IS SOMETHING. The analytical philosopher Quentin Smith pointed out to Kuhn that it is a logical fallacy to talk about "nothing" as if it were "something"; that is, to suggest that "there might have been nothing" implies "it is possible that there is nothing." As Kuhn articulates Smith's argument:

> "There is" means "something is." So "there is nothing" means "something is nothing," which is a logical contradiction. His suggestion is to remove "nothing" and replace it by "not something" or "not anything," since one can talk about what we mean by "nothing" by referring to *something* or *anything* of which there are no instances (i.e., the concept of "something" has the property of not being instantiated). The common sense way to talk about Nothing is to talk about something and negate it, to deny that there is something.[6]

Here we are bumping up against the problem of defining what we mean by "nothing" and the restrictions that language imposes on the problem. The very act of talking about "nothing" makes it a "something," or else what are we talking about?

NOTHING WOULD INCLUDE GOD'S NONEXISTENCE. In Kuhn's taxonomy of "nothings" he lists what *categories of things* might be included in "something" that would be negated by "nothing": physical, mental, Platonic, spiritual, and God. *Physical*: all matter, energy, space, and time, and all the laws and principles that govern them (known and unknown). *Mental*: all kinds of consciousness and awareness (known and unknown). *Platonic*: all forms of abstract objects (numbers, logic, forms, propositions, possibilities – known and unknown). *Spiritual and God*: anything that could possibly fit this nonphysical category (all forms of religious and spiritual belief).[7] If by "nothing" is meant no physical objects or matter of any kind, for example, there can still be energy from which matter may arise by natural forces guided by the laws of nature. Physicists, for example, talk about empty space as seething with virtual particles, from which particle–antiparticle pairs come into existence as a consequence of the uncertainty principle of quantum physics. From this "nothingness" universes may "pop" into existence.[8]

But if by "nothing" is meant that there is no physical, mental, Platonic, or nonphysical entity of any kind, then there can be no God or gods, which means that there cannot be anything outside of nothing out of which to create something. If God is proposed to be outside of or preexisting the "nothing" from which the "something" was created, then why can't the laws of nature that give rise to "somethings" (like universes) be outside of or preexisting nothing?

Some theologians argue that God is a "necessity," by which they mean it is impossible for God *not* to exist. This is the famous ontological argument for the existence of God, first proposed by St. Anselm of Canterbury in 1078, which defines God as "that than which nothing greater can be conceived." The argument is that God is necessary because necessity is a higher form of perfection that can be conceived than is contingency.[9] The argument has been refuted time and again. In his *Dialogues Concerning Natural Religion*, for example, the Scottish Enlightenment philosopher David Hume countered: "Nothing, that is distinctly conceivable, implies a contradiction. Whatever we conceive as existent, we can also conceive as non-existent. There is not being, therefore, whose non-existence implies a contradiction. Consequently there is no being, whose existence is demonstrable."[10]

To my ears this is all just word play, armchair speculation of what we can or cannot conceive of without once looking out the window to see what is actually in nature that may confirm or disconfirm our imaginary ideas.[11] I can just as easily argue that the laws of nature are a necessity for existence because they give rise to the universe, which makes them "that than which nothing greater can be conceived." Or that abstract objects like circles, squares, rectangles, and the geometric principles that govern them necessarily exist because the existence of a circle is a higher form of perfection than the nonexistence of a circle. If circles did not exist, then what would the formula for the area of a circle, $A = \pi r^2$, describe? In any case, the concept of "perfection" is once again bound by the cognitive restrictions of thought and language we faced with consciousness and nothingness. How can an imperfect being conceive of what perfection even means? Who knows what an extraterrestrial intelligence with a brain ten times the size of ours would be capable of conceiving or what a post-Singularity AI with an intelligence capacity a million times greater than humans would be able to conceptualize?

GOD DID IT EX NIHILO. For the many millennia that people have been asking these questions, the most common answer given was some version of "God did it": A creator existed before the universe and brought it into existence *ex nihilo – out of nothing*. Revealingly, Genesis does not actually say that God created the universe ex nihilo – that is a later inference made by theologians. Genesis 1:1 reads simply: "In the beginning God created the heavens and the earth." It does not elaborate on what God made the heavens and the earth *out of,* which theologians have presumed to be nothing. As *Skeptic* magazine religion editor Tim Callahan notes, the Hebrew word for creation in Genesis 1:1 is "bara," which can mean create but can also mean "choose" or "divide." Callahan cites the Old Testament scholar Ellen van Wolde, who argues that the most accurate translation of "bara" is "separate," so Genesis 1:1 should read "In the beginning God *separated* the heavens and the earth."[12] This, says Callahan, better fits the context of Genesis 1,

> in which the creation is presented as a series of separations: light is created and separated from darkness, the firmament of heaven is created to separate the waters above it from the waters below it, and the separation of land from water. This is followed by a series of creation events

populating the separated realms – the land populated with plants, the firmament populated with heavenly bodies, the sea populated with fish and sea monsters, the air with birds, and the land, again, with animals – followed finally by the creation of humans in the image of God.[13]

Even if one rejects this interpretation of Genesis 1:1 and opts for creation *ex nihilo*, this just begs the question of who or what created the creator? Theists retort that God is that which does not need to be created. But why can't the universe be in the same ontological and epistemological category as God, wherein we could simply say that the universe is that which does not need to be created? Theists counter that the universe had a Big Bang beginning and everything that begins to exist has a cause. But not everything in the universe is strictly causal, such as some quantum effects, and even though our universe in its current state can be traced back to a Big Bang beginning, that doesn't mean there was not a previous universe that gave birth to our universe through the Big Bang.

Theists also note that that the universe is a thing, whereas God is an agent or being. But don't things and beings all need a causal explanation? Why should God be exempt from such causal reasoning? Because, rejoins the theist, God is *supe*rnatural – outside of space, time, and matter – whereas everything in the universe, and the universe itself, is *natural* – made up of space and time, matter and energy – so God and the universe are ontologically different. But if that is so, then how would we detect God with our instruments? If a *supernatural* deity used *natural* forces to, say, cure someone's cancer by reprogramming the cancerous cells' DNA, wouldn't that make God nothing more than a highly skilled genetic engineer along the lines of a sufficiently advanced ETI or far-future human? And if God used unknown *supernatural* forces to effect change in our *natural* world, how do they interact with the known forces of our universe? And if such supernatural forces could somehow stir the particles in our universe, shouldn't we be able to detect them and thereby incorporate them into our theories about the natural world? If so, wouldn't that bring God into the universe as a natural being and thus subject him to the search for a natural causal explanation for his existence? Finally, if God made the universe *ex nihilo* – literally out of *nothing* – then apparently it *is* possible for something to come from nothing, so this brings us back to searching for the best causal explanation for anything: natural or supernatural.

NATURAL V. SUPERNATURAL EXPLANATIONS OF SOMETHING.
The history of science has been one long and steady replacement of the supernatural with the natural. Weather events once attributed to the supernatural scheming of deities are now understood to be the product of natural forces of temperature and pressure. Plagues formerly ascribed to women cavorting with the devil are today known to be caused by bacteria and viruses. Mental illnesses previously imputed to demonic possession are currently sought in genes and neurochemistry. Accidents heretofore explained by fate, karma, or providence are nowadays accredited to probabilities, statistics, and risk. If we follow this trend to encompass all phenomena, what place is there for supernatural agents like gods and demons? Do we know enough to know that they cannot exist? Or is it possible there are unknown forces within our universe, or intentional agents outside of it, that we have yet to discover? According to the Caltech physicist Sean Carroll, in his 2016 book *The Big Picture: On the Origins of Life, Meaning, and the Universe Itself,* "All of the things you've ever seen or experienced in your life – objects, plants, animals, people – are made of a small number of particles, interacting with one another through a small number of forces."[14] Once you understand the fundamental laws of nature, such as the thermodynamic arrow of time and the Core Theory of particles and forces, you can scale up to planets and people, and even assess the likelihood that God, the soul, and the afterlife exist, which Carroll concludes is very low.

But isn't the history of science also strewn with the remains of failed theories like geocentrism (the Earth is the center of the solar system), phlogiston (a fire-like element that causes objects to burn), miasma (the "bad air" source of disease), spontaneous generation (fully formed living organisms can abruptly arise out of inanimate matter), and the luminiferous ether (the medium filling outer space for the propagation of light)? Yes, and that's how we know we're making progress. The postmodern belief that discarded ideas means that there is no objective reality and that all theories are equal is wronger than all of the wrong theories combined. I have called this *Asimov's Axiom*, after an observation by the science writer Isaac Asimov:

> When people thought the earth was flat, they were wrong. When people thought the earth was spherical, they were wrong. But if you think that thinking the earth is spherical is just as wrong as thinking the earth is flat, then your view is wronger than both of them put together.[15]

There is real progress in science. Think of it as an expanding sphere of knowledge. As the sphere of the known expands into the ether of the unknown, the proportion of ignorance seems to grow – the more you know, the more you know how much you don't know. But in this mathematical analogy, note what happens when the radius of a sphere increases: The expansion of the surface area is squared while the increase in the volume is cubed. So as the sphere of scientific knowledge expands, the volume of the known increases geometrically over the surface area of ignorance and the unknown. (The ratio of volume to area of a sphere scales as the radius to the three-halves power.) The more you know, the more of the unknown becomes known. It is at this boundary where we can stake a claim of true progress in the history of science.

Take the Core Theory of the forces and particles that make up the universe. This includes the four forces of gravity, electromagnetism, and the strong and weak nuclear forces, along with the Standard Model of elementary particles making up the nucleus of the atom: quarks, leptons, and bosons, plus the underlying Higgs boson. Carroll says this Core Theory is "indisputably accurate within a very wide domain of applicability," such that "a thousand or a million years from now, whatever amazing discoveries science will have made, our descendants are not going to be saying 'Ha-ha, those silly twenty-first-century scientists, believing in "neutrons" and "electromagnetism"'." Thus, Carroll concludes that the laws of physics rule out supernatural and paranormal claims. Why? Because the particles and forces of nature don't allow us to bend spoons, levitate, read minds, or perform miracles, and "we know that there aren't new particles or forces out there yet to be discovered that would support them. Not simply because we haven't found them yet, but because we definitely would have found them if they had the right characteristics to give us the requisite powers."[16]

It is at the horizon where the known meets the unknown that we are tempted to inject supernatural forces to explain hitherto unsolved mysteries, but we must resist the temptation, for such efforts can never succeed, not even in principle. Humans have always filled in such gaps in our knowledge with gods, and it never leads to any useful or productive theory. Let us try to overcome this psychological propensity to fill in the gaps with supernatural forces and follow the path of science in searching for natural forces.

NOTHING IS UNSTABLE, SOMETHING IS STABLE. Asking why there is something rather than nothing presumes "nothing" is the natural state of things out of which "something" needs an explanation. Maybe "something" is the natural state of things and "nothing" would be the mystery to be solved. As the physicist Victor Stenger notes in his 2011 book, *The Fallacy of Fine Tuning*, "Current cosmology suggests that no laws of physics were violated in bringing the universe into existence. The laws of physics themselves are shown to correspond to what one would expect if the universe appeared from nothing. There is something rather than nothing because something is more stable."[17]

In his 2012 book, *A Universe from Nothing*, the cosmologist Lawrence Krauss attempts to link quantum physics to Einstein's gravitational theory of general relativity to explain the origin of something (including a universe) from nothing: "In quantum gravity, universes can, and indeed always will, spontaneously appear from nothing. Such universes need not be empty, but can have matter and [electromagnetic] radiation in them, as long as the total energy, including the negative energy associated with gravity [balancing the positive energy of matter], is zero." And: "In order for the closed universes that might be created through such mechanisms to last for longer than infinitesimal times, something like inflation is necessary." Observations have revealed that, in fact, the universe is flat (there is just enough matter to eventually halt its expansion), its energy is zero, and it underwent rapid inflation, or expansion, shortly after the Big Bang as described by inflationary cosmology. Thus, Krauss concludes, "quantum gravity not only appears to allow universes to be created from nothing – meaning ... the absence of space and time – it may require them. 'Nothing' – in this case no space, no time, no anything! – *is* unstable."[18]

In his follow-up 2017 work, *The Greatest Story Ever Told – So Far*, Krauss notes that "Einstein was one of the first physicists to demonstrate that the classical notion of causation begins to break down at the quantum realm." Although many physicists objected to the idea of something coming from nothing, Krauss adds that "this is precisely what happens with the light you are using to read this page. Electrons in hot atoms emit photons – photons that didn't exist before they were emitted – which are emitted spontaneously and without specific cause. Why is it that we have grown at least somewhat comfortable with the idea that photons can be created from nothing without cause, but not whole universes?"[19]

EXPLANATIONS FOR OUR UNIVERSE

The anthropic principle invoked to explain our universe troubles most scientists because of its antithesis known as the "Copernican principle," which states that we are not special. The anthropic principle puts humans right back in the center of the cosmos, not geographically but anthropocentrically – it is all about *us*. There are a number of counterexplanations for our universe that continue in the scientific tradition of defenestrating humans from the Tower of Babel.

INCONSTANT CONSTANTS. The various numbers invoked in the "fine-tuning" argument for our universe being special, such as the speed of light and Planck's constant, are, in fact, arbitrary numbers that can be configured in different ways so that their relationship to the other constants do not appear to be so remarkable. As well, such constants may be *inconstant* over vast spans of time, varying from the Big Bang to the present, making the universe finely tuned only now but not earlier or later in its history. The physicists John Barrow and John Webb call these numbers the "inconstant constants," and they have demonstrated how in particular the speed of light, gravitation, and the mass of the electron have in fact been inconstant over time.[20]

GRAND UNIFIED THEORY. In order to explain our universe, we need a comprehensive theory of physics that connects the subatomic world described by quantum mechanics to the cosmic world described by general relativity. As the cosmologist Sean Carroll notes in his 2010 book *From Eternity to Here*:

> Possibly general relativity is not the correct theory of gravity, at least in the context of the extremely early universe. Most physicists suspect that a quantum theory of gravity, reconciling the framework of quantum mechanics with Einstein's ideas about curved spacetime, will ultimately be required to make sense of what happens at the very earliest times. So if someone asks you what really happened at the moment of the purported Big Bang, the only honest answer would be: "I don't know."[21]

That grand unified theory of everything will itself need an explanation, but it may be explicable by some other theory we have yet to comprehend out of our sheer ignorance at this moment in history. And as I repeat *ad nauseum* to audiences curious about unsolved mysteries and anxious to fill in scientific gaps with questionable pseudoscientific conjectures, it's always okay to say, "I don't know" and leave it at that.

BOOM-AND-BUST CYCLES. Perhaps our bubble universe is just one episode of an eternal boom-and-bust cycle of expansion and contractions of the universe, with the bubble's eventual collapse and re-expansion in an eternal cycle. Sean Carroll argues "that space and time did exist before the Big Bang; what we call the Bang is a kind of transition from one phase to another." As such, he says, "there is no such thing as an initial state, because time is eternal. In this case, we are imagining that the Big Bang isn't the beginning of the entire universe, although it's obviously an important event in the history of our local region."[22] Although there does not appear to be enough matter in our universe to halt the expansion and bring it back into a big crunch that could launch it back into a new bubble out of another Big Bang, the relevant observation here is that something existed before the Big Bang, thereby obviating the need to invoke a supernatural creator.[23]

DARWINIAN UNIVERSES. According to the cosmologist Lee Smolin, the evolution of the universe may include a Darwinian component in the form of a "natural selection" of differentially reproducing bubble universes. Like its biological counterpart, Smolin's hypothesis is that there might be a selection from different "species" of universes, each containing different laws of nature. Universes like ours will have lots of stars, which means they will have lots of black holes that collapse into singularities, a point at which infinitely strong gravity causes matter to have infinite density and zero volume, which many cosmologists believe gave birth to our universe from the Big Bang singularity. Perhaps collapsing black holes create new baby universes out of these singularities, and those baby universes with laws of nature similar to ours will be fine-tuned to life, whereas universes with radically different laws of nature that disallow stars, planets, and people will go extinct. The result of this cosmic evolutionary process would be a preponderance of universes like ours, so we should not be surprised to find ourselves in a universe fine-tuned for life.[24]

MULTIPLE CREATIONS COSMOLOGY. In his 1997 book *The Inflationary Universe*, the cosmologist Alan Guth proposes that our universe sprang into existence from a bubble nucleation of spacetime. If this process of universe creation is natural, then there may be multiple bubble nucleations that give rise to many universes that expand but remain separate from one another without any causal contact between them. Of course, if these universes were truly causally disconnected, then there is no way to get information from them, which would make this an untestable hypothesis.[25] But, again, there is much we still don't know about the cosmos, and I am encouraged by the startling discovery of gravitational waves, which could open up possibilities of obtaining information from other bubble universes, if they exist.

MANY-WORLDS MULTIVERSE. According to the "many worlds" interpretation of quantum mechanics, there are an infinite number of universes in which every possible outcome of every possible choice that has ever been available, or will be available, has happened in one of those universes. This model is grounded in the bizarre findings of the famous "double-slit" experiment, in which light is passed through two slits and forms an interference pattern of waves on a back surface (like throwing two stones in a pond and watching the concentric wave patterns interact, with crests and troughs adding and subtracting from one another). The spooky part comes when you send single photons of light one at a time through the two slits – they still form an interference wave pattern even though they are not interacting with other photons. How can this be? One answer is that the photons are interacting with photons in other universes! In this type of *multiverse*, you could meet your doppelganger, and, depending on which universe you entered, your parallel self would be fairly similar or dissimilar to you, a theme that has become a staple of science fiction (see, for example, Michael Crichton's *Timeline*). I am skeptical that this version of the *multiverse* will pan out, however, because the idea of there being multiple versions of me and you out there – and in an infinite universe there would be an infinite number of me and you – seems to me to be even less likely than the theistic alternative "God did it." Still, as Richard Feynman famously quipped, "no one understands quantum mechanics,"[26] so who am I to write off this theory considered legitimate by many quantum physicists?

BRANE AND STRING UNIVERSES. Universes may be birthed when three-dimensional "branes" (a membrane-like structure on which our universe exists) moves through higher-dimensional space and collides with another brane, the result of which is the energized creation of another universe.[27] A related multiverse is derived through string theory, which by at least one calculation allows for 10^{500} possible worlds, all with different self-consistent laws and constants.[28] That's a 1 followed by 500 zeros possible universes. The number is so large that it would be miraculous if there were not intelligent life in a number of them. In his 2008 book *God: The Failed Hypothesis*, the late physicist Victor Stenger created a computer model that analyzes what just 100 different universes would be like under constants different from our own, ranging from five orders of magnitude above to five orders of magnitude below their values in our universe. Stenger found that long-lived stars of at least one billion years – necessary for the production of life-giving heavy elements – would emerge within a wide range of parameters in at least half of the universes in his model.[29]

QUANTUM FOAM UNIVERSE CREATIONS. In this model, universes are created out of nothing, but in the scientific version of *ex nihilo* the nothing of the vacuum of space actually contains quantum foam, which may fluctuate to create baby universes. In this configuration, any quantum object in any quantum state may generate a new universe, each one of which represents every possible state of every possible object.[30] This is Stephen Hawking's explanation for the fine-tuning problem that he himself famously presented in the 1990s:

> Why is the universe so close to the dividing line between collapsing again and expanding indefinitely? In order to be as close as we are now, the rate of expansion early on had to be chosen fantastically accurately. If the rate of expansion one second after the big bang had been less by one part in 10^{10}, the universe would have collapsed after a few million years. If it had been greater by one part in 10^{10}, the universe would have been essentially empty after a few million years. In neither case would it have lasted long enough for life to develop. Thus one either has to appeal to the anthropic principle or find some physical explanation of why the universe is the way it is.[31]

Hawking's collaborator Roger Penrose layered on even more mystery when he noted that the "extraordinary degree of precision (or 'fine tuning') that seems to be required for the Big Bang of the nature that we appear to observe . . . is one part in $10^{10^{123}}$ at least." Penrose suggested two pathways to an answer, either it was an act of God, "or we might seek some scientific/mathematical theory."[32] Hawking opted for the second, with this explanation: "Quantum fluctuations lead to the spontaneous creation of tiny universes, out of nothing. Most of the universes collapse to nothing, but a few that reach a critical size, will expand in an inflationary manner, and will form galaxies and stars, and maybe beings like us."[33]

M-THEORY GRAND DESIGN, OR AUTO-EX-NIHILO. Stephen Hawking continued working on this question, and he and the physicist Leonard Mlodinow presented their answer in their 2010 book *The Grand*

Design.[34] They approach the problem from what they call "model-dependent realism," based on the assumption that our brains form models of the world from sensory input, that we use the model most successful at explaining events, and that when more than one model makes accurate predictions "we are free to use whichever model is most convenient." Employing this method, they write, "it is pointless to ask whether a model is real, only whether it agrees with observation." The dual wave/particle models of light are an example of model-dependent realism, where each one agrees with certain observations but neither one is sufficient to explain all observations. To model the entire universe, Hawking and Mlodinow employ "M-Theory," an extension of string theory that includes eleven dimensions and incorporates all five current string theory models. "M-theory is the most general supersymmetric theory of gravity," Hawking and Mlodinow explain. "For these reasons M-theory is the only candidate for a complete theory of the universe. If it is finite – and this has yet to be proved – it will be a model of a universe that creates itself." Although they admit that the theory has yet to be confirmed by observation, if it is, then no creator explanation is necessary because the universe creates itself. Call it *auto-ex-nihilo.*

A SENSE OF AWE OUT OF NOTHING

By no means does this list exhaust the possible explanations for why there is something rather than nothing and why our universe is the way it is, but it perhaps gives one a sense that the questions are answerable through science, through natural and testable hypotheses and theories, without resort to supernatural intercession. It is good to reflect on the fact that the history of science is relatively young compared to the history of religion – roughly 500 v. 5,000 years – so it is premature to say that because science does not yet have a definitive explanatory theory accepted by most scientists, it means that one is not forthcoming. Despite the optimism derived from my expanding sphere of knowledge metaphor in which the known expands into the unknown at a geometric or exponential rate, there is still much we do not understand about the cosmos and everything in it. But given science's track record over the past five centuries, this only means there are remarkable and exciting new discoveries and theories yet to come. As Carl Sagan expressed it in his 1985 Gifford Lecture Series titled *The Search for Who We Are* (published in book form posthumously in 2007 as *The Varieties of Scientific Experience*):

> By far the best way I know to engage the religious sensibility, the sense of awe, is to look up on a clear night. I believe that it is very difficult to know who we are until we understand where and when we are. I think everyone in every culture has felt a sense of awe and wonder looking at the sky. This is reflected throughout the world in both science and religion.[35]

PART III

DEFERRED DREAMS: REFLECTIONS ON POLITICS AND SOCIETY

CHAPTER 12

Another Dream Deferred

How Identity Politics, Intersectionality Theory, and Tribal Divisiveness Are Inverting Martin Luther King, Jr.'s Dream

PREAMBLE

In 2017/2018 there rose to cultural prominence an electronic magazine of extraordinary vision called *Quillette* (Quillette.com, @Quillete), founded by the equally visionary Claire Lehmann (@clairlemon), who curated into publication articles on topics almost no one else would touch, such as gender differences in cognition and career preference, sexual harassment and the #metoo/#timesup movement, income inequality, race and IQ, evolutionary psychology and human nature, human violence and its causes, social justice, intersectionality theory, and especially identity politics. Claire's magazine has skyrocketed in online readership and with it crowd-funded financial support (www.patreon.com/Quillette) to enable her to hire top-notch editors like Jonathan Kay and regular contributors such as Coleman Hughes, Toby Young, and Clay Routledge. I was, therefore, pleased and honored to compose this essay and the one that follows for *Quillette*, on topics that are outside my normal wheelhouse of science and skepticism and beyond the scope of my regular publishing venues of *Scientific American* and *Skeptic*. That Claire and her team have stepped in to fill a void in mainstream media, and that they have done so with both literary and financial success, gives me hope that, in an age of fake news and alternative facts, real news and verifiable facts are not only protected (as in "protected speech") but welcomed by a great many readers.

* * *

I have a dream that my four little children will one day live in a nation where they will not be judged by the color of their skin but by the content of their character.

W HEN DR. MARTIN LUTHER KING, JR. DELIVERED WHAT, IN the fullness of time, would become his most memorable vision from his 1963 magisterial "I Have a Dream" speech, he could not have known how much progress in civil rights would ensue over the coming half-century, in no small measure because of his work.

Human progress in general, and moral advancement in particular, have been documented in detail in a number of recent books, including Hans Rosling's *Factfulness* (2018, Flatiron Books), Yuval Noah Harari's *21 Lessons for the 21st Century* (2018, Spiegel & Grau), Steven Pinker's *Enlightenment Now* (2018, Penguin) and *The Better Angels of Our Nature* (2011, Penguin), Greg Easterbrook's *It's Better Than it Looks* (2018, PublicAffairs), Johan Norberg's *Progress* (2017, OneWorld), my own *The Moral Arc* (2015, Henry Holt), and Matt Ridley's *The Rational Optimist* (2010, HarperCollins). Regular updates on humanity's development are provided with copious data on such sites as HumanProgress.org by Marian Tupey and OurWorldinData.org by Max Roser, aggregated with statistics from the World Bank, the UN, OECD, Eurostat, and other sources. There has never been another time in history when it has been better to be alive than today, including and especially for people of color, women, and minorities of any type. Ever since the two major rights revolutions of the late eighteenth and mid-twentieth centuries, the moral sphere has been expanding to encompass all of humanity – a "brotherhood of man" in the parlance of the 1960s' pre-feminist influence on gendered language. Fifty-five years on we should be celebrating the instantiation of Dr. King's visage:

I have a dream that one day this nation will rise up, live out the true meaning of its creed: "We hold these truths to be self-evident, that all men are created equal." I have a dream that one day on the red hills of Georgia sons of former slaves and the sons of former slave-owners will be able to sit down together at the table of brotherhood.

Lamentably, the past decade has witnessed what appears to be a reversal of Dr. King's dream in the form of identity politics, or the collectivization of individuals into groups competing for status and power and perceived persecution by privileged identities. In Dr. King's time, race was the primary political power dimension. Since the 1960s, identity politics has expanded to include not only race but gender identity, sexual orientation, class, religion, ethnicity, language, dialect, education, generation, occupation, political party, disability, marital status, veteran status, and more, all competing for political power in the public sphere.

Added to this new instantiation of ancient tribalism is intersectionality theory, in which membership in multiple intersecting identity groups brings more or less power, more or less persecution. Thus, for example, the historical subjugation of blacks by whites is measured along a single axis of race, while the oppression of women by men is assessed along a single axis of gender; that black women have different experiences than black men or white women can be traced along two intersecting axes of race and gender; a nonwhite transgender lower-class disabled Muslim woman faces a world different from that of a white cisgender upper-class able-bodied Christian man along these multiple intersecting axes, of which there are more than a dozen, including:

White–Non-White, Male–Female, Light–Dark, Cisgender–Transgender, Heterosexual–Homosexual, Gender-typical–Deviant, Young–Old, European–Non-European, Anglophone–English as Second Language, Gentile–Jews, Rich–Poor, Fertile–Infertile, Able-bodied–Disabled, Credentialed–Nonliterate.

As philosopher Kathryn Pauly Morgan explained intersectionality, each of us may be identified and judged on where we fall "on each of these axes (at a minimum) and that this point is simultaneously a locus of our agency, power, disempowerment, oppression, and resistance." The Chicana feminist activist Elizabeth Martinez worried what such hierarchical assessments might lead to: "There are various forms of working together. A coalition is one, a network is another, an alliance is yet another. But the general idea is no competition of hierarchies should prevail. No Oppression Olympics."

Unfortunately, as detailed in three new books, *Suicide of the West* by Jonah Goldberg (2018, Crown), *The Diversity Delusion* by Heather Mac Donald (2018, St. Martin's Press), and *The Coddling of the American Mind* by Greg Lukianoff and Jonathan Haidt (2018, Penguin), the Oppression Olympics are well past their opening ceremonies in colleges, corporations, and Congress, tearing institutions asunder as conflicting cohorts vie for who has suffered the most historical inequities. It is also known as "competitive victimhood," and it has resulted in a race to the bottom through what Lukianoff and Haidt call "The Untruth of Us Versus Them: *Life is a battle between good people and evil people.*" They write, "As a result of our long evolution for tribal competition, the human mind readily does dichotomous, us-versus-them thinking. If we want to create welcoming, inclusive communities, we should be doing everything we can to turn down the tribalism and turn up the sense of common humanity."

That historical injustices were degrading, destructive, and deadly none of these authors (including me) denies, and even the most optimistic of us acknowledges that prejudices and disparities still exist, as poignantly highlighted by the #blacklivesmatter and #metoo movements. Racism and misogyny, while in historical decline, may still be found in too many places in our society, as nightly news stories (with dramatic body-camera footage) show black citizens being shot by white cops, or powerful males being perp-walked in the media before the testimonies of women they sexually harassed. Inequalities still abound in too many institutions of Western democracies, but these realities should not be mistaken as trendlines in reverse, as if we are lurching backward to the disenfranchisement of women or a return to weekly lynchings of blacks. Once civil rights and liberties are achieved, the people now enjoying them are disinclined to give them back, despite the racist rhetoric of a handful of tiki-torch wielding Alt-Right kooks or the misogynistic mumblings of elderly rat-packers.

Among its many elements, Dr. King's dream included his faith that one day "we will be able to transform the jangling discords of our nation into a beautiful symphony of brotherhood." Within our culture in general, and on social media and talk radio and television in particular, the jangling discords of identity politics are said to be pulling us into another civil war, this one cultural instead of martial. With discordance arising from these many identities competing for power and influence that have brought out the worse demons of our nature, it is prudent to recall the dream of a civil rights crusader from an earlier century – Abraham

Lincoln – as his country was on the eve of a real civil war over the enslavement of millions of people, who wanted nothing more than to be treated equally as fully human with the same rights and privileges as those enslaving them. Speaking to the southerners who had already seceded from the union and formed the Confederate States of America, the Great Emancipator implored:

> We are not enemies, but friends. We must not be enemies. Though passion may have strained it must not break our bonds of affection. The mystic chords of memory, stretching from every battlefield and patriot grave to every living heart and hearthstone all over this broad land, will yet swell the chorus of the Union, when again touched, as surely they will be, by the better angels of our nature.

Today's cultural civil war is not remotely comparable to the one that killed over half a million Americans, but the division of people into such aggregate identities is a perverse inversion of Dr. King's dream, now deferred by these movements for identity politics and intersectionality theory, however well-intentioned their practitioners. My lament is echoed by the African American jazz poet Langston Hughes in his 1951 poem "Harlem," when he asked, "What happens to a dream deferred?", which he answered in a series of rhetorical questions, most famously: "Does it dry up / like a raisin in the sun?"

Let us not allow Dr. King's noble dream of judging others by the content of their character alone to wither on the vine under the collectivist drought brought on by these politically intersecting tribal identities, which we must shed if we are to return to the moral path leading to a unifying humanity.

CHAPTER 13

Healing the Bonds of Affection

The Case for Classical Liberalism

PREAMBLE

When I was an undergraduate at Pepperdine University in the 1970s, everyone was reading a cinderblock of a book called *Atlas Shrugged*, penned by the novelist-philosopher Ayn Rand, with whom I was unfamiliar. Its size was so intimidating that I begged off reading it until my friends cajoled me to just get through the first hundred pages after which, they assured me, plot momentum would carry me through to the end. It did, and for a time I was enamored with Rand's philosophy of Objectivism, based on four fundamental principles: 1. Metaphysics: Objective Reality; 2. Epistemology: Reason; 3. Ethics: Self-interest; 4. Politics: Capitalism. In my 1997 book, *Why People Believe Weird Things*, I devoted a chapter to the cult-like following that developed around Rand and her philosophy (I called it "The Unlikeliest Cult in History"), in an attempt to show that extremism of any kind, even the sort that the eschews cultish behavior, can become irrational. And although I now disagree with her theory of human nature and her ethics of self-interest (science shows that in addition to being selfish, competitive, and greedy, we also harbor a great capacity for altruism, cooperation, and charity), reading Rand led me to the extensive body of literature on politics and economics.

I do not know if it was the practical outcomes of fiscal conservatism and free market economics that convinced me of their value or if it was my temperament that reverberated so well with this worldview. As it is for most belief systems we hold, it was probably a combination of both, inasmuch as I was raised by parents who could best be described as fiscally conservative and socially liberal, who themselves were raised during the Depression and were motivated by the fear of falling back into abject poverty. Throughout my childhood I was inculcated with the fundamental principles of economic conservatism: hard work, personal responsibility, self-determination, financial autonomy, small government, and free markets. Even though they were not in the least religious (as so many conservatives are today), my parents were exceedingly generous to those who were less fortunate. Thus, when asked as an adult what my politics are, I have called myself a libertarian, that is, someone who is socially liberal and fiscally conservative.

Like most liberals, I am pro-choice and fully support women's reproductive and economic rights; I am in favor of free speech and free thought; I believe in the separation of church and state and am against prayer in school; I believe in liberal democracy and voters' rights; I believe in some gun-control measures; I support environmental protection laws and agree that global warming is real, human-caused, and something we should work toward mitigating; I work toward reducing animal suffering and expanding animal rights; I think that we need judicial reform because of our broken criminal justice system that incarcerates far too many people for victimless crimes; I think we should legalize all drugs and regulate them like tobacco and alcohol; I believe we have a moral obligation to help those who cannot help themselves; and, of course, I hold that science is the best tool ever devised for understanding the world and changing it for the better.

Like most conservatives, I believe in limited and accountable government, along with low taxes, low spending, and a balanced budget; I believe in the Constitution and the rule of law along with our system of constitutional republicanism with checks and balances to prevent power from accruing to any one person or agency; I believe in property rights, and that one of the primary functions of government is to protect our rights; I believe in individual liberty, personal responsibility, and the philosophy of individualism in contrast with collectivism and identity politics; I contend that free trade and free markets are by far and away the best economic system for wealth production and lifting people out of poverty; I believe that there are objective moral values that apply to most people in most places most of the time (although I do not believe they were derived from God); and I reject moral relativism in all its forms.

When I was writing *The Moral Arc*, I found my libertarianism challenged on so many fronts that I began to reconsider my politics and look for a new label, one that better described what I came to believe was the right balance between Left and Right, between liberalism and conservatism. I believe I may have found it in classical liberalism, a defense of which follows in this essay, originally published in the online magazine *Quillette.*

* * *

A party of order or stability, and a party of progress or reform, are both necessary elements of a healthy state of political life.

John Stuart Mill, *On Liberty*, 1859

O N THE DAY I PENNED THE INTRODUCTION TO THIS ARTICLE (April 18, 2018), Starbucks announced that they would close more than 8,000 of their retail stores for part of a day so that their 175,000 employees could undergo bias sensitivity training for the "implicit racism" that, apparently, everyone in the company unconsciously harbors. This was the result of the action of a single store manager in Philadelphia named Holly, who called the police when two African American men wanted to use the bathroom but were not paying customers. Setting aside the contentious issue of measuring (much less correcting in half a day) unconscious bias, which I and others have been skeptical of,[1] that the unconscious motives of an entire corporate collective can be inferred by the actions of one individual reveals another form of bigotry lurking beneath our cultural commitment to individual freedom, this time inverting the direction of prejudice from the one to the many.[2]

In an unrelated incident but one indicative of the problem in reverse, earlier this year, students at the top-rated liberal arts Reed College in Oregon protested Humanities 110, a foundational course in the college curriculum which, in the words of a Reed professor, "seeks to introduce students in a systematic way to the various disciplines – history, literature, philosophy, aesthetics, social sciences – of which the liberal arts are composed." The problem, according to Reedies Against Racism (RAR), is that the course "is Eurocentric at its core," so RARers barged into the classroom and stood at the front with placards condemning, in the words of another professor, "the course and its faculty as white supremacists, as anti-black, as not open to dialogue and criticism, on the grounds that we continue to teach, among many other things, Aristotle and Plato."[3] That Aristotle, Plato, Shakespeare, and others are white is – or certainly ought to be – irrelevant to the assessment of their ideas, especially at an institution whose self-proclaimed liberal (and even progressive) students and faculty surely endorse the moral principle articulated by Dr. Martin Luther King, Jr. that people should be judged not by the color of their skin but by the content of their character.[4]

These are just two among hundreds of incidents that have erupted over the past few years as our society, in parallel with our politics, grows ever more divided over incidents readily identifiable in short tags: BLM, BDM, MSM, LGBTQI, SJW, #metoo, #TakeAKnee, Dreamers, Google Memo, Milo, Charlottesville, Evergreen, Berkeley, Yale, Middlebury, Parkland, Sandy Hook, fake news, alternative facts, microaggressions, safe spaces, no platforming, hate speech, etc.[5] And the accusatory labels hurled back and forth across the political divide have been shifting ever outward from the center. The Left, the Far Left, the Regressive Left, the Authoritarian Left, the Alt-Left. These are just some of the labels slapped on liberals by conservatives on the Right, the Far Right, the Radical Right, the Authoritarian Right, and the Alt-Right.[6]

Such cultural labeling and political epithet smearing brings to mind George Orwell's classic 1946 essay *Politics and the English Language*, in which the noted journalist and critic observed, "Political language – and with variations this is true of all political parties, from Conservatives to Anarchists – is designed to make lies sound truthful and murder respectable, and to give an appearance of solidity to pure wind."[7]

Language matters, and what we call people affects how we think about and act toward them. Politics has been polarizing since the earliest days of our republic. The fourth presidential contest between incumbent President John Adams of the Federalist Party and Thomas Jefferson of the Democratic-Republican Party was so bitter and contentious, for example, that it became known as the "Revolution of 1800." The election of Abraham Lincoln sixty years later to the nation's highest office resulted in a civil war and over half a million dead Americans. And the 2000 Gore v. Bush race went all the way to the United States Supreme

Court before it was ultimately decided by the Florida recount over hanging chads. But today, between left-leaning media and liberal academics on one side and right-leaning talk radio and conservative think tanks on the other side (and social media on both), the country has never been so divided.

Surveys consistently show that the political center has been shrinking over the past two decades as the Left and the Right grow ever further apart. A 2014 Pew poll of over 10,000 Americans, for example, found that the percentage of Republicans holding "mostly or consistently conservative positions" has grown from 31 to 53 percent over the past two decades, while Democrats holding "mostly or consistently liberal positions" has seen a similar shift from 30 to 56 percent. And what Republicans and Democrats think about those in the other party has been increasing in hostility: Republicans who view Democrats unfavorably has gone up from 17 to 43 percent between 1994 and 2014, and Democrats who feel as negatively about Republicans has seen a similar increase from 16 percent to 38 percent.[8] One has only to monitor talk radio and social media to feel the animosity oozing across the airwaves and cyberspace. (See Figure 13.1 and Figure 13.2 for a dramatic visual display of this difference across the decades.)[9]

What can we do about this polarization? Many good ideas have been proffered and policy changes suggested.[10] To these I would like to propose that the Left and the Right make a bargain – call it The Grand

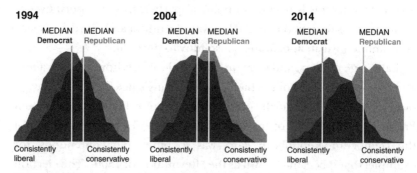

Figure 13.1 Democrats and Republicans are more ideologically divided than in the past: Distribution of Democrats and Republicans on a ten-item scale of political values. "Political Polarization in the American Public." Pew Research Center, Washington, DC (June 12, 2014). https://pewrsr.ch/2LqCD2O.

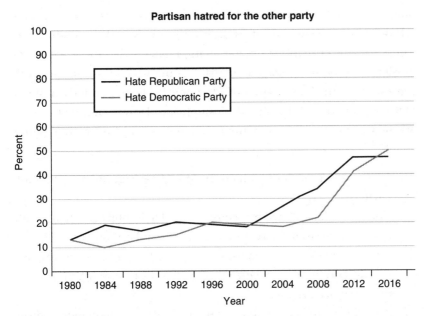

Figure 13.2 Partisan hatred for the other party. Data from a 2016 Pew Research Center survey reported in: Hetherington, Marc and Jonathan Weiler. 2018. *Prius or Pickup?* New York: Houghton Mifflin Harcourt, 129.

Bargain – of finding common ground in our political roots, now shrouded in the mists of the eighteenth-century Rights Revolution when the principles that most liberals and conservatives accept were first articulated. This bargain even has a bold and uplifting name – *classical liberalism* – and its values form the basis of most modern Western societies. Its founders are a veritable Who's Who of political and economic thought admired by liberals and conservatives alike: Thomas Hobbes, John Locke, Thomas Jefferson, Adam Smith, David Hume, Thomas Paine, Jeremy Bentham, John Stuart Mill, Alexis de Tocqueville, and many others. It has been variously described as championing individual liberty and autonomy, personal agency and responsibility, natural and civil rights, civil and economic liberties, religious liberty and church–state separation, free speech, free press, and free trade, private property and the rule of law, and others. (In the nineteenth century this political and economic philosophy became known as "liberalism," but the morphing of that word in the twentieth century toward one end of the political spectrum now requires the modifier "classical.")[11] Surely most of us on both the Left and the Right today can agree – in principle if not always in practice – that these are values we share. To be more specific in articulating what classical liberalism represents, in the final chapter of *The Moral Arc*, I enumerated a number of these principles as the "Freedom and Justice Dozen," noting that they are necessary "to quell our inner demons and to inspire our better angels."[12]

1. A liberal democracy in which the franchise is granted to all adult citizens.
2. The rule of law defined by a constitution that is subject to change only under extraordinary circumstances and by judicial proceedings.
3. A viable legislative system for establishing fair and just laws applied equally and fairly to all citizens regardless of race, religion, gender, or sexual orientation.
4. An effective judicial system for the equitable enforcement of those fair and just laws that employs both retributive and restorative justice.
5. Protection of civil rights and civil liberties for all citizens regardless of race, religion, gender, or sexual orientation.
6. A potent police for protection from attacks by other people within the state.
7. A robust military for protection of our liberties from attacks by other states.
8. Property rights and the freedom to trade with other citizens and companies, both domestic and foreign.
9. Economic stability through a secure and trustworthy banking and monetary system.
10. A reliable infrastructure and the freedom to travel and move.
11. Freedom of speech, the press, and association.
12. Mass education, critical thinking, scientific reasoning, and knowledge available and accessible for all.

And for a Baker's Dozen, let's add one more that has developed over the past century that I was slow to recognize as important for a well-functioning society:

13. Social spending to help those in need to survive and flourish, such as the homeless, mentally ill, physically handicapped, unemployed, and children, with such necessities as shelter and housing, child care, food, energy, education, job training, and medical care.

A word on this last point as it is one I never would have included in my more libertarian youth but now do in my classical liberal maturity:[13] Those on the Left feel that we do not do enough to support citizens in need, while those on the Right argue that too much social spending is enabling those who should be helping themselves. There are elements of truth in both of these extreme responses, but the fact is that today the strongest and fastest-growing economies in the world allocate anywhere from 20 to 30 percent of their GDP to social expenditures, including (in order), France (31.5%), Finland (30.8%), Belgium (29%), Italy (28.9%), Denmark (28.7%), Austria (27.8%), Sweden (27.1%), Germany (25.3%), the UK (21.5%), the USA (19.3%), and Australia (19.1%), with über-liberal Canada bringing up the rear at 17.1%.[14] When social spending made through employers instead of government (such as health care, retirement, and disability) is factored into the equation, the USA rises from twenty-fourth place to second in overall social expenditures. Nevertheless, we still boast the largest economy in the world.

Germany is a model country that has balanced highly competitive free market economics – it is by far the strongest economy in the EU – with a social welfare system that provides its citizens with cradle-to-grave security. My wife, Jennifer, is from Köln, Germany, and she is constantly amazed at what the USA fails to provide to those in need (or even the basics we all need, such as universal health care) that her country supplies without apparent harm to its robust economy. Tellingly, a 2015 study on world human development between 1870 and 2007, conducted by the economist Leandro Prados de la Escosura, reported a positive correlation between the percentage of GDP that an OECD nation allocated to social spending and its score on a composite measure of prosperity, health, and education.[15]

So it is not only moral to help those who cannot help themselves, it pays fiscal dividends to have a strong social safety net within the umbrella of a competitive free market economy. Social spending may seem like the weather – everyone complains about it (there's too much or too little), but no one does anything about it – but, in fact, it has become an integral part of all advanced nations and must be counted as a form of progress on the long arc of the moral universe. It is another grand bargain of classical liberalism that both conservatives and liberals ought to agree to support within that band of 20 to 30 percent of GDP, the details left to jigger depending who is in power and what, specifically, voters want funded more or less.

Even core moral foundations that liberals and conservatives fight about are, in fact, shared by almost everyone in both camps, with the differences being in degree, not kind. The moral psychologist Jonathan Haidt, for example, collected data from hundreds of thousands of people and distilled from them five foundations of morality:

1. **Harm/care.** This foundation underlies such moral virtues as kindness, gentleness, and nurturance and manifests in taking care of the needy.
2. **Fairness/reciprocity.** This foundation leads to such political ideals of justice, rights, and autonomy for individuals.
3. **In-group/loyalty.** This foundation underlies such virtues as patriotism and self-sacrifice for the group.
4. **Authority/respect.** This foundation underlies such virtues as leadership and followership, including esteem for legitimate authority and respect for traditions.
5. **Purity/sanctity.** This foundation underlies the striving to live in a more elevated and noble way, and it emphasizes the belief that the body is a temple that can be desecrated by immoral activities and contaminants.

To listen to political pundits on both the Left and the Right, one might conclude that conservatives care only for numbers 3, 4, and 5, while liberals are concerned only with numbers 1 and 2. In point of fact, in surveys asking questions that are proxies for these moral values, liberals do score higher than conservatives on 1 and 2 (*Harm/care* and *Fairness/reciprocity*) but lower than conservatives on 3, 4, and 5 (*In-group /loyalty, Authority/respect,* and *Purity/sanctity*), while conservatives are roughly equal on all five dimensions, lower than liberals on 1 and 2, but higher on 3, 4, and 5.[16] But to my point: both liberals and conservatives value all five; they just differ in degree.

The central dogma both liberals and conservatives embrace today that veers from the ideals of classical liberalism is in their emphasis on the group over the individual. Under the guise of "identity politics," liberals tend to treat individuals as members of an oppressed or oppressing group, as defined by race, ethnicity, gender, sexual orientation, religion, and political party. Under the pretense of "faith and flag," conservatives tend to sort people into such collectivities as nation, state, tribe, family, religion, and political party. The resulting Us v. Them tribalism results in such illiberal policies as speech censorship and destructive moralizing on the Left and political populism and economic nationalism on the Right. The racial politics of the Alt-Right is not unrelated to the identity politics of the Alt-Left. Two can play that game, but no winner emerges.

Classical liberals believe that it is *individuals* who are entitled to rights, not races, genders, ethnicities, religions, or nations, because it is individuals who perceive, emote, respond, love, feel, and suffer. Classical liberals emphasize the freedom and autonomy of individuals and the rights of *persons*, not collectives. Individuals vote, not genders. Individuals want to be treated equally under the law, not races. The Bill of Rights, in fact, was designed to protect individuals from being discriminated against as members of a group, such as by race, gender, and sexual orientation.

We are a social species, so we enjoy and even need the company of others, such as families, friends, and faiths. And we are a political species, so we revel in sorting ourselves into like-minded ideological tribes. But such consortiums should not be confused with or negate the value of the individual as the primary moral agent of our ethical concern, the axiomatic inheritor of our legal rights, the principal participant in our democracy, and the ultimate subject under our laws. The unique individual is to politics what the atom is to physics and the organism is to biology – a fundamental unit of nature. Therefore, our moral starting point ought to be *the survival and flourishing of individual sentient beings.*[17]

It is when individuals are subsumed into and sacrificed for the good of the group that abuses of freedom have been most widespread and body counts have been driven highest. It is when people are judged not by the content of their character but by the color of their skin – or by their gender chromosomal constitution, or by whom they prefer to share a bed with, or by what accent they speak with, or by which political or religious affiliation they identify with – that freedom falls and liberty is lost.

CHAPTER 14

Governing Mars

Lessons for the Red Planet from Experiments in Governing the Blue Planet

PREAMBLE

I originally penned this essay in the summer of 2018, stimulated by a Twitter exchange I had with Elon Musk, itself triggered by the SpaceX CEO's previously announced decision to colonize Mars. This led me to wonder if this visionary had given any thought to what sort of government he would set up on the Red Planet, and if he already had a team of social scientists working on the problem or whether he was just going to wing it when they got there. Surely not, but what source for research would a team of social engineers (let's call them) working at SpaceX (or NASA, since it too plans to send people to Mars in the coming decades) access? There are no working models. Or are there? There are. Since it is Earthlings going to Mars, experiments in governance on the Blue Planet are a useful resource for lessons on how to govern the Red Planet. This essay, originally published in *Quillette*, is my modest contribution to future Martians on what they should take with them when they, in the words of the poet John Gillespie Magee, Jr., "slipped the surly bonds of earth ... high in the sunlit silence ... where never lark or even eagle flew ... the high untrespassed sanctity of space."

* * *

Politics, the crooked timber of our communal lives, dominates everything because, in the end, everything – high and low and, most especially, high – lives or dies by politics. You can have the most advanced and efflorescent of cultures. Get your politics wrong, however, and everything stands to be swept away.

Charles Krauthammer, *Things that Matter*, 2013

I N SEPTEMBER OF 2017 ELON MUSK ANNOUNCED HIS INTENTION
to establish a Martian colony by the mid 2020s, thereby assuring our
survival as an interplanetary species. "If there's a third world war we want
to make sure there's enough of a seed of human civilization somewhere
else to bring it back and shorten the length of the dark ages," he told an
SXSW (South by Southwest) audience in March of 2018, while also
admitting that the endeavor will be "difficult, dangerous, a good chance
you'll die."

Setting aside for the moment the many physical and biological problems that must be overcome to establish a permanent base on Mars, just
as intractable is determining how to govern such a remote colony.
Curious to know his thoughts on the subject, on June 16, 2018,
I whimsically tweeted at the SpaceX CEO (Figure 14.1).

Minutes later I received this reply from Musk (Figure 14.2).

Michael Shermer ✔ @michaelshermer · Jun 16
When you start the 1st Mars colony @elonmusk what documents would you
recommend using to establish a governing system? U.S. Constitution/Bill of
Rights? Universal Declaration of Human Rights? Humanist Manifesto? Atlas
Shrugged? Against the State: An Anarcho-Capitalist Manifesto?

🗨 158   ↻ 277   ♡ 2.9K   ࿚

Figure 14.1 Tweet from Michael Shermer (@michaelshermer), June 16, 2018. The thread
is available at: https://bit.ly/30uUrNy

Elon Musk ✔ @elonmusk · Jun 16
Replying to @michaelshermer
Direct democracy by the people. Laws must be short, as there is trickery in
length. Automatic expiration of rules to prevent death by bureaucracy. Any rule
can be removed by 40% of people to overcome inertia. Freedom.

🗨 1.9K   ↻ 2.5K   ♡ 18K   ✉

Figure 14.2 Tweet reply from Elon Musk (@elonmusk), June 16, 2018.

There's a lot packed into those 217 characters, but a tweet does
not a constitution make. At that SXSW conference interview, when
asked what type of government he envisions for the first Mars
colony, Musk elaborated:

Most likely, the form of government on Mars would be somewhat of a direct democracy where people vote directly on issues instead of going through representative government. When the United States was formed representative government was the only thing that was logistically feasible. There was no way for people to communicate instantly. A lot of people didn't have access to mailboxes, the post office was primitive. A lot of people couldn't write. So you had to have some form of representative democracy or things just wouldn't work at all. On Mars, everyone votes on every issue and that's how it goes. There are a few things I'd recommend, which is keep laws short. Long laws ... that's like something suspicious going on if there's long laws.[1]

Musk's sentiments about fewer laws and more freedom sound sensible. Can't reasonable people get along with just a handful of rules, such as "don't hurt other people and don't take their stuff" (the title of Matt Kibbe's libertarian manifesto) or golden rules like "do unto others as you would have them do unto you" (and its silver derivative "don't do to others what you don't want done to yourself")?[2] Unfortunately, no.

Reasonable people – not to mention the unreasonable, of whom there are plenty – can disagree on a great many things even when the rules are clear and simple. One reason is human nature, as James Madison articulated it in *Federalist Paper* No. 51, one of the founding documents of the inchoate United States, an analogue to what we're about to embark on in colonizing the Red Planet:

> But what is government itself, but the greatest of all reflections on human nature? If men were angels, no government would be necessary. If angels were to govern men, neither external nor internal controls on government would be necessary. In framing a government which is to be administered by men over men, the great difficulty lies in this: you must first enable the government to control the governed; and in the next place oblige it to control itself.[3]

A second reason is the emergent property of complex systems in which potential interactions of – and disagreements between – people multiply astronomically as population increases. Initial Martian colonies will be roughly the size of hunter-gatherer bands, and as the UCLA geographer Jared Diamond has calculated from his studies of the hunter-gatherer peoples of Papua New Guinea, a small band of 20 people generates 190 possible dyads, or two-person interactions (20 x 19 ÷ 2), small enough for informal conflict resolution. But increase that 20 to 2,000 and you're facing 1,999,000 possible dyads (2000 x 1999 ÷ 2). Here a 100-fold population increase produces a 10,000-fold dyadic rise. Scale that up to cities of 200,000 or 2,000,000 and the potential for conflict multiplies beyond comprehension and, along with, it the laws and regulations needed to insure relative harmony and efficiency. As Diamond explains in his 1996 book *Guns, Germs, and Steel,*

> Once the threshold of "several hundred," below which everyone can know everyone else, has been crossed, increasing numbers of dyads become pairs of unrelated strangers. Hence, a large society that continues to leave conflict resolution to all of its members is guaranteed to blow up. That factor alone would explain why societies of thousands can exist only if they develop centralized authority to monopolize force and resolve conflict.[4]

Musk has said that "the threshold for a self-sustaining city on Mars or a civilization would be a million people." That number generates nearly 500 billion dyadic combinatorial possibilities (1,000,000 x 999,999 ÷ 2 = 499,999,500,000), meaning any hoped-for manual of "short laws" would soon become tomes of bureaucratic legalese and all that entails in Earthly political and legal systems – suffocating regulations, entangling restrictions, government overreach, and suppression of individual freedom and autonomy. Martian colonists will need to figure out how to prevent a bureaucracy from expanding in response to the accelerating dyadic combinations as their population increases, which has happened in every government on Earth as if it were a law of nature.

Thus, the general challenge for Martians is the same as it has been for Earthlings for millennia: to strike the right balance between freedom and security. It would be interesting for Martian colonists to experiment with and design new systems of governance never tried on Earth, but these Martians will be Earthlings with all the inner demons that come bundled with the better angels of our nature.

* * *

We are about to colonize the Red Planet and set up a permanent base there with the intention that it will grow into a sustainable civilization. In time, such a civilization will likely become a founding population that will spread outward throughout the solar system, establishing colonies on the moons of Jupiter and Saturn. Eventually our descendants will make it to another star system, and from there island-hop their way around the galaxy, just as our Paleolithic ancestors spread across Earth, eventually making their way to the most remote islands of the Pacific Ocean. Given that these twenty-first-century planetary colonists (and twenty-third-century stellar colonists) will have the same human natures as our Paleolithic colonists had when they undertook to spread their cultures around the Earth, we need to determine *now* what science has learned about how best to govern a civilization. That is, for a century, social scientists have studied the variety of political, economic, and social systems tried around the world over the past 10,000 years. What have we learned?

Elon Musk, for example, thinks Mars should be governed by a *direct democracy*. Well, in theory this sounds good, but in practice such a system can easily slide into a tyranny of the majority – aka mob rule – which is why they are historically rare. Switzerland is an exception, although it is a hybrid, or semidirect democracy, with federalism-like vertical separation of powers mixed in.

In recent centuries we have learned that some sort of representational system appears to be necessary to obviate the inherent flaws with direct democracies. The *representational democracy* of the sort practiced in the USA constitutional republic works fairly well, although as is all too apparent representatives can be heavily influenced by special-interest groups and corporations. Perhaps a variation of *delegative democracy* might be tried, in which voters have an option to delegate their vote to others, although that could quickly degenerate into trading or selling votes. In *Federalist* No. 10, Madison outlined the problem with competing factions in a direct democracy ("a landed interest, a manufacturing interest, a mercantile interest, a moneyed interest ... "):

> [A] pure democracy, by which I mean a society consisting of a small
> number of citizens, who assemble and administer the government in

person, can admit no cure for the mischiefs of faction. A common passion or interest will be felt by a majority, and there is nothing to check the inducements to sacrifice the weaker party. Hence it is, that democracies have ever been found incompatible with personal security or the rights of property; and have, in general, been as short in their lives as they have been violent in their deaths.

As Thomas Jefferson wrote in 1804, "No experiment can be more interesting than that we are now trying, and which we trust will end in establishing the fact, that man may be governed by reason and truth."[5]

* * *

A number of scientists and science fiction writers have made the analogy of Europeans colonizing the Americas in discussions of establishing colonies on other worlds, but this only goes so far given the fact that those incipient settlers at least had air to breath, water to drink, and plenty of potential food on the hoof, in the ground, and in oceans, lakes, and rivers. The lack of these basic commodities generates additional problems for the political governance of Mars – there's no air, food, or (that we know of yet) water there! As well, the 1967 Outer Space Treaty that the USA signed prohibits anyone from "owning" Mars. What would be the incentive to colonize Mars if there's no guarantee that the work you do to live there would result in any type of ownership? Although working the land and air to produce resources is not directly proscribed by the treaty, doing so in a manner that doesn't lead to tyranny is another matter entirely.

These and related problems were addressed by the University of Edinburgh astrophysicist Charles S. Cockell in a series of meetings with scientists and scholars from varied fields in two conference proceedings titled *Human Governance Beyond Earth* and *The Meaning of Liberty Beyond Earth*. To learn more about what to do when the most basic necessities of life – oxygen, water, and food – are under the control of one company (SpaceX?) or one government (the US of Mars?), I spoke with Dr. Cockell by Skype, starting with the observation that Earthlings colonizing Mars will be nothing like Europeans colonizing

North America.[6] "Space is an inherently tyranny-prone environment," Cockell told me. "You are living in an environment where the oxygen you breathe is being produced by a machine." On Earth, he notes, governments can rob their people of food and water, "but they can't take away your air, so you can run off into a forest and plan revolution, and you can get your friends together and you can try to overthrow a government."

In habitats on the moon or Mars where oxygen production is controlled by a single entity, there must be some guarantee that the air supply cannot be cut off to citizens. It would seem, then, that common ownership of the air and the machines that produce it through a single entity would follow, and I suggested as much to Cockell. But to my surprise he responded, "I would go in completely the opposite direction. I would fragment as much as possible. I would try to create plurality in the means of production and great competition and have many people able to produce oxygen. So what you're trying to do is decentralize," he and his team concluded after studying Earth-bound systems, because "centrally planned governments generally end up as not very good experiments."

What about corporations that capture a majority market share and become so dominant that they can monopolize the market and turn tyrannical, I inquire? "Well, these things happen on the Earth," Cockell historicized, noting that documents like the Bill of Rights are designed to keep tyranny in check. True, but not without violence, revolutions, and wars, I rejoin. "It's hard work to get people to believe in freedom and to fight for it," Cockell admitted, "and I think in space it's going to be even more hard work. So you've got to give people freedom of movement, freedom of information – it's really no different from the Earth, it's just more expanded and more vigorous of what we need to do on the Earth to maintain freedom."

If he were to recommend to the first Mars colonists what documents they should take with them to help design their new society, Cockell unhesitatingly offered, "The US Constitution, Bill of Rights, and the Declaration of Independence," adding that the latter "is not just about independence; it's also about the ideals of free governance." Here the analogue is fitting, given that on a planet in which nearly every square foot of land (and much of the sea) is already under some form of governmental legislation, there are few opportunities to try anew, so the US experiment in governance is one well worth emulating. "One of the moments of genius of the founding fathers . . . was they recognized that human beings can never be made perfect. Ambition must be made to counteract ambition. You can't make people perfect. You must take a cynical view and assume they are very imperfect and create the checks and balances to hold those slightly more negative aspects of humans in check."

Among the new ideas Cockell and his colleagues came up with is modularity, literally incorporating liberty into architecture. "You could modularize a settlement so that there's lots of oxygen production machines, lots of food production machines, such that the failure of any one of them does not threaten the whole settlement." Decentralization "allows people to do their own thing. The disasters happen when you try to artificially construct societies that are wholly controlled from the center, or where there's no organization and you create an anarchic society. The best forms of society have always been ones that are flexible and modify themselves over time as fashions and ideas change, and that's why, I think, Western democracies are reasonably successful at keeping people happy to the maximum extent you can try and do that. And I think in space there is going to be nothing different there."

* * *

Science fiction authors have been considering extraterrestrial political systems for far longer than scientists and legal scholars. In *The Dispossessed*, for example, Ursula K. Le Guin explores tensions between capitalist/individualist societies like ours and that of collectivist systems like the Soviet Union, or even anarcho-syndicalist systems involving industrial unionism. In his Mars trilogy (*Red Mars*, *Green Mars*, *Blue Mars*), Kim Stanley Robinson plays out the consequences of transnational corporations ("transnats") gaining enough control and power over Martian citizens, leading to a balance between a global government overseeing relatively autonomous settlements and cities and a blended economic system of capitalism, socialism, and environmental conservationism; this works so well that soon Martians face the problem of illegal immigration – from Earthlings whose planet has suffered from environmental ruin.

According to the renowned science fiction author (and physicist) David Brin (*The Postman, Kiln People, Uplift War*), whom I queried on the matter, "New, cyber technologies do offer a chance for meaningful revisions of democracy that would make it more responsive while retaining some benefits of delegation."[7] He suggests two: (1) *Self-sorted constituencies*: "Let any 750,000 Americans gather and claim a US Congressional Representative. Let them sort themselves out, online. If radical environmentalists or gunfolks can muster the absolute minimum of 700,000, they get a rep. Yes, you'll get fifty or a hundred really zealous representatives of special interests, but you've got that today. And other groups, or the remaining geographic districts, would choose more moderate ones." (2) *Preferential ballots*, as used in Australia and in the Hugo Awards, "letting voters rank order the candidates or issues. Had this been available, Brexit would have settled on ... 'negotiate harder with Brussels.' Voters would get to bracket and calibrate and give more nuanced guidance to their representatives."

In a cyber-linked society, says Brin, "there will be ever stronger pressures for direct democracy, or 'demarchy,' which were portrayed by Joan Vinge in *Outcasts of the Heaven Belt*." The American founders opted for a republic to strike a "balance between popular sovereignty and the calm deliberation of 'wiser heads.'" And notice what happened in France just two years after the US Constitution was ratified, "when anger boiled over to swamp any chance of rational discourse." As Edmund Burke noted in his *Reflections on the Revolution in France*: "Nothing turns out to be so oppressive and unjust as a feeble government."

How can we avoid establishing feeble government on Mars? I put the question to Robert Zubrin, aerospace engineer, President of the Mars Society, author of *The Case for Mars* and *The Case for Space*, and one of the most visionary scientists I have ever known. "I'm not going to specify a government for Mars," Zubrin began.

> There will be groups of people that go to Mars and they'll have different ideas on what the best government should be and what form of government will maximize human potential and opportunity. In fact, I think this will be a major driver for the colonization of Mars – there will

be groups of people who have novel ideas in these respects and will not be popular and they'll need a place to go where they can give these ideas a spin.[8]

Invoking Darwin's idea of natural selection, Zubin went on to suggest that those with governance ideas that work will succeed and those that don't, won't. This, he suggests, is not unlike what happened with the founding of the United States. The liberal ideas from the Enlightenment that the founders evoked were not unknown in Europe, but the long-established power structures prevented them from flourishing there. "Mars won't be utopia," Zubrin concluded, invoking instead the US founders' description of America as a grand experiment in governance. "It will be a lab. It will be a place where experiments are done." But what if a Martian tyrant turns off the air of the people in order to control them, I inquire? "Specialization leads to empowerment," Zubrin countered, explaining that autocrats could control peasants in medieval Europe because they were living in such a simple society that tyrants could do away with them if they didn't obey. On Mars, everyone will be critical to everyone else's survival, so "extraterrestrial tyranny is impossible."

* * *

There are, as well, a variety of social experiments in setting up new societies here on Earth that differ from nations and states, and these come in the form of *unintentional communities*, such as shipwrecked sailors stranded on an island, *intentional communities*, such as the communes established in America in the nineteenth century and the Kibbutzim founded in Israel in the twentieth century, and *artificial communities*, such as online gaming communities developed in the twenty-first century. These natural experiments in living that differ from those I've been discussing are deeply explored by the evolutionary sociologist Nicholas Christakis in his 2019 book *Blueprint: The Evolutionary Origins of a Good Society*. Let's look at a few examples from unintentional communities and see what light might be shown on what the first Martians should do to set up a good society.

First, says Christakis, at the core of all good societies is a suite of eight social characteristics, including (1) The capacity to have and recognize individual identity, (2) Love for partners and offspring, (3) Friendship, (4) Social networks, (5) Cooperation, (6) Preference for one's own group (that is, "in-group bias"), (7) Mild hierarchy (that is, relative egalitarianism), and (8) Social learning and teaching. Whatever the right balance of these characteristics will be for the first Martians remains to be seen, but the overall balance to be sought is between individualism and group living – individual autonomy balanced with commitment to the community.

As I have argued in *The Moral Arc* (and Chapters 21 and 22 in this volume) we are a hierarchical social primate species that needs one another to survive and flourish in the teeth of entropy, which nature throws at us at every turn, but a moral starting point is *the survival and flourishing of individual sentient beings* because (1) the individual is the primary target of natural selection in evolution, and (2) it is the individual who is most affected by moral and immoral acts. Societies succeed or fail depending on whether or not they get this balance right between the survival and flourishing of the individual and that of the community.

Unintentional communities are natural experiments that have struggled to find this balance, a type of "forbidden experiment" that would never get the approval of a research IRB (Institutional Review Board). Being stranded in a remote place is one such natural experiment, and, believe it or not, there's a database of such forbidden experiments in the form of shipwrecks with survivors, or in the subtitle of an 1813 work in this genre, "A Collection of Interesting Accounts of Naval Disasters with Many Particulars of the Extraordinary Adventures and Sufferings of the Crews of Vessels Wrecked at Sea, and of Their Treatment on Distant Shores." Christakis includes a table of twenty-four such small-scale shipwreck societies over a 400-year span from 1500 to 1900, with initial survival colony populations ranging from 4 to 500, with a mean of 119 (2,870/24 = 119.5), but with much smaller numbers of rescued survivors, ranging from 3 to 289, with a mean of 59 (1,422/24 = 59.25), reflecting their success or failure at striking the right balance. The duration of these unplanned societies ranged from two months to fifteen years, with a mean of twenty months (461.5/23 = 20.06; one group was rescued after thirteen days, so I didn't count them).

Some of the survivors killed and ate each other (murder and cannibalism), while others survived and flourished and were eventually rescued. What made the difference? "The groups that typically fared best were those that had good leadership in the form of mild hierarchy (without any brutality), friendships among the survivors, and evidence of cooperation and altruism," Christakis concludes. The successful shipwreck societies shared food equitably, took care of the sick and injured survivors, and worked together digging wells, burying the dead, building fires, and building escape boats. There was little hierarchy – for example, while on board their ships, officers and enlisted men were separated, but, on land, successful castaways integrated everyone in a cooperative, egalitarian, and more horizontal structure, putting aside prior hierarchical class differences in the interest of survival. Camaraderie emerged and friendships across such barriers were formed.

The closest thing to a control experiment in this category was when two ships (the *Invercauld* and the *Grafton*) were wrecked on the same island (Auckland) at the same time in 1864. The island is 26 miles long and 16 miles wide and lies 290 miles south of New Zealand, truly isolated. The two surviving groups were unaware of one another, and their outcomes were starkly different. For the *Invercauld*, nineteen out of twenty-five crew members made it to the island, but only three survived when rescued a year later, whereas all five of the *Grafton* crew made it to land, and all five were rescued two years later. "The differential survival of the two groups may be ascribed to differences in initial salvage and differences in leadership, but it was also due to differences in social arrangements," Christakis explains. "Among the *Invercauld* crews, there was an 'every man for himself' attitude, whereas the men of the *Grafton* were cooperators. They shared food equitably, worked together toward common goals (like repairing the dinghy), voted democratically for a leader who could be replaced by a new vote, dedicated themselves to their mutual survival, and treated one another as equals." Take note, future Martians.

* * *

In between unintentional and intentional communities is arguably the most famous of these forbidden experiments, which began in the early morning hours of April 28, 1789, when Fletcher Christian, the Master's Mate of the HMS *Bounty* – a modest-size merchant ship crewed by forty-five men and loaded with over a thousand pots of breadfruit trees bound for the Caribbean islands where they would be delivered as cheap slave fodder for the British colony there – seized control of the ship from Captain William Bligh, released the captors into a 23-foot launch, and sailed the *Bounty* into the mists of history where they were not found until 1808, when only one member of the original crew, John Adams, survived to tell the tale of what happened. I researched and wrote about this event in my book *Science Friction*, employing evolutionary psychology as a deeper explanation of what happened and why. It is a valuable lesson for future Martians on how not to set up a new society.

The *Bounty* departed Portsmouth on December 23, 1787. Ten months and 27,010 miles later it arrived in Matavai Bay, Tahiti, where it was anchored for five months, plenty of time for the young male crew members, including Fletcher Christian, to become romantically involved with the native women. After departing Tahiti, a number of the smitten men grew restless without their love interests, which, when coupled to the normal discipline imposed on them by Bligh for relatively minor offenses, led to the explosive response that fateful April morning in 1789. After the mutiny, Bligh and his loyal followers sailed the little launch 3,618 miles to safety – one of the greatest open-ocean voyages in recorded history – affording him the chance to tell the world what happened and why. Here is Bligh's explanation provided in his published account:

> It however may very naturally be asked what could be the reason for such a revolt, in answer to which I can only conjecture that they have Idealy assured themselves of a more happy life among the Otaheitians than they could possibly have in England, which joined to some Female connections has most likely been the leading cause of the whole business.

After seizing the ship, Christian and his followers returned to Tahiti, and on September 23, 1789, they left the island for good, carrying a total of nine male mutineers, six Tahitian men, and eleven Tahitian women, knowing the Royal Navy would track them down and execute them. On January 15, 1790 they arrived at one of the remotest rocks in the Pacific,

Pitcairn Island, unloaded the ship, and a week later torched it in a final gesture of commitment to their new life on this far-flung outpost. The seeds for the failure of governing a long-term society were already apparent in the sex ratio: fifteen men, eleven women. Not good. After three years, the woman living with mutineer John Williams died, so he took the wife of one of the Polynesian men, leading to jealousy, violence and, on September 20, 1793, retribution when five of the mutineers were killed, including Fletcher Christian, along with all of the Polynesian men. In subsequent years after the massacre, one mutineer committed suicide, another was killed by one of the other mutineers, and yet another died of asthma. By 1800, the only male survivor was John Adams, who lived until 1829, long enough to tell the tale of the fate of the *Bounty*'s mutineers and why the Pitcairn society failed.

In my analysis I made the distinction between proximate causes (e.g., imbalanced sex ratio) and ultimate causes (e.g., attachment and jealousy) for the failure both of Captain Bligh on the *Bounty* and of Fletcher Christian on Pitcairn, starting with certain basic facts about human nature: we are a hierarchical social primate species and one of the most sexual of all primates, whose males are more openly and intensely obsessed with obtaining sexual unions and equally preoccupied with protecting those unions from threats from other males. The evolutionary foundation for the mutineers' heightened state of emotions is born out in modern neuroscience, which shows that the attachment bonds between men and women are powerful forms of chemical addiction, especially in the early stages of a relationship. Dopamine is a neurotransmitter substance secreted in the brain that, according to Helen Fisher in her book, *Why We Love*, produces "extremely focused attention, as well as unwavering motivation and goal-directed behaviors," and elevated levels during bonding "produce exhilaration, as well as many of the other feelings that lovers report – including increased energy, hyperactivity, sleeplessness, loss of appetite, trembling, a pounding heart, accelerated breathing, and sometimes mania, anxiety, or fear." Attachments this strong are literally addictive, stimulating the same region of the brain that is active in drug addictions. The mutineers were literally going through withdrawal when they seized the *Bounty* and returned to Tahiti.

On Pitcairn, the mutineers failed to find the right balance between hierarchy and egalitarianism. Both Bligh and Christian were products of the Royal Navy, very much steeped in hierarchy and the accompanying status (or lack thereof). Anthropologists tell us that most social mammals, all social primates, and every human community ever studied, shows some form of hierarchy and social status. On the *Bounty* the hierarchical tensions between Bligh and Christian led to the mutiny, and on Pitcairn island the hierarchical tensions between Christian and the mutineers, and between the mutineers and the male Tahitians (with the racist attitudes of the former toward the latter, common for the day), when coupled to the sex ratio imbalance and accompanying jealousy and violence, led to its demise.

The lessons for Martian colonists from Pitcairn mutineers are clear enough: start off with a balanced sex ratio, structure a political system more horizontal than hierarchical, eliminate racist and misogynist attitudes, and accentuate cooperation and attenuate competition.

* * *

Martian political, economic, and legal institutions will likely vary from Earthly ones according to the most basic needs of the first colonists, but any such variation will be necessarily bounded by human nature. Perhaps SpaceX or NASA will create a division of social engineers – a team of legal scholars, political scientists, economists, social psychologists, and conflict resolution scholars – and they'll come up with a wholly different system of governance.

Or maybe the Martian colonists themselves will think of something new as they experiment with different solutions to social problems. Who knows what that space seed might sprout in the coming centuries and millennia? The prospects of a new form of government being discovered on Mars and exported back to Earth makes any such exploratory mission to the Red Planet worthwhile. Either way, governing Mars is also an analogue for governing Earth, inasmuch as we do not have the final answers here in order to ensure the survival of our own civilization.

The prospects of establishing a human colony – and eventually a human civilization – on Mars, not only boggles the mind and fires the imagination, it is a call to action to gather the best science we have on how best to live there, based on what we know and understand about how we live here. This project is not just for Martians and their descendants, but for Earthlings and their descendants, and for all humanity, wherever we reside in the solar system and, eventually, the galaxy. Perhaps one day we shall read the following Martian Declaration of Independence:

> *When in the Course of human events it becomes necessary for one people to leave their planet and dissolve the political bands which have connected them to the people of the home planet, and to assume among the powers of Mars, the separate and equal station to which the Laws of Nature entitle them, a decent respect to the opinions of Earthlings requires that they should declare the causes which impel them to the separation to become Martians.*

and this Preamble to a Martian Constitution:

> *We the People of United States of Mars, in Order to form a more perfect Union, establish Justice, insure domestic Tranquility, provide for the common defense, promote the general Welfare, and secure the Blessings of Liberty to ourselves and our Posterity, do ordain and establish this Constitution of the United States of Mars.*

More unlikely things have happened in the history of our civilization, but as Robert Browning stirred,

> Ah, but a man's reach should exceed his grasp,
> Or what's a heaven for?

CHAPTER 15

The Sandy Hook Effect

What We Can and Cannot Do about Gun Violence

PREAMBLE

After the massacre at the Sandy Hook Elementary School on
December 14, 2012, my lecture agent Scott Wolfman, whose offices are
located only eight miles from the site of the deadliest school shooting in
history, contacted me to inquire if I would be willing to engage in
a debate over gun control. He felt the need to do something – anything –
to address the problem, and as gun violence was a subject I had done
some research on, I undertook a thorough review of the social science
literature and, in the process of preparing to debate the pro-gun advocate John Lott, penned this research article, first published in *Skeptic* for
a special issue on gun violence (Vol. 18, No. 1). In brief, I concluded that
while preventing highly improbable mass murders like that at Sandy
Hook is impossible, there are some things we can do to decrease violence
and reduce the carnage, which has only gotten worse since that tragic
event.

* * *

O N DECEMBER 14, 2012, TWENTY-YEAR OLD ADAM LANZA
broke into Sandy Hook Elementary School in Newtown, CT,
killing twenty children and six adults – and then himself – after first
slaying his mother Nancy Lanza in their home. He used a .223 caliber
Bushmaster XM-15 semiautomatic rifle in the killing spree, but also had
on him a 10mm Glock 20 SF handgun and a 9mm SIG Sauer handgun.
He had a shotgun in his car, and at home police found a .45 Henry
repeating rifle, a .30 Enfield rifle, and a .22 Marlin rifle, the latter of
which he used to shoot his mother in the head four times.[1] All of the guns
were legally owned and registered, and preliminary reports note that

Nancy Lanza was a gun enthusiast who owned at least a dozen firearms and taught her son how to shoot them at gun clubs in her neighborhood.[2] Every one of the victims is a heartbreaking story, perhaps best captured by the sole survivor in a first-grade classroom who, after narrowly escaping Lanza's bullets by playing dead, exclaimed to her mother, "Mommy, I'm okay, but all my friends are dead."[3] Just imagining a first grader uttering those words is beyond horrific.

The response to the tragedy was as emotional as it was predictable, with pundits and the public demanding stricter gun-control measures and more funding for mental-health research and facilities.[4] The National Rifle Association (NRA) called on Congress to appropriate funds enough to post armed police officers at every school in America.[5] President Obama pronounced, "We're going to have to come together and take meaningful action to prevent more tragedies like this, regardless of the politics," then vowed to do everything in his power to prevent such an event happening again, "Because what choice do we have? We can't accept events like this as routine."[6]

That such reactions are emotionally understandable should not distract us from having a rational discourse over whether or not the national obsession over highly improbable events like Sandy Hook is the best use of our time, energy, and resources toward the overall goal of reducing violence in our society. In fact, the evidence overwhelmingly shows that, contra President Obama's characterization, such events are far more random than they are routine. They are what are known as Black Swan events, but, in this context, I shall refer to them as *Sandy Hook Events – high-profile, improbable, rare, and unpredictable mass murders.* We cannot and never will be able to predict *Sandy Hook Events.* We can *postdict* them, looking for factors common to the killers, but the most we can ever do is make statistical-based generalizations about the likelihood of a Sandy Hook Event happening somewhere sometime in the future.

This does not mean we can or should do nothing. It is, perhaps, ironically fitting that the same day as the Sandy Hook tragedy, a Chinese man stabbed with a knife twenty-two children and one adult outside a primary school in the village of Chengping in Henan Province in central China, resulting in *zero fatalities.*[7] There really is a difference between a gun and a knife, and in this case that difference is measurable in the number of survivors. However, it is doubtful that Americans would vote to change our government into a Chinese-like Communist regime in which controlling guns is possible – but at a considerable cost to other freedoms. Nevertheless, we can build a science-based rational response in the form of a two-pronged approach: (1) bottom-up actions by private citizens, experts, and scientists to identify those most likely to commit mass murder in order to try to reduce the odds that they will do so through various interventions (while recognizing that we can never prevent them entirely); (2) top-down measures by government, police, and law-enforcement agencies to continue the centuries-long trend in the overall decline of violence.

MURDER V. MASS MURDER

According to the FBI's crime reports, between 2007 and 2011 the USA experienced an annual average of 13,700 homicides, with guns responsible for 67.8 percent of those.[8] That's an average of 9,289 people shot dead by a gun, or 774 a month, 178 a week, 25 a day, or a little more than one per hour. It's a disquieting thought that every hour of every day someone is shot to death. By contrast, according to James Alan Fox, Northeastern University Professor of Criminology, Law, and Public Policy, between 1980 and 2010 there was an average of 20 mass murders per year (defined by the FBI as "a number of murders (four or more) occurring during the same incident, with no distinctive time period between the murders")[9] for an average annual death toll of about 100, or 5 per shooting.[10] Figure 15.1 graphs Fox's data.

This averages out to one mass murder every 2.6 weeks, which when clustered in time and covered in explosive media attention intuitively feels like a veritable plague of violence. But an average annual death rate of 100 constitutes a mere 0.01 percent of the average homicide total, a tiny figure in the statistical noise among overall gun deaths. As well, predicting which week, much less which day and where the mass murders will occur is not possible. If we want to save lives by preventing gun deaths, the larger problem of individual homicides, suicides, and accidents is the place to begin, not *Sandy Hook Events*.

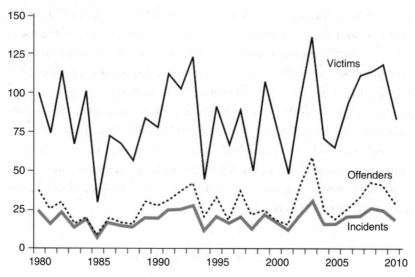

Figure 15.1 Mass Shootings in the United States, 1980–2010, tracking incidents, offenders, and victims. In any given year the number of each bounces around wildly, but the overall averages come out to around 20 mass murders and 100 victims per annum.

According to a 1998 study published in the *Journal of Trauma and Acute Care Surgery* on "Injuries and Deaths Due to Firearms in the Home," "every time a gun in the home was used in a self-defense or legally justifiable shooting, there were four unintentional shootings, seven criminal assaults or homicides, and 11 attempted or completed suicides." In other words, a gun is twenty-two times more likely to be used in a criminal assault, an accidental death or injury, a suicide attempt, or a homicide, than it is for self-defense. "Guns kept in homes are more likely to be involved in a fatal or nonfatal accidental shooting, criminal assault, or suicide attempt than to be used to injure or kill in self-defense."[11]

The raw figures are staggering. According to the National Center for Injury Prevention and Control, in 2010 a total of 19,392 US residents killed themselves with a firearm;[12] in 2010 there were 11,078 gun-caused homicides, and in 2011 there were 55,544 gun-caused injuries treated in emergency rooms;[13] in 2010, 606 people died by unintentional shooting while, in 2011, 14,675 were wounded in an unintentional shooting.[14] Ironically – and tragically – the fate of Nancy Lanza was that of most victims of a gun-homicide: killed by her own gun in her own home by someone she knew.

The problem is murder, not mass murder; individual homicides, not *Sandy Hook Events.*

WHO ARE THESE MASS MURDERERS, ANYWAY?

Perhaps if we knew more about mass murders that could ameliorate the problem. Not likely. The pop diagnosis of Adam Lanza as having "Asperger's syndrome," for example, whether true or not, is irrelevant and unhelpful because millions of people have Asperger's and related disorders on the Autism spectrum, and 99.99 percent of them will never commit an act of mass murder. So the moment we turn to diagnostic labels we risk a plethora of Type I false-positive errors of suspecting or accusing innocent people.

Perhaps a suite of characteristics or symptoms can help narrow the search. For example, research shows that these are three of the most common characteristics of mass murderers:[15]

1. *Psychopathy or mental illness.* Although some forms of mental illness such as schizophrenia have been identified as possible triggers of violent behavior, the best candidate we have for a psychological condition that leads to violence and criminal behavior is psychopathy. According to Robert Hare (*Without Conscience*), Simon Baron-Cohen (*The Science of Evil*), and Kevin Dutton (*The Wisdom of Psychopaths*), the latter of whom I queried for this article, "estimates of the incidence of psychopathy tend to vary from 1–3 percent in men and 0.5–1 per cent in women," and in prison populations, "around 50 percent of the most serious crimes on record – crimes such as murder and serial rape, for instance – are committed by psychopaths."[16]

2. *A sense of victimization or an ideological cause.* The thirty-two-year old Norwegian Anders Behring Breivik is a case in point: On July 22, 2011, he opened fire on participants in a Labour Party youth camp on Utoya island after exploding bombs in Oslo, resulting in a death toll of seventy-six, the worst tragedy in Norway since the Second World War. He said he did it to "send a strong message to the people and

cause maximum amount of damage to the Labour Party to stop a deconstruction of Norwegian culture and mass-import of Muslims."[17] Perpetrators of violence always have their reasons, including taking the law into their own hands when the state won't do what they think it should.

3. *The desire for fame and glory.* Forget *American Idol*, if you want instant media coverage there is no surer way to gain it in real time than by killing innocent people, especially children. In the case of the Chinese man who stabbed twenty-two children – reported to be "a long-term epilepsy sufferer" named Min Yongjun who was also "psychologically affected by rumors of the upcoming end of the world" – was quoted as saying: "I learned from the media two years ago that killing children would get me on TV."[18]

There are additional factors that increase the probability of a *Sandy Hook Event.* According to Columbia University Medical School psychiatrist Paul S. Applebaum: "There are characteristics that when they occur together markedly increase the risk of violent behavior: youth, male gender, substance abuse, paranoid view of the world, hostility and difficulty controlling anger, and preoccupation with weapons. Put those things together and you have identified a group of people who are at much greater risk than the average person of committing a violent act."[19] The problem, Applebaum continues, "is that there are tens of thousands of people who fall into that category and the majority of them will never commit a violent act, and that's the limit of our predictive abilities today."[20]

THE PREDICTION AND PREVENTION PROBLEM

Psychopathy is subject to the same false-positive problem. As a back-of-the-envelope calculation, let us employ the midrange figure of 2 percent psychopathy for men only. The current US population is approximately 314 million, about half of which are males, so if 2 percent of the 157 million American men are psychopathic, this results in a figure of 3,140,000. Most of these men are not violent; in fact, as Kevin Dutton reveals in his book, many successful CEOs, politicians, Wall Street traders, and special forces soldiers employ their psychopathic personality traits of tough-minded and emotionless impulsive decision making to great effect in the rough-and-tumble world of business, politics, and war. So let's conservatively estimate that if only 1 percent of these 3,140,000 men commit any kind of violent act, this results in 31,400 acts of violence per year, a nontrivial number. If only 1 percent of those violent acts involve murders, this leaves us with 314 tragic deaths caused by psychopaths. And, finally, if only 1 percent of those murderous violent acts involves killing four or more people in one setting, this results in a rate of 3.14 *Sandy Hook Events* per year in America. Add schizophrenia, severe depression, and paranoid delusion into the formula and we quite likely have accounted for most of the *Sandy Hooks Events.*

Perhaps we can just administer the Psychopathic Personality Inventory (PPI) developed by the Emory University psychologist Scott Lilienfeld to everyone and then monitor those who score above a certain number? No. The PPI consists of a wide swath of personality dimensions measured by 187 questions, factor analyzed into a cluster of combined characteristics, such as Machiavellian Egocentricity, Impulsive Nonconformity, Blame Externalization, Carefree Nonplanfulness, and the like. The problem is that most of us have most of these personality traits in some measure. As Lilienfeld told Dutton in an interview, "You and I could post the same overall score on the PPI. Yet our profiles with regard to the eight constituent dimensions could be completely different. You might be high on Carefree Nonplanfulness and correspondingly low on Coldheartedness, whereas for me it might be the opposite."[21]

An additional prediction problem arises from the fact that we find such factors at work in most mass murderers and terrorists *after the fact.* But *before the fact,* predicting which individuals who harbor such characteristics will act on them is impossible, and any attempt to target such individuals would result in trapping in our net millions of innocent people who would never act on such impulses. For example, researchers at the University of Connecticut announced on December 28, 2012 that they had obtained a sample of Adam Lanza's DNA in order to search for a possible mass murderer mutation.[22] This is problematic on several levels. First, it is virtually impossible that violent behavior is caused by a single gene, since no complex behavior studied to date is. The most that can be hoped for is a complex set of genes that code for violent tendencies, which may then be triggered by any number of environmental factors. As such, it is entirely possible – highly probable in fact – that millions of people could have such a gene complex and never act on their violent tendencies, and then we're back to the problem of Type I false-positive errors in our search, and in the process violate the civil liberties of many innocent people.

What about the brains of mass murderers? Harvard University neuroscientist Joshua W. Buckholtz uses CAT scans and MRIs on the brains of those who commit acts of violence, explaining in an interview on a PBS *Frontline* special *After Newtown*: "When we compare people who commit violent acts against those who do not commit violent acts, some brain differences begin to emerge – differences in brain circuitry involved in emotional arousal and emotion regulation."[23] For example, the prefrontal cortex normally regulates the amygdala – our brain's emotion center that becomes active whenever a threat is perceived. If the threat is not real, the prefrontal cortex overrides amygdala activity, resulting in no response. But if the circuit between the prefrontal cortex and the amygdala is broken or mis-wired, the inhibitory signals may be blocked or rerouted, resulting in a false-positive response of violence when none was called for, as Buckholtz explained: "In those folks it seems like the circuit is broken in such a way that they are more likely to respond with greater amygdala activity and greater emotional arousal when they think they are being faced with some kind of threat."[24] The problem with brain scan research is that such patterns emerge only after examining a large number of brains, from which computers generate statistical averages that do not apply to any one brain.[25]

Additional mass murder myths abound that confound the prediction and prevention problem. For example, according to the aforementioned criminologist James Alan Fox:[26]

- Mass shootings are not on the rise, but have held steady over three decades, randomly clustering in time to trick our brains into finding a pattern of increase where none actually exists.
- Mass murderers do not snap and kill indiscriminately, but "plan their assaults for days, weeks, or months. They are deliberate in preparing

their missions and determined to follow through, no matter what impediments are placed in their path."

- Enhanced background checks do not keep dangerous weapons away from mass murderers because "Most mass murderers do not have criminal records or a history of psychiatric hospitalization. They would not be disqualified from purchasing their weapons legally." And even if they could not legally purchase the firearms needed, "mass killers could always find an alternative way of securing the needed weaponry, even if they had to steal from family members or friends."

- Restoring the federal ban on assault weapons will not stop *Sandy Hook Events* because "The overwhelming majority of mass murderers use firearms that would not be restricted by an assault-weapons ban. In fact, semiautomatic handguns are far more prevalent in mass shootings."

- Mass murders are unlikely to be deterred by increasing security in public places because "Most security measures will serve only as a minor inconvenience for those who are dead set on mass murder," as in the case of Columbine, whose armed guard was unable to stop Eric Harris and Dylan Klebold.

IS THERE NOTHING WE CAN DO?

If we cannot predict or prevent Sandy Hook Events, what can we do? I suggest three evidence-based actions we can take right now that could save lives.

1. Run, Hide, or Fight. There is an excellent video on self-defense on YouTube called "Run. Hide. Fight. Surviving an Active Shooter Event."[27] It is for people in offices, schools, or any public facility in which gunfire is heard. After calling 911, the first thing to do is to *run* – escape from the building as quickly as possible, taking as many people with you as you can. If people hesitate, encourage them to join you but leave them behind if they do not move at once. You have seconds to act and cannot afford to delay. If there is no clear escape route, *hide* underneath a desk, behind a wall or door, or inside any container in which you can fit. If you are in a room, lock the door and barricade it with furniture. Remain as quiet as possible and silence your cell phone. If these two actions do not work and you encounter the shooter, *fight* with anything and everything you've got – a chair, purse, fist, leg, anything you can throw, swing, or hit with. Do not hesitate. Attack like your life depends on it, because it does. At that moment you will likely either be killed or stop the killer long enough for others to join in.

2. A National Mental-Health Hotline. A joint effort between such governmental agencies as the National Institutes of Mental Health, the American Psychological Association, the Association for Psychological Science, the American Psychiatric Association, and the FBI could result in a national mental-health hotline for potentially violent psychopaths, schizophrenics, and severely depressed and delusional people who *also* exhibit behaviors indicative of violence *and* purchase large quantities of firearms and ammo. A *Mother Jones* study on "A Guide to Mass Shootings in America,"[28] for example, found that more than half (thirty-eight out of sixty-two) were committed by individuals with mental-health problems who had exhibited signs noticed by family, friends, or colleagues indicative that something was wrong and that violence of some kind was possible.[29] Depression, delusion, and paranoia were common features of the killers in this cohort, and thirty-six of them committed suicide at the end of their killing spree, with another seven opting for "suicide by cop" in a final Götterdämmerung with the police. A national database of people (1) reported as exhibiting a set of symptoms of mental disturbance such as acute depression, schizophrenia, extreme psychopathy, paranoid delusions, *and* (2) a clear sign of potential violence such as comments or letters or journal entries about killing people, *and especially* (3) the purchase of multiple weapons, ammunition, body armor, and other equipment, might be cause for authorities to at least pay a visit to the residence of the person in question.

A case in point is James Holmes, the Aurora, Colorado killer, who showed clear signs of a mental breakdown during the May to July timeframe in which he amassed an arsenal of 6,295 rounds of ammunition, two handguns, a shotgun, an assault rifle, ballistic gear, laser sights and holsters, and tear gas canisters, all delivered to his doorstep.[30] Competent data analysts working with such a national database could easily ferret out potential candidates for mass murder. This would be something like a citizens watch program in which all of us should be paying attention to the people around us, most notably our immediate family, friends, and colleagues. On the day I was writing this section (January 7, 2013), for example, ABC News reported that an eastern Alabama high school teacher turned over to the police a student journal she found that "contained several plans that looked like potential terrorist attacks, and attacks of violence and danger on the school," including targeting six students and one teacher by name. That young man, a seventeen-year old named Derek Shrout, identified in the media as a white supremacist targeting five black students and one gay student, was promptly arrested on attempted assault charges after police searched his home and found numerous cans filled with pellets that, according to the sheriff, were just "a step or two away from being ready to explode," adding that "the system worked and thank God it did. We avoided a very bad situation."[31] What system? A mass murder was averted thanks entirely to the bottom-up actions of an alert citizen, not the top-down measures of authorities.

Of course, the civil liberties of such individuals would need to be protected, and law-enforcement agencies would have to be leery of false charges made out of revenge against rivals, but surely someone reported by close friends, family, or colleagues as having severe mental-health issues, who has made violent threats involving mass murder, and who has purchased an arsenal of firearms and ammunition, might at least alert local authorities to be extra vigilant.

3. *Gun Control.* This is the most talked about option for preventing *Sandy Hook Events*, but it's a complicated route with numerous permutations. First, the most common weapon of all homicides and mass murders is a handgun, and the United States Supreme Court ruled in 2008 (in *District of Columbia v. Heller*)[32] and again in 2010 (*McDonald v. Chicago*)[33] that the Second Amendment's guarantee of the right to "keep and bear arms" includes handguns. And once the Supreme Court has ruled on a case – twice in this instance – the chances of overturning such rulings are next to nil. In any case, with over 300 million guns already in the homes and on the streets of America, short of turning the United States

into the Stasi States wherein police sweep through every home, business, garage, shack, storage unit, cabin, car, and container in every nook and cranny in every state in the union (likely resulting in multiple Ruby Ridge and Waco-type confrontations with those who resist), gun bans will most likely be honored by the people who least need them and ignored by those who need them most. Even talk of stricter gun-control laws following the Sandy Hook massacre has driven gun sales through the roof. A gun show in Ontario, California, the first weekend of 2013, for example, was overflowing with customers lined up outside the door to get in, and those who made it inside were snapping up firearms and ammunition at record rates. One customer noted "I'll tell you right now, Obama is the No. 1 gun salesman in the nation. The NRA should give him an award." The FBI reported that December 2012 was the biggest month in their history for the number of firearm background checks conducted, at 2.78 million.[34] In one month alone nearly three million people purchased guns. Staggering.

Here is a typical suggestion for a reasonable gun-control measure, from the aforementioned psychiatrist Paul Applebaum:

> Even in the face of our difficulties of predicting and preventing violent behavior in general, there is an approach we can take today that will markedly reduce the likelihood of horrific crimes like what occurred at Newtown, CT, were we to remove from easy access weapons that are designed solely for the purpose of killing large numbers of people – semi-automatic weapons, high-volume clips, bullets intended to seriously maim and kill their victims. That could have an impact today while we wait for the science to improve, while we wait to have a better capacity to identify people who are likely to behave in violent ways.[35]

Let's examine these options in more detail. Banning semiautomatic weapons is not likely to have a significant effect on *Sandy Hook Events* since most are committed by handguns, and the evidence for the effectiveness of bans on semiautomatic weapons on overall crime rates is mixed. Following the ten-year Federal Assault Weapons Ban enacted in the United States in 1994, the National Research Council (NRC) reviewed all academic studies of the assault weapon ban, concluding that the data "did not reveal any clear impacts on gun violence," and noted, "due to the fact that the relative rarity with which the banned guns were used in crime before the ban . . . the maximum potential effect of the ban on gun violence outcomes would be very small."[36]

On the pro-gun side of the debate, John Lott, whom I spent a weekend with in Santa Fe, New Mexico, at a conference and whose book *More Guns, Less Crime* has been a steady flash point for controversy, argues that gun bans have the opposite effect than intended.[37] Take Washington, DC, he says. Before the ban on handguns was implemented in August of 1976, DC ranked twentieth in murder rates out of the top fifty cities in America. After the gun ban, DC shot up to either #1 or #2, where year after year it held steady as "the murder capital of the nation," as it was dubbed by the media. As a control experiment of sorts, after the Supreme Court decision in the 2008 Heller case overturned the DC gun ban, murder rates dropped and have continued to fall ever since. According to Lott, whose data is based primarily on crime statistics provided by the FBI, once the gun ban was lifted, homicide rates plummeted 42.1 percent, sexual assault rates dropped 14.9 percent, robbery excluding guns dropped 34.3 percent, robbery with guns plunged 58 percent, assault with a dangerous weapon excluding guns sank 11 percent, assault with a dangerous weapon using guns tumbled 35.6 percent, and total violent crime nosedived 31 percent, along with total property crimes decreasing a total of 10.7 percent.

Why do more guns mean less crime? Lott says it is because it is hard to keep criminals from getting and keeping guns because gun bans are primarily obeyed by noncriminals. Criminals that already have guns do not turn them in, and potential criminals that want to get guns have no problem procuring them illegally on the street (and in any case most mass murderers obtained their guns legally). Lott cited several studies by criminologists who interviewed criminals in jail and collected data on the amount of time they spend casing a home before burglarizing it. In the UK, where gun bans are much more prevalent than in the USA, the criminals reported that they spend very little time casing a joint and that they don't really care if someone is home or not because they know the residents won't be armed (whereas they, of course, are armed). Their US counterparts, by contrast, reported spending more than double the time casing a home before robbing it, explaining that they were waiting for the residents to leave. Why? They said that they were worried they would be shot.

Lott has his critics, some of whom resort to ad hominem attacks (such as Piers Morgan and Alan Dershowitz)[38] while others more thoughtfully challenge his data.[39] I agree with Lott that gun bans have done little to reduce crime, at least in the United States, but I disagree with Lott that the lifting of gun bans is the cause of the decline of violence in the 1990s and 2000s. That cause is hotly disputed, with everything from the Freakonomics theory (that *Roe v. Wade* led to fewer unwanted children being born in the 1970s and thus fewer kids growing up in poverty and becoming criminals in the 1990s),[40] to more police on the beat and assorted other factors well summarized by Steven Pinker in *The Better Angels of Our Nature*.[41]

The most cited study in support of gun control comes out of Australia following a 1996 firearm massacre in Tasmania in which thirty-five people were murdered. State governments agreed to ban semiautomatic and pump-action shotguns and rifles. A 2006 follow-up study measured "changes in trends of total firearm death rates, mass fatal shooting incidents, rates of firearm homicide, suicide and unintentional firearm deaths, and of total homicides and suicides per 100,000 population." The data showed that in the eighteen years before the ban there were thirteen mass shootings, but in the decade following the ban there were none. Statistically significant declines were also found for total firearm deaths, firearm suicides, and firearm homicides (but not for unintentional firearm deaths). There was also "no evidence of substitution effect for suicides or homicides," and "the rates per 100,000 of total firearm deaths, firearm homicides and firearm suicides all at least doubled their existing rates of decline after the revised gun laws." The authors concluded:

> Australia's 1996 gun law reforms were followed by more than a decade free of fatal mass shootings, and accelerated declines in firearm deaths, particularly suicides. Total homicide rates followed the same pattern. Removing large numbers of rapid-firing firearms from civilians may be an effective way of reducing mass shootings, firearm homicides and firearm suicides.[42]

Is Australia comparable to America? I have my doubts. The population is much smaller and more homogeneous, and the number of guns already in circulation is orders of magnitude smaller, and the "gun culture" there is nothing like it is in America.

Another common element found among mass murderers is large-capacity magazines, most notably at Fort Hood, Texas, on the Virginia Tech campus, and in Tucson at the Gabrielle Giffords shooting where the killer used a 33-round magazine. The prohibition of high-volume ammo magazines seems like a rational response based on the fact that a number of mass murders were ended by bystanders and police when the killers stopped to reload.[43] As the aforementioned criminologist James Allen Fox noted, "limiting the size of ammunition clips would at least force a gunman to pause to reload or switch weapons."[44] The proposed legislation on the table, introduced after the 1993 Long Island Rail Road killing by Representative Carolyn McCarthy (whose husband was killed in the shooting), is called *The High Capacity Ammunition Feeding Device Act*, and it would prohibit magazines that hold more than ten bullets (the maximum now is 100).[45] That seems reasonable to me, and hunters who claim otherwise can give their game a more sporting chance of escape – if you can't nail them in ten rounds they deserve to live.

WHOSE RIGHTS?

As a lifelong libertarian I have opposed gun-control measures, primarily based on the larger principle of increasing individual freedom and decreasing government intervention. Plus, I've been a gun owner most of my life. I was raised with guns – my step-father was a hunter and we shot dove, duck, and quail with 20-gauge and 12-gauge shotguns that we owned and kept in the house. Growing up, I had a BB gun, then a pellet gun, than a 20-gauge shotgun, then a 12-gauge shotgun (the lower number is the higher caliber gun). We had black Labrador re-trievers, and we went hunting with them half a dozen times a year; we ate everything we shot, which was especially enjoyable given my father's culinary skills with wild game. As an adult, for a quarter-century I owned a Ruger 357 Magnum pistol with hollow-tip bullets designed to rip to shreds a human body intruding into my home with intent to harm my family. After I started having marital problems, I took it out of the house and eventually got rid of it, having studied the psychology of human violence and knowing the statistic cited above about a gun being twenty-two times more likely to be used on yourself or a family member than on a home invader. I own no guns now, but I am not opposed to those who believe having a gun in the home is the best way to protect themselves and their family.

Even though it is not clear that the two suggested legislations banning assault rifles and large-capacity magazines over ten bullets would have a significant effect on mass murders, there could be a net gain, and it seems to me to be no great threat to liberty if we lump them with the already-existing bans on private citizens owning and operating bazookas, tanks, drone aircraft, fighter jets, and nuclear weapons. Bans on semiau-tomatic assault rifles and high-volume ammo clips will not stop *Sandy Hook Events*, but there is some evidence that they could curtail the level of carnage, and that strikes me as a rational response that even freedom-loving libertarians can live with. Recall the words of the Aurora, Colorado shooting victim Jessica Ghawi, who was almost gunned down in a shopping mall in Toronto in another mass murder the month before, after which she reflected on her blog: "I was shown how fragile life was on Saturday. I saw the terror on bystanders' faces. I saw the victims of a senseless crime. I saw lives change. I was reminded that we don't know when or where our time on Earth will end. When or where we will breathe our last breath."[46]

CHAPTER 16

On Guns and Tyranny

PREAMBLE

Since I wrote "The Sandy Hook Effect" in 2012, gun violence has continued to fill the evening news, most notably the massacre in Las Vegas on October 1, 2017. In response to that horrific event, I penned an opinion editorial for the *New York Times*, solicited and edited by the estimable editor Bari Weiss, addressing the argument by pro-gun advocates that guns are a deterrent against tyranny. What follows is an expanded version of that op-ed that includes the problem of copycat mass murders, in which perpetrators seek fame through their murderous acts, and a simple solution to it.

* * *

I N THE WAKE OF THE LAS VEGAS MASSACRE – THE WORST IN modern American history, with 59 dead and 527 wounded – the onus falls once again to those against gun control to make their case. The two most common arguments made in defense of broad gun ownership are (a) self protection and (b) as a bulwark against tyranny. Let's consider each one.

Stories about the use of guns in self-defense – a good guy with a gun dispensing with a bad guy with a gun – are legion among gun enthusiasts and conservative talk radio hosts. But a 1998 study in the *Journal of Trauma and Acute Care Surgery*, to take one of many examples, found that "every time a gun in the home was used in a self-defense or legally justifiable shooting, there were four unintentional shootings, seven criminal assaults or homicides, and 11 attempted or completed suicides." That means a gun is twenty-two times more likely to be used in a criminal assault, an accidental death or injury, a suicide attempt, or a homicide than it is for self-defense. A 2003 study published in the journal *Annals of Emergency Medicine* examined gun ownership levels among thousands of murder and suicide victims and nonvictims and found that having guns in the home was associated with a 41 percent increase in homicide and 244 percent increase in suicide. The Second Amendment protects your right to own a gun, but having one in your home involves a risk–benefit calculation you should seriously consider.

The wording of the Second Amendment explicitly evokes the idea that guns stand as a deterrent against tyrannical governments. The proclamation that "a well regulated militia being necessary to the security of a free state, the right of the people to keep and bear arms shall not be infringed" made sense in the 1770s, when breech-loading flintlock muskets were the primary weapons tyrants used to conquer other peoples and subdue their own citizens, who could, in turn, equalize the power equation by arming themselves with equivalent firepower. That is no longer true. If you think stock piling firearms from the local Guns & Guitars store, where the Las Vegas shooter purchased some of his many weapons, and dressing up in camouflage and body armor is going to protect you from the US military's tanks delivering Navy SEALs to your door, you're delusional. The tragic outcomes of Ruby Ridge and Waco in the 1990s, in which citizens armed to the teeth collided with government agencies and lost badly, is a microcosm of what would happen were the citizenry to rise up in violence against the state today.

If you're having trouble with the government, a lawyer is a much more potent weapon than a gun. Bureaucrats, politicians, and police fear citizens armed with lawyers more than they do a public fortified with guns. The latter they can just shoot. The former means they have to appear before a judge.

A civil society based on the rule of law with a professional military to protect its citizens from external threats, a police force to protect civilians from internal dangers, a criminal justice system to peacefully settle disputes between the state and its citizenry, and a civil court system to enable individuals to resolve conflicts nonviolently have been the primary drivers in the dramatic decline of violence over the past several centuries. States reduce violence by asserting a monopoly on the legitimate use of force, thereby replacing what criminologists call "self-help justice," in which individuals settle their own scores, often violently, such as drug gangs and the Mafia. Homicide rates, for example, have plummeted a hundredfold since fourteenth-century England, in which there were 110 homicides per 100,000 people per year, compared to less than 1 per 100,000 today. Similar declines in murder rates have been documented in Germany, Switzerland, Italy, the Netherlands and Scandinavia. (US homicide rates are around five times higher than in Europe, owing primarily to the deadly combination of guns and gangs.)

There's no question that tyrannical states have abused the freedom of their citizens. But it is no longer realistic to think that arming citizens to the teeth is going to stop tyranny should it arise. Far superior are non-violent democratic checks and balances on power, constitutional guardians of civil rights, and legal protections of liberties.

What else can we do to reduce the carnage of mass murders? First, we must recognize the impossibility of ever bringing the number down to zero – as it is in most countries where guns are unavailable – because there are more guns in America than there are people, ownership of most of them is perfectly legal, and there's a black market for guns for those who could not get them otherwise. That fact isn't going to change any time soon, so our goal should be to attenuate gun violence, not eliminate it. What can we do?

Of the many proposals on the table for discussion, there is one that can be implemented today by the media: Don't name or show the mass murderers. A September 2017 article in *American Behavioral Scientist* by Adam Lankford and Eric Madfis reported that as many as twenty-four mass murderers admitted that they went on their killing rampage in order to gain fame. The 1999 Columbine shooters, for example, fantasized about movies that would be made about them, which happened. The 2007 Virginia Tech assassin made a martyrdom video and sent it to NBC News, which aired clips from it. The 2011 Tucson murderer proclaimed online "I'll see you on National T.V.!" and sure enough, there he was. The 2012 Sandy Hook school shooter wrote about "my catalog of mass murderers" that he wanted to best on his killing spree, which he did. The 2014 Isla Vista, California gunman wrote in his manifesto that "infamy is better than total obscurity . . . I never knew how to gain positive attention, only negative." That he got in spades. The 2015 Roanoke shooter mailed his suicide note to ABC News. During his rampage the

2016 Orlando nightclub killer called the local News 13 to report his own actions, then checked his social media to see if he had "gone viral" yet. "These fame-seeking offenders are particularly dangerous because they kill and wound significantly more victims than other active shooters," the authors conclude, "they often compete for attention by attempting to maximize victim fatalities, and they can inspire contagion and copycat effects."

The media already has a moratorium on naming or showing victims of sex crimes, so expanding the ban on publicity to include mass murderers is surely a step in the right direction. Don't give these guys what they want.

CHAPTER 17

Debating Guns

What Conservatives and Liberals Really Differ On about Guns (and Everything Else)

PREAMBLE

This essay began as a blog post on *Skeptic.com* that I wrote after a series of debates I did with John Lott, who has emerged as one of the strongest opponents of gun-control measures and a regular guest on Fox News. The original blog included my PowerPoint slides and accompanying commentary that I used in my debates; here I primarily focus on my experiences debating Lott, drawing on some of the more poignant data slides I used to counter his thesis that more guns equals less crime. This is followed by a discussion of a more recent debate I did with a radical gun advocate named Michael Huemer, who made the argument for guns as a necessary bulwark against governmental tyranny, which I debunked in the previous essay.

I did not fully understand where Lott and Huemer (or gun-rights advocates of any kind) were coming from until I read George Lakoff's book *Moral Politics*, which lifted the scales from my eyes and enabled me to understand what both conservatives and liberals really want, and not just in the realm of gun control but in all dominions of life. The final part of this essay addresses those insights. The next time you find yourself in a debate (formally or informally) with a gun advocate (or gun-control proponent), understand – as I now do, thanks to Lakoff – that the debate is not really about guns or gun controls. It is about something much more fundamental, and therefore the topic carries much greater emotional salience.

* * *

I N MARCH AND APRIL OF 2013, I DEBATED GUN ADVOCATE JOHN Lott four different times on four university campuses: The University of South Alabama in Mobile, the University of Texas Permian Basin, Indiana University in Pennsylvania, and Penn State University, Altoona. Here are a few of my general impressions of the debates.

Despite the fact that most college campuses (especially public universities) skew far left politically and liberals tend to be in favor of more gun control, the audiences at all four campuses were over-whelming in support of Lott, even before the debates began. I could see it in their eyes as I looked out over the audience – I've been a professional speaker for over twenty-five years and have an intuitive sense of whether or not an audience is with me, and these folks were definitely agin me, especially in Texas, where I privately suspected (and publicly joked about) half the audience packing heat. They probably were!

As for Lott himself, he has turned out to be one of the more curious characters I have ever met in my career as a public intellectual. (See Figure 17.1.) In our Altoona debate, for example, I sat in the front row while Lott delivered his twenty-five-minute opening statement, but when it came my

Figure 17.1 Michael Shermer speaking at Penn State University, Altoona. Photo credit: Marissa Carney, media and public relations coordinator at Penn State Altoona; reproduced courtesy of Penn State, Altoona.

Figure 17.2 Michael Shermer speaking at Penn State University, Altoona. Photo credit: Marissa Carney, media and public relations coordinator at Penn State Altoona; reproduced courtesy of Penn State, Altoona.

turn to deliver my opening statement, Lott just sat there on stage next to me, which, with the arrangement of the podiums right next to each other, would mean I could not walk around on stage as is my custom. I politely asked him to leave the stage, but he refused. I then asked him to at least move so I could have some space to move about a little, but he just moved his chair a bit and turned his back to me, as seen in Figure 17.2.

After the debate, someone in the audience told me that throughout my presentation Lott was rolling his eyes and making faces in response to my points. This person found Lott's behavior to be rude, but I think Lott simply can't help himself. I suspect he might be on the spectrum with something like Asperger's syndrome, where he just blurts out what is on his mind and, when asked questions, delivers long and rambling answers that are so convoluted that by the time he's done talking it's hard to remember what the original question was. This was the case even in private time with Lott, for example when we were in the limo being driven to the debate venues from our hotel. In one case, this was a long drive of about ninety minutes each way, so we spent a lot of time in a very closed space together, time he had no problem filling with long stories and mini-lectures, most of which I rather enjoyed. He's a likeable enough fellow, but I don't trust his numbers when it comes to gun control. In my opinion he's more of a committed advocate than a nonpartisan scholar. He would, of course, disagree with that assessment.

Either way, Lott is remarkably adroit with numbers, demographics, studies, and statistics related to guns, and he can rattle them off from memory in a debate or on a television show. I did my homework on Lott's research and his critics, and prepared slides summarizing studies that are (1) critical of Lott's methods and results, and (2) show the exact opposite of what he concluded in his title-by-thesis book: *More Guns, Less Crime.* As often as not, more guns is associated with *more crime*, particularly homicide.

As a quick-and-dirty guide to the gun-control debate, here are a few of the key take-home points from my PowerPoint presentation, starting with NRA Executive Vice President Wayne LaPierre's famous proclamation:

> The only thing that stops a bad guy with a gun is a good guy with a gun.

In other words, the NRA's solution to crime and violence is to arm everyone to the teeth and hope the good guys out-gun the bad guys. In essence, it's saying:

> America is a lawless society in which criminals run the show so arm yourself to the teeth.

Now, at this point in the debate I acknowledged:

> If the good guys with guns are well-armed and professionally trained police and military who routinely practice at shooting ranges, then yes, this is one among many factors in the decline of violence over the centuries. But if "good guys" means armed private citizens with little to no gun training, this could not be more wrong.

A brief scan of YouTube videos under the search string "gun mishaps and negligent discharges" (or any number of related key-words) will provide hours of mostly entertaining – but sometimes tragic – gun accidents due almost entirely to human error and ignorance. This is why I conclude:

> Arming everyone to the teeth as a solution to the problem of crime and violence is quite possibly the worst idea anyone has ever had.

Why? Because it runs counter to all of the research on the decline of violence as documented in Steven Pinker's magisterial 2011 book *The Better Angels of Our Nature: Why Violence Has Declined*. I won't review that research here as it would require an entire article to properly summarize – and I wrote my own 500-page book on the related topic of moral progress, *The Moral Arc*, that reviews this literature – but in a single observation let me quote my own PPT slide:

> On time scales ranging from years to centuries, the decline of violence and the increase in peace has been the result of *disarming* the citizens of civil societies.

How?

> A state with a monopoly on the legitimate use of force: (1) Decreases incentives for exploitative attack; (2) Reduces the need for deterrence and vengeance; (3) Replaces "self-help justice" with criminal justice; (4) Eliminates a "culture of honor" with a culture of civility.

As for guns and violence, consider the fact that crime rates in the United States are comparable to other Western countries who have few guns:

> Car theft, burglary, robbery, sexual assault, aggravated assault, and adolescent fighting rates in the U.S. are similar to those of other high-income countries. But U.S. homicide rates are off the charts higher. Why? Guns!

For every 100 Americans there are around 90 guns. Of course, many people have no guns, which means a lot of people have a lot of guns. As a consequence, homicide rates in the USA are many times greater than that of any other Western democracy and even higher than most crime-ridden lawless third-world countries. Homicide rates in European countries, for example, are less than 1 per 100,000, whereas in the USA it is about 5.5 per 100,000 (higher in cities like Chicago). The correlation is starkly clear in between-country comparisons evidenced in Figure 17.3, which shows unmistakably that *more guns means more gun deaths.*

A similarly striking correlation is seen in gun ownership v. gun deaths by state within the United States: the higher the rate of gun ownership in a state, the more gun deaths per 100,000 people, as in this graph (Figure 17.4) from *Mother Jones*. Once again, *more guns means more gun deaths.*

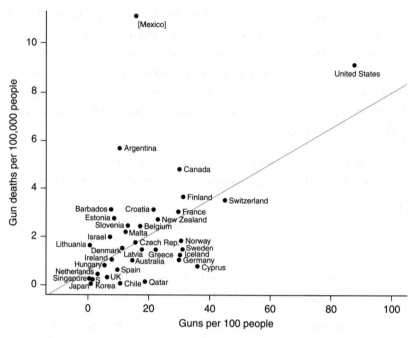

Figure 17.3 Gun deaths v. gun ownership.

In a comprehensive 2011 study on "Homicide, Suicide and Unintentional Gun Deaths among 5–14 year olds," comparing the United States to twenty-five other high-income countries, published in the *Journal of Trauma Injury, Infection and Critical Care*, David Hemenway and his colleagues found these stark mortality-rate ratios (the number on the left represents the US homicide and suicide rates for gun and non-gun causes as a ratio to the average of twenty-five other high-income countries):

Non-Gun Homicides 1.7 : 1
Gun Homicides 13.2 : 1
Non-Gun Suicides 1.3 : 1
Gun Suicides 7.8 : 1
Unintentional Gun Deaths 10.3 : 1

In other words, for non-gun related homicides and suicides, there's not that much difference between the USA and other Western nations, but the equation shifts dramatically once someone picks up a gun. The reason is as obvious as it is tragic: Guns are far less forgiving than other

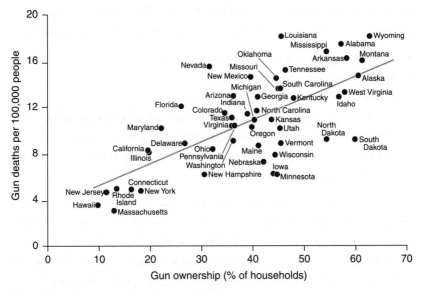

Figure 17.4 Gun ownership v. gun deaths by state.

methods of homicide and suicide. When a couple of drunken guys at a bar get into fisticuffs, it mostly results in bruised bodies and egos, but add a gun into the mix and someone is going to the morgue while the other person is headed to prison. When people attempt suicide, they don't always want to kill themselves. We know from studies on people who failed to kill themselves that, according to my friend and colleague Dr. Ralph Lewis, a psychiatrist who treats people in existential crises,

> They say "I don't know what came over me. I don't know what I was thinking." This is why suicide prevention is so important because people can be very persuasive in arguing why they believe life – their life – is not worth living. And yet the situation looks radically different months later, sometimes because of an anti-depressant, sometimes because of a change in circumstances, sometimes just a mysterious change of mind.

A misguided overdose of medications or botched attempt at slit wrists may grant someone a second chance at life. Guns are less inclined to fail.

In my debates with John Lott, he would often ask: "Can you name one place where guns have been banned that has seen its murder rate fall?"

My answer: Yes! Austria. In 1997 the Austrian government tightened its legislation on firearms to match that of EU laws about guns, including

- Required age minimum of twenty-one years old
- Required background check
- Required proof of safe firearm storage
- A three-day "cooling off" period before the gun becomes available for use
- Required reasons for a firearm purchase must be provided
- Psychological testing before obtaining handguns, semiautomatic firearms, and repeating guns.

A decade later, in 2007, the *British Journal of Psychiatry* published a study titled "Firearm Legislation Reform in the European Union: Impact on Firearm Availability, Firearm Suicide and Homicide rates in Austria," in which the authors Nestor Kapusta, et al. discovered that between 1985 and 2005 there was a marked reduction in the rate of firearm licenses associated with a significant decrease in the rate of firearm suicides, the percent of firearm suicides, and the rate of firearm homicides before and after the gun-control law was passed. The researchers concluded:

> Our findings provide evidence that the introduction of restrictive firearm legislation effectively reduced the rates of firearm suicide and homicide. The decline in firearm-related deaths seems to have been mediated by the legal restriction of firearm availability.

The findings are as visually striking as they are viscerally conclusive in this series of graphs from the paper that I presented in my PowerPoint presentation (Figure 17.5).

One final point from my debates that I didn't cover in my essay "The Sandy Hook Effect" is that gun advocates repeat like a mantra:

> When Guns Are Outlawed, Only Outlaws Will Have Guns.

In busting this myth, I point out:

- Gun control ≠ guns outlawed.
- Gun control ≠ anti-gun.
- Handguns are protected by 2nd Amendment.

(a) Firearm license rates before and after the 1997 firearm legislation was passed.

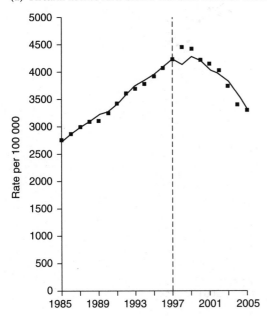

(b) Firearm suicide rates before and after the 1997 firearm legislation.

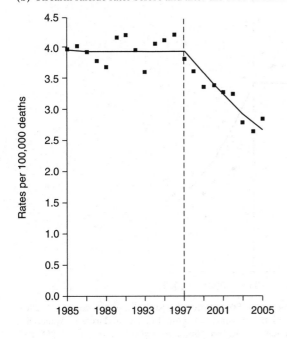

(c) Firearm suicides as a percent of total suicides before and after the 1997 firearm legislation.

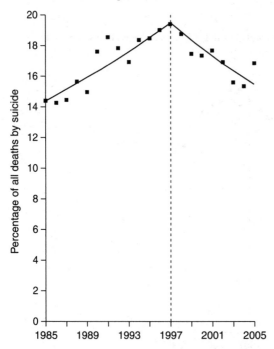

(d) Firearm homicide rates per 100,000 people before and after the 1997 firearm legislation.

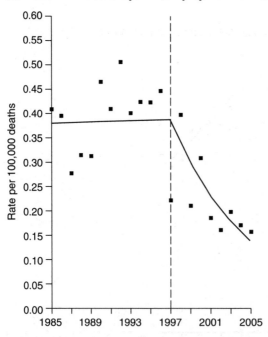

Figure 17.5 Graphs from Kapusta, N., Etzersdorfer, E., Krall, C., and Sonneck, G. 2007. "Firearm Legislation Reform in the European Union: Impact on Firearm Availability, Firearm Suicide and Homicide Rates in Austria." *British Journal of Psychiatry*, 191:3, 253–257. doi:10.1192/bjp.bp.106.032862. Reproduced by permission of Cambridge University Press.

- No "slippery slope": The licensing and regulation of cars does not mean only outlaws will drive cars!
- Police and courts need gun regulation to bar high-risk people from guns.

For example, the 1934 National Firearms Act, regulating the manufacture and sale of machine guns (and backed by the NRA!), did not result in only outlaws having machine guns! Where is today's "Machine Gun" Kelly? There are none because machine guns are regulated and restricted. This is rational gun control that even the NRA can get behind.

GUN VIOLENCE V. TERRORISM VIOLENCE

In October 2018 I participated in another gun-control debate, this one at the Center for Ethics, Economics, and Public Policy at San Diego University on "Does America Need Stricter Gun-Control Laws?" My debate opponent was the University of Colorado, Boulder philosopher Michael Huemer, whose political leanings are so far beyond libertarian (he calls himself a philosophical anarchist) that he makes me look like a big-government endorsing bleeding-heart liberal. Huemer's arguments differed from those made by John Lott, focused as they were more on political freedom and why guns represent a safeguard against governmental tyranny, so the arguments made in the previous essay ("On Guns and Tyranny") were relevant in this context. I also updated my PowerPoint slides, for example, showing that over 37,000 people died by guns in 2016 and that more people now die by guns than die in automobile accidents. I closed with a bullet-point summation of my conclusions in "The Sandy Hook Effect," points that I still contend are reasonable measures that both liberals and conservatives should be able to agree upon:

- Ban military-style assault weapons
- Ban high-capacity magazines (>10 bullets)
- Universal background check system
- Close the gun-show loophole
- Penalties for illegal gun trafficking
- Ban high-risk individuals from guns (convicted of violent crime, drugs, stalking, restraining orders)

- Ban sales to dangerous mentally ill
- Research funding on gun violence.

My concluding slide in this debate, as it was for my Lott debates, was anodyne enough to be acceptable to most politicos:

> Even though we can't do everything, we can do *something* to reduce the carnage of gun violence and further bend the arc of the moral universe toward justice, peace, and freedom.

Since I knew Huemer's tact would be a political one and that there was a good chance the audience would skew conservative, I added a data set comparing the number of American deaths caused by terrorism v. guns between 2004 and 2013: 313 died by terrorism, 316,545 died by gun. It's a shocking comparison: in that time frame, for every American killed by terrorism in the United States and abroad more than 1,000 died by gun violence in the USA (by all causes: homicide, suicide, and accident). I then made the following point, directed more at the conservatives in the room rather than my opponent, who probably agrees with me:

> Conservatives think nothing of suspending civil rights and ramping up big government intrusion into our private lives in the name of "Homeland Security" over terrorism deaths that are not even in the statistical noise compared to gun deaths. If over 30,000 people died annually from terrorism in the U.S. – the equivalent of over ten 9/11's every year – conservatives would declare a national emergency, quadruple the national defense budget, and suspend the Constitution (except for the 2nd Amendment, of course).

WHAT CONSERVATIVES AND LIBERALS REALLY DIFFER ON ABOUT GUNS (AND EVERYTHING ELSE)

This nonbenign hypocrisy is emblematic of an even larger inconsistency in the political narrative that one often hears on the Right, particularly when it comes to guns: Conservatives believe in "small government" and "limited government." No, they don't. In addition to the massive government buildup in response to terrorism since 9/11, conservatives believe in substantial government intervention in social, political, and economic life when it supports their preferred worldview. What worldview is that?

According to the cognitive psychologist George Lakoff, in his deeply insightful book *Moral Politics: How Liberals and Conservatives Think* (University of Chicago Press, 1996), all of us use metaphors to navigate the world. Scientists, for example, employ such metaphors as the universe is like a clock or a machine, natural selection is like artificial selection used by breeders, neurons operate like digital computer chips, the mind works like a parallel processing computer, and so forth. In the social and moral world, Lakoff, who studies how the use of such metaphors alters how we perceive the world, has identified a core metaphor of the nation as a family, of which there are two types: Conservatives employ a "Strict Father" family model, while liberals embrace a "Nurturant Parent" family model. Before we turn to what conservatives and liberals really differ on with regard to guns, let's look at these metaphors more deeply.

The Strict Father model predictably adheres to the traditional nuclear family "with the father having primary responsibility for supporting and protecting the family as well as the authority to set overall policy, to set strict rules for the behavior of children, and to enforce the rules" while the mother "has the day-to-day responsibility for the care of the house, raising the children, and upholding the father's authority." Obedience is the key to building character and self-reliance. "Self-discipline, self-reliance, and respect for legitimate authority are the crucial things that children just learn." Much follows from understanding how this family metaphor plays out in the political arena. With the nation as a family and the government as the parents, it is clear why conservatives contend that the purpose of government is to demand its citizens be self-disciplined, self-reliant, and to help themselves, and why liberals hold that the purpose of government is to help those who cannot help themselves through social programs. Lakoff summarized the implications of these metaphor differences in an interview, starting with the conservative's Strict Father model, which

> assumes that the world is dangerous and difficult and that children are born bad and must be made good. The strict father is the moral authority who supports and defends the family, tells his wife what to do, and teaches

his kids right from wrong. The only way to do that is through painful discipline – physical punishment that by adulthood will become internal discipline. The good people are the disciplined people. Once grown, the self-reliant, disciplined children are on their own. Those children who remain dependent (who were spoiled, overly willful, or recalcitrant) should be forced to undergo further discipline or be cut free with no support to face the discipline of the outside world.

So, project this onto the nation and you see that to the right wing, the good citizens are the disciplined ones – those who have already become wealthy or at least self-reliant – and those who are on the way. Social programs, meanwhile, "spoil" people by giving them things they haven't earned and keeping them dependent. The government is there only to protect the nation, maintain order, administer justice (punishment), and to provide for the promotion and orderly conduct of business. In this way, disciplined people become self-reliant. Wealth is a measure of discipline. Taxes beyond the minimum needed for such government take away from the good, disciplined people rewards that they have earned and spend it on those who have not earned it.

By contrast, the Nurturant Parent model emphasizes love, empathy, and nurturance as the key to raising responsible and self-disciplined children. Obedience follows naturally from a child's love and respect for parents, and "when children are respected, nurtured, and communicated with from birth, they gradually enter into a lifetime relationship of mutual respect, communication, and caring with their parents." In his interview description of the Nurturant Parent family model, Lakoff noted that it

assumes that the world is basically good and can be made better and that one must work toward that. Children are born good; parents can make them better. Nurturing involves empathy, and the responsibility to take care of oneself and others for whom we are responsible. On a larger scale, specific policies follow, such as governmental protection in the form of a social safety net and government regulation, universal education (to ensure competence, fairness), civil liberties and equal treatment (fairness and freedom), accountability (derived from trust), public service (from responsibility), open government (from open communication), and the promotion of an economy that benefits all and functions to promote these values, which are traditional progressive values in American politics.

Awareness of these underlying metaphorical structures helps clarify apparent contradictions, paradoxes, and hypocrisies. When conservatives say that they are in favor of small government and limited governmental powers, for example, liberals rightly point out their hypocrisy when they call for an increase in military spending, demand that the borders be enforced, increase the reach of the Department of Homeland Security and the National Security Agency, step up police presence, insist on law and order, expand the power of the courts, and the like, all of which require bigger government and more federal intrusion into the private lives and individual liberties of American citizens. All of these measures expand government, but the inconsistency vanishes when one realizes that conservatives are not in favor of small government (despite what they proclaim); they are favor of a Strict Father government to impose discipline on the nation and provide security for its children. Similarly, when conservatives proclaim their belief in "freedom," liberals counter that being "pro-life" on the abortion issue restricts the freedom of adult women citizens by denying their constitutionally guaranteed reproductive rights. But it isn't "freedom" that conservatives value; it is discipline and self-control through the foundation of a two-parent nuclear family, so women getting pregnant out of wedlock or when they are not prepared to raise a child is a failure of the family patriarch that must be corrected.

Of course, conservatives are not aware that this is what they are doing – cognitive biases are rarely apparent to those subject to their influence, which is all of us – and so they couch their arguments in terms of protecting defenseless fetuses and asserting that they care about the lives and safety of children more than liberals. But we can see cognitive biases in others, so when conservatives cut the Aid to Families with Dependent Children (AFDC), which provided food and sustenance to starving children, liberals accused them of being hypocritical. (That program was replaced by the more restrictive Temporary Assistance for Needy Families program). But for conservatives, AFDC wasn't about helping those in need; instead they argued that it incentivized single-parenthood and disincentivized marriage, the very antithesis of the Strict Father family model. In like manner, when pro-life conservatives support capital punishment, liberals accused them of being pro-death. (As someone joked, conservatives are pro-life right up to the birth of the baby; after that, it's "hang 'em all and let God sort it out," as the country-and-western song says. Or, as some other wag quipped, conservatives are pro-life right up to the moment their mistress gets pregnant.) Lakoff shows why these are not hypocrisies in the context of these different cognitive metaphors as evidenced in the words and phrases used by each. For example, in embracing the Nurturant Parent family model of the nation liberals speak of,

> Social forces, social responsibility, free expression, human rights, equal rights, concern, care, help, health, safety, nutrition, basic human dignity, oppression, diversity, deprivation, alienation, big corporations, corporate welfare, ecology, ecosystem, biodiversity, pollution.

By contrast, conservatives in the embrace of the Strict Father family model of the nation, speak of,

> Character, virtue, discipline, tough it out, get tough, tough love, strong, self-reliance, individual responsibility, backbone, standards, authority, heritage, competition, earn, hard work, enterprise, property rights, reward, freedom, intrusion, interference, meddling, punishment, human nature, tradition, common sense, dependency, self-indulgent, elite, quotas, breakdown, corrupt, decay, rot, degenerate, deviant, lifestyle.

Guns, then, fit into the conservative lexicon as a proxy for self-defense, self-reliance, individual responsibility, authority, property rights, freedom, and punishment of wrong-doers. "Guns are seen as the individual's form of protection in a hostile world and they are symbolic of the male role as a family protector," Lakoff elaborates. "They are an instrument of moral strength and a symbol of the power of the Strict Father. As such, they also uphold the moral order." Gun-control advocates are therefore demonized, inasmuch as "they would take guns away from those who need them to protect themselves and their families both from criminals and from possible government tyranny." These differences also help explain why certain social and political issues cluster as they do, for example, gun-control opponents are also "opposed to social programs, progressive taxation, gay rights, multiculturalism, and abortion, and so on, while proponents of gun control have the opposite views on these issues." Gun advocates are also more inclined toward survivalism of the "prepper" type because "survivalism is about self-reliance through self-discipline, the hallmark of Strict Father morality."

Before I read Lakoff's book, I did not fully understand the arguments of gun advocates and gun-control opponents, nor the apparent hypocrisy of – in my example above – obsessing over terrorism violence but not gun violence. But that's because I was arguing with facts and data alone, not seeing guns for what they represent. Guns make perfect sense in the context of a strict father protecting his family from outside threats – from foreign terrorists to domestic tyrants – particularly through individual self-defense, which the gun has represented for centuries in this country.

CHAPTER 18

Another Fatal Conceit

The Lesson from Evolutionary Economics Is Bottom-Up
Self-Organization, Not Top-Down Government Design

PREAMBLE

This review essay was originally published in the *Journal of Bioeconomics* in March 2012 (Vol. 14, No. 2) under the above title and subtitle. It was initiated by Ulrich Witt, Professor of Economics and Director of the Evolutionary Economics Group at the Max Planck Institute in Jena, Germany. He asked me to review *The Darwin Economy: Liberty, Competition, and the Common Good* (Princeton University Press) by the economist Robert H. Frank, to which Frank would reply (https://bit.ly/23m8ioW). It was an intense but constructive exchange on some of the most important political and economic issues of our time, most notably solving the "collective action" problem of getting selfish actors in a social system (i.e., each of us individually) to forego what is good for us in the short term for what is good for all of us in the long term.

* * *

WHEN I ENTERED THE WORLD OF COMPETITIVE BICYCLE racing in 1980, no serious cyclist wore a helmet in training, and the leather "hair net" required by some race organizations – thin bands of leather-wrapped cotton stuffing – did nothing more than prevent your hair from getting mussed upon impacting pavement. Bell Helmets already had the technology from their motorcycle division to make a viable crash-tested safety helmet for bicycling, but elite cyclists are an elitist cohort that follows the trends of what looks good as much as what works well. The perception at the time was that a helmet was delimiting on performance and made you look like a "Fred" – two-wheel-speak for geek. Even if an individual cyclist wanted to don protection, unless everyone else did as well the competitive choice was to race sans helmet. When I was sponsored by Bell to compete in the Race Across America – the 3,000-mile nonstop transcontinental bicycle race – they engaged me to help design a helmet that elite cyclists would wear that would, in marketing theory, inspire the masses of two-wheelers to follow in emulation. We came up with the V1-Pro, a model that aped the leather hair net in design but was made of the same compressed polystyrene foam utilized in motorcycle helmets for absorbing the energy of an impact. Nonetheless, it was shunned by the pros until the Union Cycliste International (UCI) – the governing body of professional cycling – mandated the use of safety helmets for all cyclists in all races. No helmet, no race. Period. I was relieved, as were many other cyclists I knew, because I wanted to wear a helmet but didn't want to stand out or lose a slight competitive edge. In time, as helmet use grew in popularity, market forces worked effectively to make them lighter, cooler, and colorfully trendy. Now everyone wears them, and we are all better for it.

THE COLLECTIVE ACTION PROBLEM

According to the Cornell University economist Robert Frank, this is an example of a collective action problem that requires top-down government-like regulation. Without such mandated intervention, people will not do what is best for themselves or the group, and this leads to market inefficiencies and moral failures. In his latest book, *The Darwin Economy: Liberty, Competition, and the Common Good*, Frank uses such collective action problems to make the case for why governments must intervene in economic transactions. Financial exchanges in a free market carry externalities – benefits and costs not included in the price of the transaction that is incurred by one or more of the parties involved, with or without their knowledge or agreement. In my aforementioned example, the UCI had to intervene into and mandate the use of helmets for the collective good, because individual cyclists within the collective body known as the peloton will not have the motivation to do so otherwise (Frank uses National Hockey League hockey helmet rules as his type specimen, but in principle the problem is the same). From governing bodies in sports, Frank extrapolates to government agencies in society, arguing that in order to correct for market inefficiencies and moral failures, we need more government regulations and taxes.

Frank's term for this collective action problem is the "Darwin Economy," which he derives from his understanding of Darwinism and the mechanism of natural selection. The ornate and ostentatious tail of the peacock troubled Darwin for a spell because natural selection holds that animals should evolve characteristics that protect them from predation. The peacock's radiantly colorful tail is not exactly a model of stealthy camouflage. "The sight of a feather in a peacock's tail, whenever I gaze at it," Darwin bemoaned in an 1860 letter to his colleague Asa Grey, "makes me sick."[1] Darwin resolved the paradox a decade later through his theory of sexual selection, presented in his two-volume work *The Descent of Man, and Selection in Relation to Sex*, in which he demonstrated how females select males based on certain characteristics they find attractive, and males compete with other males for status, hierarchy, and females.[2]

In Frank's view, what is good for the individual peacock in attracting peahens by building a flamboyant tail is bad for the species in making everyone a greater target for predation; as well, building ever fancier tails is a waste of resources. If the peacocks could form a governing organization to establish and enforce rules to delimit tail design, the species would be better off. In like manner, Frank continues by example, the Brobdingnagian rack of antlers on the North American bull elk may intimidate other males competing for status and mates, but it endangers the species by decreasing efficiency of escape from wolves and other predators through thickly branched forests in which said rack would become entangled. This principle of individual success versus collective failure is so important to Frank that he goes so far as to predict that his fellow economists will, in time, come to see Charles Darwin as the most important economist in history.

The human analogue of tails and antlers for Frank are McMansion homes, expensive business suits, high-heel shoes, and extravagant coming-of-age parties. Much of his thinking here is derived from research conducted by behavioral economists, who report that relative position on the economic ladder – "positional rank" – matters more than absolute value to most people. Once you have a roof over your head and three square meals a day, it doesn't matter how much more money you make above basic needs as long as it is equal to or exceeds that of your neighbors. As H. L. Mencken quipped, "A wealthy man is one who earns $100 a year more than his wife's sister's husband." Remarkably, research shows that given the choice between, say, a $500,000 home in a neighborhood of million-dollar mansions and a $400,000 home on a street surrounded by $300,000 dwellings, most people opt for the latter.[3] They are apparently willing to pay $100,000 for the opportunity to be relatively richer even while being absolutely poorer. Economists call this the hedonic treadmill. Run as fast as you like, you'll never get there because there is no there, there, without a relative context that gives you a positional rank among your fellow consumers.[4]

In like manner, men competing for limited high-paying jobs will enter an arms race with their competitors for ever nicer and more expensive suits. If everyone wore a $500 suit to the interview, the playing field would be level, but when someone ups the ante and arrives in a $1,000 suit, the rest of the field has to ... well ... follow suit. All are poorer because of it (except for suit designers, manufacturers, and retailers). Ever-increasing height in the heels of women's shoes is another example of a fashion arms race in which everyone would be better off in flats. Once a few start to inch up their heels, the fashion trend takes off, forcing those who would not otherwise do so to engage in an Achilles-tightening arms race. Coming-of-age parties suffer the same positional rank fate. When the mega rich produce a festival fit for a king for their sixteen-year old queen, the next economic tier down must up the catering bill to satisfy teenage wants that have been artificially adjusted upward. Money that should be spent on, say, food, clothes, health care, future college tuition, or mortgage payments, is being wasted on frivolous ceremonial one-upmanship.

THE HIDDEN COSTS OF MARKET FAILURES AND MORAL HAZARDS

Moving from examples to analysis, Frank employs a technical model developed by the economist Ronald Coase that shows precisely how economists can take into account such transaction costs in order to better understand macroeconomic phenomena and correct for market failures.

Here Frank claims that the transaction costs of keeping up with the Joneses are not presently included in the price of homes, suits, shoes, and parties in terms of the real benefit to the owners, so this is an example of a market failure (and, he opines, a moral hazard) that he suggests can be remedied through a progressive consumption tax wherein these new-found liabilities would not only adjust the transaction costs to account for the hedonic treadmill while simultaneously curtailing needless consumptive behavior, it would also generate additional tax revenues from the rich that could be used to shore up our crumbling Social Security and Medicare accounts.

Once you concede the point that markets fail to correct for transaction costs and that individuals must be coerced to act in ways that benefit both themselves and the collective because they would have no economic incentive to do so otherwise, it's Katy bar the door for adding rules and regulations, taxes, and incentives right and left. While we're at it, we would need to correct for the hedonic treadmill and the positional rank problems with some serious income redistribution from those who have it to those who don't. So-called "sin taxes" on alcohol and tobacco are just a start. Frank would like to tax sugared soft drinks under the rubric that obesity leads directly to diabetes and heart disease and premature deaths from other causes as well.

Although economists counter that such early deaths may save us money down the road, had these folks lived long enough to incur massive end-of-life health-care costs (in a straightforward amoral cost-benefit analysis), the sugared soft-drink consumers will be thankful in the long run that taxing their favorite sodas led them to consume less of the harmful substances. Frank admits that this could lead us down a slippery slope of taxing fried foods, ice cream, and candy, not to mention bad television sit-coms that rot the brain. "But," he concludes,

> we're forced to go part way down slippery slopes all the time. It's a concern we can set to one side until we have traveled further down this particular slope. Consuming large quantities of soda laced with high-fructose corn syrup clearly causes substantial harm. And as long as we're continuing to tax saving, job creation, and other beneficial activities, the case for replacing such taxes with taxes on harmful activities is compelling.[5]

EITHER WAY, WE'RE PAYING TAXES

Libertarians and other critics of big government might counter that if, say, you don't want to wear a helmet or pay taxes, you can go somewhere else. But where are you going to go? Just as there is only one National Hockey League and only one Union Cycliste International in which professional hockey players and cyclists can compete, so too are there no tax-free countries. As Frank notes: "Without mandatory taxation, there could be no government. With no government, there would be no army, and without an army, your country would eventually be invaded by some other country that has an army. And when the dust settled, you'd be paying mandatory taxes to that country's government."[6] Either way, we're paying taxes, so we might as well concede the point and get on with the business of determining with the best analytics available where, when and how much we should be taxing ourselves to solve these assorted market shortcomings.

Robert Frank is a gifted economist and a skilled rhetorician whose regular commentaries in the *New York Times*, coupled to his blogs, podcasts, radio and television interviews, and popular books, make him a formidable and influential public intellectual who well represents those who tend to favor top-down government solutions to social problems in a manner most closely aligned with the economic policies of John Maynard Keynes. Given the resurgence of Keynesian economics during the financial crisis and subsequent recession, Frank's ideas deserve thoughtful consideration and response, which I shall endeavor to do here from the perspective of someone who has also written extensively on evolutionary economics – what I called evonomics – in my book *The Mind of the Market*.[7] I too start with Darwin, but with a very different outcome from Frank's analysis.

EVONOMICS: THE CONNECTION BETWEEN ADAM SMITH AND CHARLES DARWIN

Charles Darwin was not an economist and never penned a single statement or treatise on economics, so it is difficult to imagine how or why a century from now, in Frank's words, "if a roster of professional economists is asked to identify the intellectual father of their discipline, a majority will name Charles Darwin."[8] Not likely. There is a connection between Darwin and economics, but it isn't in the way Frank thinks it is.[9] In October of 1825, Darwin matriculated at Edinburgh University where, as a matter of general course curricula, he studied the works of the great Enlightenment thinkers, including David Hume, Edward Gibbon, and Adam Smith. A decade later, upon his return home from the five-year voyage around the world on HMS *Beagle*, Darwin revisited these works, reconsidering their implications in light of the new theory he was developing.[10] Although Darwin does not reference Smith directly, Darwin scholars are largely in agreement that he modeled his theory of natural selection after Smith's theory of the invisible hand.[11] Compare, by example, these two descriptions from Smith and Darwin:

> Every individual is continually exerting himself to find out the most advantageous employment for whatever capital he can command. He generally, indeed, neither intends to promote the public interest, nor knows how much he is promoting it. He intends only his own gain, and he is in this, as in many other cases, led by an invisible hand to promote an end which was no part of his intention.
>
> Adam Smith, *The Wealth of Nations*, 1776

> It may be said that natural selection is daily and hourly scrutinising, throughout the world, every variation, even the slightest; rejecting that which is bad, preserving and adding up all that is good; silently and insensibly working, whenever and wherever opportunity offers, at the improvement of each organic being in relation to its organic and inorganic conditions of life.
>
> Charles Darwin, *On the Origin of Species*, 1859

These descriptors – *invisible hand* and *natural selection* – are so powerful, and so deeply annealed into our thought and culture, that it is difficult not to think of them as *forces* of nature, such as gravity and electromagnetism, or as *mechanical systems*, such as gears and pulleys. But they are not forces or mechanisms, because there is nothing acting on the agents in the system in such a causal manner. Instead, Smith's invisible hand and Darwin's natural selection are *descriptions* of processes that naturally occur in the economies of nature and society. The causal mechanisms behind the invisible hand and natural selection lie elsewhere in the system – within the agents themselves – which is why

Smith invested so much work on understanding the natural sympathies of people, and Darwin advanced so much effort toward comprehending the natural tendencies of organisms.

If there is a connection between evolution and economics – between Charles Darwin and Adam Smith – it is this: Life is intricate, complex, and looks designed, so our folk biology intuition leads us to infer that there must be an intelligent designer, a god. Analogously, economies are intricate, complex, and look designed, so our folk economic intuition is to infer that we need an intelligent designer, a government. But as Smith and Darwin demonstrated, life and economies are not intelligently designed from the top down; they spontaneously arise out of simpler systems from the bottom up. Natural selection and the invisible hand explain precisely how individual organisms and people, pursuing their own self-interest in their struggle to survive and make a living, generate the emergent property of complex ecologies and economies. Charles Darwin and Adam Smith, each in their unique way trying to solve a specific problem, independently stumbled across an elegant solution to what turns out to be a larger and overarching phenomenon of the emergence of complexity out of simplicity. Apparent design from the bottom up does not imply the necessity of intentional design from the top down.

CORPORATIONS AS SPECIES

If there is a specific analogy to make between evolution and economics beyond a description of bottom-up self-organized emergence, it is that species are analogous to companies and corporations, not to societies and nations. In evolution, extinction is the rule, survival the exception. Most species go extinct because they fail to adapt to changing environments, and in their stead arise new species that are better adapted . . . for the time being anyway. The economist Joseph Schumpeter's descriptor for this process in an economy was "creative destruction."[12] Although Schumpeter derived the concept from a Marxian analysis of the negative implications of capitalism, the term has been adopted by modern economists to describe the natural evolution of firms, companies, corporations, and even entire industries that go extinct and/or are replaced with new ventures better adapted to the ever-changing needs and wants of consumers.[13]

The meteor impact 65 million years ago that wiped out the dinosaurs opened up new niches to be filled by fledgling mammals living in the nooks and crannies on the margins of ecosystems. A good case can be made that were it not for the demise of the dinosaurs we would not be here.[14] That's life. Ditto dinosaur corporations. In 1917 Bertie Forbes published his list of the top 100 US corporations. By 1987, sixty-one of them were gone, and of the remaining thirty-nine, twenty-one were no longer in the top 100, and eighteen underperformed the average growth in stock market value. The only company to both survive and outperform the market was General Electric. Similarly, of the 500 companies that made up the Standard & Poor's original list in 1957, only seventy-four survived through 1997, at which point they had all underperformed the S&P 500 index by an average of 20 percent.[15] In both natural ecosystems and economies, extinction is part of evolution. Think Kodak.

Kodak once so dominated the film and camera industry – at one point enjoying a 96 percent market share – that government bureaucrats were wringing their interventionistic hands in panic that such a monopoly could bring about market inefficiencies, or worse, Americans would get so hooked on capturing their "Kodak moments" that the film giant would force addicted consumers to pay artificially jacked-up prices. In response, the feds sued Kodak twice for antitrust violations in 1921 and 1954, opening the door for Fuji film to jump into the market. The result? Kodak and Fuji became a duopoly, and like most gargantuan organizations both grew sclerotic and failed to keep up with the digital revolution that, in the case of Kodak, saw their stock price collapse from $60 a share in 2000 to less than 50 cents a share at the time of this writing, shortly after the story broke that the fearful giant was preparing to declare bankruptcy.[16]

Apple and Google are hot today, but who knows what a couple of grad students are dreaming up in their dorm rooms this year that in the near future will reconfigure the economic landscape? These giants – which the antitrust regulators are fretting about today – will almost assuredly turn into GM-like lumbering sloths unable to respond in time to the next shift in the economic ecology, and they too could go the way of

Neanderthals. The Darwinian focus for economists should not be on societies and nations but on companies and corporations, and, at this level of analysis, top-down interventions are neither justified by the evolutionary analogy nor necessary for the long-term prospects of either societies or nations.

PEACOCKS AND BULL ELK ARE DOING JUST FINE, THANK YOU

In evolutionary theory, "good" and "bad" for a species is measured by "reproductive success." The bottom line for organisms is getting their genes into the next generation. To that end, entertain this thought experiment: If you were a gene what would you do to survive? First you create a means of reproduction, then you build a vehicle to house your self-replication machinery. You start with chromosomes as a template to hold your self-replicating molecules, then add a surrounding nucleus with a semipermeable membrane for moving liquid nutrients in and out of the cell, then build yourself a multicellular vehicle with eyes for seeing and ears for hearing and legs for propulsion. You can greatly increase your reproductive success by reproducing sexually instead of asexually because this generates greater genetic diversity to adapt to ever-changing environments. You will also want to develop various mechanisms to avoid or prevent other vehicles that want to devour your vehicle, such as claws and teeth and wings and camouflage. You might also want to grow something on your body that will intimidate other members of your sex and to attract members of the opposite sex that is a proxy for your good genes, such as elaborate and colorful tail feathers if you are a peacock or a huge rack of antlers if you are a bull elk.

In such a thought experiment – which comes from Richard Dawkins in his 1976 book *The Selfish Gene* – we can see that there are constant conflicts and trade-offs in evolution. Heavy armor plating may be good for defending against claws but slows you up for escaping fast predators. Colorful feathers may grant you higher status and attract females, but predators will see you hiding in the bushes. Antlers may ward off challenging males and appeal to females, but you might win a Darwin Award for allowing yourself to be taken out of the gene pool by a predator. The value of such features to the species depends entirely on its overall reproductive success. If effervescent tail feathers lead to more matings with their resultant offspring than they lead to individuals being consumed by predators, then the overall reproductive success for peacocks and peahens is increased and we can say that the peacock's tail is "good" for the species. Darwin explained such effects with his theory of sexual selection, of which there are at least two forms: (1) female selection of males based on characteristics that are proxies for good genes, (2) male v. male competition for females, status and hierarchy, and dominance. These sexual selection factors can increase the reproductive success of a species far more than natural selection through predation can decrease the reproductive success of the species. In fact, both types of selection go on simultaneously and so each case must be examined in detail to determine whether or not a feature is good or bad for a species.

This interaction of natural and sexual selection is further complicated by a mechanism described by the Israeli evolutionary biologists Amotz and Avishag Zahavi as Costly Signaling Theory (CST).[17] Broadly speaking, in a CST model, people do things not just to help those related to them genetically (kin selection), and not just to help those who will return the favor (reciprocal altruism), but sometimes to send a signal that says, in essence, "my altruistic and charitable acts demonstrate that I am so successful that I can afford to make such sacrifices for others." That is, altruistic acts are a form of information that carries a signal to others of trust and status – *trust* that I can be counted on to help others when they need it so that I can expect others to do the same for me, and *status* that I have the health, intelligence, and resources to afford to be so kind and generous. In the specific context here, CST allows us to see that a large rack of antlers or radiantly colorful tail signals to other members of the group that your genes are so good that you can afford the risk that such features may bring as a result of predation.

As the UCLA evolutionary biologist Jared Diamond explained it to me in an email discussing Frank's thesis,

> animal signals have to demonstrate the validity of their intended message
> if they are to be believed. For example, if a male moose evolved to try to

signal its superior genes to a female merely by growing a small tuft of red hair on top of the head, any scrawny lousy moose could afford to grow such a tuft, and the tuft would not be a reliable signal of individual quality. When a female sees a bull moose that is lugging around a huge set of antlers and has still survived despite that handicap, then the female can be sure that that really is a superior individual bull moose. More generally, the animal signals involved in sexual displays often or usually carry some disadvantage for natural selection, offset by an advantage for sexual selection. Thus, one can't say that the peacock's tail and moose's antlers are bad for the species.[18]

In point of fact, both peacocks and bull elk are doing just fine as species, contrary to what Frank suggests in his claim that such features are inefficient and therefore not good in the long run. In any case, whether or not something is good or bad for peacocks and bull elk has nothing whatsoever to do with what is good or bad for other species, including humans, especially the political policy of humans. As Diamond summarized the problem, "In addition, analogy is dangerous guidance: regardless of whether the peacock's tail is good or bad for the peacock species, the merits of government regulation have to be assessed without reference to peacocks."[19]

I would go even further. Taking Frank's analogy seriously, not only are such features as the human equivalence of peacocks' tails and bull elk antlers not a detriment to our species, sexual selection may very well account for most of the characteristics that we so admire about our species: art, music, humor, literature, poetry, fashion, dance, and, more generally, creativity and intelligence. Science itself may be a byproduct of the cognitive process of trying to impress others in order to gain status and mates by making breakthrough discoveries and formulating important new theories. The University of New Mexico evolutionary psychologist Geoffrey Miller makes a strong case for just such selective effects in his book *The Mating Mind*.[20] Sexual selection, he argues, has driven organisms from bowerbirds to brainy bohemians to engage in the creative production of magnificent works in order to attract mates – from big blue bowerbird nests to big-brained orchestral music, epic poems, stirring literature, and even scientific discoveries. Those organisms that do so most effectively leave behind more offspring and thus pass on their creative genes into future generations.

Thus, contrary to what Frank argues, a viable case can be made that the evolutionary arms races he so detests – men's suits, women's high heels, McMansion homes, and elaborate coming-of-age parties – are products of a larger system that drives our species to be so successful. By carrying out the biological analogy into political policy, if anything we should be rewarding the most ostentatious displays of power, prestige, wealth, creativity, health, vigor, and intelligence with tax breaks and even subsidies! At the very least, one could argue that a consumption tax on the rich could very well backfire and reduce the reproductive success of our species by attenuating the creative productivity that has given us so much of our culture that we cherish.

It may sound crude and unromantic to reduce the arts and sciences to little more than the product of organisms trying to impress others in order to gain status, resources, and mates, but as the late Christopher Hitchens once advised me after we imbibed several doses of what he was fond of calling "Mr. Walker's amber restorative," once you've mastered the pen and the podium, you need never dine or sleep alone.

POSITIONAL RANKING, RELATIVE HAPPINESS, AND INDIVIDUAL LIBERTY

One of Frank's justifications for taxing the rich involves the matter of positional ranking and relative happiness. If research shows that the existence of wealthy neighbors puts me on a hedonic treadmill that I can never satisfy, legislated policy is therefore justified in forcing my neighbors to redistribute some of their wealth to me and others less fortunate. This, Frank argues, will not only adjust the positional ranking problem, it will help shore up the leaking budgets of Social Security and Medicare and Medicaid (which, with defense spending, constitutes two-thirds of the overall budget). The problem with this argument is three-fold: (1) Taxing the rich will do next to nothing for our debt crisis, (2) taxing the rich won't make the poor any happier, and (3) positional ranking exists for a range of traits, not just for wealth.

1. **Taxing away the debt crisis.** If, say, we followed Warren Buffett's proposal for taxing the "super rich" who make between $1 million and $10 million a year at an effective rate of 50 percent, according to the nonpartisan Tax Foundation using figures from the IRS, this would reduce the national debt by a grand total of 1 percent. What about the "mega rich," those making more than $10 million a year? If we taxed them at 100 percent – that is, we confiscated every last dollar made by every person in the country at this level, the national debt would be reduced by only 2 percent. Taxing the rich will not solve our debt crisis.[21]

2. **Taxing away unhappiness.** In what way, exactly, will redistributing money from the rich to the poor increase the latter's happiness or decrease their unhappiness? In fact, research shows that economic self-reliance makes people happier than economic dependency, and studies show that people are happier, healthier, and more generous when they voluntarily donate their money to causes they deem worthy, instead of having their money confiscated from them and given to causes that they may not have otherwise chosen to support. Evidence for this claim can be found in two sets of data: (a) studies on international happiness and freedom, (b) studies on national charitable giving.

    a. **International happiness and freedom.** Research on happiness and freedom internationally reveals that an increase in personal autonomy and self-control leads to greater happiness, and that people tend to be happier in societies with greater levels of individual autonomy and freedom compared to those in more totalitarian and collectivist regimes. The Erasmus University, Rotterdam social scientist Ruut Veenhoven, for example, conducted a comprehensive survey on happiness as a function of three social conditions: individualism, opportunity to choose, capability to choose. "The data show a clear positive relationship," Veenhoven concludes, "the more individualized the nation, the more citizens enjoy their life." Further, he found no "pattern of diminishing returns," meaning that "individualization has not yet passed its optimum."[22] In other words, greater levels of individual freedom and autonomy could lead to even greater levels of happiness, and this could very well counter the alleged decline of happiness due to one's lower positional rank.

b. **National Charitable Giving.** Research on the difference between forced and volunteer giving reveals a counterintuitive finding on the differences between the political Left and Right. According to the Syracuse University professor of public administration Arthur C. Brooks, when it comes to charitable giving and volunteering, numerous quantitative measures debunk the myth of "bleeding heart liberals" and "heartless conservatives." The opposite, in fact, appears to be true. Conservatives donate 30 percent more money than liberals (even when controlled for income), give more blood, and log more volunteer hours. And it isn't because conservatives have more expendable income that they are more generous. The working poor give a substantially higher percentage of their incomes to charity than any other income group, and three times more than those on public assistance of comparable income. In other words, poverty is not a barrier to charity, but welfare is. One explanation for these findings is that people who are skeptical of big government give more than those who believe that the government should take care of the poor. "For many people," Brooks explains, "the desire to donate other people's money displaces the act of giving one's own." In this sense, liberals feel that they already donated to the poor through their taxes, whereas conservatives believe that it is *their* duty, not the government's, to assist those in need. The effects on happiness are measurable in terms of societal health: Charitable givers are 43 percent more likely to say they are "very happy" than nongivers, and 25 percent more likely than nongivers to say their health is "excellent" or "very good."[23]

3. **Positional ranking exists throughout life.** The George Mason University economist Donald Boudreaux made an important observation about positional rank and relative happiness in responding to a *New Yorker* article in which the financial analyst John Cassidy argued for income redistribution because of the hypothesis that people's health is harmed by relative (instead of absolute) positional rank. In

a nature analogue, Cassidy argues that "dominant rhesus monkeys have lower rates of atherosclerosis (hardening of the arteries) than monkeys further down the social hierarchy." Boudreaux showed how, in fact, income redistribution could have the opposite effect:

> Because status among humans is determined not only by income but also by traits such as political power, athletic prowess, military heroics, intellectual success, and good looks, equalizing incomes will intensify the importance of these non-pecuniary traits as sources of status. And there's no reason why persons with low status in these non-pecuniary categories will not suffer all the stress and envy now allegedly suffered by people with low incomes.[24]

In the end, then, following Frank's line of reasoning, the government should give tax breaks to conservatives, the wealthy, and the working poor in order to reward their pro-social behavior and encourage more giving, and the government should stimulate income inequality in order to attenuate status seeking in other nonpecuniary traits. All liberals in favor of such policies please raise your hands.

OTHER HIDDEN COSTS: WHAT IS SEEN AND WHAT IS NOT SEEN IN GOVERNMENT ACTIONS

Even if evolutionary psychologists are wrong in this analysis of sexual selection and costly signaling theory, and it was determined that ostentatious displays of wealth, power, prestige, and creativity should be penalized through a consumption tax because of Frank's analysis using Coase's transaction models that reveal the hidden transaction costs of positional ranking and subsequent arms races, there are transaction costs of implementing such a tax.

In fact, once you concede the point that at least some government services are necessary and must be paid for by taxes, then to the short list of services such as military, police, courts, and tax collectors, one can bolt on any number of additional services justified under the collective action problem rubric: fire departments, roads and bridges, schools, libraries, national parks and forests, postal service, social security, welfare, Medicare and Medicaid, foreign aid, and countless others embodied in the alphabet soup that this slippery slope line of reasoning has given us. Herewith are just a handful, and these only a select few from the letter A: Administration for Children and Families; Administration for Native Americans; Administration on Aging; Administration on Developmental Disabilities; Agricultural Marketing Service; Alcohol, Tobacco, Firearms, and Explosives Bureau; American Battle Monuments Commission; Animal and Plant Health Inspection Service; Architectural and Transportation Barriers Compliance Board; Archives and Records Administration; Armed Forces Retirement Home; Arms Control and International Security; Army Corps of Engineers; Arthritis and Musculoskeletal Interagency Coordinating Committee. Imagine how long this list grows when you start tossing in all the "Bureaus," "Committees," "Councils," and "Departments" in working your way through the alphabet.[25]

The not-so-hidden costs include the fact that each of these government agencies must be located in an office rented or leased, running up monthly utility bills and staffed by people who must be paid, provided with health benefits, retirement programs, and the like. As well, once such agencies are established, they are almost impossible to terminate, not to mention that they are also subject to the usual bureaucratic inefficiencies, political favoritism, and corruption and graft that are part and parcel of what we have come to expect from the public sector. A day doesn't go by that we do not read of politicians and government bureaucrats busted for something they should not have been doing with taxpayers' money.[26]

And these are not even the hidden costs to which I refer in my subhead. The French economist Frédéric Bastiat demonstrated the difference between what is seen and what is not seen when governments intervene in the marketplace. A public-works project, such as the infamous Alaskan "bridge to nowhere," is seen by all, gloried in by its producers, and appreciated by its few users. What is not seen, however, are all the products that would have been produced or the services provided by the monies that were taxed out of private hands in order to finance the public project. It is not just that individual liberties are violated whenever governments interfere with freedom of choice in the economic realm, but that, in fact, the net result is a loss not just for the individuals directly affected by the confiscation of their monies but for the nation as a whole for which the government action was originally intended. "There is only one difference between a bad economist and a good one," Bastiat explained, "the bad economist confines himself to the *visible* effect; the good economist takes into account both the effect that can be seen and those effects that must be *foreseen.*"[27] What is not seen when tax programs are implemented is what that money would have been used for in the private sector.

There is one final hidden cost in taxing economics arms races – and a hidden benefit in not doing so – that was pointed out to me by the Hampden-Sydney College economist and Director of the Center for Entrepreneurship and Political Economy, Jennifer Dirmeyer:

> The people who jump on that hedonic treadmill and work so that they can have a yacht that is one foot longer than their neighbor's produce massive positive external benefits to the rest of us. In order to make money they must use available resources in a way that creates more value than anyone else and with lower costs. In fact, most profit is made from reducing the transactions costs associated with getting products to consumers, which means lower prices. When some guy willingly works 80 hours a week managing the distribution system of a moderately sized corporation everyone else benefits from that hard, and probably dull, work in the form of low prices and increasing quality of goods and services. So, eliminating the "yacht" incentive to reduce transactions costs will just ... increase transaction costs, making us all poorer, not just the peacocks.[28]

FATAL CONCEIT REDUX

Robert Frank strikes me as an intelligent and thoughtful man who genuinely wants to employ science and reason to improve the design of society for the betterment of all. His arguments are carefully crafted and artfully presented to make the case that, since we're in the business of designing society from top down anyway, we might as well go whole hog and do it right. It is *this* that worries me – the conceit that interventionists of all stripes hold that if a little interventionism is good, then a lot must be great. Granted, we need a military to protect us from foreign invaders, but do we really need a defense budget that currently accounts for 43 percent of all military spending in the entire world, more than the next fourteen largest defense budgets combined? Yes, we need some social services, but a century ago Americans somehow survived and thrived with a government that consumed only 8 percent of our GDP; today it is over 40 percent and climbing. Currently we spend $204 billion or 1.4 percent of GDP servicing the debt. The Congressional Budget Office is now projecting that in the next 70 years that figure will climb to $27.2 trillion, or a whopping 41.4 percent of GDP. What will happen when servicing the debt exceeds 50 percent of GDP? Agreed, we need some regulatory agencies, but according to the Small Business Administration we are presently spending $1.75 trillion annually on regulations, which is almost double the amount collected on all individual income taxes in 2010.[29] Looking at the global picture, in 2011 government spending rose on average to 35.2 percent of world GDP, up from 33.5 percent in 2010. What will happen when that figure reaches half, when half the world is completely financed through taxes paid by the other half?

This is the consequence of the fatal conceit that we can design a society from the top down. "The curious task of economics," observed the Nobel laureate economist Friedrich Hayek, "is to demonstrate to men how little they really know about what they imagine they can design." Hayek understood (more than most economists) that Darwinian evolution is a self-organized bottom-up process of design without a designer. "To the naive mind that can conceive of order only as the product of deliberate arrangement, it may seem absurd that in complex conditions order, and adaptation to the unknown, can be achieved more effectively by decentralizing decisions and that a division of authority will actually extend the possibility of overall order. Yet that decentralization actually leads to more information being taken into account." Hayak called this the "extended order," the result not of planning and design but of a system that "constitutes an information gathering process, able to call up, and put to use, widely dispersed information that no central planning agency, let alone any individual, could know as a whole, possess or control."[30] The fatal conceit of socialist planners was tested experimentally over the course of the twentieth century, and it failed in every case. Presciently, Hayak's *The Fatal Conceit* was published in 1988, just before the crumbling of the Berlin Wall and the collapse of Communism, so this was an experimentally verified prediction.

Robert Frank is not a socialist or a Communist, and neither is President Obama or anyone else working in government today. And yet the design conceit is there nonetheless. Even when gussied up in economic jargon with Darwinian overtones, hints of the totalitarian mind from millennia past creep into our thoughts and reach for the controls. Somebody should do something. Take command. Control our actions. Direct our thoughts. Dial our desires. The clan elder, the tribal leader, the chiefdom big man, the state king, the central planner, the apparatchik, the lord savior, the infallible pope, the chief rabbi, the dear leader. Someone somewhere somehow will save us by telling us what to do and how to live. The impulse is a deep one that harkens back to our Paleolithic ancestry. It's counterintuitive to think bottom up instead of top down. It is why so many people struggle to truly grasp the deep meaning of evolutionary theory, and it is why so many people fail to see that economic order is the product not of human design but of human action.

PART IV

SCIENTIA HUMANITATIS: REFLECTIONS ON SCIENTIFIC HUMANISM

CHAPTER 19

Scientific Naturalism

A Manifesto for Enlightenment Humanism

PREAMBLE

This article was initially published in the August 2017 issue of the journal *Theology and Science* under the above title and subtitle. It was commissioned by Ted Peters, Research Professor Emeritus in Systematic Theology and Ethics at Pacific Lutheran Theological Seminary and the Center for Theory and the Natural Sciences. Even though Ted and I disagree on a great many things, we share a love and respect for science, for the question of extraterrestrial intelligence and for what such a discovery would mean to humanity in general and religion in particular (his 2018 edited volume *Astrotheology: Science and Theology Meet Extraterrestrial Life* encapsulates his research on this subject). When Ted invited me to make the best case I could for a scientific defense of objective values and morals, I could not resist the challenge. My 2015 book *The Moral Arc* is a much longer and thorough defense of this worldview – especially my claim that science and reason can determine moral values – but herein I offer some new strategies for addressing the Is-Ought barrier problem to avoid the naturalistic fallacy that one cannot derive an Ought from an Is. And I relished the challenge of doing so in a more succinct statement.

* * *

IN JUNE OF 1510, SIXTY-FOUR WOMEN AND MEN WERE BURNED at the stake in Val Camonica, Italy, for causing drought and fires and for harming people, animals, and land.

In July of 1518, sixty women and men were burned at the stake in Breto, Italy, for triggering thunder and lightning and for causing sickness and death of nearly 200 people.

In June of 1582, the wife of an English sawyer named Alice Glosscock from the town of Chelmsford was stripped naked and her body searched for "the marks of a witch," which were found, leading to her conviction and execution.

In May of 1653, a Connecticut colonialist named Elizabeth Godman asked her neighbor Goodwife Thorp if she had any chickens to sell, but none were available. The next day Thorp's chickens dropped dead, leading to Godman's arrest and trial.

In May of 1692, seven teenage girls writhed on the floor of a Salem, Massachusetts courtroom during the trial of a suspected witch named Martha Carrier, crying out "There is a black man whispering in her ear!" Carrier was one of twenty people executed in what became the most famous witch trial in history.

What were these people thinking?[1] It is convenient to dismiss them as unthinking naïfs caught up in the hysterics of a moral panic, but in fact they were thinking quite clearly, and they had the authority of the Bible behind them, as in Exodus 22:18: "Thou shalt not suffer a witch to live." They also had the backing of the Roman Catholic Church. In 1484, Pope Innocent VIII issued the Papal Bull *Summis desiderantes affectibus,* in which he pronounced that many people had

> abandoned themselves to devils, incubi and succubi, and by their incantations, spells, conjurations, and other accursed charms and crafts, enormities and horrid offences, have slain infants yet in the mother's womb, as also the offspring of cattle, have blasted the produce of the earth, the grapes of the vine, the fruits of the trees, nay, men and women, beasts of burthen, herd-beasts, as well as animals of other kinds, vineyards, orchards, meadows, pasture-land, corn, wheat, and all other cereals; they hinder men from performing the sexual act and women from conceiving . . .[2]

Inspired by the Bull, two years later, the German Dominican inquisitor Heinrich Kramer published his *Malleus Maleficarum* (*Hammer of the Witch*), the infamous how-to manual on finding and prosecuting witches, which was promptly put to use, culminating in the murder of some 100,000 people.[3]

Such theological bafflegab and administrative argle-bargle was believed by most Europeans half a millennium ago. Today, no one in the West employs what I have called the *witch theory of causality*, and its disappearance gives us some insight into how moral progress is made – by employing a better understanding of causality. The primary difference between us and these early modern Europeans is, in a word, science. Lacking any systematic empirical method of determining the correct cause of things and specialized fields to explain specific phenomena – meteorology for the weather, epidemiology for plagues, medicine for illness and miscarriages, agronomy for crop production, animal husbandry for cattle diseases – they acted rationally according to what they believed to be true.[4] These inquisitors and their willing executioners were not evil so much as they were mistaken. We refrain from burning witches today not because our laws prohibit it but because we do not believe in witchcraft and so the thought of incinerating someone for it never even enters our minds.

Although the rise of science was not the only variable at work in the decline of the witch craze, in *Religion and the Decline of Magic* the historian Keith Thomas concludes that the first and most important factor "was the series of intellectual changes which constituted the scientific and philosophical revolution of the seventeenth century. These changes had a decisive influence upon the thinking of the intellectual élite and in due course percolated down to influence the thought and behavior of the people at large. The essence of the revolution was the triumph of the mechanical philosophy." By this Thomas means the Newtonian clockwork universe, the worldview that holds that all effects have natural causes and the universe is governed by natural laws that can be examined and understood. In this worldview there is no place for the supernatural, and that is what ultimately doomed the witch theory of causality, as it did other supernatural explanations for natural occurrences. "The notion that the universe was subject to immutable natural laws killed the concept of miracles, weakened the belief in the physical efficacy of prayer, and diminished faith in the possibility of direct divine inspiration."[5]

FROM SCIENTIFIC NATURALISM TO ENLIGHTENMENT HUMANISM

Scientific naturalism is the principle that the world is governed by natural laws and forces that can be understood and that all phenomena are part of nature and can be explained by natural causes, including human cognitive, moral, and social phenomena. According to a Google Ngram Viewer search, the term "scientific naturalism" first came into use in the 1820s, picked up momentum from the 1860s through the 1920s, then hit three peaks in the 1930s, 1950s, and early 2000s, where it is now established as a core component of modern science.[6] It incorporates *methodological naturalism*, the principle that the methods of science operate under the presumption that the world and everything in it is the result of natural processes in a system of material causes and effects that does not allow, or need, the introduction of supernatural forces. "Methodological naturalism" spiked dramatically in use in the mid-1990s and continues climbing into the 2000s,[7] most likely the result of the rise in popularity (and polarization) of "scientific creationism" and Intelligent Design theory, the proponents of which complained that *methodological naturalism* unfairly excludes their belief in what I have called *methodological supernaturalism*, or the principle that supernatural intervention in the natural world may be invoked to explain any allegedly unexplained phenomena, such as the Big Bang, the fine-tuned cosmos, consciousness, morality, the eye, DNA and, notoriously, bacterial flagella.[8]

In the centuries following the Scientific Revolution, the gradual but systematic displacement of religious dogmatism, authority, and supernaturalism by scientific naturalism, particularly its application toward explaining the human world, led to the widespread adoption of *Enlightenment humanism*, a cosmopolitan worldview that places supreme value on science and reason, eschews the supernatural entirely, and relies exclusively on nature and nature's laws – including human nature and the laws and forces that govern us and our societies – for a complete understanding of the cosmos and everything in it, from particles to people.

Humanism's roots, however, actually predate the Scientific Revolution, and are usually traced back to the fifteenth century when, for example, the Italian philologist Lorenzo Valla exposed the Latin document *Donatio Constantini* – the Donation of Constantine that was used by the Catholic Church to legitimize its land grab of the Western Roman Empire – as a fake, through the use of historical, linguistic, and philological evidence.

"He was skeptical, he was empirical, he drew an hypothesis, he was rational, he used very abstract reasoning (even counterfactual reasoning)," the University of Amsterdam humanities professor Rens Bod told me.[9] Inspired by Valla's philological analysis of the Bible, the Dutch Renaissance scholar Erasmus (who already carried the sobriquet "Prince of the Humanists") employed these same empirical techniques to demonstrate that, for example, the concept of the Trinity did not appear in bibles before the eleventh century. In 1606 the Leiden University professor Joseph Justus Scaliger published a philological reconstruction of the ancient Egyptian dynasties, finding that the earliest one of 5285 BC predated the Hebrew Bible chronology for the creation of the world by nearly 1,300 years. This led later scholars like Baruch Spinoza to reject the Bible as a reliable historical document. "Thus abstract reasoning, rationality, empiricism, and skepticism are not just virtues of science," Bod concluded. "They had all been invented by the humanities."

Why does this distinction matter? Because in the late twentieth century, the humanities took a turn toward postmodern deconstruction and the belief that there is no objective reality to be discovered and no idea that is closer to the truth than any other – the basis for the charge of "scientism." Because humanism as a movement became political in the late twentieth century, moving away from its roots in science and objective truth and toward progressive liberal politics and activism. And because, at a time when students and funding are fleeing humanities departments and support for and membership of humanist organizations are dwindling as a result of the alienation of all those who do not share their narrow political agenda, the argument that humanism and the humanities are at least good for "self-cultivation" misses their real value, which Bod has forcefully articulated in his 2014 book *A New History of the Humanities: The Search for Principles and Patterns from Antiquity to the Present.*[10] The transdisciplinary connections between the sciences and humanities are well captured in the German word *Geisteswissenschaften*, which means the science of expressions of the human mind. This, in fact, is everything humans do, including the scientific theories we generate about the natural world. "Too often, humanities scholars believe that they are moving towards science when they use empirical methods," Bod reflected. "They are wrong: humanities scholars using empirical methods are returning to their own historical roots in the *studia humanitatis* of the fifteenth century, when the empirical approach was first invented."

True enough, and regardless of which university brick-and-mortar building scholars inhabit, we are all working toward the same goal of improving our understanding of the true nature of things, and that is the way of both the sciences and the humanities. Call it a *scientia humanitatis.* This is what I mean by *Enlightenment humanism*, a relatively new term that a Google Ngram Viewer search shows did not come into popular use until the 1980s.[11] In 2011 it was moved center stage by Steven Pinker in his 2011 book *The Better Angels of Our Nature* (and is more fully defended in his *Enlightenment Now*) to reflect the influence of that era's scientists and philosophers on modernity. Pinker explains the logic of how the successful application of scientific naturalism in biological matters can adduce principles that lead to social and moral progress when applied to human affairs:

> When a large enough community of free, rational agents confers on how a society should run its affairs, steered by logical consistency and feedback from the world, their consensus will veer in certain directions. Just as we don't have to explain why molecular biologists discovered that DNA has four bases – given that they were doing their biology properly, and given that DNA really does have four bases, in the long run they could hardly have discovered anything else – we may not have to explain why enlightened thinkers would eventually argue against African slavery, cruel punishments, despotic monarchs, and the execution of witches and heretics.[12]

And enlightened thinkers did exactly that, which is why slavery, torture, and witch hunts were abolished, and civil rights, women's rights, children's rights, gay rights, and animal rights were legislated.

Scientific naturalism and Enlightenment humanism made the modern world. Many of the founding fathers of the United States, for example, such as Thomas Jefferson, Thomas Paine, Benjamin Franklin, James Madison, and John Adams, were either practicing scientists or were trained in the sciences, although at the time they would have considered themselves experimental or natural philosophers, as the term *scientist* wasn't coined until 1840 and did not come into common use until the

1860s.[13] They deliberately adapted the scientific method of gathering data, running experiments, and testing hypotheses to their construction of the nation. Their understanding of the provisional nature of findings led them to develop a political system in which doubt and disputation were the centerpieces of a functional polity. They thought of political governance as a *problem-solving technology* rather than as a power-grabbing opportunity. They thought of democracy in the same way that they thought of science – as a method, not an ideology. They argued, in essence, that no one knows how to govern a nation, so we have to set up a system that allows for experimentation. Try this. Try that. Check the results. That is the heart of science. "The methods of science – with all its imperfections – can be used to improve social, political and economic systems," noted Carl Sagan in the final chapter of his 1996 book *The Demon-Haunted World.* "The great waste would be to ignore the results of social experiments because they seem to be ideologically unpalatable."[14]

Think about the fifty different states, each with its own constitution and set of laws. These are fifty different experiments. Every state has different gun-control laws, for example, so we can treat these as experiments from which we can gather results and draw conclusions: States with more guns and fewer controls have higher homicide and suicide rates.[15] Every time an amendment to the Constitution is ratified and enacted into law that is an experiment. The Nineteenth Amendment that granted women the right to vote in 1920 worked, so we still abide by it. By contrast, the Eighteenth Amendment, passed in 1919, that prohibited alcohol to test the hypothesis that it would reduce drinking and crime failed, so in 1933 the Twenty-First Amendment was enacted, overturning the Eighteenth. Changing your mind when the evidence changes is a virtue in science.

These are not controlled laboratory tests, but they are nevertheless valuable experiments to social scientists, policy makers, and the public. For example, policy experiments showed that teaching abstinence in sex education classes does not stop teens from having sex,[16] and criminalizing abortions did not curb the practice.[17] In both cases, information and contraception works better.[18] We can't run laboratory-like experiments in real-world governance, but we can use the comparative method to compare the outcomes of different economic and political systems, which is what Jared Diamond did in *Guns, Germs, and Steel* to explain the differential rates of development of different peoples around the world over the past 13,000 years.[19] A dramatic experiment began in August of 1945 when North and South Korea were divided at the thirty-eighth parallel. Both countries began the experiment with an annual average per capita GDP of $854 and were in lock-step through the 1970s when South Korea implemented economic measures to grow their economy and North Korea turned into a full-fledged dictatorship. Today, the per capita GDP of North Korea is $1,800, compared to $33,000 for South Korea.[20] You can also see the difference from space: One is dark and impoverished while the other is bright and flourishing.

Foreign policy decisions are also experiments. The US intervention in Germany from 1942 to 1945 was an experiment that very likely prevented the unnecessary deaths of millions of people. The United States *not* intervening in Rwanda in 1994 was an experiment that very likely resulted in many *more* unnecessary deaths. The United States' intervention in Iraq appears to have been a failed experiment, whereas the result of today's intervention in Syria is unknown. Sometimes science can be very complicated, and its results difficult to interpret. In *The Science of Liberty*, the science writer Timothy Ferris notes of the architects of the United States: "The founders often spoke of the new nation as an 'experiment'. Procedurally, it involved deliberations about how to facilitate both liberty and order, matters about which the individual states experimented considerably during the eleven years between the Declaration of Independence and the Constitution."[21] We are all citizen scientists now.

SCIENTIFIC NATURALISM, ENLIGHTENMENT HUMANISM, AND THE IS-OUGHT FALLACY

At this point in the process of applying science to human affairs, many scientists and philosophers pull back from the precipice and dismiss such grand synthesizing as *scientism*, a calumny that I, for one, gladly embrace. Ever since the philosopher David Hume identified what is known as the Is-Ought problem (or the naturalistic fallacy), most people hold that there is an unbreachable wall between *descriptive* statements (the way something *is*) and *prescriptive* statements (the way something *ought to be*).[22] It is repeated like a mantra the moment you attempt to apply science to values, morals, and meaning. "But, but, but ... Hume!," they sputter, as if that were all that is needed to refute such an argument.

I think some confusion arises here from what is meant by *is* or *natural.* For example, I would agree that the statement, *there has always been war, so war must be natural and the way things ought to be,* is a fallacy.[23] But here I mean something different by *is.* I mean the true condition or nature or cause of a thing. When we undertake a study of war in order to understand its causes so that we may lessen its occurrence and attenuate its effects, this is an Is-Ought transition grounded in the true nature of war. And by *nature,* I do not just mean the biological propensity (or not) of humans to fight. I mean all of the factors that go into the causes of war: biology, psychology, geography, culture, politics, economics, ideology, etc. That is the *is* we want to understand so that we can do something about it (the *ought*). In this sense, if morals and values ought not to be based on the way something *is* – *reality* – then on what should they be based?

In point of fact, we have been breaching the wall separating facts and values for centuries, and in my 2015 book, *The Moral Arc,*[24] I contend that this has been a major driver of moral progress. In brief, here's how. The Scientific Revolution of Copernicus, Kepler, Galileo, and Newton that culminated in the mechanical worldview led scientists in others fields to strive to do the same. In the arena of governance, for example, the English philosopher Thomas Hobbes consciously applied the principles and methods of the physical sciences to the political and moral sciences in his 1651 book *Leviathan,* considered to be one of the most influential works in the history of political thought. In it, Hobbes deliberately modeled his analysis of the social world after the work of Galileo and the English physician William Harvey, whose 1628 *On the Motion of the Heart and the Blood* outlined a mechanical model of the workings of the human body. As Hobbes later immodestly reflected: "Galileus ... was the first that opened to us the gate of natural philosophy universal, which is the knowledge of the nature of motion ... The science of man's body, the most profitable part of natural science, was first discovered with admirable sagacity by our countryman, Doctor Harvey. Natural philosophy is therefore but young; but civil philosophy is yet much younger, as being no older ... than my own *de Cive*."[25]

A century later, the French *philosophe* Montesquieu consciously invoked Newton in his 1748 work *Esprit des lois* (*The Spirit of the Laws*), when he compared a well-functioning monarchy to "the system of the universe" that includes "a power of gravitation" that "attracts" all bodies to "the center" (the monarch). And his method was the deductive method of Descartes: "I have laid down first principles and have found that the particular cases follow naturally from them." By "spirit" Montesquieu meant "causes" from which one could derive "laws" that govern society. One such law was the relationship between trade and peace, in which he noted that hunting and herding nations often found themselves in conflict and wars, whereas trading nations "became reciprocally dependent," making peace "the natural effect of trade." The psychology behind the effect, Montesquieu speculated, was exposure of different societies to customs and manners different from their own, which leads to "a cure for the most destructive prejudices." Thus, he concluded, "we see that in countries where the people move only by the spirit of commerce, they make a traffic of all the humane, all the moral virtues."[26] This early version of the *trade theory of peace* has held up well in modern empirical studies, and here we can draw the links from empirical science to moral values: If you agree that peace is better than war (the *ought*), then the application of the principle of free trade and open economic borders between nations is a means of attaining that goal (the *is*).

Following in the natural-law tradition of Montesquieu, a group of French scientists known as the physiocrats declared that all "social facts are linked together in necessary bonds eternal, by immutable, ineluctable, and inevitable laws" that should be obeyed by people and governments "if they were once made known to them" and that human societies are "regulated by *natural laws* ... the same laws that govern the physical world, animal societies, and even the internal life of every organism." One of these physiocrats, François Quesnay – a physician to the king of France – modeled the economy after the human body, in which money flowed through a nation like blood flows through a body and ruinous government policies were like diseases that impeded economic health. He argued that even though people have unequal abilities, they have equal natural rights, and so it was the government's duty to protect the rights of individuals from being usurped by other individuals, while at the same time enabling people to pursue their own best interests. This led them to advocate for private property and a free market. It was, in fact, the physiocrats who gave us the term *laissez faire*.[27]

The physiocrats asserted that people operating in a society were subject to knowable laws of both human and economic nature not unlike those discovered by Galileo and Newton, and this movement grew into the school of classical economics championed by David Hume, Adam Smith, and others that forms the basis of all economic science and policy today. Consider Smith's monumental 1776 work. Most people think the title is *The Wealth of Nations*. Its full title is far more revealing as to its intent: *An Inquiry into the Nature and Causes of the Wealth of Nations*. Smith employed the terms "nature" and "causes" in the scientific sense of identifying and understanding the cause-and-effect relationships in the natural system of an economy, with the underlying premise that natural laws govern economies, that humans are rationally calculating economic actors whose behaviors can be understood, and that markets are self-regulated by an "invisible hand."

In these and many other examples, we see both the connection from the physical and biological sciences to the social sciences, and also the point of my focusing on this period in the history of science – our modern concepts of governance arose out of this drive to apply reason and science to any and all problems, including human social problems. In other words, we can ground human values and morals not just in philosophical principles such as Aristotle's virtue ethics, Kant's categorical imperative, Mill's utilitarianism, or Rawls' fairness ethics, but in science as well. But what about Hume and that Is-Ought fallacy? What is the ontological and epistemological justification of shifting from *is* to *ought*? Those who reject scientific naturalism tend to turn to the divine, relying on what is known as Divine Command Theory. God is the ontological foundation of morals and values, the outside source from which we can derive real *oughts*. Unfortunately for methodological supernaturalists, Plato refuted Divine Command Theory with his "Euthyphro's dilemma," in which he asked, in so many words, "Is what is morally right or wrong commanded by God because it is inherently right or wrong, or is it morally right or wrong only because it is commanded by God?" For example, if murder is wrong because God said it is wrong, what if He said it was okay? Would that make murder right? Of course not! If God commanded murder wrong for good reasons, what are those reasons and why can't we base our proscription against murder on those reasons alone and skip the divine command stage altogether? In other words, if murder is really wrong in the moral universe, then it doesn't matter what God thinks, or if there's a god or not, it's still wrong. Here are three ways we can reason our way from *is* to *ought* and derive moral values.

First, morality is derived from the Latin *moralitas*, or "manner, character, and proper behavior." Morality has to do with how you act toward others. So I begin with a *Principle of Moral Good*:

> *Always act with someone else's moral good in mind, and never act in a way that it leads to someone else's moral loss* (through force or fraud).

You can, of course, act in a way that has no effect on anyone else, and, in this case, morality isn't involved. But given the choice between acting in a way that increases someone else's moral good or not, it is more moral to do so than not. I added the parenthetical note "through force or fraud" to clarify *intent* instead of, say, neglect or ignorance. Morality involves conscious choice, and the choice to act in a manner that increases someone else's moral good, then, is a moral act, and its opposite is an immoral act.

Second, morality involves how our thoughts and actions affect the *survival and flourishing of sentient beings*. By *survival* I mean the instinct to live. By *flourishing* I mean having adequate sustenance, safety, shelter, bonding, and social relations for physical and mental health. Any organism subject to natural selection will by necessity have this drive to survive and flourish, for if they didn't they would not live long enough to reproduce and would therefore no longer be subject to natural selection. By *sentient* I mean *emotive, perceptive, sensitive, responsive, conscious*, and therefore able to feel and to suffer. Our moral consideration should be based not primarily on what sentient beings are *thinking*, but on what they are *feeling*.[28]

Third, given that moral principles must be founded on something *natural* instead of *supernatural* and that science is the best tool we have for understanding the natural world, applying evolutionary theory to the ultimate foundation of morality, it seems to me that it is *individual sentient beings* that is our starting point because, (1) the individual is the primary target of natural selection in evolution, and (2) it is the individual who is most affected by moral and immoral acts. Thus:

> *The survival and flourishing of individual sentient beings* is *the foundation for establishing values and morals, and so determining the conditions by which sentient beings best survive and flourish* ought to be *the goal of a science of morality.*

Here we see a smooth transition from the way nature *is* (the individual struggling to survive and flourish in the environment of our evolutionary ancestry) to the way it *ought to be* (given a choice, it is more moral to act in a way that enhances the survival and flourishing of other sentient individuals). In *The Moral Arc*, I proposed an analogy with what I called "a public health model of moral science," noting the startling advances in improving health and prolonging life for more people in more places over the past two centuries through flush toilets, sewers and waste disposal technologies, clean water, vaccinations, Pasteurization, occupational safety, family planning, and nutrition and diet, and many others. If you agree that it is better that millions of people no longer suffer from and die of yellow fever and small pox, cholera and bronchitis, dysentery and diarrhea, consumption and tuberculosis, measles and mumps, and many other assaults on the body, then you have offered your provisional assent that the way something *is* (diseases cause suffering and death) means we *ought* to prevent them through vaccinations and other medical and public health technologies.

Or consider the fact that according to the World Bank the percentage of people living on less than $2.50 a day (poverty) and $1.25 a day (extreme poverty) has fallen by more than half since 1990 and is projected to disappear entirely by around 2035.[29] The end of poverty – imagine that![30] If the *survival and flourishing of individual sentient beings* is the foundation of values and morals, then we can say objectively and absolutely that ending poverty is real moral progress. On what basis can we make such a claim? *Ask the people who are no longer living in squalor.* They will tell you that surviving on more than $2.50 a day or $1.25 a day is better than suffering on less. Why is it better? Because it is in our nature to prefer flourishing to suffering. Or consider the fact that the number of polio cases has decreased from 350,000 in 1988 to 222 in 2012. Is that an absolute moral good? Ask the 349,778 people who did not die of polio. They'll tell you. If that is not objectively quantifiable moral progress, then I don't know what is.

Thanks to the worldview of *scientific naturalism* and *Enlightenment humanism,* never again need we be the intellectual slaves of those who would bind our minds with the chains of dogma and authority. In their stead, we use reason and science as the arbiters of truth and knowledge. As I said in my 2012 Reason Rally speech before a crowd of over 20,000 humanists and science enthusiasts on the mall in Washington DC:[31]

Instead of divining truth through the authority of an ancient holy book or philosophical treatise, people began to explore the book of nature for themselves.

Instead of looking at illustrations in illuminated botanical books scholars went out into nature to see what was actually growing out of the ground.

Instead of relying on the woodcuts of dissected cadavers in old medical texts, physicians opened bodies themselves to see with their own eyes what was there.

Instead of human sacrifices to assuage the angry weather gods, naturalists made measurements of temperature, barometric pressure, and winds to create the meteorological sciences.

Instead of enslaving people because they were a lesser species, we expanded our knowledge to include all humans as members of the species through evolutionary sciences.

Instead of treating women as inferiors because a holy book says it is a man's right to do so, we discovered natural rights that dictate that all people should be treated equally through the moral sciences.

Instead of the supernatural belief in the divine right of kings, people employed a natural belief in the legal right of democracy, and this gave us political progress.

Instead of a tiny handful of elites holding most of the political power by keeping their citizens illiterate and unenlightened, through science, literacy, and education people could see for themselves the power and corruption that held them down and began to throw off their chains of bondage and demand their natural rights.

The constitutions of nations ought to be grounded in the constitution of humanity, which science and reason are best equipped to understand. That is the heart and core of scientific naturalism and Enlightenment humanism.

CHAPTER 20

Mr. Hume: Tear. Down. This. Wall.

A Response to George Ellis' Critique of My Defense of Moral Realism

PREAMBLE

Following the publication of the article in Chapter 19, the journal received a well-reasoned critique by the physicist George Ellis, which they published in a subsequent issue of *Theology and Science*,[1] along with my response, which appears here. These two essays constitute my manifesto for *Enlightenment humanism* through the worldview of *scientific naturalism* and, in fact, are the cornerstone of an even larger worldview I am working on now, hinted at in the subtitle of this book, *scientific humanism*.

* * *

I AM DEEPLY APPRECIATIVE THAT UNIVERSITY OF CAPE TOWN professor George Ellis took the time to read carefully, think deeply about, and respond thoughtfully to my *Theology and Science* paper "Scientific Naturalism: A Manifesto for Enlightenment Humanism" (August 2017),[2] itself an abbreviation of the full-throated defense of moral realism and moral progress that I present in my 2015 book, *The Moral Arc*.[3] As a physicist, he naturally reflects the methodologies of his field, wondering how a social scientist might "discover" moral laws in human nature as a physical scientist might discover natural laws in laboratory experiments. It's a good question, as is his query, "Is it possible to say in some absolute sense that specific acts, such as the large scale massacres of the Holocaust, are evil in an absolute sense?"

Pace Abraham Lincoln, who famously said, "If slavery is not wrong, then nothing is wrong,"[4] I hereby declare in an unequivocal defense of moral realism:

If the Holocaust is not wrong, then nothing is wrong.

Since Professor Ellis is a physicist, let me approach this defense of moral realism from the perspective of a physical scientist. It is my hypothesis that, in the same way that Galileo and Newton discovered physical laws and principles about the natural world that really are out there, so too have social scientists discovered moral laws and principles about human nature and society that really do exist. Just as it was inevitable that the astronomer Johannes Kepler would discover that planets have elliptical orbits – given that he was making accurate astronomical measurements and given that planets really do travel in elliptical orbits, he could hardly have discovered anything else – scientists studying political, economic, social, and moral subjects will discover certain things that are true in these fields of inquiry. For example, that democracies are better than autocracies, that market economies are superior to command economies, that torture and the death penalty do not curb crime, that burning women as witches is a fallacious idea, that women are not too weak and emotional to run companies or countries, and, most poignantly here, that blacks do not like being enslaved and that the Jews do not want to be exterminated. Why?

My answer is that it is in human nature to struggle to survive and flourish in the teeth of nature's entropy, and having the freedom, autonomy, and prosperity available in free societies – built as they were on the foundation of Enlightenment philosophers and scientists seeking to discover the best way for humans to live – best enables individual sentient beings to live out their evolved destinies. Let me unpack that sentence. As I noted in my manifesto, my moral starting point is *the survival and flourishing of individual sentient beings,* by which I mean the evolved instinct to live and to have adequate sustenance, safety, shelter, bonding, and social relations for physical and mental health. Any organism subject to natural selection will by necessity have this drive to survive and flourish. If it didn't, it would not live long enough to reproduce and would no longer be subject to natural selection.

From here, we can derive the purpose of life: It is to push back against the entropy of nature, as described by the Second Law of Thermodynamics. Entropy is a fundamental physical rule that closed systems (those not taking in energy) move from order to disorder, from organization to disorganization, from structured to unstructured, and from warm to cold. Although entropy can be temporarily reversed in an open system with an outside source of energy, such as heating cold food in a microwave, isolated systems decay as entropy increases. We can never get around this fundamental law of nature, as the eminent astrophysicist Sir Arthur Stanley Eddington explained in his classic 1928 book *The Nature of the Physical World*:

> The law that entropy always increases – the second law of thermodynamics – holds, I think, the supreme position among the laws of Nature ... [I]f your theory is found to be against the second law of thermodynamics I can give you no hope; there is nothing for it but to collapse in deepest humiliation.[5]

The Second Law of Thermodynamics is the First Law of Life. As the evolutionary psychologists Leda Cosmides, John Tooby, and Clark Harrett argued in their paper exploring the ultimate purpose of evolution: "The most basic lesson is that natural selection is the only known natural process that pushes populations of organisms thermodynamically uphill into higher degrees of functional order, or even offset the inevitable increase in disorder that would otherwise take place."[6] This "extropy" only happens in an open system with an energy source, such as our planet with the sun providing the energy that temporarily reverses entropy, and replicating molecules like RNA and DNA that enable living organisms to send near-duplicates out into the world that provide fodder for natural selection. Once this system is up and running, evolution can move away from the left wall of minimum order and simplicity and toward the right wall of maximum order and complexity. If you do nothing, entropy will take its course and you will move toward a higher state of disorder (ultimately causing your demise). So the most basic purpose in life is to combat entropy by doing something extropic – expending energy to survive, reproduce, and flourish.

Consider another analogy from mathematics, one made by the Harvard psychologist Steven Pinker. Certainly, moral truths don't instantiate in some physically measurable form like the mass of a particle or the gravitational force of a star, but there are abstract Platonic truths that most scientists agree exist, such as those in mathematics. Pinker writes:

On this analogy, we are born with a rudimentary concept of number, but as soon as we build on it with formal mathematical reasoning, the nature of mathematical reality forces us to discover some truths and not others. (No one who understands the concept of two, the concept of four and the concept of addition can come to any conclusion but that $2 + 2 = 4$.) Perhaps we are born with a rudimentary moral sense, and as soon as we build on it with moral reasoning, the nature of moral reality forces us to some conclusions but not others.[7]

In his book *Nonzero*, by way of example, Robert Wright documents an ever-increasing prevalence of nonzero-sum games through the history of life and civilization.[8] Over billions of years of natural history and thousands of years of human history, there has been an increasing tendency toward the playing of cooperative "nonzero" games between organisms. This tendency has allowed more nonzero gamers to survive. Although competition between individuals and groups was common in both biological evolution and human history, Wright argues that symbiosis among organisms and cooperation among people have gradually displaced competition as the dominant form of interaction. Why? Natural selection: Those who cooperated by playing nonzero games were more likely to survive and pass on their genes for cooperative behavior. And this process has been ongoing, Wright says, "from the primordial soup to the World Wide Web." From the Paleolithic to the present, human groups have evolved from bands of hundreds to tribes of thousands, to chiefdoms of tens of thousands, to states of hundreds of thousands, to nations of millions. This could not have happened through zero-sum exchanges alone. The hallmarks of humanity – language, tools, hunting, gathering, farming, writing, art, music, science, and technology – could not have come about through the actions of isolated zero-sum gamers. Thus, reasoning moral agents would eventually conclude that both should cooperate toward mutual benefit rather than compete to either a zero-sum outcome in which one gains and the other loses, or both lose in a defection cascade. Pinker draws out the implications for moral realism:

> If I appeal to you to do anything that affects me – to get off my foot, or tell me the time or not run me over with your car – then I can't do it in a way that privileges my interests over yours (say, retaining my right to run you

over with my car) if I want you to take me seriously. Unless I am Galactic Overlord, I have to state my case in a way that would force me to treat you in kind. I can't act as if my interests are special just because I'm me and you're not, any more than I can persuade you that the spot I am standing on is a special place in the universe just because I happen to be standing on it.[9]

Then there is the principle of the interchangeability of perspectives, which is at the core of the oldest moral principle discovered multiple times around the world: the Golden Rule. Pinker notes that it also forms the basis of

> Spinoza's Viewpoint of Eternity, the Social Contract of Hobbes, Rousseau and Locke; Kant's Categorical Imperative; and Rawls's Veil of Ignorance. It also underlies Peter Singer's theory of the Expanding Circle – the optimistic proposal that our moral sense, though shaped by evolution to overvalue self, kin and clan, can propel us on a path of moral progress, as our reasoning forces us to generalize it to larger and larger circles of sentient beings.[10]

Professor Ellis asserts that my attempt to base moral values in science fails, but, in fact, as I document in *The Moral Arc* (and more briefly in my manifesto), the moral progress we have witnessed over the centuries – the abolition of slavery, torture, and the death penalty; the expansion of rights to blacks, women, children, workers, and now even animals – has its origin in the scientific and reason-based concept that the world is governed by laws and principles that we can understand and apply, whether it is solar systems, eco systems, political systems, economic systems, or social and moral systems. Whether or not you consider "ought" to be a scientific category (Ellis, along with most philosophers and scientists, concurs with David Hume that it is not – one cannot derive an *ought* from an *is*), for centuries we have been treating the *is* of the world – the way things really are that we can discover – as a basis for determining what we *ought* to do morally. Thus, he concludes, "science *per se* does not in any recognizable sense imply that survival and flourishing is either good or bad, because there is no scientific test for good or bad and no scientific proof that they are positive or negative in moral terms, i.e. that this is the way things *ought* to be."

Excuse me? We have, in fact, been running such experiments for centuries – the natural experiments of societies and their social, political, and economic systems. Every state or national constitution is an experiment in social and moral living, and we can compare them through the comparative method social scientists and policy makers routinely use. Different laws and systems produce different outcomes. We can study and learn from them, with our evaluative criteria grounded in human nature and our desire to survive and flourish.

A couple of important corrections: First, Ellis claims that Sam Harris' defense of moral realism in *The Moral Landscape*[11] (and elsewhere) has received a "drubbing" from "competent philosophers" so, he concludes, "let's discard it." Not so fast. While there have been many critiques of Harris' hypothesis, he has actively sought critical feedback and robustly defended his position.[12] In my opinion, his defense of moral realism still stands, but at the very least a thorough and honest review of the literature cannot lead one to simply discard it. Second, Ellis naively rejects standard natural selection theory with the individual as the target of selection, and in its stead embraces multiselection theory with its concomitant acceptance of group selection theory, as if this were no longer controversial. Nothing could be further from the truth, as even a cursory review of the literature in evolutionary theory reveals. Group selection, if it has any basis in reality – and even that is questionable – is at most a minor player in the evolution of organisms, including humans, and has been nearly universally rejected by most evolutionary biologists since the 1960s, and more recently debunked by Steven Pinker.[13]

Finally, intellectual humility requires me to admit that it is possible that my entire program may be, in Ellis' words, "sociologically based – it is that of a WEIRD (Western, Educated, Industrialized, Rich, and Democratic) culture – taken for granted by those living in such cultures, but not necessarily by others. People brought up in Eastern cultures are likely to make the opposite assumption." Sure, future scientists may one day discover that humans do not have an instinct to survive and flourish, that most people do not want freedom, autonomy, and prosperity, that women want to be lorded over by men, that animals enjoy being tortured, killed, and eaten, that some people like being enslaved, and that large populations of people don't object to being liquidated in gas chambers. But I doubt it.

Through science and reason, we have followed a path of discovery that has led more people in more places to lead better lives and enjoy more moral rights, respect, and consideration. The Is-Ought fallacy is a red herring. Mr. Hume: Tear. Down. This. Wall.

CHAPTER 21

Kardashev's Types and Sparks' Law

How to Build Civilization 1.0

PREAMBLE

A shorter version of this essay was originally published in the *Los Angeles Times* opinion editorial pages on July 22, 2008, as "Toward a Type 1 Civilization: Along with energy policy, political and economic systems must also evolve." With hindsight the date is especially ominous as two months later, on September 29, 2008, the Dow Jones Industrial Average fell 777.68 points, the single largest one-day drop in history to that date, and that was only the beginning of what would turn out to be the worst financial crisis since the Great Depression. By the time the carnage was cleared, the Dow had collapsed 53.5 percent from its pre-recession high on October 9, 2007 of 14,164 to its nadir on March 5, 2009 of 6,594. Keep this in mind when sensing my optimism which, had I penned this piece six months or a year later, would surely have been more tempered with caution. Still, that the Dow closed at 25,063 on Friday February 1, 2019 (the day I wrote this introduction) – a 380 percent increase in eleven years – is a testament to Adam Smith's famous quip "there's a lot of ruin in a nation." Civilizations are equally robust, as I hope to show in this essay on how we can transition from a zero-sum tribal world to a nonzero global world.

* * *

POLITICS, ECONOMICS, AND RELIGION HAVE, AT VARIOUS times in recent history, been identified as the cause of strife and conflict between nations. Politicos argue that we need a new political system, either more left-leaning or more right-leaning, depending on the politician. Economists forecast and prescribe monetary solutions to social problems, again either more left-leaning or more right-leaning, depending on the economist. And religionists of various stripes call for either more or less tolerance of other religious beliefs while atheists ask us to "imagine no religion" as the means to eliminate most wars, revolutions, conflicts, intolerance, bigotry, and the like.

That's too easy. In many instances, particular political, economic, and religious ideologies are just excuses for land grabbing and power mongering. Remove those specific excuses and others would quickly fill the void. Revolutionary Marxism as a faux religion fills the bill as a recent historical example that predates the current problem with radical Islam.

Politics, economics, and religion are tertiary or secondary causes of the problem. A deeper ultimate cause is tribalism. We are a social primate species, and as such we are exceptionally tribal. Group identity is essential to our sense of self. Political tribalism (e.g., nations v. nations, states v. states), economic tribalism (e.g., favorable balances of trade and most favored tariffs), and religious tribalism (e.g., Sunnis v. Shiites, Protestants v. Catholics) are simply type specimens of the broader species of tribalism.

The unfortunate byproduct of such in-group/out-group tribalism is xenophobia. We have a natural aversion to Others, and we show a remarkable ability to sort people into in-group/out-group categories on the most minute levels of criteria – the Crips and the Bloods, the Hutus and the Tutsis, the Albanians and the Serbs, or closer to home, the conservatives and the liberals.

Liberals describe conservatives as stingy, heartless, dour, dim-witted authoritarians who appeal to voters' emotions through threat and fear-mongering. Conservatives, we are told, avoid uncertainty, have a "need for order, structure, closure," are "resistant to change" and "endorse inequalities."

In turn, conservatives believe that liberals are a bunch of sandal-wearing, tree-hugging, whale-saving, hybrid-driving, trash-recycling, peacenik flip-flopping bed-wetters. Liberals, say conservatives, lack a moral compass that leads to an inability to make clear ethical choices, an inordinate lack of certainty about social issues, a pathological fear of clarity that leads to indecisiveness, a naive belief that all people are equally talented, and a blind adherence in the teeth of contradictory evidence that culture and environment determine one's lot in society and therefore it is up to the government to remedy all social injustices.

To move beyond this political tribalism, I suggest we adopt the approach that considers liberals and conservatives as emphasizing different moral values, rather than one being right and the other wrong. Or in the words of the psychologist Jonathan Haidt,

> that morality is not just about how we treat each other (as most liberals think); it is also about binding groups together, supporting essential institutions, and living in a sanctified and noble way. When Republicans say that Democrats "just don't get it," this is the "it" to which they refer. Conservative positions on gays, guns, god, and immigration must be understood as means to achieve one kind of morally ordered society.

Ever since 9/11, it has become clear that other tribes pose a serious threat to us, a threat that I think conservatives take more seriously than liberals. My favorite filmic example, which I've used before, comes from Rob Reiner's 1992 film *A Few Good Men*, in which Jack Nicholson's character – the battle-hardened Marine Colonel Nathan R. Jessup – is being cross-examined by Tom Cruise's naive rookie Navy lawyer Lieutenant Daniel Kaffee. Kaffee is defending two marines accused of killing a fellow soldier. He thinks Jessup ordered a "code red," an off-the-books command to rough up a lazy marine trainee in need of discipline, and that matters got tragically out of hand. Kaffee wants answers to specific questions about the incident. Jessup wants to lecture him on the meaning of freedom and the need to defend it. The ensuing dialogue includes Jessup's penetrating testimony about the true nature of human nature:

> *Jessup:* Son, we live in a world that has walls. And those walls have to be guarded by men with guns. Who's gonna do it? You? You don't want the truth. Because deep down, in places you don't talk about at parties, you want me on that wall. You need me on that wall. We use words like honor, code, loyalty ... we use these words as the backbone to a life spent defending something. You use 'em as a punchline. I have neither the time nor the inclination to explain myself to a man who rises and sleeps under the blanket of the very freedom I provide, then questions the

manner in which I provide it. I'd prefer you just said thank you and went on your way. Otherwise, I suggest you pick up a weapon and stand a post.

The simple observation that we live in a world with walls – and have for at least 6,000 years of recorded history – implies that those walls are needed. The constitutions of states cannot alter the constitution of man.

One long-term solution is to shift from the zero-sum tribal world of our past to a zero-sum global world of our future, what I am here calling Civilization 1.0. Let me explain. In a 1964 article on searching for extra-terrestrial civilizations, the Soviet astronomer Nikolai Kardashev suggested using radio telescopes to detect energy signals from other solar systems in which there might be civilizations of three levels of advancement: A Type 1.0 Civilization can harness all of the energy of its home planet; a Type 2.0 Civilization can harvest all of the power of its sun; and a Type 3.0 Civilization can master the energy from its entire galaxy.

Based on our energy efficiency at the time, in 1973 the astronomer Carl Sagan estimated that Earth represented a Type 0.7 Civilization on a scale ranging from Type 0.1 to Type 1.0. (More current assessments put us at 0.72.) As the Kardashevian scale is logarithmic – where any increase in power consumption requires a huge leap in power production – we have a stretch to go before we reach Civilization 1.0. Fossil fuels won't get us there. Renewable sources such as solar, wind and geothermal are a good start, but we need nuclear power to get us to Civilization 1.0.

The hurdles are not solely – or even primarily – technological ones. We have a proven track record of achieving remarkable technological solutions to survival problems – as long as there is the political will and economic opportunities that allow the solutions to flourish. In other words, we need a 1.0 polity and economy, along with the technology, in order to become a Civilization 1.0.

If we use the Kardashevian scale to plot humanity's progress, it shows how far we've come in the long history of our species from Type 0.1, and it leads us to see what a Type 1.0 Civilization might be like:

Type 0.1: Fluid groups of hominids living in Africa. Technology consists of primitive stone tools. Intragroup conflicts are resolved through dominance hierarchy, and between-group violence is common.

Type 0.2: Bands of roaming hunter-gatherers that form kinship groups, with a mostly horizontal political system and egalitarian economy.

Type 0.3: Tribes of individuals linked through kinship but with a more settled and agrarian lifestyle. The beginnings of a political hierarchy and a primitive economic division of labor.

Type 0.4: Chiefdoms consisting of a coalition of tribes into a single hierarchical political unit with a dominant leader at the top, and with the beginnings of significant economic inequalities and a division of labor in which lower-class members produce food and other products consumed by nonproducing upper-class members.

Type 0.5: The state as a political coalition with jurisdiction over a well-defined geographical territory and its corresponding inhabitants, with a mercantile economy that seeks a favorable balance of trade in a win-lose game against other states.

Type 0.6: Empires that extend their control over peoples who are not culturally, ethnically or geographically within their normal jurisdiction, with a goal of economic dominance over rival empires.

Type 0.7: Democracies that divide power over several institutions, which are run by elected officials voted for by some citizens. The beginnings of a market economy.

Type 0.8: Liberal democracies that give the vote to all citizens. Markets that begin to embrace a nonzero, win-win economic game through free trade with other states.

Type 0.9: Democratic capitalism, the blending of liberal democracy and free markets, now spreading across the globe through democratic movements in developing nations and broad trading blocs such as the European Union.

Type 1.0: Globalism, or Civilization 1.0, includes worldwide wireless Internet access, with all knowledge digitized and available to everyone. A completely global economy with free markets in which anyone can trade with anyone else without interference from states or governments. A planet where all states are democracies in which everyone has the franchise.

The forces at work that could prevent us from making the great leap forward to a Civilization 1.0 are primarily political and economic. The resistance by nondemocratic states to turning power over to the people is considerable, especially in theocracies whose leaders would prefer we all revert to Type 0.4 chiefdoms. The opposition toward a global economy is substantial, even in the industrialized West, where economic tribalism still dominates the thinking of most politicians, intellectuals, and citizens.

For thousands of years, we have existed in a zero-sum tribal world in which a gain for one tribe, state, or nation meant a loss for another tribe, state, or nation – and our political and economic systems have been designed for use in that win-lose world. But we have the opportunity to live in a win-win world and become a Civilization 1.0 by spreading liberal democracy and free trade, in which the scientific and technological benefits will flourish. I am optimistic because in the evolutionist's deep time and the historian's long view, the trend lines toward achieving Civilization 1.0 status tick ever upward.

The free market is the best system yet devised for allowing the most individuals, in the most places, to achieve the most prosperity and highest standard of living most of the time. But there must be strictly enforced rules and conditions in which the free market operates. There are too many defectors and cheaters, too much greed and avarice for the system to operate effectively outside of a political system.

In order to keep the free market both free and fair, we need political states based on:

1. The rule of law.
2. Property rights.
3. A secure and trustworthy banking and monetary system.
4. Economic stability.
5. A reliable infrastructure and the freedom to move about the country.
6. Freedom of the press.
7. Freedom of association.
8. Mass education.
9. Protection of civil liberties.
10. A clean and safe environment.

11. A robust military for protection of our liberties from attacks by other states.

12. A potent police force for protection of our freedoms from attacks by other people within the state.

13. A viable legislative system for establishing fair and just laws.

14. An effective judicial system for the equitable enforcement of those fair and just laws.

The case for democracy has been powerfully made by Natan Sharansky in his book by that title, so let me note here that there is a well-documented correlation between liberal democracy and peace – the more a nation embraces liberal democracy, the less likely it is to go to war, especially against another liberal democracy. The political scientist Rudolf J. Rummel has researched this relationship thoroughly, showing in one study, for example, that of the 371 international wars that occurred between 1816 and 2005 in which at least 1,000 people were killed, there were 205 wars between nondemocratic nations, 166 wars between democratic and nondemocratic nations, and 0 wars between democratic nations. Writes Rummel:

> First, well established democracies do not make war on and rarely commit lesser violence against each other. Second, the more two nations are democratic, the less likely is war or lesser violence between them. Third, the more a nation is democratic, the less severe its overall foreign violence. Fourth, in general the more democratic a nation, the less likely it will have domestic collective violence. Finally, in general the more democratic a nation, the less its democide [the murder of its own citizens].

Conclusion: *Power kills, democracy saves.* Solution: *Spread democracy.*

There is another deduction to be drawn from the historical data: *Trade leads to peace and prosperity.* Therefore: *Spread trade.*

For example, 2007 marked the fiftieth anniversary of the signing of the Treaty of Rome, in which France, Italy, Belgium, West Germany, Luxembourg, and the Netherlands formed what would eventually become the European Union. By opening their borders to free trade, they moved from being half as productive as the United States to being on an equal footing, in only half that time.

By comparison, Denmark, Ireland, and the United Kingdom were on economic par with those six countries before they (the six) signed the treaty, but they subsequently fell behind the six. When Denmark, Ireland, and the UK opened their economic borders to trade with the original Treaty of Rome six, they eventually caught up, with the UK today, for example, being as productive as Germany.

Such examples do not represent controlled experiments, but we can employ the comparative method as an additional test, in which we compare social outcomes where influencing factors are varied by natural means. Employing the comparative method adds additional support for the power of free markets and capitalism.

In the 1980s, for example, Spain, Portugal, and Greece joined the free market club, quickly bringing Spain up to equal footing with the original Rome six, with Portugal and Greece not far behind. Austria, Sweden, and Finland joined in 1995, and their economic fortunes have taken an upward turn. Ten more countries have joined since 2004, and they are beginning to show early signs of upward economic mobility.

Similarly, the five wealthiest East Asian countries of Taiwan, Singapore, Japan, South Korea, and Hong Kong experienced upturns in their economies once they loosened the chains that bound their markets. By comparison, research shows the effects of protectionism on the wealth of a nation. From 1950 to 2001, for example, the per capita GDP for Europe increased 68 percent compared to the United States, while Asia increased 244 percent relative to the USA; by comparison, those Latin American countries closed to international trade saw a relative *decrease* of 21 percent, whereas in 1950 those same Latin American countries exceeded Asia's by 75 percent.

The comparative method can also be employed to an unfolding economic experiment in the form of the Central American Free Trade Agreement (CAFTA). In the year since CAFTA was signed in March of 2006 and the USA began trading with El Salvador, Guatemala, Nicaragua, and Honduras, imports from America to these Central America countries increased significantly, along with investment capital into key industries.

In the second half of 2006, for example, after it joined CAFTA, total trade in Guatemala grew by 17 percent, compared with a 5 percent growth in the first half of the year. Nicaragua is experiencing similar economic improvement. Since it signed on to CAFTA in April of 2006, total trade increased by more than 20 percent compared to the same period in 2005.

How do we get from Civilization 0.72 to Civilization 1.0? Freedom. The freedom to try. To explain, consider the following thought experiment. Imagine that it is the year 1900 and you are tasked with solving the following problems:

1. To build and maintain roads adequate for use of conveyances, their operators, and passengers.
2. To increase the average span of life by thirty years.
3. To convey instantly the sound of a voice speaking at one place to any other point or any number of points around the world.
4. To convey instantly the visual replica of an action, such as a presidential inauguration, to men and women in their living rooms all over America.
5. To develop a medical preventive against death from pneumonia.
6. To transport physically a person from Los Angeles to New York in less than four hours.
7. To build a horseless carriage of the qualities and capabilities described in the latest advertising folder of any automobile manufacturer.

This thought experiment was proposed in 1954 – the year I was born – by an entrepreneur named John C. Sparks, in a short essay entitled "If Men Were Free to Try." Sparks noted that of these seven problems, the first one would have been the easiest to solve, since there were already roads on which to improve, while the other six would have seemed like the wildest of science-fiction fantasies.

By 1954, however, the first problem had yet to be solved because the roads were made public and the government put itself in charge of building and maintaining them. And today we still drive on congested roads on which 37,332 died in 2008, the lowest in four decades and yet the equivalent of more than ten 9/11s every year. By contrast, the other six problems were not only solved but were so effectively implemented that by 1954 they were simply taken for granted. Why? Because, Sparks explained, "solutions have been found wherever the atmosphere of freedom and private ownership has prevailed wherein men could try out their ideas and succeed or fail on their own worthiness."

Imagine, however, if in 1900 the roads had been privatized and the automobile industry had been nationalized. As Sparks suggested, instead of racing competitions between automobile manufacturers, "we would have likely participated in a contest sponsored by the privately owned highway companies to suggest how to improve the government's horse-less carriage so that it would keep pace with the fine and more-than-adequate highways." Why? "We never do think creatively on any activity preempted by government. It is not until an activity has been freed from monopoly that creative thought comes into play ... as long as men are free to try their ideas in a competitive and voluntary market."

As we transition from 2008 to 2009, I would like to propose this thought experiment. It is 1954 and you are challenged to solve the following problems:

1. Build and maintain an educational system that will provide the highest-quality education at the lowest price for the greatest number of students.
2. To convey instantly verbal and visual communication between two or more people anywhere in the world with or without wires.
3. To manufacture and distribute high-quality powerful computers small enough to sit on your lap and cheap enough for almost anyone to afford.
4. To design and distribute software programs to run on personal com-puters such that anyone can operate them with minimal experience or training.
5. To create a world wide web of connectedness with virtually instanta-neous access between servers, computers, and people anywhere in the world with or without wires.
6. To innovate a computer engine that allows all knowledge to be catalogued, searched, and downloaded for free or at a minuscule cost by anyone, anywhere, anytime with or without wires.
7. To make available, for free or at a minuscule cost, all the world's knowledge for use by anyone, anywhere, anytime with or without wires.

Once again, innovators and entrepreneurs in 1954 would have thought the first problem the easiest to solve and the other six problems the product of a mind mired in madness. And yet, over half a century later, the first problem has yet to be solved, while problems two through six are not only solved but continue to be improved at an exponential rate and, assuming the continued application of Moore's Law of accelerating growth, the seventh problem will likely be complete by 2054, the centennial celebration of what we might call Sparks' Law: *Innovations are best generated when people are free to try their ideas in a competitive and voluntary market.*

Why can we talk to nearly anyone, anywhere, anytime on wireless communication systems? Because innovators and entrepreneurs were free to try. Why can most of us afford powerful laptop computers that run easy-to-use software programs that allow us to access other computers, web pages, and digital books, movies, and music for free or at a minuscule cost? Because inventors and businessmen were free to try. Why is America's public school system an abysmal failure (UNICEF, for example, ranked it eighteenth out of twenty-four industrialized countries in 2008)? Because the public education system has not been allowed to thrive and grow in a competitive and voluntary market. Only when it is, will significant innovation be generated.

This is why private schools are so superior to government schools, and why even pro-public-school liberal presidents such as Bill Clinton and Barack Obama send their children to private schools – just as most pro-public-school liberals do who can afford it. Why can't most Americans afford private schools? Because education has not been allowed to flourish in a free market in which, like wireless communications systems and computer hardware, software and search engine technologies, education quality would grow exponentially while the price would drop precipitously. This can only happen if education innovators and entrepreneurs are free to try.

CHAPTER 22

How Lives Turn Out

Genes, Environment, and Luck – What We Can and Cannot Control

PREAMBLE

Long-time readers of my work will note a shift in my political orientation in earlier essays in this volume, from libertarian to classical liberal. The differences are not huge, but neither are they trivial, especially when it comes to fiscal issues. My social attitudes about civil rights, women's rights, gay rights, animal rights, individual freedom and autonomy, and personal responsibility have not changed. But as I've gown older, and especially since the Great Recession of 2008/2009 and, more personally, the unraveling of my beloved sport of cycling in one drug scandal after another, has made it abundantly clear to me that human nature is darker than I previously realized. Our inner demons overwhelm our better angels just often enough that I've come to believe that in the same manner that sports need rules, markets need regulations, and societies need fair and just laws. As well, there is the issue of what moral obligation we have to help those who cannot help themselves, most notably as it relates to social spending. After further reflection, I now realize how unfortunate life can be to a sufficiently large number of people that I no longer think that private charity alone can do the job of shoring up a social safety net for the unlucky.

In recent years social justice activists have issued a challenge to "check your white privilege." Inasmuch as I oppose the inherent racism ingrained in identity politics (see Chapter 12), my initial replies were of a snarky nature, such as "I just checked my white privilege and it's doing just fine, thank you." But, as I engaged the task more introspectively, it wasn't my "white privilege" that I discovered so much as it was my good fortune. This led to my November 2017 column in *Scientific American*, in which I enumerated a few of the ways that luck has favored many people (myself included) that led to their success, much of which was not "earned" in the purist sense that conservatives conceive of it, in which the successful deserved it and the unsuccessful got what they had coming. The deeper I looked into the matter of how lives turn out, in fact, the more I realized how much is out of our control. This essay, an expansion of that *Scientific American* column that was originally published in *Quillette* in January 2019, is a result of my continued research on the subject of, as the above title notes, how lives turn out.

* * *

WHY DO SOME PEOPLE SUCCEED IN LIFE WHILE OTHERS fail? Is it because they are naturally smarter and harder working, or is it because they were raised to be ambitious and disciplined, or could it be that they were simply lucky along the way and got all the good breaks? For centuries, philosophers, theologians, scholars, and ordinary people have speculated on these and related questions, for example, why there are class differences between people; why some people seem to have more power, wealth, and privilege than others; and what's the best way to structure political and economic systems in order to create a fair and just society in the teeth of such obvious inequalities of natural ability, drive, and chance.

As with so many issues today, these are not ideological-free questions. Conservatives, for example, tend to embrace a *Just World Theory* of how lives turn out: If you are rich, successful, and happy it is because you are hard-working, intelligent, creative, risk-taking, and justly rewarded with happiness for your discipline and self-control; if you are poor, unsuccessful, and unhappy it is because you are lazy, ignorant, unimaginative, risk-averse and duly punished with unhappiness for your lack of will power and self-persuasion. In other words, for conservatives, the world is already just, so any injustices are the result of the natural order of things, which should be left well alone. People get what they deserve, so a just society is one in which there are equal opportunities for natural inequalities to form, so let the chips fall where they may.

By contrast, liberals tend to hold an *Unjust World Theory* of how lives turn out: If you are rich, successful, and happy it is because you were fortunate to be born with genes for intelligence, drive, and ambition; were raised in a stable family that inculcated into you the virtues that produce behaviors that translate into hard work, creativity, and risk taking; and you were nourished along the way by people who enabled your success, such as your parents, teachers, mentors, and communities that were nurturing and caring. For those people who did not have the good fortune to have been born into wealth, prosperity, stable families, nurturing communities, and safe environments, we have a moral obligation to alter society in a manner to level the playing field and to allow all members of our community or society to flourish to the best of their natural talents.

These differences in how conservatives and liberals see the world very much determine their attitudes toward social policies that affect how lives turn out for the citizens of a society. Believing that the world is already just, conservatives emphasize institutions and traditions, faith and family, nation and creed, and they want to maintain the order and stability of the present structure of society even at the cost of those at the bottom falling through the cracks. Believing that the world is unjust, liberals question authority, celebrate diversity, often flout faith and tradition in order to care for the weak and oppressed, and they want change and justice even at the risk of political and economic disorder.

One's vision of *human nature* also determines how one approaches the subject of how lives turn out. Conservatives, for example, tend to see human nature as *constrained* while liberals see it as *unconstrained* (in Thomas Sowell's configuration in his book *A Conflict of Visions*), and these differences account for the different positions people hold on a number of seemingly unrelated social issues, such as immigration, health care, social security, welfare, taxes, criminal justice reform, police, and war. If human nature is constrained by our biology, the narrative goes, then there isn't much anyone can do to change people's lives, short of locking up the criminals and disciplining the downtrodden. If human nature is unconstrained, the narrative continues, then social inequalities are primarily the result of bad or broken families, inadequate health care and education, or repugnant social policies that must be changed. "In the unconstrained vision, there are no intractable reasons for social evils and therefore no reason why they cannot be solved, with sufficient moral commitment," Sowell explains. "But in the constrained vision, whatever artifices or strategies restrain or ameliorate inherent human evils will themselves have costs, some in the form of other social ills created by these civilizing institutions, so that all that is possible is a prudent trade-off." Which of these theories of human nature you believe to be true will largely shape which solutions to changing how lives turn out will be most effective, such as the size of the government (big versus small), the amount of taxation (high versus low), immigration (open versus closed borders), health care (universal versus individual), environment (protect it versus leave it alone), crime (caused by social injustice versus caused by criminal minds), the constitution (judicial activism for social justice versus strict constructionism for original intent), trade (fair versus free), and others.

In my 2011 book *The Believing Brain*, I sought a nonpolitical perspective and presented evidence for a *realistic vision* that human nature is *relatively constrained* by our heredity and biology, *along with* the constraints from our families, communities, culture, and society. How lives turn out very much depends on both heredity and environment, genes and culture, our evolutionary history and our life trajectory, and how they all interact. People are not blank slates so malleable and responsive to social programs that governments can engineer their lives into a great society of its design, yet we are not so biologically programmed that there is nothing for anyone to do to help those who cannot help themselves because their restraints are greater than most.

A *realistic vision* of human nature recognizes the importance of family, custom, law, and traditional institutions for social harmony, as well as the need for strict moral education through parents, family, friends, and community. We are born with a dual human nature of competing motives: selfish and selfless, competitive and cooperative, greedy and generous, and so we need rules and guidelines and encouragement to do the right thing. A *realistic vision* also recognizes that people vary widely both physically and intellectually – in good part because of natural inherited differences – so the goal must always be to create environments and societies that are truly fair and just, where those who can help themselves can rise (or fall) to their natural levels, and those who cannot help themselves can get the help they need from these nurturing societal institutions.

In addition to the role of chance in how lives turn out, there is the related concept of *contingency*, or an *unpredictable sequence of antecedent states*, which is slightly different from how we usually think of chance as randomness. Contingency may be contrasted with necessity, which is in the domain of natural law. In a model I developed in the late 1980s and early 1990s to explain how history unfolds – the Model of Contingent-Necessity[1] – I defined *contingency* as: *a conjuncture of events occurring without design*; and *necessity* as: *constraining circumstances compelling a certain course of action*. Contingencies are the sometimes small, apparently insignificant, and usually unexpected events of life – the kingdom hangs in the balance awaiting the horseshoe nail. Necessities are the large and powerful laws of nature and trends of history – once the kingdom has collapsed, the arrival of 100,000 horseshoe nails will not save it. The past is composed of both contingencies and necessities. Therefore, it is useful to combine the two into one term that expresses this interrelationship – *contingent-necessity* – taken to mean: *a conjuncture of events compelling a certain course of action by constraining prior conditions*. In other words, we are not free to do just anything we like because there are constraining prior conditions compelling our future actions, but neither are we completely determined by everything that came before since there is an element of self-aware volition in human lives – we can become aware of our genes, environment, and luck and tweak the variables going forward to initiate a different life outcome. What follows are some of the many ways that both contingency and necessity influence how lives turn out.

* * *

At a campaign rally in Roanoke, VA before the 2012 election, President Barack Obama hinted at the role of the environment and society in helping shape the outcome of lives:

> If you were successful, somebody along the line gave you some help. There was a great teacher somewhere in your life. Somebody helped to create this unbelievable American system that we have that allowed you to thrive.

Somebody invested in roads and bridges. If you've got a business – you didn't build that. Somebody else made that happen. The Internet didn't get invented on its own. Government research created the Internet so that all the companies could make money off the Internet.[2]

Although Obama was making a larger point about the power of collective action, like building dams and the Internet, conservative heads exploded at the central sentiment. "I did build that!" is an understandable rejoinder to which I can relate. I research my books, edit my magazine, teach my courses, and write my articles for journals and my monthly columns for *Scientific American*. If I don't make them happen, nobody else will. But then I started thinking as a social scientist on the role of chance and contingency in how lives turn out. It's a sobering experience to realize just how many variables are out of our control.

First, there is the luck of being born at all. The ratio of the number of people who could have been born to those who actually were born is incalculably large – trillions to one. Then there is the luck of being born in a Western country with a stable political system, a sound economy, and a solid infrastructure (roads and bridges), rather than, say, in lower-caste India, war-torn Syria, or anarchic Somalia. If you were unlucky enough to be born in one of those countries, you can hardly be blamed for a life outcome of poverty and destitution, and if you managed to get out of such a horrific environment, there's a good chance that, in addition to being intelligent, creative, and a high-risk taker, you probably had some help along the way.

Second, there is the luck of having loving and nurturing parents who raised you in a safe neighborhood and healthy environment, provided you with a high-quality K–12 education, and who instilled in you the values of personal responsibility. If your family was also financially successful, that's an added bonus because one of the best predictors of someone's earning power is that of their parents. If you were unlucky enough to be raised in an impoverished home by a single parent in an unsafe neighborhood with crappy schools with underpaid and uninspiring teachers, you can hardly be blamed for not waltzing your way into Harvard followed by a six-figure corporate salary with country-club privileges. If you did manage to pull yourself up by your bootstraps into such a privileged world out of such an impoverished environment, there's a good chance that, in addition to being intelligent, creative, and a high-risk taker, you had help along the way.

Third, there's the luck of attending a college where you happened upon good or inspiring professors or mentors who guided you to your calling, along with a strong peer cohort to challenge and support you, followed by finding a high-paying job or a fulfilling career that matches your education, talents, and interests. If you were unlucky enough to have never been mentored by nurturing teachers and professors, did not befriend smart and ambitious peers in your age range in school, could not land a high-paying job out of school, and never found your calling in life that could be converted into a lucrative career, the fault is not entirely in your stars; it is, in fact, more prudently found in your background, including and especially the constraining prior conditions, both biological and environmental.

Fourth, there is the luck of being born at a time in history when your particular aptitudes and passions fit that of the zeitgeist. Would Google's co-founders Larry Page and Sergey Brin be among the richest and most successful people in the world had they been born in 1873 instead of 1973? Both are brilliant and hard-working, so they would probably have been successful in any century, but at the equivalent of $35 billion each? It seems unlikely. If you had the bad luck to have the talents and interests in a task or subject for which your society has next to no interest, you can hardly be blamed for that, short of not having the foresight to see what is coming around the next bend, which few people save the Google boys have. That's contingency.

Fifth, there is the luck of being born with a certain personality, or the unique pattern of relatively permanent traits that make an individual similar to but different from others. Today's most popular personality trait theory is what is known as the Five Factor Model, or the Big Five, given in the acronym OCEAN – (1) Openness to Experience (fantasy, feelings, values), (2) Conscientiousness (competence, order, dutifulness), (3) Extraversion (gregariousness, assertiveness, excitement seeking), (4) Agreeableness (trust, altruism, modesty), and (5) Neuroticism (anxiety, anger, depression). Decades of research on the Big Five by behavior geneticists leads to the unmistakable conclusion that these personality traits are at least 50 percent heritable, so although this leaves much room for environment and volition (50 percent room in fact), the luck of the genetic draw also plays an undeniable role.

Sixth, there is the luck of where you fall in the family structure, namely your birth order. In Frank Sulloway's 1996 book, *Born to Rebel*, the UC Berkeley psychologist presents a summary of 196 controlled birth-order findings classified according to the Big Five:[3]

> *Openness to Experience*: Firstborns are more conforming, traditional, and closely identified with parents.
>
> *Conscientiousness*: Firstborns are more responsible, achievement oriented, and planful.
>
> *Extroversion*: Firstborns are more extroverted, assertive, and likely to exhibit leadership.
>
> *Agreeableness*: Laterborns are more easygoing, cooperative, and popular.
>
> *Neuroticism*: Firstborns are more jealous, anxious, and fearful.

What is the connection between birth order and personality? Sulloway's theory is that firstborns – by the pure luck of being first – receive substantially more attention from their parents than do laterborns, who tend to enjoy greater freedom and less indoctrination into the ideologies of and obedience to authorities. Firstborns generally have greater responsibilities, including the care and liability of their younger sibs. Laterborns are frequently a step removed from the parental authority, and thus less inclined to obey and adopt the beliefs of higher authorities in general. Sulloway summarized the connection between birth order and personality thusly:

> Sandwiched between parents and younger siblings, the firstborn child occupies a special place within the family constellation and, for this reason, generally receives special treatment from parents. Moreover, as the eldest, firstborns tend to identify more closely with parents, and through them, with other representatives of authority. This tendency is probably reinforced by the firstborn's frequent role as a surrogate parent to younger siblings. Consistent with these developmental circumstances, firstborns are found to be more respectful of parents and other authority

figures, more conforming, and more conscientious, conventional, and religious. Laterborns, who tend to identify less closely with parents and authority, also tend to rebel against the authority of their elder siblings.[4]

Applying his theory to the history of science, Sulloway found that laterborns were far more likely to be receptive to radical new ideas, whereas firstborns were more inclined to defend the status quo. Specifically, coding the positions of 2,784 participants in twenty-eight diverse scientific controversies spanning over 400 years of science history, Sulloway discovered, "using multiple regression models with these and other variables, that birth order consistently emerges as the single best predictor of intellectual receptivity." Needless to say, one doesn't choose one's birth order; nevertheless, the effects on something as seemingly unrelated to it as one's openness to new ideas, is unmistakably influenced by it.

In these and many other ways do chance and contingency shape how lives turn out. But by now you must surely be asking, What about intelligence and hard work? Surely they matter as much as luck. Yes, but as with personality traits, behavior geneticists tell us that at least half of intelligence is heritable, as is having a personality that is high in openness to experience, conscientiousness, need of achievement, and risk taking, all factors that shape success. The nongenetic components of aptitude, scrupulousness, and ambition matter too, of course, but most of those environmental and cultural variables were provided by others or circumstances not of your making. If you wake up in the morning full of vim and vigor, bounding out the door and into the world to take your shot, you didn't choose to be that way.

By contrast, and as a test of sorts, there are the counterexamples of über-smart, creative, hardworking people who never prosper. If genes and environment are everything (or nearly so), then why do so many people with good genes and lugubrious environments fail (or at least fail to succeed, if only living mediocre lives)? We cannot simply employ the hindsight bias by taking only successful people and looking to see what they did to become successful and then back-engineer those traits, package them into a program (or self-help book!), and dispense it into the world for consumers to imbibe and prosper. That's not how science works. I call this the *Biography Bias*, evident in the reception of Walter

Isaacson's bestselling biography of Steve Jobs, as readers scrambled to understand what made the mercurial genius so successful. Want to be the next Steve Jobs and create the next Apple? Drop out of college and start a business with your buddy in the garage of your parents' home. How many people have followed the Jobs model and failed? Who knows? No one writes books about them and their failed companies. But venture capitalists (VC) have data on the probability of a garage start-up becoming the Next Big Thing, and here the survivor bias is of a different sort. David Cowan, a VC at Bessemer Venture Partners in Menlo Park, California (and a good friend), told me in an email:

> For garage-dwelling entrepreneurs to crack the 1 percent wealth threshold in America, their path almost always involves raising venture capital and then getting their startup to an Initial Public Offering (IPO) or a large acquisition by another company. If their garage is situated in Silicon Valley they might get to pitch as many as 15 VCs, but VCs hear 200 pitches for every one we fund, so perhaps 1 in 13 startups get VC, and still they face long odds from there. According to figures that the National Venture Capital Association diligently collects through primary research and publishes on their web site, last year was somewhat typical in that 1,334 startups got funded but only 13 percent as many achieved an IPO (81 last year) or an acquisition large enough to warrant a public disclosure of the price (95 last year). So for every wealthy startup founder, there are 100 other entrepreneurs who end up with only a cluttered garage.[5]

Consider the plethora of business books readily available in airport bookstalls that feature the most successful companies. In the 2001 book *Good to Great* (over four million copies sold), for example, the author Jim Collins culled eleven companies out of 1,435 whose stock beat the market average over a forty-year time span, and then searched for shared characteristics among them that he believed accounted for their success. Instead, as the Pomona College economist Gary Smith explained in his insightful 2014 book, *Standard Deviations* (Overlook), Collins should have started with a list of companies at the *beginning* of the test period, then employed a set of criteria to predict which eleven companies should do better than average. To do otherwise – to summarize the characteristics of the companies that did best *after the fact* – is not prediction; it's *postdiction.* In fact, as Smith goes on to show, from 2001 through 2012, the stock of six of Collins' eleven "great" companies did *worse* than the overall stock market, meaning that this system of post hoc analysis is fundamentally flawed. Smith finds a similar problem with the 1982 book *In Search of Excellence* (over three million copies sold) in which the authors Tom Peters and Robert Waterman identified eight common attributes of forty-three "excellent" companies. Since then, of the thirty-five companies with publicly traded stocks, twenty have done *worse* than the market average.[6]

* * *

There are, as well, additional factors that determine life outcomes over and above genes, environment, and chance, such as good or bad choices. Here I must briefly engage with the contentious issue of free will and determinism and consider the role of *volition* in any evaluation of life outcomes. In two of my books (*The Science of Good and Evil* and *The Moral Arc*), in a couple of my *Scientific American* columns, and in several articles and essays,[7] I have defended the compatibilist position in the free will–determinism debate, so I don't want to unduly burden the patience of my readers by bolting on a long sidebar on the issue here. In brief, I believe I have worked out how one can accept the fact that we live in a determined universe without that assumption precluding us from making volitional choices and thus retaining personal responsibility and moral accountability for our actions (our choices). Here are my four compatibilist workarounds: (1) *modular mind* – even though a brain consists of many neural networks in which one network may make a choice that another network finds about later, they are all still operating in a single brain; (2) *free won't* – vetoing competing impulses and choosing one thought or action over another; (3) *choice as part of the causal net* – wherein our volitional acts are part of the determined universe but are still our choices; (4) *degrees of moral freedom* – a range of choice options varying by degrees of complexity and the number of intervening variables.

Underlying these four factors is a fifth, deeper layer of *self-awareness*, and *awareness of the influencing factors* that shape how your life turns out. How? Knowing your strengths and weaknesses and selecting paths more likely to result in the desired effect, you can become aware of the internal and external influencing variables on your life and self-aware of how you respond to them and then make adjustments accordingly, however restrictive the degrees of freedom may be. I realize that this will not satisfy determinism purists, but then I contend that they don't *act* like determinists anyway, given that the illusion they think free will is, is so powerful that – like placebos – it can affect life outcomes.

In the end, if the cosmic dice rolled in your favor, how should you feel? *Modest pride in one's hard work is no vice, but boastful arrogance at one's good fortune is no virtue.* Cultivate gratitude. What if you've been unlucky in life? There is consolation in the fact that studies show what's important in the long run is not success so much as living a meaningful life, which is the result of having family and friends, setting long-range goals, and meeting challenges with courage and conviction. As Polonius advised (*Hamlet*, Act 1, scene 3), "This above all: to thine own self be true."

PART V

TRANSCENDENT THINKERS: REFLECTIONS ON CONTROVERSIAL INTELLECTUALS

CHAPTER 23

Transcendent Man

An Elegiac Essay to Paul Kurtz – A Skeptic's Skeptic

PREAMBLE

This essay was commissioned by the Center for Inquiry (CFI) and
Prometheus Books to remember and celebrate the life and work of
Paul Kurtz, one of the central figures in the birth of the modern skeptical
and humanist movements, in conjunction with his passing on
October 20, 2012. It was published as a Foreword for a new addition of
Paul's magnum opus, *The Transcendental Temptation* (Prometheus Books,
2013), which I read initially when it was originally published in 1987 (and
whose material I incorporated into a course I taught in the history of
ideas at Glendale College), and then reread in the 1990s for inspiration
during our inchoate efforts to contribute to the skeptical movement
through the Skeptics Society and *Skeptic* magazine. Paul was a university
professor (SUNY Buffalo) but he was also an entrepreneur of ideas and –
unbeknownst to him – served as a mentor and role model to me. I was
honored to be asked to pen this elegiac essay.

* * *

SKEPTICISM DATES BACK TO THE ANCIENT GREEKS, WELL
captured in Socrates' famous quip that all he knows is that he
knows nothing. Skepticism as nihilism, however, gets us nowhere and,
thankfully, almost no one embraces it. The word "skeptic," in fact,
comes from the Greek *skeptikos*, for "thoughtful" – far from modern
misconceptions of the word as meaning "cynical" or "nihilistic."
According to the *Oxford English Dictionary*, "skeptical" has also been
used to mean "inquiring," "reflective," and, with variations in the ancient
Greek, "watchman" or "mark to aim at."

What a glorious meaning for what we do! We are thoughtful, inquiring, and reflective, and, in a way, we are the watchmen who guard against bad ideas, consumer advocates of good thinking who, through the guidelines of science, establish a mark at which to aim. And here I would like to apply it to my friend, colleague, and hero Paul Kurtz, who, as one of the founders of the modern skeptical and humanist movements, not only embodied the principle of skepticism as thoughtful inquiry but was also our watchman who provided a mark at which we skeptics may all aim. Paul Kurtz was the embodiment of excellence in all things, and this book, *The Transcendental Temptation*, is not only his magnum opus, but it transcends his body of work and takes its place among the greatest works of Enlightenment humanism.

The Enlightenment, on one level, was a century-long skeptical movement, for there were no beliefs or institutions that did not come under the critical scrutiny of such thinkers as Voltaire, Diderot, Rousseau, Locke, Jefferson, and others. Immanuel Kant in Germany and David Hume in Scotland were skeptics' skeptics at the birth of skepticism that was the foundation of the Age of Reason and the Enlightenment, and their influence continues unabated to this day. Closer to our time, Charles Darwin and Thomas Huxley were skeptics par excellence, not only for the revolution they launched and carried on (respectively) against the dogma of creationism, but also for their stand against the burgeoning spiritualism movement that was sweeping across America, England, and the Continent. Although Darwin was quiet about his skepticism of the new form of spiritualism spreading across the cultural landscape and worked behind the scenes, Huxley railed publicly against the movement, bemoaning, in one of the great one-liners in the history of skepticism, "Better live a crossing-sweeper than die and be made to talk twaddle by a 'medium' hired at a guinea a séance." In the late nineteenth century, the "Great Agnostic" Robert Ingersoll carried the torch of reason to the century's end, which was picked up in the first half of the twentieth century by the likes of Bertrand Russell and Harry Houdini, who stand out as representatives of skeptical thinkers and doers (respectively), railing against the irrationality and hucksterism of their age. Skepticism in the second half of the century began with Martin Gardner's *Fads and Fallacies in the Name of Science*, launching what we think of today as "the skeptical movement," which Paul Kurtz so courageously organized and led to the end of the century, launching us into a new millennium of reason and science.

There has been some debate (and much quibbling) about who gets what amount of credit for the founding of the modern skeptical movement through the Committee for the Scientific Investigation of Claims of the Paranormal (CSICOP, now Center for Inquiry, or CFI) and its journal *Skeptical Inquirer*. Along with Martin Gardner, magician James Randi, psychologist Ray Hyman, and, most notably, philosopher Paul Kurtz played primary roles in the foundation and planning of the organization and the subsequent movement it launched that led to the formation of a worldwide phenomenon of humanists, skeptics, atheists, agnostics, and free thinkers of all stripes.

Regardless of who might be considered the "father" of the modern skeptical movement, everyone I have spoken to (including the other founders) agrees that it was Paul Kurtz more than anyone else who actually made it happen. All successful social movements have someone who has the organizational skills and social intelligence to get things done. Paul Kurtz is that man. When he founded the organization that launched the modern skeptical movement, I was a graduate student in experimental psychology. About this time (the mid-1970s) Uri Geller entered my radar screen. I recall *Psychology Today* and other popular magazines published glowing stories about him, and reports were afloat that experimental psychologists had tested the Israeli psychic and determined that he was genuine. My advisor – a strictly reductionistic Skinnerian behavioral psychologist named Doug Navarick – didn't believe a word of it, but I figured there might be something to it, especially in light of all the other interesting research being conducted on altered states of consciousness, hypnosis, dreams, sensory deprivation, dolphin communication, and the like. I took a course in anthropology from Marlene Dobkin de Rios, whose research was on shamans of South America and their use of mind-altering plants. It all seemed entirely plausible to me and, being personally interested in the subject (the Ouija board consistently blew my mind), I figured that this was rapidly becoming a legitimate subfield of psychological research. After all, Thelma Moss had a research laboratory devoted to studying the paranormal, and it was at UCLA no less, one of the most highly regarded psychology programs in the country.

Then I discovered the "skeptics" – people like Gardner, Hyman, Randi, and Kurtz – who entered the public sphere through popular publications that debunked and explained all these apparently paranormal phenomena, exposing them as either deceptions or self-deceptions. It was, in fact, on Johnny Carson's *Tonight Show* that I saw Randi duplicate much of what Geller and other so-called "psychics" were doing, such as levitating tables, bending spoons, performing psychic surgeries, and the like. I recall thinking that if some of these psychics were fakes, perhaps they all were (and if not fakes, at least self-deceived shut-eyes). Herein lies an important lesson. There is little to no chance that we can convince True Believers of the errors of their thinking. Our purpose is to reach that vast middle ground between hard-core skeptics and dogmatic believers – people like me who thought that there might be something to these claims but had simply never heard a good counterexplanation. There are many reasons why people believe weird things, but certainly one of the most pervasive is simply that most people have never heard a good explanation for the weird things they hear and read about. Short of a good explanation, they accept the bad explanation that is typically proffered. This alone justifies all the hard work performed by skeptics toward the cause of science and critical thinking. It does make a difference.

For twenty years now, I have been at the head of the Skeptics Society and *Skeptic* magazine, and, as such, as much as I admire Randi, Gardner, and the other early heroes of skepticism, I have come to respect more than ever what Paul Kurtz did for our movement, most notably in terms of the day-to-day grind of keeping it afloat through the constant battering and assaults that come from variegated sources. Running a nonprofit organization and keeping a movement alive past the initial excitement of press conferences and television appearances requires a special type of drive and intelligence, which Paul Kurtz had in spades. The inglorious job of fund-raising and the essential task of making payroll to keep a movement alive fly under the radar of observers, but without that there would be no skeptical organization. It was Paul Kurtz more than anyone else who showed us all how to build a movement. So I close this brief remembrance with my favorite excerpts from Kurtz's finest work that should be mandatory reading for all graduates of a Skepticism 101 course. If you want to learn to be a good skeptic, *The Transcendental Temptation* is the place to start.

The temptation, says Kurtz, "lurks deep within the human breast. It is ever-present, tempting humans by the lure of transcendental realities, subverting the power of their critical intelligence, enabling them to accept unproven and unfounded myth systems." Specifically, Kurtz argues that myths, religions, and claims of the paranormal are lures tempting us beyond rational, critical, and scientific thinking, for the very reason that they touch something in us that is sacred and impor-tant – life and immortality: "This impulse is so strong that it has inspired the great religions and paranormal movements of the past and the present and goaded otherwise sensible men and women to swallow patently false myths and to repeat them constantly as articles of faith." What drives this temptation? The answer Kurtz provides is both insight-ful and elegant:

> Let us reflect on the human situation: all of our plans will fail in the long run, if not in the short. The homes we have built and lovingly furnished, the loves we have enjoyed, the careers we have dedicated ourselves to will all disappear in time. The monuments we have erected to memorialize our aspirations and achievements, if we are fortunate, may last a few hundred years, perhaps a millennium or two or three – like the stark and splendid ruins of Rome and Greece, Egypt and Judea, which have been recovered and treasured by later civilizations. But all the works of human beings disappear and are forgotten in short order. In the immediate future the beautiful clothing that we adorn ourselves with, eventually even our cherished children and grandchildren, and all of our possessions will be dissipated. Many of our poems and books, our paintings and statues will be forgotten, buried on some library shelf or in a museum, read or seen by some future scholars curious about the past, and eventually eaten by worms and molds, or perhaps consumed by fire. Even the things that we prize the most, human intelligence and love, democratic values, the quest for truth, will in time be replaced by

unknown values and institutions – if the human species survives, and even that is uncertain. Were we to compile a pessimist's handbook, we could easily fill it to overflowing with notations of false hopes and lost dreams, a catalogue of human suffering and pain, of ignominious conflict, betrayal, and defeat throughout the ages.

Although this sounds pessimistic, Paul Kurtz is a realist, even an optimist, as in his cataloguing of the triumphs of the human spirit:

Were I to take an inventory of the sum of goods in human life, they would far outweigh the banalities of evil. I would outdo the pessimist by cataloguing laughter and joy, devotion and sympathy, discovery and creativity, excellence and grandeur. The mark made upon the world by every person and by the race in general would be impressive. How wonderful it has all been. The pessimist points to Caligula, Attila, Cesare Borgia, Beria, or Himmler with horror and disgust; but I would counter with Aristotle, Pericles, da Vinci, Einstein, Beethoven, Mark Twain, Margaret Sanger, and Madame Curie. The pessimist points to duplicity and cruelty in the world; I am impressed by the sympathy, honesty, and kindness that are manifested. The pessimist reminds us of ignorance and stupidity; I, of the continued growth of human knowledge and understanding. The pessimist emphasizes the failures and defeats; I, the successes and victories in all their glory.

The most important point Kurtz makes in *The Transcendental Temptation* comes toward the end in his discussion of the meaning and goals of skepticism. It is an admonition we should all bear in mind, a passage to be read once a year:

The skeptic is not passionately intent on converting mankind to his or her point of view and surely is not interested in imposing it on others, though he may be deeply concerned with raising the level of education and critical inquiry in society. Still, if there are any lessons to be learned from history, it is that we should be skeptical of all points of view, including those of the skeptics. No one is infallible, and no one can claim a monopoly on truth or virtue. It would be contradictory for skepticism to seek to translate itself into a new faith. One must view with caution the promises of any new secular priest who might emerge promising a brave new world – if only his path to clarity and truth is followed. Perhaps the best we can hope for is to temper the intemperate and to tame the perverse temptation that lurks within.

RIP Paul Kurtz. We all owe you a great debt of gratitude for making the world a better place. You will be missed. But you live on in your words, so powerfully and beautifully expressed in this magnificent work.

CHAPTER 24

The Real Hitch

Did Christopher Hitchens Really Keep Two Sets of Books About His Beliefs?

PREAMBLE

Two events led to the two essays related to Christopher Hitchens that are here stitched into one: (1) a book published after his death claiming that Hitch kept "two sets of books" about his religious beliefs – his public set as an atheist and his private set flirting with believing in God and religious faith; (2) Hitch's death on December 15, 2011. My motives for each are self-evident within, so let me add parenthetically here that, eight years on after he left us, Hitch's voice is needed now more than ever. He was such a penetrating thinker on the deepest questions of our time – of all time really – and what I wouldn't give to read a *Vanity Fair* essay by Hitch on Trump or Putin or Saudi Arabia or North Korea or Iran or immigration or Islam or, or, or ... We live in troubled times; then again, Hitch lived in troubled times, and his stabilizing voice of reason and rationality gave us a deeper understanding of what was going on in our world, and lacking that intellectual foundation on which to rest our anxious souls only adds to the grief those of us who knew him already feel.

* * *

RECENTLY, A NUMBER OF PEOPLE HAVE ASKED ME ABOUT A newly published book entitled *The Faith of Christopher Hitchens* by the Christian apologist Larry Alex Taunton, who runs the Fixed Point Foundation and whom I have gotten to know through public debates and private conversations. The Religious News Service (RNS), for example, interviewed me about the book (http://bit.ly/1YH2X4V), explaining that they had never heard of the author and were wondering why I blurbed the book (a "blurb" is a short quote on the back jacket of books encouraging people to read it). Here is what I wrote (only the final sentence made it onto the book's cover, but the entire quote is on the book's webpage):

> If you really want to get to know someone intimately, go on a multi-day cross-country road trip, share fine food and expensive spirits, and have open and honest conversations about the most important issues in life. And then engage them in public debate before thousands of people on those very topics. In this engrossing narrative about his friendship with the atheist activist Christopher Hitchens, the evangelical Christian Larry Taunton shows us a side of the man very few of us knew. Apparent contradictions dissolve before Taunton's penetrating insight into the psychology of a man fiercely loyal to his friends and passionately devoted to leading a life of integrity. This book should be read by every atheist and theist passionate about the truth, and by anyone who really wants to understand Hitch, one of the greatest minds and literary geniuses of our time.

I thought the statement was a fair appraisal of the book, but now I am having second thoughts because of the reception of the book, in which many people seem to think that its author implies that Hitch had a deathbed conversion, or that he had serious doubts about his atheism, or that he was earnestly considering Christianity as a viable belief system. That is not the assessment of Hitch's close friend of thirty years, Steve Wasserman, who told the RNS reporter, Kimberly Winston, "I am not in the position to dispute what Taunton says were private conversations . . . but I really think it is a shabby business. It reveals a lack of respect. This is not a way to debate Christopher Hitchens' beliefs—to report unverifiable conversations, which amazingly contradict everything Christopher Hitchens ever said or stood for."

Hitch's *Vanity Fair* editor Benjamin Schwarz, who also knew the man quite well, opined, "That Christopher had friends who were evangelicals is testimony to his intellectual tolerance and largeness of heart, not to any covert religiosity."

In his Noachian deluge of tweets about his book, Taunton gainsays these criticisms, insisting that he makes no such claim in his book. According to RNS, Taunton "stood firm in the face of such criticism," maintaining, "What I am saying is this: If Christopher Hitchens is a lock, the tumblers don't line up with the atheist key and that upsets a lot of atheists. They want Christopher Hitchens to be defined by his atheism, and he wasn't."

In *The Faith of Christopher Hitchens*, Taunton employs a metaphor for Hitch that the man himself used in their conversations, which is "keeping two sets of books." What does this expression mean? According to Taunton:

> The original meaning of the phrase "keeping two sets of books" refers to a fraudulent bookkeeping method in accounting, where one set of books is public and one is private; the public book is made to appear in accordance with the law, while the private book records all the shady financial dealings behind the scene. The implication, in using this phrase in regard to himself, is that the discovery of his private set of books, would reveal that his public set of books were somehow fraudulent.

But what did Hitch mean by the idiom? Taunton interpreted it this way: "For Hitchens, 'Keeping two sets of books' often meant that he had two real aspects of his personality and of his real beliefs that existed in real tension: one that he would reveal to the public and another that he revealed only to certain people."

In one example Taunton says that the phrase came up in their discussions of politics and Hitch's apparent "contradictions." For example, before 9/11 Hitch was adamantly anti-militaristic; after 9/11 he defended George W. Bush's war in Iraq. Taunton: "He moved from one book to the other, from public repudiation of military defense, to public recognition of its necessity against real evil" (p. 31). That's not an example of dual bookkeeping, but of changing one's mind. A duplicitous dialogue would have Hitch telling Taunton that he was privately against the Iraq war even while endorsing it publicly. That is not the case.

Taunton also says that Hitch complained about being made to "sit through lessons in the sinister fairy tales of Christianity" at The Leys School he attended in his youth, but he also said that "I can't pretend that I hated singing the hymns or learning the psalms, and I enjoyed being in the choir and was honored when asked to read from the lectern on Sundays" (p. 31). Again, this isn't fraudulent bookkeeping; it is simply the man's honest appraisal of his own multilayered emotions. I can relate. When I was a Christian, I found church services boring and pedantic, even while admiring the magnificent cathedrals of Europe and the music of Bach. Even now, as an ardent atheist, whenever I'm in Europe, I make it a point to visit cathedrals and attend classical music concerts, most of which were religiously inspired. Does that mean I have two sets of books? No.

I suspect what Hitch meant by "two sets of books" – public and private – is something far more quotidian: Most of us say things in private to our friends and family that we would never say in public. To suggest that something more is at play in this phrase is to imply that Hitch was dishonest with the public in all those essays, reviews, articles, lectures, debates, and bestselling books – including the definitive statement of his beliefs about religion in *God is Not Great* and in his autobiographical narrative of how his beliefs were formed and changed (or not) in *Hitch-22*. It would also mean he was mendacious with his most intimate friends and family – including his brother Peter, who is a Christian (and so ought to know if his brother was wavering) – but revealed his true feelings to Taunton. This does not stand to reason, figuratively and literally. But don't take my word for it. Listen to Hitch himself.

Shortly before his death, in a videotaped interview at his home conducted by the *Atlantic*'s Jeffrey Goldberg, with the evidence of chemotherapy's ravages on his face, Hitch reflected on the matter of whether or not he was reconsidering his religious views, or even contemplating the possibility that Christianity was true and that Jesus was the Messiah. As he said, point blank and in no uncertain terms, and in front of Martin Amis, whom he had just introduced to his interlocutor as "my dearest friend" (http://bit.ly/241e3W2): "Now might be the time to say that in the event of anyone ever hearing or reading a rumor of such a thing, it would not have been made by me ... No one recognizable as myself would ever make such a ridiculous remark."

Goldberg then asks Hitch if he thinks anyone might try to make such a claim about him, to which he emphatically replies, "No," reflecting further:

This is a very old game that goes back to Thomas Paine and David Hume and Voltaire, in whose company I have no right to be mentioned, and even with Darwin, to circulate outright lies about deathbed conversions.

Goldberg pressed the point: "When you received your diagnosis did you have a fleeting moment of asking yourself 'I wonder if prayer would help . . . I wonder if there is anything . . . '" at which point Hitch cut him off, unhesitatingly answering, "No. I can quite safely say that." When Goldberg lingered on topic Hitch again interrupted him:

> In the same way that I can absolutely assure you that while cornered in Sarajevo thinking, "Jeez, I wish I hadn't gotten into this building and how am I going to get back to the hotel?" or pounced on by fascists in Beirut or traveling far from home in Afghanistan where I thought "I can absolutely see how I might not get out of this," the foxhole foolishness quite literally did not cross my mind.

Does this sound like a man who kept two sets of books in the double-dealing manner Taunton implies? I think not. To suggest otherwise would be calumnious.

I knew Hitch moderately well (more on this below). We first met in 1997, when he came to LA for a film premiere of *FairyTale*, the story of how Sir Arthur Conan Doyle got duped by two girls in the famous Cottingley Fairies fake photographs story, which Hitch was reviewing for *Vanity Fair*. We stayed in touch over the years and met up periodically at conferences and dinners (that often included "Mr. Walker's amber restorative" as he affectionately called his favorite whisky). I would not call Hitch a close friend, but I believe I knew him well enough to suspect what was really going on here. On his road trips with Taunton, Hitch was merely doing what he often did with people who differed with him – spend personal time with them in order to penetrate their public façade and see what is inside their private thoughts.

I do this myself, and it's an illuminating exercise. I've spent time with and gotten to know most of the leading Holocaust deniers (e.g., David Irving), creationists (e.g., Duane Gish), Intelligent Design advocates (e.g., Bill Dembski), 9/11 truthers, JFK conspiracy campaigners, electric universe advocates, alien abductee claimants, UFO believers, ghost hunters, near-death experiencers, etc. You can learn so much more about a person's real motives and motivated reasoning by talking to them off stage and off print than you can by limiting yourself to debating them in public and reading their published works. Particularly effective is to dine and drink with them, because after a time they open up and reveal what they're really thinking and feeling. This is not at all "keeping two sets of books" in the two-faced manner that phrase implies. It is just being friendly and respectful to better understand someone's inner self.

I believe that is what Hitch did in general, and in particular with Taunton. Naturally, because he's an evangelical, Taunton hoped that perhaps, possibly, maybe – just maybe – Hitch imbibed the gospel message from their discussions about the Book of John (among other related topics) so that Hitch would be spared eternal damnation. By definition, evangelicals evangelize, so it would be surprising if the evangelical Taunton did not himself have two sets of books, including one that hoped for Hitch's conversion. Alas, Taunton admits at the end of the book that there was no deathbed conversion or anything close.

Taunton did not record his conversations with Hitch, but a similar "road trip" experience Hitch had with evangelical Doug Wilson was turned into a documentary film that is well worth watching (http://bit .ly/22Oo2vo). It's called *Collision* and it follows Wilson and Hitch in debates, on the road, in taxis, restaurants, elevators, homes, etc. Hitch was certainly not a one-dimensional man. His motives were complex, but mostly I think he loved engaging with people to challenge them and learn from them, and of course to stir things up and get people thinking, including himself.

That was the real Hitch.

Post Script. I gave Larry Taunton a chance to clarify what, exactly, he means by the "two sets of books" phrase: the public/private distinction we all make or intentional deception concealing his true beliefs from the public and his closest friends and revealing his true beliefs to Taunton. Taunton responded: "I stand by what I've written, Michael. A few – very few – of the hateful atheist crowd have read it, but almost none of the trolls. That is a quotation that I allowed to be used in an article." I personally find that interpretation unbelievable.

MY DINNER (AND DRINKS) WITH CHRISTOPHER

When I first heard the news that Christopher had been diagnosed with esophageal cancer, I penned the following essay and published it at Skepticblog.org on July 20, 2010, wishing to pay tribute to the man before it would become an obituary, which unfortunately it did become when we republished it on the occasion of his death on December 15, 2011, a sad day for all who knew him, and a loss to our intellectual culture.

First, I'm half way through listening to the unabridged audio book of *Hitch 22,* which I wholeheartedly recommend because Christopher reads it himself in that inimitable classically educated British accent with his style of flowing quiet narrative punctuated by occasional bursts of accented emphasis. In other words, Hitchens sort of mumbles modestly along, then suddenly his voice rises into crystal clarity when he wants you to get the point hard and fast. *Hitch 22* is a literary masterpiece, an absolute joy to listen to. I'll leave it to his literary/politico peers to critique the ideas within (see, for example, the latest issue of the *New York Review of Books* with Ian Buruma's review, as well as David Horowitz's insightful analysis of Hitchens' evolving political beliefs).

Although I'm a self-professed libertarian (fiscally conservative and socially liberal), I'm really not much of a politico or social commentator, especially when it comes to foreign affairs, about which I am woefully ignorant compared to Hitchens' vast database he has accumulated throughout his many travels abroad. So I'm just enjoying the ride listening to Christopher's many amusing stories. (One humorous anecdote: In an early writing assignment for a publication, Hitchens recalls that his editor said something to him that, as he explained it, made it simply impossible for him to continue employment there. It turned out that the editor told him, "You're fired.")

My intersection with Hitchens is through our mutual concern about the influence of religion on science and society. Hitchens, of course, has many other worries about the effects of religious beliefs on political, economic, and social conditions around the world (particularly the Middle East), but he was kind and generous enough to provide a back-jacket blurb for my book, *Why Darwin Matters,* and noted in his letter to me containing said blurb that he had found a couple of minor errors in the book, adding parenthetically (in case I missed it) that this meant that he did, indeed, actually read the book. (In the book publishing business, it is common practice for authors who are friends and colleagues to blurb each other's books, and sometimes I suspect this means that the blurb is generated based on a cursory scan of the manuscript. To his credit and energy – considering how many blurb requests he must have received over the years – Christopher really did read my manuscript.)

I first met Christopher in Hollywood in 1997 at a preview showing of the film *FairyTale: A True Story*, starring Harvey Keitel as Harry Houdini and Peter O'Toole as Sir Arthur Conan Doyle, which recounted the story of the two giants' collision over the fake fairy photographs that Doyle fell for and Houdini did not. Hitch and I had dinner (well lubricated with whisky) before the preview, and although I was a bit distressed at the ending of the film that implied that fairies may actually be real (after showing that Doyle was duped), I rather enjoyed this artfully edited and beautifully presented film. Christopher's review in *Vanity Fair*, which included a thoughtful and much appreciated endorsement of the Skeptics Society and *Skeptic* magazine, was much deeper and more insightful than anything I thought of during the screening. Even though I'm a professional skeptic, for some reason, when I watch a film, I willingly suspend disbelief in order to enjoy the experience, and this sometimes interferes with my critical thought processes. Not Hitch.

A decade later, in 2007, as I was meandering through the sensorially overloaded Las Vegas airport on my way to The Amazing Meeting (TAM) 5 and Freedom Fest, conferences at which Hitchens and I were both speaking, we encountered each other in search of our respective limo drivers, so we ended up sharing a ride to the hotel. Checking in early (it was around 11:00 am), our rooms were not yet ready, so Hitch suggested that we put the time to good use at the bar. Before noon. So there we were, me nursing a Corona with lime for as long as I could socially get away with it while Hitchens ordered a Johnny Walker Black, a red wine, and a bottle of water to mix with JWB in what appeared to be a well-choreographed routine. A couple of rounds later, Hitch seemed completely unfazed, while my empty-stomach imbibing on that single beer left me feeling less than adequate to keep up with the conversation. (Hey, when you drink with a professional, come prepared – I didn't have the training miles.) When the bill came, I had the singular honor of buying Christopher Hitchens' drinks because (1) his wallet was in his baggage with the bellman, and (2) the room keys were not yet activated to put it on his room. I didn't mind – blurb reciprocity and all that, you know.

After hammering down two rounds of the Hitch Mix, Christopher was nearly (but not quite) ready for his noon luncheon speech, so he ordered a third round to go. At the podium where Hitch stood, before him were a glass of whisky, a glass of red wine, and a bottle of water. (Just as we cyclists always ride with water bottles filled with fluid replacement drinks, Christopher apparently never speaks without his Hitch Mix to top off his energy needs.) I can't for the life of me remember what his speech was about (politics, I think) but I recall that Hitchens was extemporaneous, clever, and worldly.

That night, the host of Freedom Fest, Mark Skousen, invited Christopher and myself to join a group of VIP guests and speakers at an exclusive (and quite expensive, I'm sure) dinner at a posh restaurant in Las Vegas (no prices on the menu is all you need to know). Even though everyone at the table was someone of some import and standing, it was clear throughout the evening that Hitch was Sol and we were his orbiting planets, gathering up the warmth of his verbal rays. He told stories – lots and lots of stories – about his travels, his encounters with names we would all surely know, and especially about his intellectual battles with this and that ideologue. Other people's comments were, for the most part, stimulants for another Hitch story. I can see why some people might find that this rubs them up the wrong way, but for some reason – at least for me – that was how it should have been. If you invite Christopher Hitchens to your dinner, expect to be entertained, and the more the waiter poured expensive wine, the more histrionic Hitchens became, until four hours and who-knows-how-many-drinks later, I detected a slight slowing of his verbal and cognitive skills ... so there are limits after all.

The next time I saw Hitch was at a party in Washington DC, when I was touring for the release of my book, *The Mind of the Market*. *Reason* magazine kindly arranged for a book party at a bar and restaurant that was so crowded and so loud that it was physically uncomfortable. After an obligatory drink and a few stories to entertain the troops, Hitchens leaned in and said, "Michael, why don't we retire to a restaurant down the street, where they know me?" Exiting the cacophony, we walked a few blocks to what turned out to be one of Hitch's regular haunts. "The usual place, Mr. Hitchens?" the maître d' inquired. We were escorted to a quiet corner of the restaurant where Hitch positioned himself to be able to scan the room, and soon we were joined by his wife and an occasional passerby who recognized him and dropped in for a story (and drink) or two.

Shortly after the waiter took our drink orders ("the usual?" was all Hitch needed to hear, to which he nodded affirmatively), the Hitch Mix was on the table, followed by a fabulous dinner and, of course, lots of stories, none of which was repeated from my previous dinner (at least that I could remember – I too imbibed). After a couple hours at the restaurant, Hitch invited me to his home, not far from the restaurant, where I was treated to a visual delight: mountains of books, oceans of books, a sea of books – pick your geographical metaphor. As the recipient myself of bound galleys and newly published volumes sent to *Skeptic* magazine for review, I know how quickly a mass accumulates on my desk that then migrates to the floor and eventually peaks above the desk again. But in my case, these are just science books. As a literary polymath, Hitch receives books for review from virtually every category in the Dewey decimal system. And he actually seems to read the books he reviews.

But the library is not where we adjourned for the evening. It wasn't long before I found myself at a rectangular table in the dining room chockablock full of whisky bottles from around the world. I'm not a whisky connoisseur so I couldn't tell you the brand names, but even a teetotaler like me could tell from the labels and bottle designs that here was a collection of the very best whiskys money can buy from all over the world, and I suspect that Hitch didn't have to buy many of them, since such gifts seem to naturally flow his way. So I sampled and sipped and sauced my way into a late-night bliss that I paid for dearly the next day. I think I had an interview for an early-morning television show, but I honestly don't remember because I barely recall even having a next day.

Was it worth it? I once had an opportunity to ride my bike 50 miles on a fund-raising event next to the great Belgian cycling champion Eddy Merckx, considered the greatest cyclist of all time. I was so nervous about crashing and taking him down that I just concentrated on the bumper in front of us that we were drafting behind at 30 miles per hour. But just the experience of riding side by side with one of the greatest athletes to ever grace the planet was enough for me. That's how I felt drinking and dining and delighting in the presence of Christopher Hitchens.

CHAPTER 25

The Skeptic's Chaplain

Richard Dawkins as a Fountainhead of Skepticism

PREAMBLE

In 2005 I was contacted by Latha Menon from Oxford University Press, who was commissioning essays on the occasion of Richard Dawkins' sixty-fifth trip around the sun, which also happened to coincide with the thirtieth anniversary of the first publication of his now-classic book, *The Selfish Gene*. "We are therefore putting together a small collection of pieces about the nature and influence of Richard's ideas and his role as a public intellectual," Latha wrote, adding, thankfully, "This is planned as an intelligent tribute, not a eulogy." That volume was published in 2006 under the title *Richard Dawkins: How a Scientist Changed the Way We Think*, edited by two of Richard's former students, Alan Grafen and Mark Ridley. I was honored to contribute to this delightful volume, which included contributions from Steven Pinker, Matt Ridley, Daniel Dennett, David Deutsch, Michael Ruse, A. C. Grayling, David Barash, Simon Blackburn, and Philip Pullman, among others, the list alone a tribute to the esteem in which Richard and his work is held.

My essay title plays on Richard's 2003 anthology *A Devil's Chaplain: Reflections on Hope, Lies, Science, and Love*. Richard, of course, got his book title from Charles Darwin, who in an 1856 letter wrote to his friend and colleague the botanist Joseph Hooker: "What a book a Devil's Chaplain might write on the clumsy, wasteful, blundering low and horridly cruel works of nature." In 1860 Darwin elaborated on this issue in a letter to his American colleague, the Harvard biologist Asa Gray, recalling a species of wasp that paralyzes its prey (but does not kill it), then lays its eggs inside the paralyzed insect so that upon birth its offspring can feed on live flesh:

> I cannot persuade myself that a beneficent God would have designedly created the *Ichneumonidae* with the express intention of their feeding

within the living bodies of Caterpillars, or that a cat should play with mice. Not believing this, I see no necessity in the belief that the eye was expressly designed.

Darwin was more conciliatory on religious matters than Dawkins, but he was nevertheless deeply troubled by the implications of his theory for theodicy, or the problem of evil. To one correspondent, for example, Darwin wrote:

> That there is much suffering in the world no one disputes. Some have attempted to explain this with reference to man by imagining that it serves for his moral improvement. But the number of men in the world is as nothing compared with that of all other sentient beings, and they often suffer greatly without any moral improvement.

The death of Darwin's beloved ten-year-old daughter Annie put an end to whatever faith he still had in God's benevolence, much less existence. According to the highly regarded Darwin biographer Janet Browne: "This death was the formal beginning of Darwin's conscious dissociation from believing in the traditional figure of God."

Nonetheless, Darwin mostly kept his religious skepticism to himself, issuing just a handful of public statements on the matter, for example, in 1879, just three years before he died, Darwin responded to a correspondent who inquired about his religious beliefs: "In my most extreme fluctuations I have never been an Atheist in the sense of denying the existence of God. I think that generally (and more and more as I grow older), but not always, that an Agnostic would be the more correct description of my state of mind." The following year he clarified his reasoning to the British socialist Edward Aveling, who was seeking an endorsement from Darwin for a book with a militant antireligious flavor. Darwin declined the offer, adding:

> It appears to me (whether rightly or wrongly) that direct arguments against christianity & theism produce hardly any effect on the public; & freedom of thought is best promoted by the gradual illumination of men's minds which follow[s] from the advance of science. It has, therefore, been always my object to avoid writing on religion, & I have confined myself to science.

By contrast, after decades of illuminating the minds of millions of people through his popular science writing, Richard Dawkins turned his keen mind to religion, and the result was the birth of the New Atheist movement, which began shortly after this tribute volume was published.

* * *

OVER THE WEEKEND OF AUGUST 12–14, 2001, I PARTICIPATED in an event titled "Humanity 3000," whose mission it was to bring together "prominent thinkers from around the world in a multidisciplinary framework to ponder issues that are most likely to have a significant impact on the long-term future of humanity." Sponsored by the Foundation for the Future – a nonprofit think tank in Seattle founded by aerospace engineer and benefactor Walter P. Kistler – long-term is defined as a millennium. We were tasked with the job of prognosticating what the world will be like in the year 3000.

Yeah, sure. As Yogi Berra said, "It's tough to make predictions, especially about the future." If such a workshop were held in 1950 would anyone have anticipated the World Wide Web? If we cannot prognosticate fifty years in the future, what chance do we have of saying anything significant about a date twenty times more distant? And please note the date of this conference – needless to say, not one of us realized that we were a month away from the event that would redefine the modern world with a date that will live in infamy. It was a fool's invitation, which I accepted with relish. Who could resist sitting around a room talking about the most interesting questions of our time, and possibly future times, with a bunch of really smart and interesting people. To name but a few with whom I shared beliefs and beer: science writer Ronald Bailey, environmentalist Connie Barlow, twins expert Thomas Bouchard, neuroscientist William Calvin, educational psychologist Arthur Jensen, mathematician and critic Norman Levitt, memory expert Elizabeth Loftus, evolutionary biologist Edward O. Wilson, and many others, all highly regarded in their fields, well published, often controversial, and always relevant.

Also in attendance, there to receive the $100,000 Kistler Prize "for original work that investigates the social implications of genetics," was the Oxford University evolutionary biologist Richard Dawkins. (Ed Wilson was the previous year's winner and was there to co-present the award, along with Walter Kistler, to Richard.) Dawkins was awarded a gold medal and a check for his work "that redirected the focus of the 'levels of selection' debate away from the individual animal as the unit of evolution to the genes, and what he has called their extended phenotypes." Simultaneously, the award description continues, Dawkins "applied a Darwinian view to culture through the concept of memes as replicators of culture." Finally, "Dr. Dawkins' contribution to a new understanding of the relationship between the human genome and society is that both the gene and the meme are replicators that mutate and compete in parallel and interacting struggles for their own propagation." The prize ceremony was followed by a brilliant acceptance speech by Richard, who never fails to deliver in his role as a public intellectual (the number *one* public intellectual in England, according to *Prospect* magazine) and spokesperson for the public understanding of science.

This is not what most impressed me about Richard, however, since any professional would be expected to shine in a public forum, especially with a six-figure motivator hanging around his neck. It was during the two full days of round-table discussions, breakout sessions, fishbowl debates, and (most interestingly) coffee-break chats, where Richard stood out head-and-shoulders above this august crowd. Despite his reputation as a tough-minded egotist, Richard is, in fact, somewhat shy and quiet, a man who listens carefully, thinks through what he wants to say, and then says it with an economy of words that is a model for any would-be opinion editorialist. In one session, for example, we were to debate "Conscious Evolution – Fantasy or Fact?" After about twenty minutes of discussion of a topic none of us had carefully defined, Richard spoke up:

> I wanted to listen around the table to see if I could make out what conscious evolution is. I still haven't. It seems to be a mix-up of two, or three, or four very different things. There is the evolution of consciousness; there is what Julian Huxley would have called "consciousness of evolution" or, the way he put it was "man is evolution become conscious of itself." But entirely separate from that . . . forget about consciousness and just talk about deliberate control of evolution, and then we bifurcate again into two entirely different kinds of evolution. That is genetic evolution and cultural evolution. I am not going to

utter the "m" word [memes]; everybody else keeps saying it and then looking at me, and I am going to duck out of that. I used not to think this, but I am increasingly thinking that nothing but confusion arises from confounding genetic evolution with cultural evolution, unless you are very careful about what you are doing and don't talk as though they are somehow just different aspects of the same phenomenon. Or, if they *are* different aspects of the same phenomenon, then let's hear a good case for regarding them as such.

The first response was from the futurist Michael Marien, who said, "I would like to start back at the point where Richard Dawkins honestly said he had never heard the term *conscious evolution.* Sometimes a statement of ignorance can be very illuminating." Indeed it can be, and Richard's candid comments throughout the weekend illuminated the conference like no one else's.

Outside of additional specifics of what Richard said, here is my overall impression of that weekend in Seattle, an observation with broader implications for Dawkins' impact on science and culture: A discussion would ensue over some issue, such as "the factors most critical to the long-term future of humanity," and most of us panelists would jump in with our opinions, banter some particular theme back and forth for a while, then leap to another topic, hammer that into the faux-mahogany table, and so forth round and round. Richard would sit there listening, processing the verbosities of us long-winded opinionators, select his moment to lean forward and make a short observational remark or inductive inference, then sit back and collect more data. It was through what happened after Richard spoke that I came to realize this is a man on a different plane, above even these stellar minds. The conversation changed, bifurcated in a new direction, with references to its source: "You know, Richard has a point ...", "I'd like to comment on Richard's observation ...", "Going back to what Professor Dawkins said ...", and so on. Richard Dawkins changed the conversation. He has been changing the conversation ever since 1976 when his book *The Selfish Gene* changed the way we look at ourselves and our world.

* * *

Humans are a hierarchical social primate species who, despite centuries of democratic rule, still long to sort themselves into pecking orders within families, schools, peer groups, social clubs, corporations, and societies. We can't help it. It is in our nature, courtesy of natural selection operating in the social sphere. As an intellectual social movement in which I am intimately involved, skepticism is subject to the same hierarchical social forces. As such, we scientists and skeptics look up to and model ourselves after our alpha leaders. In my own intellectual development, there have been several who served me well in this capacity, including Carl Sagan, Stephen Jay Gould, and Richard Dawkins. They are, in fact, candles in the darkness of our demon-haunted world (in Carl's apt phrase from his skeptical manifesto). Lamentably, we lost Carl and Steve too early. How I long for one more poetic narrative on our pale-blue dot in the vast cosmos or one more elegant essay on life's complexity and history's contingency.

But thank the fates and his hearty DNA that we have Richard, who stands as a beacon of scientific skepticism and a hero to skeptics around the world. Dawkins' work has touched the skeptical movement in three areas of common concern: pseudoscience, creationism, and religion.

Dawkins' primary work on pseudoscience is *Unweaving the Rainbow,* a collection of essays centered on "Science, Delusion and the Appetite for Wonder" (the book's subtitle). Here we see almost no limits to the breadth of Richard's interests, as he skeptically analyzes astrology, coincidences, conjurors, eyewitness accounts, fairies, flying saucers, the Gaia hypothesis, gambling fallacies, hallucinations, horoscopes, illusion, imagination, intuition, miracles, mysticism, paranormalism, postmodernism, psychic phenomena, reincarnation, Scientology, superstition, telepathy, and even *The X-Files.* Richard's analysis of these and other delusions is not debunking as such, but more positively directed toward helping us better grasp what science is by looking at what science isn't and showing us how we can recognize good science by seeing bad science for what it is. Deeper still is the take-home message embodied in the book's title from Keats, "who believed that Newton had destroyed all the poetry of the rainbow by reducing it to the prismatic colours. Keats could hardly have been more wrong." Instead, Richard offers us this insight: "I believe that an orderly universe, one indifferent to human preoccupations, in which everything has an explanation even if we still have a long way to go before we find it, is a more beautiful, more wonderful place than a universe tricked out with capricious, *ad hoc* magic."

Creationism is a form of pseudoscience, and the connection here is an obvious one for an evolutionary biologist who holds the job title of "Professor of the Public Understanding of Science." In America, at least, there is no better example of a public *mis*understanding of science than creationism, and Richard has written broadly and deeply on the subject, mincing no words (and it is with creationists especially that Richard does not "suffer fools gladly," as he has been accused). After the May 2005 hearings in Kansas on the proposed introduction of "Intelligent Design" into the public school science curriculum, Dawkins fired off an opinion editorial in the *Times* (London) on May 21, entitled "Creationism: God's Gift to the Ignorant," that included this poignant observation that cut through yards of creationist verbiage with clarity and wit:

> The standard methodology of creationists is to find some phenomenon in nature that Darwinism cannot readily explain. Darwin said: "If it could be demonstrated that any complex organ existed which could not possibly have been formed by numerous, successive, slight modifications, my theory would absolutely break down." Creationists mine ignorance and uncertainty in order to abuse his challenge. "Bet you can't tell me how the elbow joint of the lesser spotted weasel frog evolved by slow gradual degrees?" If the scientist fails to give an immediate and comprehensive answer, a default conclusion is drawn: "Right, then, the alternative theory, 'intelligent design', wins by default."

At least three of Richard's books – *The Blind Watchmaker, Climbing Mount Improbable,* and *River Out of Eden* – are direct challenges to creationists' arguments, although presented not as straight debunking works but as science-advancing treatises on evolutionary theory. And Richard's latest book, *The Ancestor's Tale,* is one long answer to creationists' demand to "show me just one transitional fossil." Dawkins traces innumerable transitional forms, as well as numerous common ancestors, or what he calls "concestors" – the "point of rendezvous" of the last common ancestor shared by a set of species – from *Homo sapiens* back four billion years to the origin of heredity and the emergence of evolution. No one concestor proves that evolution happened, but together they reveal a majestic story of process over time. Richard is the Geoffrey Chaucer of life's history and our most articulate public defender of evolution.

Creationism, of course, is nothing more than thinly disguised religion masquerading as science, as an end-run around the US Constitution's First Amendment prohibition on the government establishment of religion. Richard's views on religion, particularly when it intersects with science, are so public and controversial that they have even inspired a book by the Oxford University Professor of Historical Theology, Alister McGrath, *Dawkins' God* (Blackwell, 2004), a book I reviewed in *Science* (8 April 2005, 205–206). The connection between science and religion for Dawkins runs like this: Before Darwin, the default explanation for the apparent design found in nature was a top-down designer – God. The eighteenth-century English theologian William Paley formulated this into the infamous watchmaker argument: If one stumbled upon a watch on a heath, one would not assume it had always been there, as one might with a stone. A watch implies a watchmaker. Design implies a designer. Darwin provided a scientific explanation of design from the bottom up: natural selection. Since then, arguably no one has done more to make the case for bottom-up design than Dawkins, particularly in *The Blind Watchmaker*, a direct challenge to Paley. But if design comes naturally from the bottom up and not supernaturally from the top down, what place, then, is there for God?

Although most scientists avoid the question altogether or take a conciliatory stance along the lines of Stephen Jay Gould's nonoverlapping magisteria (NOMA), Dawkins unequivocally states in *The Blind Watchmaker*, "Darwin made it possible to be an intellectually fulfilled atheist." And in *River Out of Eden*: "The universe we observe has precisely the properties we should expect if there is, at bottom, no design, no purpose, no evil and no good, nothing but blind pitiless indifference."

Herein lies the crux of the issue, and Dawkins brooks no theological obfuscation. For example, after debunking all the quasi-scientific and pseudoscientific arguments allegedly proving God's existence, scientists are told by theologians like Alister McGrath that we should come to know God through faith. But what does that mean, exactly? In *The Selfish Gene*, Dawkins wrote that faith "means blind trust, in the absence of evidence, even in the teeth of evidence." This, says McGrath, "bears little relation to any religious (or any other) sense of the word." In its stead, McGrath presents the definition of faith by the Anglican theologian W. H. Griffith-Thomas: "It commences with the conviction of the mind based on adequate evidence; it continues in the confidence of the heart or emotions based on conviction, and it is crowned in the consent of the will, by means of which the conviction and confidence are expressed in conduct." Such a definition – which McGrath describes as "typical of any Christian writer" – is what Dawkins, in reference to French postmodernists, calls "continental obscurantism." Most of it describes the psychology of belief. The only clause of relevance to a scientist is "adequate evidence," which raises the follow-up question, "Is there?" Dawkins' answer is an unequivocal No.

* * *

Does a scientific and evolutionary worldview such as that proffered by Richard Dawkins obviate a sense of spirituality? I think not. If we define spirituality as a sense of awe and wonder about the grandeur of life and the cosmos, then science has much to offer. As proof, I shall close with a final story about Richard, and a moment we shared inside the dome of the 100-inch telescope atop Mt. Wilson in Southern California. It was in this very dome, on October 6, 1923, that Edwin Hubble first realized that the fuzzy patches he was observing were not "nebula" *within* the Milky Way galaxy, but were separate galaxies, and that the universe is bigger than anyone imagined, a *lot* bigger. Hubble subsequently discovered through this same telescope that those galaxies are all red-shifted – their light is receding from us and thus stretched toward the red end of the electromagnetic spectrum – meaning that all galaxies are expanding away from one another, the result of a spectacular explosion that marked the birth of the universe. It was the first empirical data indicating that the universe had a beginning and thus was not eternal. What could be more awe-inspiring – more numinous, magical, spiritual – than this cosmic visage of deep time and deep space?

Since I live in Altadena, on the edge of a cliff in the foothills of the San Gabriel mountains atop which Mt. Wilson rests, I have had many occasions to make the trek to the telescopes. In November 2004, I arranged a visit to the observatory for Richard, who was in town on a book tour for *The Ancestor's Tale*. As we were standing beneath the magnificent dome housing the 100-inch telescope, and reflecting on how marvelous, even miraculous, this scientific vision of the cosmos and our place in it all seemed, Richard turned to me and said, "All of this makes me so proud of our species that it almost brings me to tears."

I would echo the same sentiment about the works and words of Richard Dawkins.

CHAPTER 26

Have Archetype – Will Travel

The Jordan Peterson Phenomenon

PREAMBLE

This essay needs little introduction and is the most recently written one in this anthology, triggered as it was by the sudden rise in popularity of Jordan Peterson in 2017 and 2018. As his platform grew, I received frequent queries on when we were going to "debunk" Peterson, "put him in his place," "refute his ideas," and so forth. There were a few voices of support but, surprisingly (given our readers' purported critical thinking skills), most people seemed to pre-judge Peterson based on a handful of snippets from his writings and, especially, video clips taken out of context (that when looked at in a fuller picture rarely reveal what the critics think they do). Peterson seems to engender passionate emotions (both for and against) his ideas presented in YouTube videos, podcasts, books, and his multicity lecture tour routinely selling out large theaters. At a November 2018 public event I did with Richard Dawkins in Berlin, an "in conversation" in which we said nothing about Jordan Peterson, during the Q&A we received no fewer than four questions as to our opinions of the man and his ideas. To the first questioner, I briefly summarized my own (as articulated more fully in this chapter), and Richard simply said he didn't have an opinion because he hadn't studied Peterson. That didn't stop three more people from pressing us for more, one upbraiding me (and Sam Harris) for "letting Peterson off the hook," adding that we "should have put him away" when we had the chance. For Richard's part, he became exasperated and elevated to a principle the idea that one shouldn't opine on matters one knows nothing about. That produced a rousing round of applause. Given all this, I felt it was time to examine with a skeptical eye Jordan Peterson's ideas and, especially, the phenomenon surrounding him, so this was my introduction to a special issue of *Skeptic* we published in 2018 on the man.[1]

* * *

WHEN I WAS A LAD, ONE OF THE MOST POPULAR TELEVISION series of the early 1960s was the western *Have Gun – Will Travel*, staring Richard Boone in the title role as Paladin, a mercenary gunslinger whose name echoes the knights in Charlemagne's court (he was the "knight without armor"). The chivalrous Paladin wore custom-made suits, was schooled in philosophy, classical literature, opera, piano, poker, and chess, and was preternaturally gifted in fighting skills – from Chinese martial arts and western fisticuffs to swordsmanship and fire-arms. Paladin usually tried to resolve his clients' problems nonviolently, but, as signaled on his title business card embossed with the knight chess piece (also emblazoned on his holster), more often than not he relied on his custom-made Colt .45 single-action revolver with a unique rifled barrel for increased accuracy.[2] (See Figure 26.1). "With this gun, I could have stopped murder tonight," Paladin reflects in an early episode. "In all my life I've only seen a dozen real killers, but I've seen ten thousand people that would stand by and let it happen. Which is the greater evil?"

THE PALADIN ARCHETYPE

Paladin is an archetype – a recurring symbol, a prototype, a Platonic ideal – in this case representing the hero myth (in black-and-white TV simplicity no less) that may well capture the Jordan Peterson Phenomenon (JPP) that has arisen around the Canadian clinical

Figure 26.1 Business card: "Have Gun Will Travel, Wire Paladin, San Francisco."

Figure 26.2 Still from the Jordan B. Peterson Podcast episode with Michael Shermer and Jordan Peterson.

psychologist cum public intellectual who has embraced the Paladin archetype of the hero in Paladin-style dress, manners, and erudition. And given his professed lifelong goal of understanding human evil – particularly that of twentieth-century Fascism and Communism – Paladin's greater evil question above may well have been asked by Peterson, who has for the past several years been cajoling his fans to stand up instead of stand by. But I'm getting ahead of myself.

I was first introduced to Peterson on Joe Rogan's podcast in 2016,[3] shortly after I first appeared on the show,[4] when podcast numbers were surpassing those of even the most popular cable news and talk shows, launching what would later become known as the Intellectual Dark Web, of which I am a member.[5] Peterson has his own podcast as well,[6] on which I appeared as a guest in early 2018 in conjunction with the publication of my book *Heavens on Earth*,[7] just a few months before his *12 Rules for Life* was published, launching its author into the cultural stratosphere (see Figure 26.2).

This was a propitious time to enter the public arena, when alternative and social media gave many people a platform hitherto unavailable to all but a handful of noted academic scholars and scientists. Where once only Kenneth Clark (*Civilization*), Jacob Bronowski (*The Ascent of Man*), and Carl Sagan (*Cosmos*) were able to land a documentary series on one of only four networks (PBS), today anyone with a computer, an Internet connection, and a few apps can become a media sensation. As Peterson's YouTube subscriber list exceeded a million people, and many millions more tuned in to hear each appearance on various popular podcasts,

Peterson refined his talking points and wove them into a narrative that seem to resonate with a great many people. I wanted to find out why, so in late spring of 2018 we determined that *Skeptic* magazine should look into Peterson – not just his claims, such as doling out self-help advice in podcasts and public talks or explaining the meaning of myths and biblical stories in YouTube videos – but the seemingly insatiable media coverage and public consumption of everything he says and does. I arranged for my contributing editor, Stephen Beckner (see his article in the special section of *Skeptic*, Vol. 23, No. 3), and I to attend Peterson's public performance at the 1,800-seat Fred Kavli Theater in Thousand Oaks, California (sold out, as most of his events are), and he was generous enough to spend an hour in the green room talking informally with us about his ideas and all that has unfolded over the past two years (while signing *12 Rules for Life* posters). Our goal in this is not to "debunk" Peterson, which many readers have asked us to do as if it were a given that he's a quack selling snake-oil, but rather to analyze his claims and the JPP in the spirit of *Skeptic's* motto from the Dutch philosopher Baruch Spinoza: "I have made a ceaseless effort not to ridicule, not to bewail, not to scorn human actions, but to understand them" (see Figure 26.3).

JORDAN PETERSON, BILL C-16, AND FREEDOM OF SPEECH

Before 2016 Jordan Peterson was indistinguishable from any other relatively successful academic with a respectable scholarly pedigree: BA in political science from the University of Alberta (1982), BA in psychology from the same institution (1984), PhD in clinical psychology from McGill University (1991), postdoc at McGill's Douglas Hospital (1992–1993), assistant and associate professorships at Harvard University in the psychology department (1993–1998), full tenured professorship at the University of Toronto (1999 to present), private clinical practice in Toronto, and a scholarly book with a reputable publishing house (Routledge). This ordinary career path turned extraordinary in 2016 when the controversial Bill C-16, a federal amendment to the Canadian Human Rights Act and Criminal Code, was passed, "to protect individuals from discrimination within the sphere of federal jurisdiction and from being the targets of hate propaganda, as a consequence of their gender

Figure 26.3 Photo of Jordan Peterson at the Fred Kavli Theater in Thousand Oaks, California, June 30, 2018.

identity or their gender expression."[8] That sounds reasonable enough: If we're going to protect people from discrimination based on race, age, sex, and religion, why not gender identity or expression as well? Who would disagree with this clause in the bill?

> [A]ll individuals should have an opportunity equal with other individuals to make for themselves the lives that they are able and wish to have and to have their needs accommodated, consistent with their duties and obligations as members of society, without being hindered in or prevented from doing so by discriminatory practices based on race, national or ethnic origin, colour, religion, age, sex, sexual orientation, marital status, family status, disability or conviction for an offence for

which a pardon has been granted or in respect of which a record suspension has been ordered.

To me, this reads like another step on the moral arc bending toward justice. But in a series of YouTube videos Peterson outlined his concerns (dread, really) that Bill C-16 could turn into "compelled speech" that, if not obeyed, could land one in jail for not addressing someone by their preferred pronoun (zie, xem, hir, ve, xe, xyr ...).[9] Peterson went on record stating, "I'm not using the words that other people require me to use, especially if they're made up by radical left-wing ideologues. And that's that."[10] Even more emphatically, he told a television audience, "If they fine me, I won't pay it. If they put me in jail, I'll go on a hunger strike."[11] The image of a Canadian psychology professor on a hunger strike over gender pronouns is a little hard to equate with Gandhi's emaciating efforts to free his country from British rule, but it's a sign of moral progress that we've shifted from condemning colonization to protesting pronouns.

To his credit, Peterson has said that, if he were asked to address someone by a preferred pronoun, he might oblige him or her (or zhe or zher), assuming it was asked for the right reasons; i.e., not for political motives or a Borat-like gotcha.[12] Fair enough. When I was an undergraduate at Pepperdine University, I had a roommate who changed his name from Duane to D'Artagnan (the fourth member of the Three Musketeers), after which he respectfully asked us to address him by his new name – eventually shortened to D'Art – which we did (after a few Spock-like raised eyebrows). But that's a personal matter. It is an entirely different issue for the government to legislate speech, especially because the law is backed by violence or the threat thereof (as in Max Weber's classic definition of the state as having a "monopoly of the legitimate use of physical force"). Threatening people with physical violence for refusing to address someone by their preferred pronoun does smack of anti-Enlightenment illiberalism, government overreach, and even tyranny.

Would Bill C-16 result in Canadian professors (or anyone else) being fined, jailed (and, presumably, force-fed) at the point of a gun for not using preferred gender pronouns? Is it, as Peterson described it in an opinion editorial in the *National Post*, "frighteningly similar to the Marxist doctrines that killed at least 100 million people in the 20th century"?[13] I don't think so. As I read the Bill, there is, as in most legislation, much room for interpretation and many steps between legal language and the gulag archipelago. I don't think Peterson was ever in danger of losing his job, much less residing in the Graybar Hotel.

Still, given the number of professors who have faced Title IX inquiries, been shamed on campus and on social media over political peccadillos, or even lost employment over ideological conflicts, Peterson's stated concerns about job security at the University of Toronto (which helped propel his Patreon account into numbers only one-percenters could identify with) are not entirely without precedent. The highly publicized ousting of the biologists Bret Weinstein and Heather Heying at Evergreen University is the most blatant example, and many more have been documented by Laura Kipnis in her 2017 book *Unwanted Advances* and by Greg Lukianoff and Jonathan Haidt in their 2018 book *The Coddling of the American Mind*. There is no doubt that many college campuses today are being swept up by an East German Stasi-like climate of ideological conformity, political suppression, speech censorship, interpersonal suspicion, and preemptive denunciation – denouncing others before they denounce you – leading to the unhealthiest climate for free speech since the 1950s McCarthyism. So when Jordan Peterson said "enough" to Bill C-16, it was symbolic of this larger problem, and he became an archetypal hero willing to stand up to this perceived evil. And just as Peterson's critics were accusing him of exaggerating the dangers of the Bill, in 2017, a graduate student at Wilfrid Laurier University in Canada named Lindsay Shepherd was formally censured by her superiors for merely showing her class a video clip of Peterson debating Bill C-16 on a television news program, accusing her of creating a "toxic climate" and, in accordance to Godwin's Rule, comparing Peterson's words to a "speech by Hitler."[14]

At this point Peterson would have been fully justified in pronouncing, "I rest my case," and anyone who would join a Fair Play for Political Correctness Committee would be seriously out of touch with reality.

THE ARCHETYPAL THEORY OF TRUTH

In an episode of *Star Trek, The Next Generation* titled "Chain of Command,"[15] Captain Jean-Luc Picard is captured and tortured by a Cardassian interrogation expert who has implanted a pain generation device in Picard's chest that can be turned on with the push of a button, which will stop functioning if the Enterprise Captain will reveal the Federation's plans for disputed space. Throughout days of agonizing torture, Picard is confronted with four blindingly bright lights and told there are five. The torturer knows that he can break Picard if he can get him to confess to the false number. Throughout the ordeal the indefatigable captain grunts through the pain that "there are four . . . *four* lights," only to confess to the ship's counselor at the end of the episode that he actually came to believe that there were five lights.

How many lights were there, really? Four, of course, but I'm not at all sure Jordan Peterson would agree, given his preference for a pragmatic interpretation of truth, which holds that what works for an observer in a given context is what is true. In two excruciating podcast episodes lasting over four hours in total,[16] the philosophical realist Sam Harris could not convince the philosophical pragmatist Peterson that there is, for example, a correct order of US presidents if, in Sam's thought experiment, terrorists told their captive that disaster could be averted if the correct order of US presidents were recited . . . with this wrinkle: The terrorists have a mistaken order of the presidency, so their hostage would need to enumerate the wrong sequence to forestall the looming calamity. Surely Peterson would agree that there really is a correct temporal sequence of presidents and that the terrorists are simply mistaken (and their prisoner knows he's regurgitating an erroneous list), but no! Instead, Peterson waxed archetypal, calling religious claims, mythological stories, and literary masterpieces "meta-true" and "more true than scientific truth" inasmuch as they are mediated by sociopolitical and cultural factors related to our Darwinian need to survive and reproduce. There is no "truly independent" truth, he says, only useful or not useful truths pertaining to our evolutionary needs. The use-value of a claim at a particular time and place is what makes it true.

Peterson's theory – call it the *Archetype Theory of Truth* (ATT) – is very much in line with that of the cognitive psychologist Donald Hoffman's

Interface Theory of Perception (ITP), which holds that percepts about the world are a species-specific user interface that directs behavior toward survival and reproduction, not truth.[17] Objects in nature are like desktop icons, Hoffman analogizes, and the physical environment is like the desktop. Our senses form a biological user interface (BUI) – analogous to a computer's graphical user interface (GUI) – between our brains and the outside world, transducing physical stimuli such as photons of light into neural impulses processed by the visual cortex as things in the environment. GUIs and BUIs are useful because you don't need to know what is inside computers and brains. You just need to know how to interact with the interface well enough to accomplish your task. Adaptive function, not veridical perception, is what is important to evolution.

I'm skeptical of Peterson's ATT for the same reasons I am of ITP. My refutation of ITP in *Scientific American*[18] applies to Peterson's ATT:

First, how could a more accurate perception of reality *not* be adaptive? Hoffman's answer is that evolution gave us an interface to hide the underlying reality because, for example, you don't need to know how neurons create images of snakes; you just need to jump out of the way of the snake icon. But how did the icon come to look like a snake in the first place? Natural Selection. And why did some nonpoisonous snakes evolve to mimic poisonous species? Because predators avoid *real* poisonous snakes. Mimicry only works if there's an objective reality to mimic.

Hoffman claims, "A rock is an interface icon, not a constituent of objective reality." But a real rock chipped into an arrow point and thrown at a four-legged meal really works even if you don't know physics and calculus. Is that not veridical perception with adaptive significance?

Hoffman says perception is species specific and that we should take predators seriously, but not literally. Yes, a dolphin's icon for "shark" no doubt looks different than a human's, but there really are sharks and they really do have powerful tails on one end and a mouthful of teeth on the other end, and that is true no matter how your sensory system works.

This repudiation of Hoffman's ITP (and, thereby, Peterson's ATT) is an expression of the *correspondence theory of truth*, which, according to the *Stanford Encyclopedia of Philosophy* (*SEP*),[19] "is the view that truth is correspondence to, or with, a fact" and "more broadly to any view explicitly embracing the idea that truth consists in a relation to reality." ITP and ATT are also refuted by *scientific realism*, which the *SEP* characterizes as "a commitment to the idea that our best theories have a certain epistemic status: they yield knowledge of aspects of the world, including unobservable aspects,"[20] and *ontological realism*, or the belief that there is a world external to human minds, and that this world is knowable. The vast majority of professional philosophers trained to think about truth embrace these positions, as revealed in a 2009 survey of 3,226 philosophy professors and grad students asked to weigh in on thirty different subjects of concern in their field, from free will and God to knowledge and mind.[21] On the topic of the external world, 81.6 percent accept or lean toward *nonskeptical realism*, 75.1 percent accept or lean toward *scientific realism*, and 50.8 percent accept or lean toward the *correspondence theory of truth*. No matter what beliefs about the world a torturer may evoke in his victim, if there are four lights, there cannot be five, and Washington, Adams, Jefferson, Madison, and Monroe were the first five presidents. And that's that!

Nevertheless, I will grant Jordan his emphasis on the power of literary "truths" to explore deep themes and move people to change their lives. "There is great truth revealed in Dostoevsky, Tolstoy, and Shakespeare," Peterson proclaims. Of course there is. That's what makes great literature great. But there's that word again. Truth. Presumably there were no brothers named Karamozov in nineteenth-century Russia, but whether there were or not is beside the point because Dostoevsky's *The Brothers Karamozov* is a novel exploring profound philosophical issues of God, morality, volition, and the human struggles with faith and doubt during a time of social and political upheaval, not a scientific history of Russian modernity. Here truth is symbolic, or archetypal, inasmuch as the characters and plots of a novel reflect a type of reality as the author interprets it, and to that end a new field of Darwinian literary studies has taken root that explores why certain themes appear again and again in fiction in the context of our evolved nature, such as sex, love, jealousy, power, hierarchy, aggression, violence, and murder. If Peterson would be willing to forego his Archetype Theory of Truth, I will agree that literature, myths, and even biblical stories add much value to the understanding of the human condition.

THE ARCHITECTURE OF ARCHETYPES

During the hour and a quarter that Jordan and I talked on his podcast, he described a recently published neuroscience paper on the structure of neural cortical columns that shows they're not randomly connected to other neurons in the brain, "and what this scan shows is an underlying superhighway of built-in connections so that the columns themselves can wire into the already existing superhighways, so it was like there was an underlying architecture that was highly probable that it would manifest itself, and I thought 'well that looks like the neuro-architecture of something like an archetype'." To which I replied, "Um ... maybe."[22]

Peterson's magnum opus *Maps of Meaning*, in fact, is subtitled *The Architecture of Belief*, a 564-page mishmash of evolutionary theory, biology, psychology, philosophy, literature, comparative mythology, theology, the Bible, Nietzsche, Dostoevsky, Jung, Freud, and others, which may have been more accurately subtitled *The Architecture of Archetypes*. I undertook listening to the unabridged audio edition read by the author, but the book is so dense and convoluted that I DNF'd after six hours. Perhaps reading it makes more sense, or perhaps there isn't much sense to be made – at least for my more literalist wired brain – but it's hard to know what to make of passages like these, which fill page after page, hour after hour ...

> The Great Mother aborts children, and is the dead fetus; breeds pestilence, and is the plague; she makes of the skull something gruesomely compelling, and is all skulls herself. To unveil her is to risk madness, to gaze over the abyss, to lose the way, to remember the repressed trauma. She is the molestor of children, the golem, the bogey-man, the monster in the swamp, the rotting cadaverous zombie who threatens the living. She is progenitor of the devil, the "strange son of chaos." She is the serpent, and Eve, the temptress; she is the femme fatale, the insect in the ointment, the hidden cancer, the chronic sickness, the plague of locusts, the cause of drought, the poisoned water. She uses erotic pleasure as bait to keep the

world alive and breeding; she is a gothic monster, who feeds on the blood of the living.[23]

It goes on like this for over thirty hours. As Peterson told the *Chronicle of Higher Education*: "I don't think people had any idea what to make of the book, and I still think they don't."[24] Whew! So it's not just me.

I had more success with *12 Rules for Life*, making it through all fifteen hours. Although still too long by half for my tastes, most of the advice Peterson offers resonates reasonably well with the findings of cognitive behavior therapy, as noted by the clinical psychologist Jonathan N. Stea in his assessment (also in the special section of *Skeptic*)[25] of Peterson's advice: "The potential benefits from understanding and consuming his material can approximate what one can glean from successful psychotherapy. Whether a person wants to mitigate mental health concerns or improve their quality of life, self-help materials can be thought of as the lowest rung on the ladder in a stepped-care model of mental health treatment." To that end I recommend Jocko Willink's 2017 book *Discipline Equals Freedom* and Amy Alkon's 2018 book *Unfuckology: A Field Guide to Living with Guts and Confidence*, both of which I'm confident Peterson would endorse given that so many of his rules – such as "stand up straight with your shoulders back," "compare yourself to who you were yesterday, not to who someone else is today," and "set your house in perfect order" – are similar to those outlined by Willink and Alkon and supported by the findings of science, such as the value of "small wins" (e.g., make your bed, clean your room) that build confidence for larger challenges that can lead to big wins.

ENTROPY AND EXTROPY, CHAOS AND ORDER

One friend and colleague described Jordan Peterson to me as "one pair of mirrored sunglasses away from being a cult leader." This is too clever by half. The people I met at the Thousand Oaks event were nothing like glaze-eyed Jim Jones followers, nor were they mostly angry young white men as Peterson's critics repeat like a mantra. As I gazed around the auditorium, an informal head count put the gender ratio at roughly 65 : 35 Male : Female, their ages varying wildly from teenagers to senior citizens, and the evening wasn't even remotely political (observations that I confirmed about other audiences with Dave Rubin, who has opened for Peterson in dozens of cities). "They're not coming for a political discussion," Peterson has said about his audiences. They're "coming because they're trying to put themselves together. And there isn't anything about that that isn't good."

In point of fact, the subtitle of *12 Rules for Life* is *An Antidote to Chaos,* which leads me to a final point on the JPP, namely his worldview, which is well aligned with the reality most people experience and another contributing factor to his popularity. Life can be, in the oft-quoted observation of the political philosopher Thomas Hobbes, "solitary, poor, nasty, brutish, and short." The ultimate reason for this state of affairs is the Second Law of Thermodynamics, or entropy. Without an outside source (like the sun), energy dissipates, systems run down, warm things turn cold, metal rusts, wood rots, weeds overwhelm gardens, and . . . bedrooms get cluttered. Entropy decrees that there are more ways for things to be disordered than ordered, so Peterson's counsel to get your life in order is simpatico with a great many people. As I explained in *Heavens on Earth,* the Second Law of Thermodynamics leads to the First Law of Life, which is to get your life in order:

> If you do nothing, entropy will take its course and you will move toward a higher state of disorder (ultimately causing your demise). So your most basic purpose in life is to combat entropy by doing something extropic – expending energy to survive, reproduce, and flourish. In this sense, evolution granted us a purpose-driven life by dint of the laws of nature.

> That a meaningful, purposeful life comes from struggle and challenge against the vicissitudes of nature more than it does a homeostatic balance of extropic pushback against entropy reinforces the point that the Second Law of Thermodynamics is the First Law of Life. We must act in the world. The thermostat is always being adjusted, balance sought but never achieved. There is no Faustian bargain to be made in life. We may strive for immortality while never reaching it, as we may seek utopian bliss while never finding it, for it is the striving and the seeking that matter, not the attainment of the unattainable. We are volitional beings, so the choice to act is ours, and our sense of purpose is defined by reaching for the upper

limits of our natural abilities and learned skills, and by facing challenges with courage and conviction.[26]

Which brings us back to the Paladin archetype and his ratio of real killers to bystanders who enable evil through inaction (12 : 10,000). If we include entropy as a form of evil, then as the original conservative Edmund Burke famously said, "The only thing necessary for the triumph of evil is that good men do nothing."[27]

Standing up to evil – and to entropy – is an antidote to chaos.

CHAPTER 27

Romancing the Past

Graham Hancock and the Quest for a Lost Civilization

PREAMBLE

This essay grew out of several threads of commentary on Graham Hancock, the author of numerous bestselling books about ancient human prehistory, whose work I had encountered many times over the years. I had never had the opportunity to engage with Hancock until Joe Rogan invited us to have an informal debate in his studio for his popular podcast, which we did on May 16, 2017. It was, in fact, my third appearance on the Joe Rogan Experience, one of the most popular podcasts in the world. According to Joe, as of that week, he was averaging over 120 million downloads a month, putting him on par with the biggest talk-show hosts on television, both cable and broadcast. He has a huge and diverse following, and for good reason – he's a remarkable conversationalist. My previous two appearances lasted for three hours each, without any sense of time passing. Unlike most talk-show hosts I have engaged with over the decades, a dialogue with Joe Rogan is like talking to an old friend. He is warm, receptive to all ideas, and allows the conversation to advance organically without an agenda. For my solo appearances he was as sympathetic to my ideas as he was to those of Hancock in his prior appearances on his show.

In noting that many millions of people seemed to accept his radically challenging ideas uncritically, however, I thought someone needed to defend mainstream science and put Hancock's alternative archaeological theories into perspective. What follows is an original essay stitched together from my notes for the show, my postmortem blog about it afterward, my *Scientific American* column about Hancock's work, and a few thoughts about the book he published after our studio collision.

On a personal note, I like Graham very much as a person despite our differences over scientific issues. After the tension we both felt during and immediately after our debate, we struck up a correspondence and became friends. He is a warm, thoughtful, caring, generous, and intelligent man whose life's work I find compelling even while rejecting its central premise, with which this essay shall engage.

* * *

GRAHAM HANCOCK IS AN ALTERNATIVE ARCHAEOLOGIST AND audacious autodidact who believes that tens of thousands of years before ancient Mesopotamia, Babylonia, and Egypt, there existed an even more glorious civilization that was so thoroughly wiped out by a comet strike around 12,000 years ago that nearly all evidence of its existence vanished, leaving only the faintest of traces, which he thinks include a cryptic warning that such a celestial catastrophe could happen to us.

Hancock has put forth variations on this general theme in numerous well-written and wildly popular bestselling books, including *Fingerprints of the Gods: The Evidence of Earth's Lost Civilization* (1995), *The Message of the Sphinx: A Quest for the Hidden Legacy of Mankind* (1997), *Underworld: The Mysterious Origins of Civilization* (2002), *Magicians of the Gods* (2015), and most recently *America Before: The Key to Earth's Lost Civilization* (2019). I listened to the audio editions of *Magicians of the Gods* and *America Before*, both read by the author, whose British accent and breathless revelatory storytelling style is confessedly compelling. But is it true? I'm skeptical. As I explained in my June 2017 column in *Scientific American*:

First, no matter how devastating an extraterrestrial impact might be, are we to believe that after centuries of flourishing every last tool, potshard, article of clothing, and, presumably from an advanced civilization, writing, metallurgy, and other technologies – not to mention their trash – was erased? Inconceivable.

Second, Hancock's impact hypothesis comes from scientists who first proposed it in 2007 as an explanation for the North American mega-faunal extinction around that time and has been the subject of vigorous scientific debate. It has not fared well. In addition to the lack of any impact craters dated to around that time anywhere in the world, the radiocarbon dates of the layer of carbon, soot, charcoal, nanodiamonds, microspherules, and iridium, asserted to have been the result of this catastrophic event, vary widely before and after the mega-faunal extinction, anywhere from 14,000 to 10,000 years ago. Further, although 37 mammal species went extinct in North America (while most other species survived and flourished), at the same time 52 mammal genera went extinct in South America, presumably not caused by the impact. These extinctions, in fact, were timed with human arrival, thereby supporting the more widely accepted overhunting hypothesis.

Third, Hancock grounds his case primarily in the *argument from ignorance* (since scientists cannot explain X, then Y is a legitimate theory), or the *argument from personal incredulity* (because *I* cannot explain X, then my Y theory is valid). These are "God of the Gaps" type reasoning that creationists employ, only in Hancock's case the gods are the "Magicians" who brought us civilization. The problem here is twofold: (1) scientists *do* have good explanations for Hancock's Xs (e.g., the pyramids, the Sphinx), even if they are not in total agreement, and (2) ultimately one's theory must rest on *positive* evidence in favor of it, not just *negative* evidence against accepted theories.

Hancock's biggest X is Göbekli Tepe in Turkey, with its megalithic T-shaped 7- to 10-ton stone pillars cut and hauled from limestone quarries and dated to around 11,000 years ago when humans lived as hunter-gatherers without, presumably, the knowhow, skills, and labor to produce them. Ergo, Hancock concludes, "At the very least it would mean that some as yet unknown and unidentified people somewhere in the world had already mastered all the arts and attributes of a high civilization more than twelve thousand years ago in the depths of the last Ice Age and sent out emissaries around the world to spread the benefits of their knowledge." This sounds romantic, but it is the bigotry of low expectations. Who's to say what hunter-gatherers are or are not capable of doing? Plus, Göbekli Tepe was a ceremonial religious site, not a city, as there is no evidence that anyone lived there. Further, there are no domesticated animal bones, no metal tools, no inscriptions or writing, and not even pottery – all products that much later "high civilizations" produced.

Fourth, Hancock has spent decades in his vision quest to find the sages who brought us civilization. Yet, decades of searching have failed to produce enough evidence to convince archaeologists that the standard timeline of human history needs major revision. Hancock's plaint is that Mainstream Science is stuck in a uniformitarianism model of slow gradual change and so cannot accept a catastrophic explanation. Not true. From the origin of the universe (big bang), to the origin of the moon (big collision) to the origin of lunar craters (meteor strikes), to the demise of the dinosaurs (asteroid impact), to the numerous sudden downfalls of civilizations documented by Jared Diamond in his book *Collapse*, catastrophism is alive and well in Mainstream Science.

The real magicians are the scientists who have worked this all out.

Quite by chance, my *Scientific American* column came out the same week that the popular podcaster Joe Rogan hosted a debate between me and Graham, along with his colleague Randall Carlson, plus our hand-selected "phone-a-friend" Skyped-in guests (geologist Marc Defant for me, planetary scientist Malcolm LeCompte for Hancock and Carlson). It was a three-hour-and-thirty-five-minute marathon that, at the time of this writing, many millions of people have heard or viewed on the usual podcast platforms. In preparation for the debate, I put together half a dozen reasons why alternative archaeologists in general, and Graham Hancock in particular, have failed to convince most scientists and archaeologists to abandon the theory about the timeline of the development of civilization over the past 13,000 years and to embrace his theory of an ancient lost advanced civilization dating back tens of thousands, perhaps even hundreds of thousands of years. Hancock's is an extraordinary claim, and as skeptics and scientists like to say, *extraordinary claims require extraordinary evidence.* Unfortunately for his extraordinary claim, Hancock's evidence is less than ordinary. Here are six reasons why I am skeptical of the claims for an ancient lost civilization.

1. *There isn't just one "alternative" to mainstream archaeology, there are dozens of alternative theories. To name a few that have not fared well in the marketplace of ideas:*
   • The theory that lost tribes of Israel colonized the Americas (and other places).

- The Mormon archaeological theory that Native Americans are descended from one of these lost tribes of Israel.
- The claim that the Kensington Runestones of Minnesota prove the theory of the Nordic Viking peopling of the Americas centuries before Columbus.
- The Black Athena theory that the Greeks got Western culture from the ancient Egyptians, who were predominantly black because Egypt is in Africa.
- Thor Heyerdahl's theory that the peopling of Polynesia was from South America, not Southeast Asia.
- The archaeological theory that South American Olmec statues look African in their features, suggesting therefore that the peopling of the Americas also included voyages from Africa to South America.
- The theories of Erich von Däniken, Zecharia Sitchin, and other ancient alien alternative archaeologists, proposing that ancient monumental architecture is best explained as the products of extraterrestrial intelligences visiting Earth in the distant past.

In response to this litany, Hancock reasonably responded "what does this have to do with me and my theory?" The answer is "nothing" and "everything." Nothing, because to his credit Graham is just as skeptical as I am of these alternative archaeologies and makes that clear in his writings and speeches. Everything, because Hancock portrays himself as a lone rogue scholar being unfairly ignored by mainstream archaeologists, whereas in fact there are hundreds of such rogues, all equally convinced of the veracity of their claims. Hancock gripes about the cold-shoulder he's been given by Zahi Hawass, the Egyptian archaeologist, Egyptologist, and former Minister of State for Antiquities Affairs who oversees the Giza pyramid complex and other archaeological sites in Egypt. But I've met Hawass and followed his career as it relates to this issue of alternative archaeology and can attest to the fact that he routinely receives requests from nonprofessionals who want to come to these sites to explore their own alternative theories. Time and energy simply don't permit him – and most mainstream professional archaeologists – to engage everyone who has a pet theory about the ancient past.

The problem with all of these "alternative" theories is that they lack convincing evidence and are based almost entirely on a handful of anomalies allegedly not explained by mainstream archaeologists, along with gobs of conjectures about what "might" have happened to explain this or that archaeological feature.

To borrow a line from skeptics of alternative medicine, do you know what you call alternative archaeology with evidence? Archaeology.

2. *Cherry picking data, the confirmation bias, and starting with a conclusion and working backward through the evidence to make it fit. For example:*

• Christian Fundamentalists start with the assumption of a flood and go in search of Noah's Ark and evidence of floods.

• Creationists begin with a belief in a young Earth and instant creation in seven days, so they reject the theory of evolution and look for any anomaly in science that seems to go against the findings that support a 4.6-billion-year-old Earth.

• Hindu creationists believe in an exceptionally ancient human lineage that dates back tens of millions of years, and therefore accuse the scientific establishment of suppressing the fossil evidence of extreme human antiquity. For example, the self-identified "Vedic archaeologist" Michael Cremo, in his book *Forbidden Archaeology*, believes his findings support the story of humanity described in the Hindu Vedas.

Having personally interacted with advocates of these positions – and many more like them – I can assure readers that these writers believe as strongly in the veracity of their ideas as Graham Hancock does in his. That these challengers to mainstream science are wrong, however, doesn't mean Hancock is also wrong. We must assess each claim individually. But it does strongly suggest that if your alternative explanation is based primarily on the cherry picking of data to fit only your hypothesis, and if it begins with a conclusion and works backward through the evidence to make it fit what you'd like to be true, it very likely means that you're subject to the *confirmation bias*, which is a cognitive feature we are all subject to in which we look for and find confirming evidence for our beliefs and ignore or rationalize disconfirming evidence. Everyone does it. As the great Caltech physicist Richard Feynman once said, "The first principle is that you must not fool yourself – and you are the easiest person to fool."

Evidence for the confirmation bias abounds. In a classic 1981 experiment, for example, the psychologist Mark Snyder tasked subjects to assess the personality of someone whom they were about to meet, but only after they reviewed a profile of the person. One group of subjects were given a profile of an introvert (shy, timid, quiet), while another group of subjects were given a profile of an extrovert (sociable, talkative, outgoing). When asked to make a personality assessment, those subjects who were told that the person would be an extrovert tended to ask questions that would lead to that conclusion; the introvert group did the same in the opposite direction.

In a 1983 study, psychologists John Darley and Paul Gross showed subjects a video of a child taking a test. One group was told that the child was from a high socioeconomic class while the other group was told that the child was from a low socioeconomic class. The subjects were then asked to evaluate the academic abilities of the child based on the results of the test. Even though both groups of subjects were evaluating the exact same set of numbers, those who were told that the child they were evaluating was from a high socioeconomic class rated the child's abilities as above grade level, and those who thought that the kid was from a low socioeconomic class rated the kid as below grade level in ability.

Finally, in a study by the psychologist Deanna Kuhn, when people were exposed to evidence inconsistent with a theory they preferred, they failed to notice the contradictory evidence, or, if they did acknowledge its existence, they tended to reinterpret it to favor their preconceived beliefs.

The confirmation bias is succinctly articulated in the biblical idiom: "seek and ye shall find." It's not that alternative scientists are subject to the confirmation bias while mainstream scientists are immune; rather, by working within the scientific community instead of outside of it, science is a social process in which others challenge your hypotheses before they are presented in final form, a practice which tends to emphasize disconfirming evidence enough to ensure that wrong ideas are usually filtered out.

Now, to be sure, Graham Hancock is correct when he points out the many theories in the history of science that themselves have been subject to the confirmation bias where entire communities of scientists have prevented alternative challenges to the mainstream from getting a fair hearing. Agreed, the system is not perfect. But that doesn't mean every alternative theory to the mainstream is correct. It only means we must be vigilant.

3. *Patternicity: the tendency to find meaningful patterns in both meaningful and meaningless noise. For example:*
    *   Matching the alignment of buildings on the ground with stars in the sky, which Graham Hancock does in comparing the layout of the Great Pyramid complex in Egypt to the constellation of Orion in the winter sky (primarily the three stars in Orion that make up the figure's "belt"), is an example of patternicity. There is no independent evidence that the ancient Egyptians intended the layout of their buildings to match that constellation, and in any case it doesn't – the pattern on the ground is upside down compared to that in the sky.
    *   The comparison between disparate cultures of artifacts and monuments from one society and highlighting similarities with those of another to conclude a common source, when in fact they are more likely explained by independent invention. In many instances in his books, Hancock rejects both cultural diffusion and "coincidence" as explanations, and instead strongly suggests that cultural features between civilizations that appear to match are the result of a common ancient source – his sought-for lost civilization. But "coincidence" is not an explanation on offer from archaeologists. Instead, conceive of them as *cognitive commonalities* in thinking about the world: There are only so many variations on a handful of themes in human life, so we shouldn't be surprised when people come up with ideas similar to one another across time and space. The similarity of rituals and symbols, for example, does not automatically mean either cultural diffusion or ancient origin but instead could be the result of cognitive commonalities – there are only so many rituals and symbols that people can think of, so we shouldn't be surprised when some of them seem to match.
    *   John Taylor provides a splendid example of patternicity in his 1859 book *The Great Pyramid*, when he computed that if you divide the

height of the pyramid into twice the side of its base, you get a number close to pi; he also thought he had discovered the length of the ancient cubit as the division of the Earth's axis by 400,000 – both of which Taylor found to be too incredible to be coincidental. Other alternative archaeologists "discovered" that the base of the Great Pyramid divided by the width of a casing stone equals the number of days in the year, and that the height of the Great Pyramid multiplied by 109 approximately equals the distance from the Earth to the Sun. And so on.

In his classic 1952 book *Fads and Fallacies in the Name of Science*, during his discussion of the many alternative theories about the Great Pyramid of Egypt, Martin Gardner revealed the poignant problem with patternicity when "just for fun" he analyzed the Washington Monument and "discovered" the property of fiveness to it:

> Its height is 555 feet and 5 inches. The base is 55 feet square, and the windows are set at 500 feet from the base. If the base is multiplied by 60 (or 5 times the number of months in a year) it gives 3,300, which is the exact weight of the capstone in pounds. Also, the word "Washington" has exactly 10 letters (2 times 5). And if the weight of the capstone is multiplied by the base, the result is 181,500 – a fairly close approximation of the speed of light in miles per second.

After musing that "it should take an average mathematician about 55 minutes to discover the above 'truths,'" Gardner concludes "how easy it is to work over an undigested mass of data and emerge with a pattern, which at first glance, is so intricately put together that it is difficult to believe it is nothing more than the product of a man's brain."

In my opinion, the many patterns Graham Hancock has found in the archaeological record are primarily in his mind, not in the soil. As interesting as the many speculative patterns he has strung together in his books are, I strongly suspect that what we are witnessing is patternicity at work.

4. *Alternative archaeologists disparage mainstream archaeologists and accuse them of being closed-minded dogmatists in a conspiracy to silence the truth.*

This calumny is gainsaid by a paper published in the prestigious journal *Nature* just weeks before Graham and I collided in Joe Rogan's studio, in which scientists put forth evidence that they believe indicates humans (or possibly Neanderthals) inhabited the San Diego area of Southern California some 130,000 years ago, an order of magnitude earlier than mainstream archaeologists' timeline for the peopling of the Americas. The evidence for this conjecture, however, is not as strong as the popular media made it out to be in the considerable press coverage this paper received. The "butchered" mammoth bones may, in fact, have been broken in the excavation of a road recently constructed at the site, and the "stone tools" were nothing at all like the finely crafted Clovis points found all over North America and instead might be just broken rocks. That was, in fact, the conclusion in another paper published in the journal *PaleoAmerica* after our debate and as Hancock's *America Before* was going to press and is what most mainstream archaeologists now believe about the find.

The problem here is what to do with such anomalies. The vast majority of evidence indicates the peopling of the Americas happened sometime around 13,000 years ago, perhaps a few thousand years earlier, depending on the accuracy of the dating of these earlier artifacts and the margins of error around the calibrated date. But if people were in the Americas 130,000 years ago, where is all the evidence for their existence between 13,000 years ago and that much older date? Where are their stone tools, their homes, their trash? Hancock responds to this plaint that the spiral of silence around challenging the Clovis-first dogma has prevented archaeologists from searching for such chronologically intermittent artifacts. That may be – scientific paradigms do direct scientists and graduate students down certain paths and not others (literally in the case of archaeology) – but not one unequivocal artifact of this ancient lost civilization has been stumbled upon by farmers, hikers, cave divers, construction workers, well diggers, and the like. Not one?

How Hancock handles the pre-Clovis evidence is indicative of the problem. First, he sets up his straw-man by claiming that Clovis-first dogma prevents scientists from looking for older sites, then he contradicts himself by documenting that, even before Clovis, archaeological finds have kept pushing back the age of the peopling of the Americas to older and older dates; then he lists every possible pre-Clovis claim as if they were all of equally valid and documented veracity (which they're not); then he leaps across nearly 100,000 years to the San Diego site, as if this were a smooth transition. As Jason Colavito concluded in his extensive and detailed review of *America Before* in *Skeptic* (Vol. 24, No. 2, 2019): "Even accepting the most extreme pre-Clovis arguments, the presence of humans implies nothing about the existence of a lost Atlantis-like civilization. For example, Aboriginal Australians have been present Down Under for 65,000 years or more, but their traditional way of life did not include Atlantis-style cities."

After the *Nature* paper was published and before my debate with Hancock, I queried the renowned scholar of human history and prehistory, UCLA geographer Jared Diamond, who has for half a century followed the claims of pre-Clovis peoples populating the Americas, about his opinion on the matter. He replied with this one-liner: "The latest semi-annual new-paradigm pre-Clovis claim with a credibility half-life of two days." That has, in fact, been the fate of the 130,000-year-old claimed human presence in America.

5. *Falsifiability, conjectures and refutations, and the burden of proof.*

During our debate I asked Hancock several times, "What would it take to refute your hypothesis?" I never received a reply. In his 1959 book, *The Logic of Scientific Discovery*, the philosopher of science Karl Popper proposed a solution to "the demarcation problem" of distinguishing science from pseudoscience: "the criterion of the scientific status of a theory is its falsifiability, or refutability, or testability." In his 1963 book *Conjectures and Refutations*, Popper outlined how scientists operate by conjecturing ideas to their colleagues and considering the refutations in response. There's nothing wrong with making conjectures – it is the life blood of science in fact – but most ideas that scientists propose are wrong so the constant dialogue with one's fellow experts in a field through letters (and today emails), phone calls, papers, books, conferences, and the like, is crucial for determining if one has gone off the rails. This is why it is dangerous to work in isolation, which is an inherent limitation of being an outsider to a field. It's not that outsiders can't or don't make contributions – occasionally they do. But usually they don't because most of us most of the time are wrong about our conjectures, so refutations from colleagues are vital.

A few days before our debate, my monthly column in *Scientific American* about Graham Hancock was published (quite by chance), and so in the studio he made his annoyance known that he had not been given the chance to respond. After our debate, I wrote him this letter, in which I outlined my concerns about this problem of a lack of falsifiability:

Dear Graham,

I get that you're upset, and why, and I no doubt owe a great deal to that fact by how and what I said and wrote. To that end I am truly sorry that you feel I "rubbished" your life's work. That was certainly not my intention, and it goes against my philosophy of giving people a fair hearing. Clearly I failed in that regard. But there is nothing factual in my column that I would change, even after our long dialogue.

To wit: you still have no evidence whatsoever for the lost civilization. Not a single tool. No writing. Not even any pottery. Even after nearly four hours in Joe's studio I still have no idea what you mean by "advanced", despite my asking you repeatedly. Your comments were filled with many modifiers like "perhaps", "maybe", "possibly" etc. It's fine to speculate, and you may even be right. But to overturn the mainstream theory in any field you need to do more than that.

If mainstream archaeologists are all wrong about how they define "advanced" (writing, metallurgy, pottery, etc.) then it is incumbent on you to redefine it in a way to convince them that the evidence points to your claims. That they don't accept your theory is simply how most science in most fields works, a point I tried (and mostly failed) to make in bringing up other examples. I realize these other theories have nothing to do with you, but my point is that in the Popperian sense of falsification science you need to explain how your theory could be falsified. Maybe I missed it but I don't think I know how you would answer that question.

I then recommended to Graham that he read Jared Diamond's short essay in the January 2017 issue of the online salon Edge.org about this matter (https://bit.ly/2h7n95g):

The first well-attested settlement of the Americas south of the Canada/ U.S. border occurred around 13,000 years ago, as the ice sheets were melting. That settlement is attested by the sudden appearance of stone tools of the radiocarbon-dated Clovis culture, named after the town of Clovis, New Mexico, where the tools and their significance were first recognized. Clovis tools have now been found over all of the lower 48 U.S. states, south into Mexico. That sudden appearance of a culture abundantly filling up the entire landscape is what one expects and observes whenever humans first colonize fertile empty lands.

But any claim by an archaeologist to have discovered "the first X" is taken as a challenge by other archaeologists to discover an earlier X. In this case, archaeologists feel challenged to discover pre-Clovis sites, i.e. sites with different stone tools and dating to before 13,000 years ago. Every year nowadays, new claims of pre-Clovis sites in the U.S. and South America are advanced, and subjected to detailed scrutiny. Eventually, it turns out that most of those claims are invalidated by the equivalent of technical errors at step 37: e.g., the radiocarbon sample was contaminated with older carbon, or the radiocarbon-dated material really wasn't associated with the stone tools. But, even after complicated analyses and objections and rebuttals, a few pre-Clovis claims have not yet been invalidated. At present, the most widely discussed such claims are for Chile's Monte Verde site, Pennsylvania's Meadowcroft site, and one site each in Texas and in Oregon. As a result, the majority of American archaeologists currently believe in the validity of pre-Clovis settlement.

To me, it seems instead that pre-Clovis believers have fallen into [a] fallacy. It's absurd to suppose that the first human settlers south of the Canada/U.S. border could have been airlifted by non-stop flights to Chile, Pennsylvania, Oregon, and Texas, leaving no unequivocal signs of their presence at intermediate sites. If there really had been pre-Clovis settlement, we would already know it and would no longer be arguing about it. That's because there would now be hundreds of undisputed pre-Clovis sites distributed everywhere from the Canada/U.S. border south to Chile.

Finally, there is the matter of whether the absence of evidence is the evidence of absence. In *America Before*, Hancock writes:

When, I wonder, will archaeologists take to heart the old dictum that absence of evidence is not the same thing as evidence of absence, and learn the lessons that their own profession has repeatedly taught – namely that the next turn of the excavator's spade can change everything? So little of the surface area of our planet has been subjected to any kind of archaeological investigation at all that it would be more logical to regard *every* major conclusion reached by this discipline as provisional – particularly when we are dealing with a period as remote, as tumultuous, and as little understood as the Ice Age.

That may be, but in science whether or not the absence of evidence is the evidence of absence is a secondary issue to the falsifiability of a hypothesis. Just as SETI scientists grumble to their critics that the absence of evidence for extraterrestrial signals from space is not evidence for the absence of ETs anywhere in the galaxy – it's a big place, and we've only begun searching. The next turn of the astronomical spade could change everything! Yes, but the burden of proof is on claimants to provide positive evidence in favor of their hypotheses, not on skeptics to provide negative evidence, whatever that would be in the absence of evidence. In the end, all archaeologists and skeptics will change their mind about Hancock's lost civilization when that spade upturns unequivocal evidence. Until then, it is reasonable to be skeptical.

6. *The dangers of reading the past from the present.*

Before my debate with Graham Hancock I consulted the professional archaeologist and skeptic of alternative archaeology Ken Feder about the symbolism found on the monumental stone structures at Göbekli Tepe. Hancock thinks these symbols represent constellations of stars or carry some deeper meaning about nature at the time they were carved. Feder replied:

There appears to be a conceit on the part of modern people that all ancient art must in some way be representational, depicting things the artists actually saw and experienced. But we don't insist on that for modern artists. Their art requires no concrete explanation. We allow them to be creative, imaginative, and to just make shit up because it's cool or

represents stuff they hallucinated in trance and then interpreted through
the prism of religion.

Feder added that the paintings of Magritte, if we took them literally,
would represent the "period when gravity was abolished, at least for men
in suits and apples," and

My favorite; there's a version of a Kokopelli that I've seen in Utah
[Kokopelli is a fertility deity, usually depicted as a humpbacked flute
player with feathers or antenna-like protrusions on his head, who has
been venerated by some Native American cultures in the Southwestern
United States]. Only instead of being a hump-backed, flute-playing man,
it's a bipedal bighorn sheep playing a flute. This reflects a time when *Ovis
canadensis* [big horn sheep] was far more musically inclined. Probably
because of the comet.

Satire aside, the point is that we must be extremely cautious about
reading into the past our own ideas, and the further back in time we go,
the more problematic it is to do so. The archaeoastronomer Ed Krupp,
Director of the Griffith Park Observatory in Los Angeles and the author
of several books on when it is appropriate (or not) to interpret archaeological sites as astronomical in nature, offered these insights, including
the problem of employing astronomical computer programs that allow
one to see how the night sky would have looked to people thousands of
years ago (a technique Graham has employed in his research). Here
again, we see the problem of patternicity, or finding patterns that exist
only in the mind's eye.

The broad account of the interpretation makes me very skeptical. We have
no dictionary for the symbolic vocabulary of Göbekli Tepe imagery. This
appears to start with the assumption the figures are recognized
constellations (several problems right there) and then goes back in time
with planetarium software in search of a fit. Starry Night and Stellarium
have a lot to answer for. They are dangerous weapons in the hands of
amateurs.

Regarding the carving of a scorpion on one of the T-shaped pillars at
Göbekli Tepe, Krupp noted of Hancock's interpretation:

It all seems to rest on the Scorpion, which he argues must be Scorpio (sic. He means "Scorpius"). Then he turns the other images, which have no known relationship to any known constellation imagery into constellations in the same territory. This gives him the Milky Way in Sagittarius, although it is not depicted. Then he takes the disk, calls it a sun symbol, and says it is in the center of the Milky Way in Sagittarius, à la the 2012 Maya Calendar End Times Follies. Because the Maya calendar allegedly marked the start of a New Age, he implies the Göpekli Tepe carving also marks the start of a New Age (and the end of the earlier era). That, in turn, is linked to the alleged Dryas impact. It all appears to be contrived data of high order.

* * *

Of the many thousands of comments in response to the debate Graham and I did on Joe Rogan's show, I have become painfully aware that, to roughly half of the audience, I seemed hide-bound and dogmatically closed-minded to the possibility of a lost advanced civilization. As I told Hancock on the show and in writing after, I'm not. Honestly. I don't have a dog in the fight. I haven't written anything on the subject save the *Scientific American* column. I would happily change my mind, as I have on many other subjects (evolution, climate change, gun control, the death penalty, etc.). But the further back in time we push the origins of civilization, the more problematic the dates become, and, having followed this area since the 1970s when I read the alternative archaeology of that time with wide-eyed naivete, I've seen earlier date after earlier date not stand up to scrutiny. An uncontested conjecture does not a new civilization make. And Hancock's confession at the end of *America Before* about what he really believes doesn't help his case:

> I suppose the time has come to say in print what I have already said many times in public Q&A sessions at my lectures, and that in my view the science of the lost civilization was primarily focused upon what we now call *psi* capacities that deployed the enhanced and focused power of human consciousness to channel energies and to manipulate matter . . .
>
> My speculation, which I will not attempt to prove here or to support with evidence but merely present for consideration, is that the advanced civilization I see evolving in North America during the last Ice Age had

transcended leverage and mechanical advantage and learned to manipulate matter and energy by deploying powers of consciousness that we have not yet begun to tap. In action such power would look something like magic even today and must have seemed supernatural and godlike to the hunter-gatherers who shared the Ice Age world with these mysterious adepts.

Finally, I truly believe that science needs outsiders and mavericks who poke and prod and push accepted theories until they either collapse or are reinforced even stronger. Of all the alternative archaeology theories I've read, I found Hancock's to be the most intriguing and the most compelling, in the romantic sense of Golden Age myths and what they may mean for us. But I do not think he has convinced professional archaeologists of the factual nature of this particular story, and that's how it usually goes in science. Most ideas turn out to be wrong. The standard timeline of how civilizations unfolded over the past 13,000 years may be one of them, but so far it has held up fairly well. It could be that, in Graham's constant refrain on social media, "stuff keeps getting older," and civilization may be tens or hundreds of thousands of years older than we think it is. It's a romantic idea – one that conjures in the mind Godlike elder statesmen from the distant past communicating their wisdom to us through symbols and artifacts. But I doubt it. I love romancing the past, but I prefer to know the truth, whether or not it is romantic.

Notes

INTRODUCTION

1. Hitchens, Christopher. 2006. "Free Speech Talk." November. Available on YouTube here: https://bit.ly/1FwOJ1f and transcribed here: https://bit.ly/2vPp4AI

2. Holmes, O. W. 1919. "Opinion. Schneck v. United States." Legal Information Institute. Cornell Law School. https://bit.ly/1NSOD88

3. Schenck v. United States Leaflet. 1918. Record, Schenck v. United States. Supreme Court of the United States. https://bit.ly/2BbQWBv

4. Espionage Act of 1917. Enacted by the Senate and House of Representatives of the United States of America in Congress assembled. https://bit.ly/2IWiVQY

5. Sheldon, Novick. 1992. "The Unrevised Holmes and Freedom of Expression." *Supreme Court Review*, 303, 389. See also Sheldon, Novick. 1989. *Honorable Justice: The Life of Oliver Wendell Holmes*. New York: Little Brown and Co.

6. Milton, John. 1644. *Areopagitica: A Speech of Mr. John Milton for the Liberty of Unlicenc'd Printing, To the Parlament of England*. Available online: http://bit.ly/2HFcDjd; Paine, Thomas. 1794. *The Age of Reason: Being an Investigation of True and Fabulous Theology*. London: E. I. Eaton. Available online: https://bit.ly/1GczhaF; Mill, John Stuart. 1759. *On Liberty*. London: John W. Parker and Son. Available online: https://bit.ly/2xKHu5u

7. Shermer, Michael. 2010. "The Skeptic's Skeptic." *Scientific American*, November. https://bit.ly/2dntC8F

8. Bolt, Robert. 1960. *A Man for All Seasons*. London: Heinemann. Reprint 1990 Vintage Books. The complete script of *A Man for All Seasons* is available online at https://bit.ly/1vY6H3s

9. Helterbran, Valeri R. 2008. "Devil's Advocate Definition." *Exploring Idioms*. Gainesville, FL: Maupin House, 40.

10. Hitchens, 2006, "Free Speech Talk."

11. Strossen, Nadine. 2018. *Hate: Why We Should Resist It with Free Speech, Not Censorship*. New York: Oxford University Press, 16.

12. King, Martin Luther, Jr. 1958. *Stride Toward Freedom: The Montgomery Story*. Boston: Beacon Press, 74. Available online: https://bit.ly/29IMzOD

13. Pinker, Steven. 2015. "Why Free Speech is Fundamental." *Boston Globe*, January 27. https://bit.ly/1Cg8M1Z

CHAPTER 1 GIVING THE DEVIL HIS DUE

1. Shermer, Michael and Alex Grobman. 2000 (2009 Expanded Edition). *Denying History: Who Says the Holocaust Never Happened and Why Do They Say It?* Berkeley: University of California Press.
2. Douglas, L. 1996. "The Memory of Judgment: The Law, the Holocaust, and Denial." *History and Memory*, 7:2, 100–120.
3. In Rauch, J. 1993. *Kindly Inquisitors: The New Attacks on Free Thought*. Chicago: University of Chicago Press, 1–2.
4. Post, R. 1995. "Go Home, Irving." *Daily Californian*, February 7, 1.
5. Personal correspondence, January 2000.
6. Bolt, Robert. 1960. *A Man for All Seasons*. London: Heinemann. Reprint 1990, Vintage Books. The complete script of *A Man for All Seasons* is available online at http://bit.ly/1vY6H3s
7. Popper, Karl. 1963. *Conjectures and Refutations: The Growth of Scientific Knowledge*. New York: Harper & Row.
8. Shermer, Michael. 2011. *The Believing Brain*. New York: Henry Holt.
9. Flynn, James. 2012. *Are We Getting Smarter?: Rising IQ in the Twenty-First Century*. Cambridge, UK: Cambridge University Press.
10. Lukianoff, Greg. 2014. *Freedom from Speech*. New York: Encounter Books.
11. Ibid., 31.
12. Ibid., 38.
13. Shermer, Michael. 2015. *The Moral Arc: How Science and Reason Lead Humanity Toward Truth, Justice, and Freedom*. New York: Henry Holt, 135–136.
14. In Cunningham, N. 1987. *In Pursuit of Reason: The Life of Thomas Jefferson*. Baton Rouge: Louisiana State University Press, 77.
15. Ibid., 49.

CHAPTER 2 BANNING EVIL

1. Chapman, S., P. Alpers, K. Agho, and M. Jones. 2006. "Australia's 1996 Gun Law Reforms: Faster Falls in Firearm Deaths, Firearm Suicides, and a Decade without Mass Shootings." *Injury Prevention*, 12:6, 365–372. https://bit.ly/29xuyrz
2. Shermer, Michael. "The Sandy Hook Effect." *Skeptic*, 18:1, 26–35. https://bit.ly/2U7kURU
3. Shermer, Michael and Alex Grobman. 2000 (2009 Expanded Edition). *Denying History: Who Says the Holocaust Never Happened and Why Do They Say it?* Berkeley: University of California Press.
4. Shermer, Michael. 2018. "Have Archetype—Will Travel: The Jordan Peterson Phenomenon." *Skeptic*, 23:3, 36–43. https://bit.ly/2YizQvR
5. Reddit commentary on 2019 Tweet: "Jordan Peterson was cool with this photo." March 15. https://bit.ly/2kHCQTE
6. Anti-Defamation League (ADL). ND. "Pepe the Frog. General Hate Symbols." https://bit.ly/2r3fqIv

7. Long View on Education. ND. Photo of Jordan Peterson with Pepe the Frog banner. https://bit.ly/2kQSYSH

8. Spangler, Todd. 2017. "YouTube's PewDiePie Apologizes for Using the N-Word: 'I'm Just an Idiot.'" *Variety*, September 12. https://bit.ly/2koCkJU

9. Romano, Aja. 2017. "The Controversy Over YouTube star PewDiePie and his anti-Semitic 'jokes,' explained." *Vox*, February 17. https://bit.ly/2lTW6xj

10. Solzhenitsyn, Aleksandr. 1973. *The Gulag Archipelago*. New York: Harper, 442.

11. Richardson, Louis Fry. 1960. *Statistics of Deadly Quarrels*. Pittsburgh: Boxwood Press, xxxv.

CHAPTER 4 FREE TO INQUIRE

1. Sulloway, Frank. 1983. "The Legend of Darwin's Finches," *Nature*, 303, 372.

2. Letter to Joseph Hooker dated January 14, 1844, quoted in Browne, Janet. 1995. *Voyaging: Charles Darwin. A Biography*. New York: Knopf, 452.

3. For a detailed account of the "priority dispute" between Darwin and Wallace, see: Shermer, Michael. 2002. *In Darwin's Shadow: The Life and Science of Alfred Russel Wallace*. New York: Oxford University Press.

4. All quotes on the reaction to Darwin's theory are in Korey, Kenneth. 1984. *The Essential Darwin: Selections and Commentary*. Boston: Little, Brown.

5. Pew Research Center. 2005. "Religion a Strength and Weakness for Both Parties. Public Divided on Origins of Life," http://bit.ly/2kFVHu6

6. Israel, Hans, Erich Huckhaber, Rudolf Weinmann (Eds.). 1931. *Hundert Autoren gegen Einstein*. Leipzig: Voigtländer.

7. Adopted and paraphrased from Mayr, Ernst. 1982. *The Growth of Biological Thought*. Cambridge: Harvard University Press, 501.

8. Huxley, Thomas H. 1860."The Origin of Species" (review). *Westminster Review*, 17, 541–570.

9. Mayr, Ernst. 1988. *Toward a New Philosophy of Biology*. Cambridge: Harvard University Press, 161.

10. Dobzhansky, Theodosius. 1973. "Nothing in Biology Makes Sense Except in the Light of Evolution." *American Biology Teacher*, 35, 125–129.

11. Pew, "Religion a Strength and a Weakness." 2005.

12. Pew Research Center. 2013. "Public's Views on Human Evolution," http://pewrsr.ch/19BIvfh

13. Gallup. 2017. "In U.S., Belief in Creationist View of Humans at New Low," http://bit.ly/2CJ7Hm4

14. Bryan, William Jennings. 1925. *Bryan's Last Speech: The Most Powerful Argument Against Evolution Ever Made*. Sunlight Publishing Society.

15. The three-hour briefing was held on May 10, 2000. Quoted in Wald, D. 2000. "Intelligent Design Meets Congressional Designers." *Skeptic*, 8:2, 16–17.

16. Quoted in Bailey, Ron. 1997. "Origin of the Specious." *Reason*, July.

17. Dembski, William. 2004. *The Design Revolution: Answering the Toughest Questions About Intelligent Design.* Downers Grove, IL: InterVarsity Press, 41.
18. Quoted in Benen, Steve. 2000. "Science Test." *Church & State,* July/August.
19. Dembski, William. 1999. "Signs of Intelligence: A Primer on the Discernment of Intelligent Design." *Touchstone,* 84.
20. Benen, "Science Test." 2000.
21. Quoted in Grelen, Jay. 1996. "Witnesses for the Prosecution." *World,* November 30.
22. Johnson, Phillip. 2000. *The Wedge of Truth: Splitting the Foundations of Naturalism.* Downers Grove, IL: InterVarsity Press.
23. These and other variations on creationism are discussed on the website of the National Center for Science Education: www.ncse.com
24. Matsumura, Molleen and Louise Mead. "Ten Major Court Cases about Evolution and Creationism." National Center for Science Education, http://bit.ly/29XQZpy
25. Quoted in *The World's Most Famous Court Trial. Tennessee Evolution Case: A Complete Stenographic Report of the Famous Court Test of the Tennessee Anti-Evolution Act, at Dayton, July 10–21, 1925, Including Speeches and Arguments of Attorneys.* 1999. Clark, NJ: The Lawbook Exchange, Ltd. Google eBook, 87: http://bit.ly/1MMj2SZ
26. Lukianoff, Greg. 2014. *Freedom from Speech.* New York: Encounter Books.

CHAPTER 6 WHAT WENT WRONG? CAMPUS UNREST, VIEWPOINT DIVERSITY, AND FREEDOM OF SPEECH

1. In Kennedy, Deborah. 2002. *Helen Maria Williams and the Age of Revolution.* Lewisberg, PA: Bucknell University Press, 113. http://bit.ly/1o2XEA8
2. There has been considerable media coverage of these incidents. See, for example: Friedersdorf, Conor. 2015. "The Illiberal Demands of the Amherst Uprising." *Atlantic,* November 18. http://theatln.tc/1HY8lNG; Haidt, Jonathan and Greg Lukianoff. 2018. *The Coddling of the American Mind: How Good Intentions and Bad Ideas Are Setting Up a Generation for Failure.* New York: Penguin; Kronman, Anthony T. 2019. *The Assault on American Excellence.* New York: Free Press.
3. McNally, Richard. J. 2014. "Trigger Warnings: More Harm than Good?" *Telegraph,* October 4. http://bit.ly/1nPTLi6
4. Neff, Blake. 2015. "Oberlin Students Release Gargantuan 14-Page List of Demands." *Daily Caller,* December 17, http://bit.ly/1NzTPcm
5. This list comes from a memo sent to all faculty at Chapman University in the context of a workshop we were all invited to attend on safe spaces related to students who fall into one of these categories.
6. McNally, Richard J. 2017. "Hazards Ahead: The Problem with Trigger Warnings, According to the Research." *Pacific Standard.* June 14. http://bit.ly/1nPTLi6
7. Girls Best Friend Foundation and Advocates for Youth. 2005. Creating Safe Space for GLBTQ Youth: A Toolkit. Washington, DC: Advocates for Youth. http://bit.ly/1HtRHpd
8. "Tool: Recognizing Microaggressions and the Messages They Send." In "Diversity in the Classroom." Adopted by UCLA Diversity and Faculty Development from:

Derald Wing, Sue. 2010. *Microaggressions in Everyday Life: Race, Gender and Sexual Orientation.* New York: Wiley & Sons. http://bit.ly/2pcnKn1

9. Ibid.

10. Kukianoff, Greg and Jonathan Haidt. 2015. "The Coddling of the American Mind." *Atlantic.* September. http://theatln.tc/1EkIxUW

11. FIRE. 2014. "List of Campus Disinvitation Attempts, 2000–2014." Foundation for Individual Rights in Education. June 3. http://bit.ly/1E4lPyL

12. FIRE. Disinvitation Database. 1998–Present. http://bit.ly/1K5EHHG

13. Perez-Pena, Richard and Tanzina Vega. 2014. "Brandeis Cancels Plan to Give Honorary Degree to Ayaan Hirsi Ali, a Critic of Islam." *New York Times,* April 8. http://nyti.ms/1ixwyIY

14. De Benedetti, Chris. 2016. "Comedian Bill Maher Speaks Amid Handful of Protesters at UC Berkeley Commencement." *Mercury News,* August 12. http://bayareane.ws/1Re3ECb

15. Logue, Josh. 2015. "Uninvited to Williams." *Inside Higher Education.* October 21. http://bit.ly/2m9ZvrS

16. Hirsi Ali, Ayaan. 2014. "Here's What I Would Have Said to Brandeis." *Wall Street Journal,* April 10. http://on.wsj.com/1nPV3K9

17. Shermer, Michael. 2015. *The Moral Arc: How Science and Reason Lead Humanity Toward Truth, Justice, and Freedom.* New York: Henry Holt.

18. *Loving et ux. c. Virginia.* 1967. Supreme Court of United States. 388 U.S. 1(1967) No. 395. http://bit.ly/1QTA3yX

19. Campbell, Bradley and Jason Manning. 2014. "Microaggression and Moral Cultures." *Comparative Sociology,* 13:6. http://bit.ly/1PkUaoh

20. Haidt, Jonathan. 2014. "Where Microaggressions Really Come From: A Sociological Account." *The Righteous Mind.* http://bit.ly/1PZlogZ

21. Johnson, Catherine. 2016. "How I Became a Feminist Victim." *Spiked.* February 10. http://bit.ly/1Si7Q56

22. Malm, Sara. 2014. "'Twitter gave me PTSD': Woman claims mean comments and 'cyberstalking' gave her illness usually suffered by war veterans." *Daily Mail,* April 17. http://dailym.ai/1jOPxkq

23. French, David. 2016. "It is Only Going to Get Worse—Jonathan Haidt on the Crisis on Campus." *National Review,* February 4. http://bit.ly/1Q0wDUL

24. Shermer, Michael. 1993. "The Unlikeliest Cult in History: Ayn Rand, Objectivism, and the Cult of Personality." *Skeptic,* 2:2, 74-81. http://bit.ly/1QNNc9I

25. Foundation for Individual Rights in Education. 2015. "Yale University Students Protest Halloween Costume Email." November 6. http://bit.ly/1nPVKmJ

26. Nawaz, Maajid. 2015. "Je Suis Muslim: How Universal Secular Rights Protect Muslim Communities the Most." *Big Think,* November 17. http://bit.ly/1Nfw1j4

27. Eagan, Kevin, Ellen Bara Stolzenberg, Jennifer Berdan Lozano, Melissa C. Aragon, Maria Ramirez Suchard, Sylvia Hurtado. 2014. *Undergraduate Teaching Faculty: The 2013-2014 HERI Faculty Survey.* Los Angeles: Higher Education Research Institute, UCLA. http://bit.ly/1unvu3c

28. Duarte, Jose L., Jarret T. Crawford, Charlotta Stern, Jonathan Haidt, Lee Jussim, and Philip E. Tetlock. 2014. "Political Diversity Will Improve Social Psychological Science." *Behavioral and Brain Sciences*. July, 10.1017/S0140525X14000430. http://bit.ly/1jnzcHX

29. Barry Goldwater's famous line, which I've reversed, comes from the 1964 Republican Convention: "Let me remind you that extremism in the defense of liberty is no vice. And let me remind you also that moderation in the pursuit of justice is no virtue." A clip of the speech can be seen here: http://bit.ly/1W0hGXm

30. The original French sentence, from the final chapter of Hugo's book *Histoire d'un crime* (*The History of a Crime*), is "*On résiste à l'invasion des armées; on ne résiste pas à l'invasion des idées.*" "One can resist the invasion of armies; one cannot resist the invasion of ideas." https://bit.ly/1K1dXCL

31. Shermer, Michael and Alex Grobman. 2000. *Denying History: Who Says the Holocaust Never Happened and Why Do They Say it?* Berkeley: University of California Press, 13–14.

32. Institute for Historical Review. 1996. "Debating the Undebatable: The Weber-Shermer Clash." *Journal of Historical Review*, 16:1, 23–34. https://bit.ly/2lOBXZt

CHAPTER 9 THE CURIOUS CASE OF SCIENTOLOGY

1. Lippard, Jim. 2011. "The Decline (and Probable) Fall of the Scientology Empire." *Skeptic*, 17:1, 17–19. https://bit.ly/2DOU3Bz

2. Rosenfeld, Jean E. 2008. "Scientology Stands a Chance." *Los Angeles Times*, February 22. https://lat.ms/2KyjRmI

3. About the Series. *Leah Remini: Scientology and the Aftermath.* A&E TV. https://bit.ly/2Ge2Awn

CHAPTER 11 WHY IS THERE SOMETHING RATHER THAN NOTHING?

1. Hawking, Stephen. 1988. *A Brief History of Time.* New York: Bantam Books, 190.

2. Rees, Martin. 2000. *Just Six Numbers: The Deep Forces That Shape the Universe.* New York: Basic Books.

3. Barrow, John D. and Frank Tipler. 1988. *The Anthropic Cosmological Principle.* Oxford: Oxford University Press, vii.

4. Leslie, John and Robert Lawrence Kuhn. 2013. *The Mystery of Existence: Why is There Anything at All?* Wiley-Blackwell. See also Holt, Jim. 2012. *Why Does the World Exist: An Existential Detective Story.* New York: Liveright.

5. Kuhn, Robert Lawrence. 2007. "Why This Universe?: Toward a Taxonomy of Possible Explanations." *Skeptic*, 13:2, 28–39.

6. Ibid., 35.

7. Kuhn, Robert Lawrence. 2013. "Levels of Nothing: There Are Multiple Answers to the Question of Why the Universe Exists." *Skeptic*, 18:2. http://bit.ly/1S7Mn9i

8. Vilenkin, Alex. 2006. *Many Worlds in One: The Search for Other Universes.* New York: Hill and Wang.

9. O'Connor, Timothy. 2008. *Theism and Ultimate Explanation: The Necessary Shape of Contingency.* Oxford: Blackwell.

10. Hume, David. 1776. *Dialogues Concerning Natural Religion*, 92: http://bit.ly/1sIsq4p

11. See also the clever take-down of the ontological argument in Dawkins, Richard. 2006. *The God Delusion.* New York: Houghton Mifflin, 109–112.

12. Alleyne, Richard. 2009. "God is not the Creator, Claims Academic." *Telegraph*, October 8.

13. Callahan, Tim. 2012. "The Genesis Creation Myth is Not Unique." *eSkeptic*, April 25, http://bit.ly/1UlVqbi

14. Carroll, Sean. 2016. *The Big Picture: On the Origins of Life, Meaning, and the Universe Itself.* New York: Dutton, 148.

15. Shermer, Michael. 2006. "Wronger Than Wrong." *Scientific American.* November, 40.

16. Carroll, *The Big Picture*, 2016, 149–150.

17. Stenger, Victor. 2008. *God: The Failed Hypothesis.* Buffalo: Prometheus Books.

18. Krauss, Lawrence. 2012. *A Universe from Nothing: Why There is Something Rather Than Nothing.* New York: Free Press, 169–170.

19. Krauss, Lawrence. 2017. *The Greatest Story Ever Told – So Far: Why Are We Here?* New York: Atria Books.

20. Barrow, John and John Webb. 2005. "Inconstant Constants." *Scientific American*, June, 57–63.

21. Carroll, Sean. 2010. *From Eternity to Here. The Quest for the Ultimate Theory of Time.* New York: Dutton/Penguin, 50.

22. Ibid., 51, 64.

23. Steinhardt, Paul J. and Neil Turok. 2002. "A Cyclic Model of the Universe." *Science*, 296:5572, 1436–1439.

24. Smolin, Lee. 1997. *The Life of the Cosmos.* Oxford: Oxford University Press. See also Smith, Quentin. 1990. "A Natural Explanation of the Existence and Laws of Our Universe." *Australasian Journal of Philosophy*, 68, 22–43. For an elegant summary, see Gardner, James. 2003. *Biocosm.* Maui, HI: Inner Ocean Publishing.

25. Guth, Alan. 1981. "The Inflationary Universe: A Possible Solution to the Horizon and Flatness Problems." *Physical Review D*, 23, 347–356; Guth, Alan. 1997. *The Inflationary Universe: The Quest for a New Theory of Cosmic Origins.* Boston: Addison-Wesley; Linde, Andrei. 1991. "The Self-Reproducing Inflationary Universe." *Scientific American*, November, 48–55; Linde, Andrei. 2005. "Current Understanding of Inflation." *New Astronomy Reviews* 49, 35–41; Vilenkin, Alex. 2006. *Many Worlds in One: The Search for Other Universes.* New York: Hill and Wang.

26. Feynman, Richard. 1967. *The Character of Physical Law.* Cambridge, MA: MIT Press, 129.

27. Khoury, Justin, Burt A. Ovrut, Paul J. Steinhardt and Neil Turok. 2002. "Density Perturbations in the Ekpyrotic Scenario." *Physical Review D*, 66, 046005; Ostriker, Jeremiah P. and Paul Steinhardt. 2001. "The Quintessential Universe." *Scientific American*, January, 46–53.

28. Bousso, Raphael and Joseph Polchinski. 2004. "The String Theory Landscape." *Scientific American*, September.

29. Stenger, Victor. 2007. *God: The Failed Hypothesis.* Buffalo: Prometheus.

30. Everett, Hugh. 1957. "'Relative State' Formulation of Quantum Mechanics." *Reviews of Modern Physics* 29:3, 454–462. Reprinted in DeWitt. B.S. and N. Graham (Eds.). 1973. *The Many-Worlds Interpretation of Quantum Mechanics.* Princeton, NJ: Princeton University Press, 141–149. Wheeler, John Archibald. 1998. *Geons, Black Holes & Quantum Foam.* New York: W.W. Norton, 268–270.

31. Hawking, Stephen. 1996. "Quantum Cosmology." In Hawking, Stephen and Roger Penrose. *The Nature of Space and Time.* Princeton, NJ: Princeton University Press, 89–90.

32. Penrose, Roger. 2005. *The Road to Reality: A Complete Guide to the Laws of the Universe.* New York: Knopf, 726–732, 762–765.

33. Hawking, Stephen. 2002. "The Future of Theoretical Physics and Cosmology: Stephen Hawking 60th Birthday Symposium," Lecture at the Centre for Mathematical Sciences, Cambridge, UK, 11 January.

34. Hawking, Stephen and Leonard Mlodinow. 2010. *The Grand Design.* New York: Bantam Books.

35. Sagan, Carl. 2007. *The Varieties of Scientific Experience.* New York: Penguin, 2.

CHAPTER 13   HEALING THE BONDS OF AFFECTION

1. Shermer, Michael. 2017. "Are We All Racists?" *Scientific American,* August: https://bit.ly/2vib4PS

2. Disis, Jill. 2018. "Starbucks Will Close 8,000 US Stores May 29 for Racial-Bias Training." *CNN Business.* April 17. https://cnnmon.ie/2H7p6az

3. Greenbaum, Daniella. 2018. "The Latest Example of Political Correctness Run Amok: A Misguided Revolt at One of the Most Liberal Colleges in America." *Business Insider.* April 18. https://read.bi/2Hyrs5L

4. King Jr., Martin Luther. 1963. "I Have a Dream. . ." Speech by the Rev. Martin Luther King at the "March on Washington". US Government Archives. https://bit.ly/2fmjJXA

5. BLM (#blacklivesmater), BDM (Boycott, Divestment, Sanctions of Israel), MSM (Main Stream Media), LGBTQI (lesbian, gay, bisexual, transsexual, questioning, intersex), SJW (Social Justice Warriors), #metoo (Harvey Weinstein), #TakeAKnee (NFL national anthem protests), Dreamers (children of illegal immigrants born in the USA), Google Memo (the firing of James Demore), Milo (Yiannopoulos), Charlottesville (neo-Nazis), Evergreen (protests against professor Bret Weinstein), Berkeley (protests against Milo, Ann Coulter, et al.), Yale (protests over Halloween costumes), Middlebury (protests against Charles Murray), Parkland (school shooting), microaggressions (offensive words or phrases), safe spaces (places for students to go after hearing offensive speech), no platforming (disinvitation of speakers), hate speech (v. free speech).

6. These labels are necessarily time dependent and were in vogue in 2017 and 2018.

7. Orwell, George. 1946. "Politics and the English Language." *Horizon.* April.https://bit.ly/18z9Ikb

8. Pew Research Center. 2014. "Political Polarization in the American Public." June 12, Washington, DC: https://pewrsr.ch/1v23UXF

9. Ibid.: https://pewrsr.ch/1pbUFVO

10. See, for example: Pinker, Steven. 2018. *Enlightenment Now: The Case for Science, Reason, Humanism and Progress.* New York: Penguin; Campbell, Bradley and Jason Manning. 2018. *The Rise of Victimhood Culture: Microaggressions, Safe Spaces, and the New Culture Wars.* New York: Palgrave; Greene, Joshua. 2013. *Moral Tribes: Emotion, Reason & the Gap Between Us and Them.* New York: Penguin.

11. Epstein, Richard. 2014. *The Classical Liberal Constitution: The Uncertain Quest for Limited Government.* Cambridge, MA: Harvard University Press.

12. Shermer, Michael. 2015. *The Moral Arc: How Science and Reason Lead Humanity to Truth, Justice, and Freedom.* New York: Henry Holt, 407–408.

13. See my *Scientific American* column on the problem of how ideology can trump data in science and why I became skeptical of my libertarianism: Shermer, Michael. 2013. "When Science Doesn't Support Beliefs." *Scientific American,* October, 95: https://bit.ly/2H7jb9I

14. 2018. "List of Countries by Social Welfare Spending." *Wikipedia.* https://bit.ly/2H7erAE

15. Prados de la Escosura, Leandro. 2015. "World Human Development, 1870–2007." *The Review of Income and Wealth,* 61, 220–247: https://bit.ly/2J3wcxm

16. Haidt, Jonathan. 2012. *The Righteous Mind: Why Good People Are Divided by Politics and Religion.* New York: Random House; Haidt, Jonathan. 2003. "The Moral Emotions." In R. J. Davidson, K. Scherer, and H. H. Goldschmidt (Eds.). *Handbook of Affective Sciences.* Oxford: Oxford University Press; Haidt, Jonathan. 2001. "The Emotional Dog and its Rational Tail: A Social Intuitionist Approach to Moral Judgment." *Psychological Review,* 108, 814–834.

17. For a fuller defense of this moral starting point, see *The Moral Arc* and Chapters 19 and 20 in this volume.

CHAPTER 14 GOVERNING MARS

1. Musk, Elon. 2018. "Elon Musk Answers Your Questions." SXSW conference, March, https://bit.ly/2tD8zsx

2. Kibbe, Matt. 2014. *Don't Hurt People and Don't Take Their Stuff: A Libertarian Manifesto.* New York: William Morrow.

3. Quoted in Madison, James. 2006. *Selected Writings of James Madison.* Ralph Ketcham (Ed.). Indianapolis, IN: Hackett Publishing, 122.

4. Diamond, Jared. 1996. *Guns, Germs, and Steel.* New York: W. W. Norton, p. 268.

5. Jefferson, Thomas. 1804. "Letter to Judge John Tyler Washington." June 28. https://bit.ly/292vEbR

6. Personal correspondence, June 30, 2018. https://bit.ly/2KruEIT

7. Personal correspondence, August 3, 2018.

8. Personal correspondence, June 17, 2019. https://bit.ly/2J181SN

CHAPTER 15 THE SANDY HOOK EFFECT

1. Barron, James. 2012. "Children Were All Shot Multiple Times with a Semiautomatic, Officials say." *New York Times,* December 15.

2. Flegenheimer, Matt and Ravi Somaiya. 2012. "A Mother, a Gun Enthusiast and the First Victim." *New York Times*, December 15. https://nyti.ms/2FW2DkC

3. Sanchez, Raf. 2012. "Connecticut School Shooting: Six-Year Old Stayed Alive by Playing Dead." *The Daily Telegraph*, December 17.

4. McDuffee, Allen. 2012. "After Sandy Hook What Can Be Done to Curb Gun Violence in America? *Washington Post*, December 19. https://wapo.st/2RweJT2

5. Lichtblau, Eric and Motoko. 2012. "N.R.A. Envisions 'a Good Guy With a Gun' in Every School." *New York Times*, December 21. https://nyti.ms/2UevJii

6. Obama, Barack. Office of the Press Secretary. 2012. The White House. "Remarks by the President at Sandy Hook Interfaith Prayer Vigil." December 16. https://bit.ly/2RzE7XP

7. Associated Press. 2012. "Man Stabs 22 Children in China." December 15. https://nyti.ms/2G0QATl

8. US Department of Justice. 2019. "Gun Violence in America." National Institute of Justice. February 26. https://bit.ly/2lZOSrB. See also Bureau of Justice Statistics, *Nonfatal Firearm Violence, 1993–2011*, special tabulation from the Bureau of Justice Statistics' National Crime Victimization Survey, provided to NIJ January 2013. https://bit.ly/2knTHuk

9. Morton, Robert J. ND. "Serial Murder. Definition of Serial Murder." National Center for the Analysis of Violent Crime. Federal Bureau of Investigation. https://bit.ly/2nCRw5X

10. Fox, James Alan. 2012. "Top Ten Myths About Mass Shootings." *Chronicle of Higher Education*, December 18. https://bit.ly/2QDCpHI

11. Kellermann, Arthur L., 1998. "Injuries and Deaths Due to Firearms in the Home." *Journal of Trauma* 45:2, 263–267.

12. Kegler, Scott R., Linda L. Dahlberg, and James A. Mercy. 2018. "Firearm Homicides and Suicides in Major Metropolitan Areas–United States, 2012–2013 and 2015–2016." Centers for Disease Control and Prevention. https://bit.ly/2DcxS8b

13. Ibid.

14. Ibid.

15. Lankford, Adam. 2012. "What Drives Suicidal Mass Killers." *New York Times*, December 17. https://nyti.ms/2zIByfn

16. Personal interview, July 23, 2012. See also Dutton, Kevin. 2012. *The Wisdom of Psychopaths: What Saints, Spies, and Serial Killers Can Teach Us About Success*. New York: Farrar, Straus and Giroux; Hare, Robert. 1999. *Without Conscience: The Disturbing World of the Psychopaths Among Us*. New York: Guilford Press; and Baron-Cohen, Simon. 2011. *The Science of Evil: On Empathy and the Origins of Cruelty*. New York: Basic Books.

17. Seirstad, Asne. 2019. "The Anatomy of White Terror." *New York Times*. March 18. https://nyti.ms/2mneleJ

18. Associated Press. 2012. "Man Stabs 22 Children in China." *New York Times*, December 14.

19. "After Newtown." *Frontline*. PBS. https://to.pbs.org/2rjeNtK

20. Ibid.

21. Dutton, 2012. *The Wisdom of Psychopaths*, 61.

22. Lewis, Ricki. 2013. "Comparing Adam Lanza's DNA to Forensic DNA Databases: A Modest Proposal." *PLOS*, January 4.

23. "After Newtown."

24. Ibid.

25. Shermer, Michael. 2008. "Five Ways Brain Scans Mislead Us." *Scientific American Mind*, October.

26. Fox, 2012, "Top Ten Myths."

27. Video. 2012. "Run. Hide. Fight. Surviving an Active Shooter Event." YouTube. July 23. https://bit.ly/1GzgQOS

28. Follman, Mark, Gavin Aronsen, and Deanna Pan. 2012. "A Guide to Mass Shootings in America." *Mother Jones*, December 15. https://bit.ly/1iGWZO3

29. Follman, Mark. 2012. "Mass Shootings: Maybe What We Need is a Better Mental-health Policy." *Mother Jones*. November 9. https://bit.ly/1nlYff2

30. *CBS/AP*. 2012. "James Holmes Built Up Aurora Arsenal of Bullets, Ballistic Gear Through Unregulated Online Market." July 24.https://cbsn.ws/2ARPMKH

31. Osunsami, Steve. 2013. "Teen's Planned Bomb Plot Against School Was a Hate Crime." *ABC News*. January 7. https://abcn.ws/2QDpxl4

32. Barnes, Robert. 2008. "Justices Reject D.C. Ban on Handgun Ownership." *Washington Post*, June 27. https://wapo.st/1SWGKxR

33. Mears, Bill. 2010. "Court Rules for Gun Rights, Strikes Down Chicago Handgun Ban." *CNN*, June 28. https://cnn.it/2Qi9XvF

34. Mather, Kate. 2013. "Out in Force." *Los Angeles Times*, January 7, A1.

35. "After Newtown."

36. Wellford, Charles F., John V. Pepper, and Carol V. Petrie (Eds.). 2005. *Firearms and Violence: A Critical Review*. National Research Council, National Academy of Science, NAP.

37. Lott, John. 2010. *More Guns, Less Crime: Understanding Crime and Gun Control Laws* (3rd Edition). University of Chicago Press.

38. Feldman, Josh. 2012. "Piers Morgan and Alan Dershowitz Get in Heated Argument with Anti-Gun Control Advocate." *MEDIAite*, July 23. https://bit.ly/2EgtiH4

39. Duncan, Otis Dudley. 2000. "Gun Use Surveys: In Numbers We Trust?" *Criminologist*. January/February. https://bit.ly/2kxvCS5

40. Levitt, Steven and Stephen Dubner. 2005. *Freakonomics*. New York: William Morrow.

41. Pinker, Steven. 2011. *The Better Angels of Our Nature: Why Violence Has Declined*. New York: Viking.

42. Chapman, S., P. Alpers, K. Agho, M. Jones. 2006. "Australia's 1996 Gun Law Reforms: Faster Falls in Firearm Deaths, Firearm Suicides, and a Decade without Mass Shootings." *Injury Prevention*. 12, 365–372. https://bit.ly/29xuyrz

43. Lott, John, and William Landes. 1999. "Multiple Victim Public Shootings, Bombings, and Right-to-Carry Concealed Handgun Laws: Contrasting Private and Public Law Enforcement." *University of Chicago Law School, John M. Olin Law & Economics Working Paper* No. 73.

44. Fox, 2012, "Top Ten Myths."

45. Cassese, Sid and Tom Brune. 2013. "Rep. Carolyn McCarthy Bill Would Ban High-Capacity Ammunition Clips." *Newsday*, January 3. https://nwsdy.li/2QEhrs8

46. Peralta, Eyder. 2012. "The Tragedy of Jessica Ghawi: Spared in Toronto, She Died in Colorado Shooting. NPR *The Two-Way*. July 20. https://n.pr/2QIrEUR

CHAPTER 18   ANOTHER FATAL CONCEIT

1. Letter 2743, Darwin to Asa Gray, April 1860, Darwin Correspondence Project.
2. Darwin, Charles. 1871. *The Descent of Man, and Selection in Relation to Sex.* London: John Murray.
3. Solnick, Sara and David Hemenway. 1998. "Is More Always Better? A Survey on Positional Concerns." *Journal of Economic Behavior and Organization,* 37, 373–383.
4. Carlsson, Fredrik, Olof Johansson-Stenman, and Peter Martinsson. 2007. "Do You Enjoy Having More than Others? Survey Evidence of Positional Goods." *Economica* (Online Early Articles).
5. Frank, Robert. 2011. *The Darwin Economy.* Princeton, MA: Princeton University Press, 193.
6. Frank, 2011, *The Darwin Economy,* 6.
7. Shermer, Michael. 2008. *The Mind of the Market: Sharing Apes, Trading Humans, & Other Tales of Evolutionary Economics.* New York: Henry Holt/Times Books.
8. Frank, 2011. *The Darwin Economy,* 16.
9. I outline some of these connections and illuminate why conservatives should embrace a Darwinian view of human nature as parallel to their own here: Shermer, Michael. 2006. *Why Darwin Matters: The Case Against Intelligent Design.* New York: Henry Holt/Times Books.
10. Browne, Janet. 2000. *Voyaging: Charles Darwin. A Biography.* New York: Knopf, 36, 366.
11. Carey, Toni Vogel. 1998. "The Invisible Hand of Natural Selection, and Vice Versa." *Biology & Philosophy,* 13:3, 427–442. Ghiselin, Michael T. 1974. *The Economy of Nature and the Evolution of Sex.* Berkeley: University of California Press. Gould, Stephen Jay. 1980. "Darwin's Middle Road." In *The Panda's Thumb.* New York: W.W. Norton, 59–68. Gould, Stephen Jay. 1993. "Darwin and Paley Meet the Invisible Hand." In *Eight Little Piggies.* New York: W.W. Norton, 138–152. Khalil, Elias L. 1997. "Evolutionary Biology and Evolutionary Economics." *Journal of Interdisciplinary Economics,* 8(4), 221–244. Schweber, Silvan S. "Darwin and the Political Economists: Divergence of Character," *Journal of the History of Biology,* 13, 195–289. Ahmad, Syed. 1990. "Adam Smith's Four Invisible Hands." *History of Political Economy, Spring,* 22(1), 137–144. Walsh, Donald. 2001. "Darwin Fallen Among Political Economists." *Proceedings of the American Philosophical Society,* 145(4), 415–437.
12. Schumpeter, Joseph. 1942. *Capitalism, Socialism and Democracy.* London: Routledge.
13. Reinert, Hugo and Erik S. Reinert. 2006. "Creative Destruction in Economics: Nietzsche, Sombart, Schumpeter." In J. G. Backhaus and W. Drechsler (Eds.). *Friedrich Nietzsche: Economy, and Society.* New York: Springer.
14. Gould, Stephen Jay. *Wonderful Life: The Burgess Shale and the Nature of History.* 1988. New York: W. W. Norton, 318.
15. Foster, Richard and Sarah Kaplan. 2001. *Creative Destruction: Why Companies That Are Built to Last Underperform the Market – and How to Successfully Transform Them.* New York: Crown Business.
16. Gillespie, Nick and Matt Welch. 2011. "Death of the Duopoly." *Wall Street Journal,* June 18. https://on.wsj.com/2kIPQIG
17. Zahavi, Amotz and Avishag Zahavi. 1997. *The Handicap Principle: A Missing Piece of Darwin's Puzzle.* Oxford: Oxford University Press.

18. Personal correspondence by email, December 21, 2011.

19. Ibid.

20. Miller, Geoffrey. 2001. *The Mating Mind: How Sexual Choice Shaped the Evolution of Human Nature.* New York: Random House.

21. Logan, David S. 2011. "Warren Buffett's Proposed Tax Hikes Would Provide Insignificant Revenue." Tax Foundation. August 21. https://bit.ly/2lXUlza

22. Veenhoven, Ruut. 1999. "Quality-of-Life in Individualistic Society." *Social Indicators Research* 48, 157–186, 157. See also Veenhoven, Ruut. 2000. "The Four Qualities of Life." *Journal of Happiness Studies,* 1, 1–39.

23. Brooks, Albert. 2006. *Who Really Cares: The Surprising Truth about Compassionate Conservatism.* New York: Basic Books.

24. Boudreaux, Don. 2006. "Status Won't Go Away." *Café Hayek.* https://bit.ly/2kG3hsR

25. An A-to-Z list of government departments and agencies can be found online at http://www.usa.gov/directory/federal/index.shtml

26. See, for example, an article in the November 21, 2011 edition of *Newsweek* entitled "The Get-Rich Congress" and a few of the examples highlighted in those brief pages: Rep. Dennis Hastert, when he was Speaker of the House, added a $207-million earmark into a federal highway bill for a parkway that just happened to be near land he owned in rural Illinois. Perhaps this explains the increase in his net worth from $300,000 when he first went to Congress in 1986 to $11 million when he retired in 2007. Rep. Jared Polis invested millions of dollars in stocks and funds related to health care and pharmaceuticals during his tenure on two committees involved in drafting Obama's health-care bill. *Newsweek* cites a Roll Call study of congressional financial disclosures that revealed the net worth of members of Congress grew by 25 percent since 2008, while the average American household lost on average 20 percent of its net worth.

27. Bastiat, Frédéric. 1995. "What is Seen and What is Not Seen," in *Selected Essays on Political Economy.* George B. de Huszar (Ed.). Irvington-on-Hudson, NY: Foundation for Economic Education, 1–2.

28. Personal correspondence, January 16, 2012.

29. Mackey, John. 2011. "To Increase Jobs, Increase Economic Freedom." *Wall Street Journal,* November 16, A17.

30. Hayak, Friedrich. 1988. *The Fatal Conceit.* Chicago: University of Chicago Press, 14.

CHAPTER 19   SCIENTIFIC NATURALISM

1. These and many other accounts of witch trials are available here: Demos, John. 2008. *The Enemy Within: 2,000 Years of Witch-Hunting in the Western World.* New York: Viking; Briggs, Robin. 1996. *Witches and Neighbors: The Social and Cultural Context of European Witchcraft.* New York: Viking.

2. Medieval Sourcebook: Witchcraft Documents [15th Century] Innocent VIII: Bull Summis Desiderantes, December 5, 1484. http://bit.ly/2q0bSVs

3. The historian Brian Levack estimates that a minimum of 60,000 people were executed based on the number of trials and the rate of convictions (often close to 50 percent), while the medieval historian Anne Llewellyn Barstow pushed the total upward to 100,000 based on lost records. See Levak, Brian. 2006. *The Witch-Hunt in Early Modern Europe.* Routledge; Llewellyn Barstow, Anne. 1994. *Witchcraze: A New History of the European Witch Hunts.* New York: Harper Collins.

4. There were, of course, other factors involved in the witch crazes – including the exploitation of women, the poor, and the elderly, financial, and sexual opportunism, revenge, insanity, and preemptive denunciation (accuse others before you are accused) – but these are secondary and tertiary issues to the primary belief in supernatural agents acting in the natural world, which underlay the conviction that witches were real. Even the early judicial reformers who lobbied against the use of torture as a viable means of extracting useful information from accused witches, such as the German Jesuit Friedrich Spee, whose 1631 *Cautio Criminalis* played a role in bringing about the end of the witch mania, never doubted the existence of witches.

5. Thomas, Keith. 1971. *Religion and the Decline of Magic.* New York: Charles Scribner's Sons, 643–644.

6. A Google Ngram Viewer search for "scientific naturalism" reveals these results: http://bit.ly/2qT5Kxn

7. A Google Ngram Viewer search for "methodological naturalism" reveals these results: http://bit.ly/2pVwcJi

8. Shermer, Michael. 2006. *Why Darwin Matters: The Case Against Intelligent Design.* New York: Henry Holt.

9. Personal correspondence, June 2015.

10. Bod, Rens. 2014. *A New History of the Humanities: The Search for Principles and Patterns from Antiquity to the Present.* Oxford: Oxford University Press.

11. A Google Ngram Viewer search for "Enlightenment humanism" reveals these results: http://bit.ly/2ppE5Ui

12. Pinker, Steven. 2011. *The Better Angels of Our Nature.* New York: Penguin, 180. See also Pinker, Steven. 2018. *Enlightenment Now: The Case for Reason, Science, Humanism, and Progress.* New York: Penguin.

13. The term "scientist" was coined by the British philosopher of science William Whewell in 1833 and canonized in his 1840 classic work *The Philosophy of the Inductive Sciences.* For a history of the word, see Ross, Sydney. 1962. "Scientist: The Story of a Word." *Annals of Science,* 18:2, 65–85. This is confirmed by a Google Ngram Viewer search of "scientist": http://bit.ly/2qjFgZP

14. Sagan, Carl. 1996. *The Demon-Haunted World: Science as a Candle in the Dark.* New York: Random House, 424.

15. Shermer, Michael. 2013. "The Sandy Hook Effect." *Skeptic,* 18:1. bit.ly/1uUZL7V

16. Kohler, Pamela K., Lisa E. Manhart, and William E. Lafferty. 2008. "Abstinence-Only and Comprehensive Sex Education and the Initiation of Sexual Activity and Teen Pregnancy." *Journal of Adolescent Health*, 42:4, 344–351.

17. Raymond, E. G. and D. A. Grimes. 2012. "The Comparative Safety of Legal Induced Abortion and Childbirth in the United States." *Obstetrics & Gynecology*, 119:2. http://bit.ly/1ikYqET

18. Deschner, Amy and Susan A. Cohen. 2003. "Contraceptive Use Is Key to Reducing Abortion Worldwide." *The Guttmacher Report on Public Policy*, 6:4. http://bit.ly/1jG3rU0

19. Diamond, Jared. 1996. *Guns, Germs, and Steel: The Fates of Human Societies*. New York: W. W. Norton.

20. Bajpai, Prableen. 2015. "North Korean vs. South Korean Economies." *Investopedia*. http://bit.ly/2peBHE7

21. Ferris, Timothy. 2010. *The Science of Liberty: Democracy, Reason, and the Laws of Nature*. New York: Harper.

22. Hume, David. 1739. *A Treatise of Human Nature*. London, John Noon, 335.

23. Other solutions to the Is-Ought problem have been proposed, such as John Searle's widely cited 1964 paper "How to Derive 'Ought' From 'Is,'" in which he proposes, for example, that the act of making a promise becomes the "is" and as such it becomes an obligation that one "ought" to fulfill. Searle, John R. 1964. "How to Derive 'Ought' From 'Is.'" *Philosophical Review*, 73:1, 43–58.

24. Shermer, Michael. 2015. *The Moral Arc: How Science and Reason Lead Humanity Toward Truth, Justice, and Freedom*. New York: Henry Holt.

25. Hobbes, Thomas. 1642. *De Cive, or the Citizen*. New York: Appleton-Century-Crofts, 15.

26. All quotes from Olson, Richard. 1990. *Science Deified and Science Defied: The Historical Significance of Science in Western Culture*. Berkeley: University of California Press, 191–202 passim. See also Hankins, Thomas L. 1985. *Science and the Enlightenment*. Cambridge: Cambridge University Press, 161–163.

27. Olson, 1990, *Science Deified*, 183–189.

28. Jeremy Bentham was the first to articulate the grounding principle of animal rights: "The question is not, Can they *reason?* nor, Can they *talk?* but, Can they *suffer?*" Bentham, Jeremy. 1823. *Introduction to the Principles of Morals and Legislation*, Chapter XVII, footnote 122. See full text copy: http://bit.ly/1XdYerr

29. Data source: World Bank; Bourguignon, François and Christian Morrisson. 2002. "Inequality among World Citizens: 1820–1992." *American Economic Review*, 92:4, 727–744.

30. See also Max Roser's web page tracking progress in poverty and many other areas of human and social life http://ourworldindata.org/ along with the Cato Institute's web page http://humanprogress.org/

31. You can watch the speech here: http://bit.ly/1nUaL4L You can read the full text of the speech here: http://bit.ly/2qQ12RY You can read my essay about the rally and my experiences here: http://bit.ly/2qetArg

CHAPTER 20 MR. HUME: BREAK. DOWN. THIS. WALL.

1. Physicist George Ellis' critique was titled "Can Science Bridge the Is-Ought Gap? A Response to Michael Shermer" and is available here: https:\\bit.ly/2Eb0OPa

2. Shermer, Michael. 2017. "Scientific Naturalism: A Manifesto for Enlightenment Humanism," *Theology and Science* 15:3, 220–230.

3. Shermer, Michael. 2015. *The Moral Arc: How Science and Reason Lead Humanity Toward Truth, Justice, and Freedom.* New York: Henry Holt.

4. Lincoln, Abraham. 1864. Letter to Albert G. Hodges. Library of Congress. https:\\bit.ly /1gvohdW. The line appears in the opening of a letter to the editor of the Frankfort, Kentucky, *Commonwealth*, Albert G. Hodges, who had journeyed from Kentucky to meet with Lincoln to discuss the recruitment of slaves as soldiers in Kentucky, which was a border state and thus the Emancipation Proclamation did not apply. Nevertheless, slaves who entered the military could gain their freedom. Lincoln wrote, "I am naturally anti-slavery. If slavery is not wrong, nothing is wrong. I can not remember when I did not so think, and feel."

5. Eddington, Arthur Stanley. 1928. *The Nature of the Physical World.* New York: Macmillan, 74.

6. Tooby, John, Leda Cosmides, and H. Clark Harrett. 2003. "The Second Law of Thermodynamics is the First Law of Psychology." *Psychological Bulletin*, 129:6, 858–865.

7. Pinker, Steven. 2008. "The Moral Instinct." *New York Times*, January 13.

8. Wright, Robert. 2000. *Nonzero: The Logic of Human Destiny.* New York: Pantheon.

9. Pinker, 2008, "The Moral Instinct."

10. Ibid.

11. Harris, Sam. 2008. *The Moral Landscape: How Science Can Determine Moral Values.* New York: Free Press.

12. Harris, Sam. 2014. "The Moral Landscape Challenge." http:\\bit.ly/2f2cc1f

13. Pinker, Steven. 2012. "The False Allure of Group Selection." *Edge.org* http:\\bit.ly /2m7pU8t

CHAPTER 22 HOW LIVES TURN OUT

1. Shermer, Michael. 1993. "The Chaos of History: On a Chaotic Model that Represents the Role of Contingency and Necessity in Historical Sequences." *Nonlinear Science*, 2:4., 1–13; Shermer, Michael. 1995. "Exorcising Laplace's Demon: Chaos and Antichaos, History and Metahistory." Invited paper for *History and Theory*. Wesleyan University. 34:1, 59–83; Shermer, Michael. 1997. "The Crooked Timber of History: History is Complex and Often Chaotic. Can We Use This to Better Understand the Past?" *Complexity*, 2:6, 23–29.

2. The White House. 2012. "Remarks by the President at a Campaign Event in Roanoke, Virginia." Office of the Press Secretary. July 13. https://bit.ly/2APhuaC

3. Sulloway, Frank J. 1996. *Born to Rebel: Birth Order, Family Dynamics, and Creative Lives.* New York: Vintage Books, 73.

4. Sulloway, Frank J. 1990. "Orthodoxy and Innovation in Science: The Influence of Birth Order in a Multivariate Context." Paper presented at the meeting of the American Association for the Advancement of Science, New Orleans, LA, February 16.

5. Personal correspondence, June 7, 2014.

6. Smith, Gary. 2014. *Standard Deviations: Flawed Assumptions, Tortured Data, and Other Ways to Lie with Statistics.* New York: Overlook Press.

7. Shermer, Michael. 2003. *The Science of Good and Evil.* New York: Times Books, Chapter 4; Shermer, Michael. 2015. *The Moral Arc.* New York: Times Books, Chapter 10; Shermer, Michael. 2012. "Free Won't: Volition as Self-Control Exerts Veto Power Over Impulses." *Scientific American,* August.

CHAPTER 26   HAVE ARCHETYPE – WILL TRAVEL

1. Beckner, Stephen. 2018. "Thought Crimes: Jordan Peterson and the Meaning of the Meaning of Life." *Skeptic,* 23: 3. https://bit.ly/2BI6eih

2. "Have Gun—Will Travel." *Wikipedia.* https://bit.ly/2mqF2zj. See opening sequence "Ballad of Paladin Have Gun Will Travel." https://bit.ly/2kVWOtR

3. Rogan, Joe. 2016. "Joe Rogan Experience #877—Jordan Peterson." *Joe Rogan Experience Podcast,* November 28. https://bit.ly/2gIfvt8

4. Rogan, Joe. 2016. "Joe Rogan Experience #770—Michael Shermer." *Joe Rogan Experience Podcast,* March 7. https://bit.ly/2NA4BGm

5. Weiss, Bari. 2018. "Meet the Renegades of the Intellectual Dark Web." *New York Times,* May 8. https://nyti.ms/2IrkbW4

6. Episode Archive. *The Jordan B. Peterson Podcast.* https://bit.ly/2p5HVnt

7. Peterson, Jordan. 2018. "Heavens on Earth with Skeptical Dr. Michael Shermer." *Jordan B. Peterson Podcast,* January 22. https://bit.ly/2uCnvoO

8. Walker, Julian. 2016. "Bill C-16: An Act to Amend the Canadian Human Rights Act and the Criminal Code." Ottawa: Library of Parliament. Publications, Government of Canada. https://bit.ly/2kquorH

9. Peterson, Jordan. 2016. "Part 1: Fear and the Law." *Jordan B. Peterson Podcast.* September 27. https://bit.ly/2dzbIT2

10. Bartlett, Tom. 2018. "What's So Dangerous About Jordan Peterson?" *Chronicle of Higher Education,* January 17. https://bit.ly/2mSPCvt

11. Paikin, Steve. 2016. "Gender, Rights, and Freedom of Speech." TVO. October 26. https://bit.ly/2HCY621

12. Kivanc, Jake. 2016. "A Canadian University Professor is Under Fire for Rant on Political Correctness." *Vice,* September 29. https://bit.ly/2gla1G6

13. Peterson, Jordan. 2016. "The Right to Be Politically Incorrect: Why I Refuse to Use Genderless Pronouns." *National Post,* November 8. https://bit.ly/2uWIq5r

14. Kearns, Madeleine. 2018. "Lindsay Shepherd is Suing Wilfrid Laurier University – Here's Why." *National Review.* June 29. https://bit.ly/2uJ8L7S

15. Landau, Les. 1992. *Star Trek, The Next Generation.* "Chain of Command, Part 2." Season 6, Episode 11. The plot device was a homage to George Orwell's *Nineteen Eighty-Four* in

which the hero of the story, Winston Smith, is tortured until he admits that he sees five fingers when his torturer is holding up four fingers.

16. Harris, Sam. 2017. "What is True? A Conversation with Jordan B. Peterson." *Making Sense* podcast, episode #62, January 21. https://bit.ly/2LcrEu9 and Harris, Sam. 2017. "Meaning and Chaos: A Conversation with Jordan Peterson." *Making Sense* podcast, episode #67, March 13. https://bit.ly/2sEeTji

17. Hoffman, Donald D. and Manish Singh. 2012. "Computational Evolutionary Perception." *Perception.* January 1. https://bit.ly/2NCFanH

18. Shermer, Michael. 2015. "Perception Deception." *Scientific American*, 313:5, 75. November. Published online as "Did Humans Evolve to See Things as They Really Are?" November 1. https://bit.ly/2LFupjO

19. David, Marian. 2016. "The Correspondence Theory of Truth." *The Stanford Encyclopedia of Philosophy* (Fall 2016 Edition), Edward N. Zalta (Ed.). http://stanford.io/1SC6oKJ

20. Chakravartty, Anjan. 2011 (revised 2017). "Scientific Realism." *The Stanford Encyclopedia of Philosophy*. Edward N. Zalta (Ed.). http://stanford.io/1nqQciY

21. Bourget, David and David J. Chalmers. 2014. "What Do Philosophers Believe?" *Philosophical Studies*, 170:3, 465–500. See also The PhilPapers Surveys. https://bit.ly/1nUaL4L

22. Peterson, Jordan. 2018. "Heavens on Earth with Skeptical Dr. Michael Shermer." *Jordan B. Peterson Podcast*, January 22. At the 58-minute mark here: http://bit.ly/2uCnvoO

23. Peterson, Jordan. 1999. *Maps of Meaning: The Architecture of Belief.* New York: Routledge, 162.

24. Bartlett, Tom. 2018. "What's So Dangerous About Jordan Peterson?" *Chronicle of Higher Education*, January 17. http://bit.ly/2mSPCvt

25. Stea, Jonathan N. 2018. "Jordan Peterson's Evidence-Based Endeavor." *Skeptic*, 23:3, 16–17. http://bit.ly/2SkBn0q

26. Shermer, Michael. 2018. *Heavens on Earth.* New York: Henry Holt, 251.

27. Keyes, Ralph. 2006. *The Quote Verifier.* New York: St. Martin's Griffin, 59, 109. See also Quote Investigator. 2010. "The Only Thing Necessary for the Triumph of Evil is that Good Men Do Nothing." December 4. http://bit.ly/2CYLGk0

Index